CHINA *on the* MARGINS

CHINA *on the* MARGINS

EDITED BY
SHERMAN COCHRAN AND PAUL G. PICKOWICZ

East Asia Program
Cornell University
Ithaca, New York 14853

The Cornell East Asia Series is published by the Cornell University East Asia Program (distinct from Cornell University Press). We publish books on a variety of scholarly topics relating to East Asia as a service to the academic community and the general public. Standing orders for automatic notification and invoicing of each title in the series upon publication are accepted.

If after review by internal and external readers a manuscript is accepted for publication, it is published on the basis of camera-ready copy provided by the author who is responsible for any copyediting and manuscript formatting. Alternative arrangements should be made with approval of the Series. Address submission inquiries to CEAS Editorial Board, East Asia Program, Cornell University, Ithaca, New York 14853-7601.

Cover photo courtesy of National Archives. Photo no. 306-PS-D-70-2113.

Number 146 in the Cornell East Asia Series
Copyright ©2010 by Sherman Cochran and Paul G. Pickowicz. All rights reserved.
ISSN: 1050-2955
ISBN: 978-1-933947-16-7 hc
ISBN: 978-1-933947-46-4 pb
Library of Congress Control Number: 2009925877

24 23 22 21 20 19 18 17 16 15 14 13 12 11 10   9 8 7 6 5 4 3 2 1

CONTENTS

v

II MARGINS IN RELATION TO CENTERS

ACKNOWLEDGMENTS

This book is the result of cooperation between our respective home institutions, Cornell University and the University of California, San Diego. All essays except for the editors' introduction were originally presented at the University of California, San Diego–Cornell University Modern Chinese History Graduate Student Research Conference held at the Martin Johnson House, Scripps Institution of Oceanography, University of California, San Diego, on June 18–20, 2007. Generous support for the research projects that led to the publication of *China on the Margins* was provided by the following units of the University of California, San Diego: Program in Chinese Studies, Department of History, School of International Relations and Pacific Studies (IR/PS), Institute for International, Comparative, and Area Studies (IICAS), Dean of Arts and Humanities, Dean of Graduate Studies, Dean of Research, Hsiu Endowed Chair in Chinese Studies, Modern Chinese History Endowed Chair, Sokwanlok Endowed Chair of Chinese and International Affairs, Office of Graduate Studies (OGS), and Center for the Humanities.

Equally generous support for research that has gone into this book came from the following units at Cornell University: Graduate School, Department of History, Department of Asian Studies, East Asia Program, Hu Shih Chair of Chinese History, Michael J. Zak Chair of History for U.S.–China Relations.

We would like to thank several participants for their important contributions to the conference. Jeremy Brown, Jenwa Hsung, Ellen C. Huang, Matthew Johnson, and James Wicks presented papers; and Suzanne Cahill, Chen Jian, Joseph Esherick, David Luft, Lu Weijing, and Sarah Schneewind served as discussants.

Besides receiving comments from the graduate students and faculty members at the conference, the contributors to this volume also benefited from close readings and helpful comments on their essays by two anonymous reviewers.

For recruiting these anonymous reviewers and providing her own efficient and graceful editorial guidance, we wish to thank Mai Shaikhanuar-Cota, managing editor of the Cornell East Asia Series. We also owe thanks to Sutee Anantsuktsomsri for formatting the book and Kathryn Torgeson for adding the index.

We have greatly enjoyed the experience of bringing together graduate students and faculty from our two universities. Even though some of us had not met each other before the conference was held, all of us in attendance developed a remarkable esprit de corps, which has made the preparation of this volume surprisingly smooth and deeply satisfying.

1

CENTERS AND MARGINS IN CHINESE HISTORY

Sherman Cochran and Paul G. Pickowicz

> Of course the forces generated within Chinese society affected the ideas and lives of the leaders or would-be leaders, just as did the might or the ideas imposed on China by foreign powers. But I still feel that the attempt to make sense of these varying impulses can most fittingly—in a historical introduction of this kind—be undertaken from the center, looking out.
>
> —Jonathan D. Spence, *The Search for Modern China* (1999)

> Flexibility was characteristic of a period in which national identity was not a dominant characteristic of personal definition in Chinese society. ... That flexibility was achieved through the leverage of marginality: each side of one's doubly marginal identity was a fulcrum to leverage advantages from the other.
>
> —Philip A. Kuhn, *Chinese among Others* (2008)

Should modern Chinese history be approached from the center looking out or from the margins looking in? Jonathan Spence and Philip Kuhn, the distinguished historians quoted above, have eloquently summarized the virtues of these two different approaches. Writing the preface of the second revised edition of his influential survey of modern Chinese history, Spence has taken the position that it is advisable (at least in an introductory book like his) to begin at the center looking out because "the center provides the lens by which we can start to give a general focus to the multiple blips of light radiating from the universe of Chinese experience."[1] By contrast, Kuhn, in his recent analytical overview of the history of Chinese emigration, has shifted attention away from the center and toward the borders where a Chinese emigrant could "[find] unique opportunities in the marginal ground between jurisdictions and [use] one's comparative advantage in each environment to enhance one's position in the other."[2] In taking these positions, clearly Spence and Kuhn differ on which approach is preferable.

Confronted with contrasting views, it is worth asking what the relationship is between the center (or centers) and the margins. In this book, each contributor has given his or her own answer to this question. In this introduction, we want to give two sets of answers. In the first section, we have noted four concepts of the relationship between center and margins and used these concepts to suggest what issues our contributors have addressed in common with each other. In the remaining section, we have called attention to what is distinctive about each contributor's approach to the theme of center and margins.

Four Conceptual Schemes

We can find in our contributors' essays at least four conceptual schemes for understanding relations between the center and the margins: capital as center and provinces as margins; coast as center and interior as margins; cultural metropolis as center and parochial hinterland as margins; China as a center and bordering states also as centers with margins in between. Some contributors share one of these schemes with each other, but even the ones who share the same scheme frequently disagree about the dynamics of the relationship between the center and the margins within that scheme.

Several of the contributors have adopted the first scheme by identifying China's center as its capital and its margins as its provinces. In doing so, they have not all named the same city as the capital because China's capital has moved over time from one city to another. In fact, one advantage of this volume is that its essays span three major political eras: the Qing dynasty (1644–1912) when China's capital was in Beijing; the Republic of China (1912–1949) when its capital was in Beijing (1912–1927), Nanjing (1927–1937), Chongqing (1938–1945), and Nanjing again (1945–1949); and the People's Republic of China (1949–present) when its capital has been in Beijing. To highlight long-term comparisons and contrasts, we have included essays on all three eras in each half of the book. Part I (which is more on the center than the margins) contains essays on the Qing by Judd Kinzley and Peter Lavelle; on the Republic by Justin Jacobs, Jeremy Murray, and Tai Wei Lim; and on the People's Republic by Amy Kardos. Part II (which is more on the margins than the center) has essays on the Qing by Elya Zhang, David Chang, and Tracy Barrett; on the Republic by Soon Keong Ong and Paola Iovene; and on the People's Republic by Xiaojia Hou.[3]

Three of the volume's contributors, Kardos, Zhang, and Hou, have analyzed most closely the political and administrative relationship between the capital as the center and the provinces as the margins. All three have focused on provincial officials and have asked how they related to officials in the capital. Did provincial officials fully enforce policies emanating from the center—even policies that led them to "marginalize" fellow Han Chinese as well as local ethnic minorities (as Kardos concludes)? Did provincial officials originate policies that were accepted and carried out by leaders in the capital (as Hou argues)? Did provincial officials go so far as to reverse their hierarchical relationship with officials at the capital, making themselves "central" and the officials at the capital "marginal" (as Zhang suggests)? Zhang, Kardos, and Hou all agree that the relationship between officials in the capital and in the provinces is a revealing focal point for bringing to light tensions between the center and the margins, but they reach very different conclusions about how provincial officials dealt with this tension.[4]

Three other contributors, Lavelle, Murray, and Chang, identify the center and the margins not in administrative terms between China's capital and its provinces so much as in geo-cultural terms between its east coast and its interior. Their division of China into two cultural environments is similar to the historian Paul Cohen's "polarity between littoral and hinterland." According to Cohen, from about 1500 on, the littoral in eastern China created a new cultural zone oriented to maritime commerce overseas while the hinterland of inland China remained oriented to agriculture. Throughout the following centuries, reformers carried out cultural change across the border between littoral and hinterland in two phases: first "pioneers" from the littoral introduced new ideas into the hinterland, and then "legitimizers," who were native to the hinterland, domesticated and implemented these ideas.

The essays by Lavelle, Murray, and Chang are compatible with Cohen's model to the extent that they trace the movements of dynamic Chinese reformers across the border between littoral and hinterland, but their characterizations raise questions about how reformers have reacted to this experience. When a reformer has been born and raised in the hinterland and moved as an adult to the littoral (as in the case described by Murray), how has early life on the margins of reform affected later life at the center? When reformers ventured from littoral to hinterland, were they necessarily limited to the role of either "pioneer" or "legitimizer"? Did some extraordinary reformers with strong institutional support from the littoral succeed at not only pioneering new ideas but also legitimizing new practices in the hinterland (as in the cases presented by Lavelle and Chang)? Lavelle, Murray, and Chang seem to accept Cohen's notion of the littoral as the center and the hinterland as the margins, but as they trace reformers' movements from the littoral to the hinterland or vice versa, they differ in their assessments of how swiftly and extensively reformers brought about political and cultural transformation.[5]

Three other contributors, Jacobs, Lim, and Iovene, have described cities that were centers but were not necessarily designated as official capitals or located in the littoral. Their focus is on intellectuals—scholars, scientists, engineers, artists, filmmakers—and their historical figures considered cultural metropolises (where media were concentrated) to be the centers and regarded outlying cities and towns (where media did not reach) to be the margins. As the literary critic Leo Lee has pointed out, defining a metropolis in cultural terms is difficult to do. But Lee's "remapping" of Shanghai brings him to one unequivocal conclusion: it became the cultural center of China in the first half of the twentieth century. In his words, "By 1930 Shanghai had become a bustling cosmopolitan metropolis, the fifth largest city in the world and China's largest harbor and treaty port, a city that was already an international legend ('the Paris of Asia'), and a world of splendid modernity set apart from the still tradition-bound countryside that was China." This contrast between Shanghai as a cosmopolitan center and the rest of China as a tradition-bound countryside resembles Cohen's polarity between littoral and hinterland to some extent, but Lee identifies the center more exclusively with the city and specifically Shanghai "as the hub of the publishing industry, the place where most of this literature was produced and circulated to the country at large."

Was Shanghai China's supreme or even sole cultural center, and if so, for how long? "[N]ot until after the Sino-Japanese War ended in 1945," Lee has concluded, "did Shanghai's urban glory come to an end." But on this question, our contributors differ with Lee and each other. Unlike Lee, Jacobs has described more than one cultural center in prewar and wartime China. He notes that Chinese scholars first developed into an intelligentsia at Nanjing while it was the prewar capital of Chiang Kai-shek's Nationalist government (1927–1937) and then followed this government as it retreated in the wake of the Japanese invasion up the Yangzi River to Chongqing, Chiang's capital for the duration of the war (1938–1945). Similarly Lim describes leading Chinese engineers who fled inland and relocated their research on oil and drilling operations in northwest China for the duration of the war because of its proximity to Chongqing. But Iovene's interpretation is more in line with Lee's. She shows that not all intellectuals abandoned Shanghai and shifted China's cultural center to Chongqing during the war. Chinese filmmakers and film audiences continued to be influential participants in China's national discourse, making Shanghai a center for the country's media. So these contributors have become participants in a debate over the location and nature of China's cultural center.[6]

Three other contributors, Kinzley, Barrett, and Ong, have discussed the center and the margins not merely within China but between China as one center and other countries or colonies as other centers, and they have located the margins along the borders in between. They have agreed that Chinese officials and immigrants were aware of more than one center, but they have disagreed about who determined the immigrants' fate and what motivated their actions. Were decisions on the margins determined by the interactions of officials in two centers (as in Kinzley's analysis of negotiations over Xinjiang between officials in the Qing and Russian central governments)? As immigrants established residences on either side or both sides of China's borders, did they remain bound by informal ties primarily to China as the center (as Barrett concludes in her study of overseas Chinese under French colonial rule in Indochina)? Or were immigrants affected by their experiences in a center abroad as much as the center in China (as Ong argues in his analysis of

Chinese immigrants' motivations for returning to Xiamen from the Philippines)? The contributors agree that Chinese immigrants on the margins related to more than one center, but they disagree with each other about whether these immigrants were more strongly and enduringly committed to China than to other centers.[7] These four conceptions—capital-provinces, littoral-hinterland, metropolis-countryside, China-borderlands—are by no means the only ways of expressing the relationship between the center and the margins. We have identified these four schemes not to provide an exhaustive list of such conceptions but rather to call attention to the ones most commonly used explicitly or implicitly in our contributors' essays. We hope that these four schemes suggest how some of the contributors' interpretations relate to each other—complementing, contrasting, or conflicting with each other. But we also want to emphasize that the contributors have produced distinctive ideas that do not all fit neatly into these four schemes, and it is important to note how each one's interpretation differs from the rest.

Centers in Relations to Margins

In analyzing the dynamics between centers and margins, some of the contributors have positioned themselves primarily at a center looking out, and others have situated themselves primarily at the margins looking in. Accordingly, we have divided their essays into two parts, grouping together the ones that are more about centers in the first half of the book and the ones that are more about margins in the second half.

Contributors focusing on one or more centers have noted how radically a center's policies and perceptions could change over time. In his discussion of the Qing court's policies toward Xinjiang in the far northwest during the nineteenth century, Judd Kinzley analyzes a dramatic shift in the meaning of the concept of "opening wasteland." He notes that throughout most of the nineteenth century the Qing construed this policy to mean that Han farmers and merchants should migrate from China to the frontiers of Xinjiang and that Han miners should not. Then at the end of the century, the Qing reversed itself, dropping the stereotype of miners as "wicked people" and sanctioning their migration (along with farmers and merchants) to Xinjiang. Why did the Qing change its policy? Kinzley suggests that it responded to a threat from another political center, the Russian empire, which had served as its partner in earlier gold mining ventures but was perceived as one of the imperialist powers closing in on it in the late nineteenth century. Kinzley bases his interpretation on not only Beijing's perceptions of high diplomacy but also Qing officials' interactions with miners in the mountainous gold mining areas of the northwest corner of Xinjiang, and his vivid descriptions indicate that the Qing's reach extended to some of the most distant margins of the empire.

Peter Lavelle also documents the Qing's official reach into Xinjiang, and he focuses on one official in particular, Zuo Zongtang, who led an expedition to northwest China and Xinjiang to suppress a Muslim revolt and secure the border for the empire in the mid-nineteenth century. Zuo faithfully followed instructions from the Qing capital in Beijing, but along the way he also took inspiration from a different kind of center—the agricultural center of China along the Yangzi River in Hunan province, where he had grown up in a farming family, and Zhejiang province, where he had served as an official. While following Beijing's orders in deploying his troops for military purposes in the northwest and Xinjiang, he devised his own policies for agricultural development of these arid places, importing seeds from the lush and productive Yangzi area and supervising his soldier-farmers as they transplanted cotton, mulberry trees (for feeding silkworms and developing sericulture), and other crops in the deserts of the northwest. To what extent did Zuo obliterate the ecological distinction between Xinjiang's deserts and the Yangzi's wet lands and eliminate the administrative distinction between Xinjiang and China's provinces? Lavelle argues that Zuo did not carry out all of these plans, but in relation to China's agricultural and political centers, he did make Xinjiang less marginal.

After the fall of the Qing in 1912, the Republic was founded, and within a few decades, it moved its political center twice—from Beijing to Nanjing in 1927 after Chiang Kai-shek carried out the Northern Expedition, and from Nanjing to Chongqing in 1938 when Chiang led his Nationalist government's retreat up the Yangzi River under the onslaught of the Japanese military invasion of China. As Justin Jacobs shows, each of these relocations of the capital had significant consequences for Chinese conceptions of the relationship between the center and the margins. In each of these periods, Chinese intellectuals reformulated the basis for the Chinese center's claims of sovereignty over the northwest, and they did so by their interpretations of the archaeological handling of ancient manuscripts and objects in the Dunhuang caves, which were located in the northwest. Before the mid-1920s, Chinese intellectuals did not strenuously object to Western scholars' acquisitions of these materials and even praised their Western counterparts for making archaeological discoveries and preserving valuable old documents and objects dating from the fourth to eleventh centuries. Then in the 1920s and 1930s, especially during the Nanjing decade of 1927–1937, Chinese intellectuals cohered into a professional intelligentsia and produced an aggressively nationalistic critique of Westerners for "plundering" Dunhuang and inferring from Dunhuang documents in Sanskrit that the northwest was not an integral part of the Chinese nation. After moving westward in 1938 to Chongqing, a political center closer to the northwest, Chinese intellectuals deepened their emotional commitment to this same position, becoming even angrier with Western scholars for their "thefts" from the caves. Their lobbying ultimately culminated in the Nationalist government's decision to give state protection to Dunhuang in 1944. Jacobs's imaginative interpretation calls attention to shifts in intellectual centers as well as political ones and suggests that archaeology played a significant role in legitimating China's claim to sovereignty over the northwestern regions on the margins.

Jeremy Murray's chapter also deals with the ways in which centrally based urban professionals dealt with the special privileges enjoyed by foreign nationals in China. Citing the case of Zhang Yaozeng, who served on three occasions as Minister of Justice in the late 'teens and early 1920s, Murray analyzes the efforts made by central reformers to transform China's legal system as a way of forcing the foreign powers to give up extraterritoriality—a humiliating legal arrangement that kept foreign nationals out of Chinese courts. The result would strengthen the nation and restore China's national sovereignty. "What is the path to self-respect and self-renewal?" Zhang asked. "I would say, the answer is to establish a transparent legal system, an independent judiciary, and to maintain law and order in such a way that politics remains within the confines of the law." But Zhang and other like-minded reformers at the center of politics concluded early on that success would depend on political initiatives undertaken in the hinterlands. Zhang was an ardent nationalist who sought to foster nationalist consciousness, but he had launched his political career far from the national capital—as a law student in Japan and as a passionate advocate of the interests of his home province of Yunnan on China's southern border. As Minister of Justice, Zhang promoted a decentralized and federalist judiciary. Indeed, he saw himself as a politician caught "in the middle," trying his best to "mediate" between competing centers and margins. As a nation, China would advance when the center was able to reclaim margins in the legal sphere dominated by foreign interests. But once reclaimed by the center, these legal margins would have to be turned over to the control of independent, nonpartisan, judicial institutions that would guarantee fairness, popular access and accountability. Indeed, at various points in his career Zhang declined offers to work at the state center, preferring to travel throughout the hinterland. His efforts to balance centers and margins met with resistance—mainly from those who represented the interests of centers. Foreign powers did not want to give up their extraterritorial legal privileges even after legal reforms were carried out in China. The Nationalists and the Communists, newly emerging centralizing revolutionary parties, wanted an end to foreign extraterritorial legal privileges, but were highly suspicious of community-based and independent judicial structures in the hinterland.

Tai Wei Lim shows that another group of intellectuals, engineers and technicians, also shaped the relationship between political centers and margins. He concentrates on the Chongqing era, 1938–1945, and he notes that Chiang Kai-shek's retreat in 1938 cut his government off from oil because Chongqing, unlike Nanjing, was at the headwaters of the Yangzi River and was far from the coast and the nearest railway line. Desperate for oil in wartime, Chiang assigned Western-trained Chinese engineers the task of searching for new oil fields in parts of China not under the Japanese occupation. Just as Kinzley shows that the Qing government reached out from its capital at Beijing to the margins for gold to finance its defense against Russian imperialism in the late nineteenth century, so Lim shows that the Republican government at its capital in Chongqing reached out to the margins for oil to fuel its defense against Japanese imperialism in the 1930s and 1940s. Despite their lack of sophisticated imported equipment, the Chinese engineers and technicians under the sponsorship of the Nationalist government had surprising success at exploiting new discoveries at Yumen near Xinjiang, 865 miles northwest of Chongqing. In rich detail, Lim describes how these oil specialists overcame wartime isolation, adapted to local conditions, and devised their own technological and managerial solutions to the problems of locating and extracting oil on the margins in Yumen and transporting it to the political center in Chongqing.

Amy Kardos, like Kinzley, Lavelle, Jacobs, and Lim, describes the consequences of efforts to reach from a political center in China to the far northwest. In her chapter, the center was Beijing, the capital of China since the founding of the People's Republic of China in 1949, which deployed troops to restore order and secure the country's northwestern border in Xinjiang during the early 1950s. As Kardos points out, Beijing's aims at the time resembled those of the Qing in the nineteenth century as described by Kinzley and Lavelle, but unlike the Qing, the government of the People's Republic mobilized for this purpose soldiers from the army of a rival, Chiang Kai-shek, whose Nationalist government had been defeated by Mao Zedong and the People's Liberation Army in the Civil War of 1946–1949. In other words, in Xinjiang one political center (Beijing) used troops that had previously fought against it representing another political center (Nanjing, 1945–1949 and after Chiang was defeated and withdrew from the mainland in 1949, Taipei). Did the commanders from Beijing confine these former Nationalist troops as prisoners of war in Xinjiang or convert them into colonists expanding an empire for the People's Republic? Comparing the former Nationalist troops with groups of their fellow soldiers in Xinjiang—Han members of the People's Liberation Army and Uyghurs and Kazakhs formerly in the Army of the East Turkestan Republic— Kardos concludes that the former Nationalist troops were "twice marginalized," a historically suggestive characterization that might well apply to others who have been caught in more than one phase of relationships between the center and the margins.

All of these contributors to Part I of the book discuss both centers and margins, with their primary focus on centers. In Part II, the authors also deal with both centers and margins, but their primary focus is on margins.

Margins in Relation to Centers

All of the contributors in Part II describe Chinese efforts to exploit advantages on the margins in relation to centers as they sought to benefit (in Kuhn's words) from "the leverage of marginality." But each author characterizes a group that was marginalized, organized, and mobilized in its own distinctive way. Like Part I, Part II includes essays set in the Qing dynasty, the Republic of China, and the People's Republic of China.

In her analysis of a provincial official's network, Elya Zhang shows how he overcame his bureaucratic marginalization. In the late Qing, this official, Duanfang, was appointed to the middling rank of deputy viceroy in the inland province of Hubei far from the capital at Beijing and the coastal port of Shanghai. And yet, as Zhang documents in rich detail, Duanfang personally intervened in the Subao case of 1903 when two of the most articulate and incendiary anti-Qing revolutionaries were brought to trial in Shanghai's International Mixed Court and were accused of campaigning to overthrow the dynasty. Officially Duanfang had no role in this case, which was being tried entirely outside his jurisdiction. But as a Qing loyalist, he took a personal interest in it and started a campaign to extradite the accused from the International Mixed Court in the foreign concession area (where they would be tried under Western law) into Qing jurisdiction (where they would be tried under imperial law). With this aim he mobilized an extraordinarily diverse network consisting of Chinese officials in Beijing and Shanghai, Chinese journalists at major Chinese-language newspapers, and Western academics with ties to ambassadors representing Western governments. Zhang acknowledges that Duanfang's campaign failed, but she argues that it would have succeeded if the Qing leadership had not alienated the Westerners in Duanfang's network by having a Chinese journalist beaten to death at the time. If she is right, then provincial officials holding inland posts that might have seemed marginal were capable of making themselves central to the Chinese government's decision making—even more central than higher ranking officials serving in the capital and coastal ports.

David Chang also examines the final years of the Qing era, focusing on the elections that were held in China in 1909. He mentions actions taken by the Qing court at the capital in Beijing to authorize and implement these elections, notably the creation of a Constitutional Commission and Provincial Assembly Preparatory Bureaus. But he distinguishes between state and society (as Spence does in the epigraph above), and he argues that it was the society on the political margins, not the state at the political center, that made the election viable. At the local level, the state simply did not have the bureaucratic resources to register and mobilize voters throughout the country. By default, these tasks were left largely to non-governmental figures: the established local gentry, members of the elite who had been educated abroad or in recently founded Western-style schools in China, and the press. The efforts to register voters and convince them to vote were by no means universally welcomed, and Chang has found two instances in the hinterlands of Shaanxi and Jiangxi provinces where elections workers were attacked by villagers and killed or chased away. But despite these contrasts between attitudes in the center (at the littoral) and on the margins (inland), he concludes that the election proves China was (and is) fit for democracy, and he attributes its success largely to the press, which he lauds for daring to criticize the government, expose corrupt campaign practices, and educate voters.

Like Zhang and Chang, Tracy Barrett sets her essay mainly in the last decade of the Qing dynasty and focuses on Chinese efforts to mobilize their society in relation to the state, but she discusses overseas Chinese living outside the Qing empire in the French colony of Indochina. In her analysis, even though these overseas Chinese were officially subordinated under French rule, they—not the French—exercised decisive control over education for Chinese in Indochina. They did so primarily through Chinese congregations, which established and sustained Chinese schools and determined the outcomes for schools opened by the French for Chinese. French schools that lacked the support of Chinese congregations failed. Only the ones receiving this support survived. How the congregations achieved this control in relation to the French political center, which had its headquarters for the colony of Indochina in Hanoi, is the central question in Barrett's chapter, and she addresses it by analyzing Chinese loyalty to their native places in China as a basis for the organizational solidarity of their congregations in Indochina.

Soon Keong Ong is also interested in overseas Chinese and the organizations that they formed to mobilize along the margins, but he questions whether love of national or provincial homeland provides an adequate explanation for their solidarity and actions. He describes a movement that was led by Chinese who had emigrated from China to the Philippines and then returned to their home area in southern Fujian province in the vicinity of the coastal port of Xiamen. He concedes that they made local investments and reformed local institutions in campaigns similar to the ones for schools as described by Barrett. But he questions whether their affection for their native place was the sole or even the primary motivation for these campaigns. He points out that overseas Chinese from southern Fujian were initially pushed back to China in the 1920s by anti-Chinese discrimination in the Philippines, not pulled back by love of homeland. Once they had returned, according to his interpretation, they made investments in Fujian and China during the 1920s and 1930s more out of a self-centered profit motive than a sentimental attachment to their native place or a fervent belief in their nation. Leveraging their marginality between two centers, China and the Philippines, they showed no deep ideological commitment to either.

What motivations lay behind the process of leveraging the margins and how these motivations should be weighed one against another are fundamental questions that Ong raises in his essay. On native place as a basis for organizing on the margins, Paola Iovene's position is perhaps closer to Barrett's than to Ong's. As she points out, her historical figures differ from theirs because she is describing internal migrants rather than emigrants who have been abroad. But if her subjects were not located on or across the borders of the Chinese state, they were afraid nonetheless of being marginalized in Chinese society. Born in Yangzhou, a city north of Shanghai, they were commonly identified in Shanghai with Subei people who hailed from an area near Yangzhou and held jobs as manual laborers with low pay. Hoping to climb the social ladder, the Yangzhou people sought to become "de-marginalized" by distinguishing themselves from low-status Subei immigrants in Shanghai. Their aspirations became apparent in 1947 when a group of Yangzhou barbers in Shanghai mounted an effective campaign against a film that they believed had slandered them because it lumped them together with low status Subei people. Showing remarkable resourcefulness, they even succeeded at getting some of the offensive scenes removed from the film. How did a group of barbers manage to gain control over a major film that had been made by one of the country's leading studios? Iovene reaches the paradoxical conclusion that they both utilized their native-place association and took advantage of national discourse on morality and education. In other words, they leveraged their marginality to forge a link between themselves and China's ideological center.

Xiaojia Hou shares Iovene's interest in local initiatives from the margins in conjunction with a national center. She has set her essay in the People's Republic of China during the early 1950s, and she has written about agricultural policymaking—a process that has previously been characterized almost exclusively as a unilateral top-down phenomenon. It has been assumed by many that all significant initiatives under socialist central planning at the time came from the center and specifically from the paramount leader of the country, Mao Zedong. But Hou has challenged this view by documenting in local archives the actions of some adventuresome provincial and local cadres in the north China province of Shanxi. As she notes, this province was marginalized in 1945 when Mao and other leaders of the Chinese Communist Party moved away from their wartime base at Yan'an, which was near Shanxi, and was marginalized still farther after 1949 when these leaders set up the People's Republic's capital in more distant Beijing. Nonetheless, in the early 1950s, cadres in Shanxi captured the attention of the center. They aggressively criticized top Beijing leaders' views of land reform and rural revolution, and they urged Mao to adopt and implement their proposals on a national scale. How these aggressive cadres on the margins were able to overcome both official and unofficial barriers and decisively exercise their influence on the center is explained in Hou's essay.

Even as the essays in Part I demonstrate the need to look from centers to margins, so the essays in Part II confirm the need to look from margins to centers. At the same time, all of the essays in both parts of the book capture the dynamism of the relationships between the centers and the margins. None assumes that a center unilaterally dictated policies that were passively and uncritically accepted on the margins, and none claims that provocative positions taken on the margins went uncontested at a center. While focusing in each case on relationships between centers and margins, these essays show the need for reconsidering how the meanings of the terms "center" and "margins" vary from one historical period to another and from one political or social context to another.

The following essays bring to light many of these meanings—even more than the four that we have identified in this introduction. The authors' various conceptions of relations between centers and margins give a possible answer to the question that we posed at the beginning of this introduction or at least provide a reminder that another question is inseparable from this one. In deciding whether we should approach Chinese history from the center looking out or from the margins looking in, each of us needs to consider carefully in the context of our historical topic what we mean by "centers" and "margins."

NOTES

1. Jonathan D. Spence, *The Search for Modern China* 2nd rev. ed. (New York: Norton, 1999), xxi.

2. Philip A. Kuhn, *Chinese among Others: Emigration in Modern Times* (Lanham: Rowman and Littlefield, 2008), 235.

3. For a recent collection of essays on China's margins during the Ming dynasty (1368–1644) and Qing dynasty (1644–1912), see Pamela Kyle Crossley, Helen F. Siu, and Donald S. Sutton, eds., *Empire at the Margins: Culture, Ethnicity, and Frontier in Early Modern China* (Berkeley: University of California Press, 2006). These essays are well worth comparing to the ones in the present volume, but they differ from most of the ones included here not only in their chronological coverage but also in their sharp focus on ethnicity.

4. On relations between provincial officials and the capital in the late Qing, see Lloyd Eastman, *Throne and Mandarins: China's Search for a Policy during the Sino-French Controversy, 1880–1885* (Cambridge: Harvard University Press, 1967); Joseph W. Esherick, *Reform and Revolution in China: The 1911 Revolution in Hunan and Hubei* (Berkeley: University of California Press, 1976); Edward J. M. Rhoads, *China's Republican Revolution: The Case of Kwangtung, 1895–1913* (Cambridge: Harvard University Press, 1975). On these relations in the Republic, see Hsi-sheng Ch'i, *Warlord Politics in China, 1916–1928* (Stanford: Stanford University Press, 1976); James Sheridan, *China in Disintegration: The Republican Era in Chinese History, 1912–1949* (New York: Free Press, 1975). On these relations in the early years of the People's Republic, see essays by Jeremy Brown, Chen

Jian, Christian A. Hess, and James Z. Gao in Jeremy Brown and Paul G. Pickowicz, eds., *Dilemmas of Victory: The Early Years of the People's Republic of China* (Cambridge: Harvard University Press, 2007), part II.

5. Cohen originally introduced this model in his book, *Between Tradition and Modernity: Wang T'ao and Reform in Late Ch'ing China* (Cambridge: Harvard University Press, 1974). For an updated restatement of it, see Paul A. Cohen, "Wang Tao in a Changing World," in his *China Unbound: Evolving Perspectives on the Chinese Past* (London: Routledge Curzon, 2003), 37–44. Susan Mann has questioned the validity of Cohen's distinction between littoral and hinterland as it applies to late imperial China. For her critique, see her *Local Merchants and the Chinese Bureaucracy, 1750–1950* (Stanford: Stanford University Press, 1987), 27.

6. Leo Ou-fan Lee, *Shanghai Modern: The Flowering of a New Urban Culture in China, 1930–1945* (Cambridge: Harvard University Press, 1999), quotations from xi, 3–4, and 323. For an interpretation contrary to Lee's and more in line with Jacobs' and Lim's, see Chang-tai Hung, *War and Popular Culture: Resistance in Modern China, 1937–1945* (Berkeley: University of California Press, 1994). For a critique of Hung's argument, see Sherman Cochran, *Chinese Medicine Men: Consumer Culture in China and Southeast Asia* (Cambridge: Harvard University Press, 2006), 115–16.

7. Ong has done a critical survey of the considerable body of literature on whether overseas Chinese have been more committed to China or their adopted homeland abroad. See his "Coming Home to a Foreign Country: Xiamen, Overseas Chinese, and the Politics of Identities, 1843–1938" (Cornell University, Ph.D. dissertation, 2007), especially chapter 1.

I

CENTERS IN RELATION TO MARGINS

2

TURNING PROSPECTORS INTO SETTLERS

Gold, Immigrant Miners and the Settlement of the Frontier in Late Qing Xinjiang

Judd Kinzley

Late on the night of August 26, 1855, an inferno raged through the Russian trade concession in the Qing frontier town of Tacheng. Soldiers from the local garrison arrived on the scene in time to witness an unruly mob of five or six hundred immigrant gold miners and nomads looting the gutted compound. The fiery holocaust in this outpost located on the geographic margins of the empire (see maps on pp. 35–37) was the outgrowth of a simmering tension in the region that emerged with the expansion of the Russian empire. More significantly, the incident marked a turning point for the perpetrators, a loosely organized community of gold prospectors who had been working the region's lucrative gold veins for more than half a century. Initially labeled bandits or violent criminals, this socially marginalized group was once actively repressed by local officials. But the emergence of the imperialist threat from Russia transformed immigrant prospectors into settlers. By the late nineteenth century, this motley group would be embraced as a vital component of the Qing frontier project in this volatile border region.[1]

In 1766, less than ten years after the conquest of Xinjiang, Qing forces founded a small outpost on the farthest western edge of their rapidly expanding new empire. They named it Suijingcheng, or "Pacification Town," a name that reflected an ongoing reality in this volatile region, as attempts to pacify this newly conquered area would occupy officials and administrators for much of the next two centuries. But the nature of this process of pacification in this isolated settlement, which in later years would come to be known as Tacheng, evolved over time. Initially, Qing administrators implemented an agriculture-centered policy of "opening wasteland" with the plow. This strategy, long employed by Chinese officials desiring to pacify restive nomads (see Lavelle, chapter 3), failed in the face of Tacheng's arid, high altitude environment made up largely of "steep valleys and rocky peaks" surrounded on all sides by land that became boggy marshland in the spring and summer.[2] Stymied in their attempts to make large-scale agricultural enterprises work, by the late nineteenth century Qing officials proved increasingly willing to consider an expanded definition of pacification.

The discovery of gold in the Katu Mountain range, located 150 miles southeast of Tacheng, helped stimulate local and provincial officials to rethink their views on frontier settlement and also prompted a reevaluation of the traditional meaning of wasteland (*huang*). Merchant travelers sojourning through this isolated backwater frequently commented that the tell tale glint of gold could be made out by the naked eye as veins of laden ore wormed their way through the red ocherous shale of the Katu.[3] The region's gold veins were said to be "chaotic, like spooled out thread."[4] Dancing and twirling across a stretch of arid mountains nearly thirty-five miles in total area, the veins had a hypnotic effect on all who caught sight of them. No one knows exactly when the first gold miners came to the Katu, but by the latter years of the eighteenth century, the zigzagging maze of gold-bearing quartz veins were luring scores of impoverished peasants away from hardscrabble farms in the loess highlands of Gansu, Ningxia, and Shaanxi provinces.

The new immigrants flooded into a region with an administrative infrastructure ill-equipped to handle the expanding population. Saddled with a deep-seated mistrust of these wealth-seekers, at first Qing officials banned prospectors, typically referring to them in court memorials as "drifters," "brigands" or "wicked people." Fed by periodic episodes of violence, these suspicions would linger in the minds of officials. But by the latter years of the nineteenth century, gold mining operations and the prospectors working for them would undergo a staggering social transformation. In the late 1890s miners were no longer referred to as bandits or criminals in official Qing documents. Instead, they were transformed from socially marginalized prospectors to socially acceptable settlers, charged with the vital task of occupying and integrating this isolated border region into the Qing state.

Scholarship on the settlement of the Qing empire's geographic margins, from maritime peripheries in Taiwan to territorial ones in Mongolia, parts of Manchuria and Xinjiang, has tended to focus on the immigration of Han Chinese agrarian and merchant communities. In Xinjiang, the historian James Millward has argued that a series of rebellions in the first two decades of the nineteenth century prompted the Qing court to begin actively encouraging the migration of these more socially acceptable economic migrants to offset and pacify restive local Muslims. But by ending his study in 1864 and by focusing exclusively on agricultural and merchant communities, Millward misses the revolutionary transformation of the frontier process that did not begin until the late Qing period.

It would take more than half a century before immigrant gold miners too were invited by the Qing state to participate in the settlement of Xinjiang. The metamorphosis of the immigrant gold mining community in Tacheng from an actively repressed underclass into an army of settlers offers a window onto the Qing frontier project not only in Xinjiang but throughout China.

The transformation of mining operations in this isolated area south of the Tarbagatai Mountains reflected shifts in the domestic economic market. But more significantly it also hints at a broader reevaluation of Qing court priorities when confronted by the forces of imperialism. A more defensive stance transformed the social status of gold mining communities and indeed the mineral itself. In the face of a perceived Russian threat, gold and gold miners in Tacheng were seen as bulwarks in the Qing defense of the region. Gold was increasingly viewed as a way of funding local Qing administration and gold miners, like the agricultural colonists, banner troops, and merchants that preceded them, were now themselves charged with the important task of opening Tacheng's vast wasteland and through their patterns of settlement, drawing this region on the geographic margins of China ever closer to the center.

Learning to Accept Immigrant Gold Miners

Tucked away into a mountainous corner of the Qing empire's most distant western edge, Tacheng is isolated even today. Along the nineteenth century official network of post roads, the city was located nearly 700 miles north of Yili, the administrative center of Xinjiang. The trip would take its traveler through twenty-seven military posts and as late as 1934 could be completed in no less than twenty days of hard travel by horse cart.[5] The fact that the Manchu garrison at Dihua, located outside of modern day Urumqi, was only slightly closer at around 400 miles, would have done little to make nineteenth century immigrants from China proper feel less remote.[6]

In 1805 Tacheng had a population of more than 12,000 people and for those early nineteenth century Han Chinese travelers the city might have felt like a cultural oasis.[7] Residents could brag about Tacheng's twenty-foot-high city wall, its temple to Guandi with a biannual sacrifice in the spring and fall, and its Lama temple with a statue of the Buddha that was cast in 1770 and gilded at official expense thirty years later.[8] But any relief sojourners from the east might have felt upon arriving could not have lasted when they contemplated what lay outside those imposing walls. There, confronted by the severity of the landscape, generations of travelers captured the terror of the region's unending steppe in poems, songs, and historical legends.

But these literary images of the local topography often hid more than they revealed. One intrepid Chinese traveler who journeyed extensively through the region from 1916 to 1917 very sensibly pointed out that the high altitude grasses that could be construed as "steppe" made up only one quarter of the region's topographical mélange. He describes the other three quarters as blowing sand deserts, newly irrigated agricultural land, and craggy windswept mountain ridges.[9] The city itself was almost completely hemmed in by mountains. To the north was the Tarbagatai Mountain range, to the southeast ran the Barlyk Mountains, to the south the Ala-tau range and even farther south sat the foothills of the Tianshan, Xinjiang's towering snowcapped geographic divide. The natural environment left much to be desired for travelers venturing north from the region's population centers around Yili or Urumqi. Mountainous areas were known to be host to a long list of "pestilent poisons," and the flat land was either boggy marsh plagued by "a myriad of most vicious mosquitoes" or else was waterless, salt encrusted plains that forced many travelers into "traveling by night and pretending to rest by day."[10]

In spite of these well-publicized horrors, thousands of eighteenth- and nineteenth-century Chinese "drifters" (youmin), as Qing officials called them, pulled up stakes in their arid, overworked homesteads in Gansu, Ningxia, and Shaanxi provinces farther east and ventured into this forbidding wilderness. They came to the edge of the empire seeking gold. Competing with tales of the ominous steppe were new stories being brought back by travelers and merchants which told of Tacheng's incalculable mineral wealth. Gold sat close to the surface in this region, making the promise of wealth tantalizingly close. Even if immigrants lacked the resources to chip away at Tacheng's mesmerizing quartz veins themselves, at the very least they could earn money hauling water or collecting firewood for those who did.

For the Qing, the first indicators of northern Xinjiang's gold wealth surfaced in 1770. In that year, the court was alerted to the news that a group of men sent into the mountains to cut trees around the northern town of Manas (located south of Tacheng and just east of what is today considered the city's administrative region) had come back bearing gold nuggets.[11] The next year, military officials in the nearby town of Kuitun were surprised to come across an individual named Zhou Yiqiang chipping gold bearing quartz out of veins lining a small river valley, smashing the rock and then washing the gold-laden ore in the local river. As an immigrant miner from China proper, Zhou was seen by Qing officials as the vanguard of a potentially destabilizing force in this newly conquered and still volatile region. Inspired by a desire to profit from the wealth and also to secure the site from a further incursion of potential immigrant miners, in 1772, the court ordered a unit of soldiers from the local garrison to work the area's gold veins.[12]

Similar developments were unfolding in the Daerdamutu Mountains, later known as the Katu. In 1796, a local official sent into the mountains to survey the situation must have been surprised when he came upon a large number of prospectors chasing gold veins so numerous they were "arrayed like chess pieces or stars in the sky."[13] He recovered from his shock enough to seize nearly five pounds of gold from the miners who were forbidden from operating in this area and won the distinction of becoming the first reported incident of an authority confronting illegal prospectors in the Katu.[14] At least initially, the prospect of mineral wealth appeared to have little impact on the calculations of court officials in Beijing. Their primary concern was security. During the eighteenth century, the area around Tacheng was so critical to Qing defense that soldiers stationed at frontier guard posts in the vicinity received higher rations and wages than those at other sites. An important part of this security calculation, and a priority for the Qing court in this isolated border region was the retention of nomadic support.[15] Many local nomads with camps set up around Tacheng were in fact Qing nomadic banner troops from allied tribes in Manchuria and Eastern Mongolia who had been stationed in Xinjiang following the conquest of the region in 1759. These soldiers were seen as vital to Qing security, and were set up in seminomadic encampments near frontier guard posts and charged with defending the borders. The court feared that the presence of legions of rowdy, displaced wealth-seekers from China proper would create social instability and spark opposition from the nomadic groups. Faced with this unsettling possibility, in 1795, the Council of State in Beijing "asked for a prohibition [on entry into the Katu Mountains]."[16] The gold fields were promptly closed. And to drive the point home, that same year, the Grand Council of State and the Yili Governor-general, together called upon the local military commander to make a yearly military foray into the region "to investigate whether or not furtive gold diggers were there, [and if so] immediately apprehend them and deal with them according to precedent."[17]

The precedent, which later generations of military commanders dutifully followed, was set in 1796 when a patrol caught Zhang Tianxi and Wan Wurong leading a group of prospectors in the Katu Mountains. As the leaders, the two men were dealt with harshly: they were locked into the heavy cangue for three months and then sent to Manchuria to serve the military as slaves.[18] In later years, torture was often used as an interrogation tactic, sentences of seven years in exile were frequently handed down, and even the lightest sentences, for first time offenders, called for them to be "transported with the cangue and the rod back to their native places to be turned over to local officials."[19]

The influx of illegal prospectors had not abated by 1806, so the Yili Governor General Song Yun increased the frequency of patrols sent into the gold fields to four times per year.[20] Three years later the plan earned an endorsement from the Jiaqing Emperor who issued an imperial rescript calling on local and provincial officials to "increase investigations; if there are violators, immediately punish them. Do not be lax."[21] This, too, did little to stem the tide. An examination of the available archival papers on the Katu Mountain gold fields shows that between 1809 and 1811 more than 215 illegal gold diggers were caught and punished by Qing patrols.

In order to understand the unrelenting desire to pursue and punish illegal prospectors during this period, it is important to keep in mind the long-held view of mining held by many Qing officials and elites. E-tu Zen Sun argues that miners in late imperial China were looked upon "with a combination of curiosity, contempt and fear."[22] Immigrant metal miners in particular were viewed with a great deal of suspicion and typically banished to the social margins of High Qing society. When groups of prospectors converged in large numbers they were often seen as a dangerous destabilizing challenge to authority, different from bandits or rebels only in degree. These views were endorsed by officials in Xinjiang, who frequently referred to illegal prospectors as "wicked people" (jianmin) and generally treated them as such. Their rigidity and insistence on firm control of the region began to fade in the face of the ever-growing influx of economic refugees to the area and the commensurate increase in the cost of patrols.[23]

In an 1801 memorial to the court, the Governor-general Song Yun first raised the issue of allowing mining in the Katu. The poverty of the immigrants was a major issue for Song and subsequent advocates for allowing mining operations. These leaders argued that only by providing these legions of impoverished peasants with employment opportunities in state-sanctioned mines could they avoid turning them into bandits. Song hijacked the rhetoric frequently used by the court as an argument against mining, insisting that allowing these immigrants to work the region's lucrative gold veins would be "a way of pacifying the area."[24] Perhaps more tellingly, however, he supplemented his argument with a straightforward economic calculus. Song suggested the attractive possibility that the opening up of mining operations in the Katu could help fill provincial treasuries and cited the success of legal mining operations in the gold fields around Urumqi as proof.[25] But the court was not yet prepared to entertain such a radical shift in policy. In the second decade of the nineteenth century, despite the aggressive campaign against them, the number of immigrants to the Katu only continued to grow. But officials and soldiers charged with seizing the gold assets of illegal prospecting enterprises could not have failed to understand the extent of the region's mineral resources. Gradually they came to realize the important role that these resources could play in funding the Qing empire in this "new dominion."

The identification of this new source of provincial revenue emerged in a context of skyrocketing operational costs for the Qing in this region. The bulk of these administrative and military costs were being shouldered by the provinces of China proper. An official in the Qing Ministry of Personnel complained in 1814 that "Xinjiang's yearly military budget reaches several hundreds of thousands [of taels], and it is China proper that bears quite a lot of this burden."[26] James Millward argues that the growing financial burden of empire in nineteenth-century Xinjiang turned the region into a policy "laboratory of sorts" for Qing officials seeking a way out of the financial morass.[27] But it seems clear that his list of innovative trade, market, and currency reforms that were implemented by officials in the region should be expanded to include the evolution of mining policy. Understanding the potential for profit in local gold mines, in 1814, the Qing court reversed course and issued a precedent breaking edict that endorsed earlier plans calling for the opening of the Katu to immigrant prospectors.[28] In late May, Song Yun, who was serving in his second term as Yili Governor-general, officially declared, "Allow the people to experiment with mining."[29]

The mine taxation system implemented by provincial officials to profit off Katu Mountain gold resources mirrored the system used to manage the gold fields to the south in Kuitun and around Urumqi. They established mining "enterprises" that were in effect government organs charged with selling road passes to those entering the gold fields and collecting a monthly tax of three gold *fen* per miner.[30] The role of provincial officials and military personnel steadily decreased, however, as most of the heavy administrative work was undertaken by a handful of "gold headmen" (*jintou*) drawn from the ranks of the prospectors themselves. These men oversaw the behavior of and were ultimately responsible for the around fifty miners in their charge. They typically paid collective taxes on behalf of their group and were also accountable to Qing local officials for any disciplinary infractions committed by their gang. The local Tacheng civil-military councilor warned a group of gold headmen in 1817 that if a group "crosses the border [into Mongol territory] to cause trouble, procrastinates in paying taxes, or [harbors] any unfamiliar and suspicious fellows, you will be brought to the city to be investigated and punished."[31]

From the beginning, many of the worst case scenarios envisioned by the Council of State came to pass. In many cases, the Mongols had indeed been "stirred up." Military leaders reported that immigrants from China proper were violating Mongol shrines and illegally building houses and shops in the vicinity of nomadic encampments. They also reported that Mongols were stealing livestock and illegally participating in mining.[32] But the early memorials prepared after the lifting of the ban focused exclusively on the revenue that gold mines were offering, as a growing stream of taxable workers began to flood the area.[33] In 1814, 1,062 mining passes were issued by frontier guard posts in the region and local and provincial leaders were confident this number would only increase. Song Yun eagerly reported that local laborers "without hesitation all desire to render their services and work like dogs and horses" for a mining enterprise.[34] Two years later, the local Tacheng civil-military councilor reported that the guard post issuing mining tickets was taking in more than 326 *liang* of gold annually, all of which was being sent to the prefectural treasury in Urumqi.[35]

The Daoguang and Xianfeng reigns (1821–1861) were characterized by a great increase in the scope of mining activities in the Katu. Gazeteers reported that miners "collected in the mountains and valleys like ants or bees," and numbered in the several tens of thousands.[36] The timing of the expansion of mining operations seems to have roughly paralleled similar administrative shifts occurring in other areas of Xinjiang during this period. Millward notes that various uprisings in the southern part of the region in the early 1820s prompted the first relaxation of restrictions on Han immigration, as Qing officials sought to control restive indigenous Muslims by increasing the number of settled Han agricultural communities and urban merchants.[37] But immigrant gold miners were still viewed with suspicion. Officials were willing to tolerate their presence as a way of generating revenue for yawning provincial treasuries. Unlike agricultural and merchant immigrants to Xinjiang, who were being actively recruited as settlers in the region and charged with the vital task of "opening the wasteland," the socially marginalized miners would have to wait more than half a century before they too would be viewed as acceptable participants in the settling of Qing Xinjiang.

Nevertheless, merchant capital from China proper began to gush into the gold fields south of the Tarbagatai during these years. The new funds led to the importation of new technology in the form of massive, livestock-powered granite quartz-crushing mortars and a sizable expansion in the scope of mining operations. The gold production during those years helped earn the period the nickname the "age of the gold pack animal" (jintuozi).[38] But there was a cost involved for Qing officials. They sacrificed their control when they willingly curtailed the military presence and encouraged immigration.[39] For officials like Song Yun, this Faustian choice was one worth making. But by the mid-nineteenth century new challenges loomed. The stability of the region was ultimately threatened by the unwieldy presence of the growing population of miners and in this already tense environment, new competitors for Tacheng's gold resources soon emerged.

Striking Back against Mining Bandits

The massive expansion of gold mining operations south of the Tarbagatai Mountains screeched to a halt in the city of Tacheng on that fateful night in August of 1855, when local miners and nomads burned and looted the Russian trade compound. In the fallout from the incident Qing provincial administrators confronted a dangerous foreign policy conundrum that so disturbed one official that the Xianfeng emperor openly chastised him for exhibiting a "paralyzing anxiety that rendered him unable to make a decision."[40] After a few anxious weeks and the payment of a hefty fine of

5,500 chests of tea to the Russian traders by the Qing government, the crisis seemed to blow over. But the incident had a longer-term impact and is worth examining in greater depth because it helped Qing officials realize the limits of gold mining as a revenue-raising strategy and also highlights the impact that the expansion of the emergent Russian empire exerted on Qing policy calculations. The events that unfolded that summer night prompted Qing officials to call a halt to the inexorable expansion of gold digging in the region and reestablish some semblance of control over Tacheng's sprawling mining operations before they provoked greater hostilities with the increasingly bellicose Russian armies.

The roots of the 1855 incident must be traced back to the expansion of the region's gold mining operations beyond the Katu Mountain gold fields during the 1850s. In 1853, responding to pressure from the Qing Ministry of Finance, Tacheng's civil-military councilor Feng Shen ordered that "for the sake of paying salaries and [funding] other programs," mining should be opened at every possible site in the greater Tacheng region.[41] In 1854 provincial officials ordered miners to begin working gold fields located southwest of the city in a place known as Ya'ergetu. The site was nearly thirty miles beyond the frontier guard post line but was where Tacheng's biannual spring and fall sacrifices were held. More importantly for Qing officials well-attuned to the worsening penury of Xinjiang's provincial treasury, early reports asserted that the area's alluvial gold dust held great promise for future wealth. The order for the move itself was unusual, and its perplexing vagueness can be seen as reflective of an underlying uncertainty about allowing miners to operate this far beyond the frontier line. Insisting that Ya'ergetu "originally" sat in Qing territory, the order went on to permit mining in the area. But the sensitive nature of the order is reflected in the odd insistence that an imperial edict would not be issued "until after we see the amount of taxes being paid by the miners."[42]

The problem that would arise was one that had been anticipated by the eighteenth and nineteenth century Qing officials who had initially called for the sealing of potentially rich gold fields. It became increasingly clear that in Tacheng, the more sites thrown open to mining, the more "unemployed poor people" (wuye pinmin) flowed in. In earlier times, gold miners were said to "sometimes gather and sometimes disperse" in the region, but by the 1850s they seemed only to gather. Troublingly, as the numbers grew they pushed out to new areas well beyond the limits of Qing control.[43]

Confronted with the disturbing spectacle of a growing force of impoverished Qing subjects chasing the region's gold veins farther and farther west, officials began to get desperate. In one 1855 case, in which miners marched nearly 150 miles beyond the nearest frontier guard post, soldiers and officials sent to bring them back were forced to resort to begging. They shrilly pleaded with the miners, arguing "You all belong to the son of the heavenly dynasty and you should follow the state's law voluntarily."[44] With the population of poor gold miners growing every year, however, this tactic was limited in its persuasive power. As one official explained, "The number of unemployed poor people is not insignificant and these drifters only know they want profit. It is especially difficult to guarantee they will not sneak back." The miners were frequently threatened with the rod and cangue but sometimes it was only the point of a sword wielded by Manchu or Mongol banner troops that drove these gold digging "bandits" back into Qing territory. Often, even this motivational tactic failed. When a detachment of soldiers journeyed out to one site to convince prospectors to return to Qing territory, they encountered a large group of Chinese Muslim miners who were unwilling to leave and "who appeared especially threatening and flaunted a fierce countenance." Fearing that a trap was being laid by these miners with their "unemployed roaming bandit hearts," the unit aborted the mission and quickly scurried back to Tacheng. [45]

Based on cases like these, it soon became clear to local and provincial officials that the western expansion of gold mining operations needed to be curtailed. The growing number of belligerent prospectors was turning into a highly destabilizing force in the region. Adding to their concerns, the new presence of an increasingly aggressive Russian military force underscored the looming threat of a dreaded "border dispute" (bianxin). These fears were not completely unfounded. In July 1854 a Russian consular official delivered an ominous message to a Qing frontier administration post which argued that Chinese miners in Ya'ergetu were operating on "Kazak lands belonging to us." The letter went on to darkly warn, "We cannot guarantee the safety [of the miners]."[46] After surveying the area, the Tacheng military civil-military councilor wrote that the land did indeed lie within the Qing sphere of influence. Nevertheless, he ordered the miners to disperse and return to Tacheng because the "gold ore in this area was not lucrative."[47] The prospectors evidently disagreed with this assessment because they stubbornly refused to leave. Eventually, their intransigence led to a Russian military response, the violence of which fuelled the outrage that drove the angry, torch-bearing miners to the trade concession on the night of August 26.

The event highlighted the difficult choice that faced local and provincial officials: expand mining operations to meet ever-growing financial shortfalls and risk war with the Russian empire or reassert control over the miners to keep the peace but sacrifice revenue. In the end they tried to do both. Operations in the region continued to expand in the 1860s. However, Qing officials sought to limit the activities of the prospectors to mines within the

Qing frontier post line and focus their attention on the tempting gold veins of the Katu Mountains. The incident also highlighted the new foreign policy threat in the region. With the looming presence of Russian armies stationed only a short march away from Tacheng's gold fields, the crisis appeared to affirm an important new link between local gold and Qing foreign policy.

The Emergence of the Russian Threat

There was a time when the Russian empire was seen by Qing officials not as an avaricious competitor for the region's resources, but instead as just another group in the broadly defined *huren* category. This ethno-cultural grouping, which generally referred to non-Han foreigners from the north, also included Kazakhs, Mongols, and Uyghurs as well as historic nomadic enemies of the Chinese state like the Xiongnu.[48] It was under this moniker that a parade of Russian explorers traversed the region around Tacheng in the early years of the nineteenth century. They were first drawn to the area by tales of gold nuggets "the size of the heart and liver of a goat" being spread by merchant caravans plying the trade routes of Central Asia and Siberia.[49]

There were hints of a Russian desire to annex these precious resources as early as the early nineteenth century. One explorer, the "traveler, writer, and diplomat" E. P. Kovalevsky, disguised himself as a Central Asian merchant in the early 1840s and embedded himself in a trade caravan traveling through northern Xinjiang.[50] Passing through some alluvial gold sites south of the Tarbagatai Mountains, he breathlessly wrote that the rich resources had "not yet come to the attention of the Chinese government." Like many future travelers to the area he urged that the gold be exploited by Russian agents before the Qing court realized the extent of the region's mineral wealth.[51]

Despite their interest in gold, early Russian activities in the region were focused primarily on trade. The early nineteenth century was marked by a massive expansion of Russia's woolen manufacturing industry, a growth that drove an increasing number of Russian merchants into markets in Siberia and Central Asia.[52] Many of these merchants grew dissatisfied with the official trading regulations that limited Sino-Russian interaction to the border town of Kyakhta in modern-day Mongolia. They were seeking trade sites farther west, closer to Russian markets and centers of manufacturing, and were enticed to northern Xinjiang by an illegal yet well-established exchange there of Russian woolens, leather, and iron for Chinese tea, silks, and furs.

The amount of profit generated by the trade caravans plying the overland routes between Russian outposts and Tacheng expanded exponentially in the first half of the nineteenth century.[53] Scholars suggest that the main reason for this growth was the increasing demand for Chinese tea imports into Russia. With tea from China proper making up 95 percent of Russia's total trade through Tacheng in 1850, the commodity's centrality cannot be denied. But it would be a mistake to overlook the impact that locally mined gold had on driving the lucrative trade in this region. One Russian observer noted that while early trade was primarily conducted by barter, by the 1830s and 1840s, trade in Tacheng came to be heavily dependent on gold. Chinese merchants preferred to be paid for their tea with the unalloyed metal and as a result "gold in dust and bars formed the medium of exchange." This observer added, "The subsequent appearance of gold on the bazaars had an injurious effect on the exchange of Russian goods," as it negatively affected rates of exchange. To meet the demands of this new market, illegal gold mining by both Chinese immigrants and Kazakh nomads in the region around Tacheng grew precipitously.[54]

By 1851 and the signing of the Sino-Russian Yili Tacheng Mutual Trade Agreement (*Zhong'e Yili Ta'erbahatai Tongshang Zhangcheng*), it had become apparent to the Qing court that Russia was perhaps different from the other *huren* with whom it had been previously associated. The arrival of Russian ships in Guangzhou in 1848 and 1850 helped prompt a shift in the court's approach to the country. Increasingly, Russia was seen as one of the "maritime barbarians" (*yangren*), a categorization it shared with Britain, France, the United States, and other nineteenth-century Western powers.[55] One Qing official astutely pointed out in 1851 that Russia is "not like Korea, the Ryukyus, or Vietnamese tribute states." In fact, this commentator added that like the British, with whom the Qing court recently fought the Opium War, "this barbarian's energy is always used to secure trade agreements: it is always thinking of wealth and poverty."[56]

This characterization certainly seemed to fit. However, Russian activity in Xinjiang was not limited to economic and trade acquisition. From the 1850s onward, Russia came to be viewed by the Qing court as a major competitor for political control of Xinjiang. A series of military crises spawned a deep-seated "Russophobia" in Qing officials, who feared that Russia had its eyes set on force-fully incorporating the region into its growing empire. Prince Gong summarized these suspicions when he lamented that "Russia, whose territory is contiguous to ours, having long nourished the intention to bite off our land 'as the silkworm devours mulberry leaves' is our sickness of body while Great Britain which seeks to trade is our sickness of limb."[57] As far as late Qing elites were concerned, the most egregious of the Russian affronts was the occupation of 1,220 square miles of the Yili River Valley in June 1871. The land was eventually handed back in 1881 following a military stand-off with General Zuo Zongtang's army, but a simmering mistrust permeated Qing policy toward Russia until the end of the nineteenth century.

Suspicion of Russian intentions in Xinjiang and a generalized fear about the aggression of imperial powers was a motivating force in transforming Qing mining policy in its border areas. The incredible isolation of many of these peripheral regions on the margins of the empire, and their distance from Qing administrative centers only served to accentuate official discomfort. Provincial leaders worried that the Katu Mountain gold fields, sitting in this rugged stretch of the Western border, were "quite far away from populated centers, and governmental control could not extend to this isolated area."[58]

This logistical dilemma was not unique to Qing China. Lonely stretches of unsettled land posed a similar administrative problem for leaders in the United States, Russia, and Britain who were similarly hoping to protect their territorial sovereignty and incorporate underpopulated frontier areas. One solution to this quandary was being well publicized in China's newly emergent late-nineteenth-century newspaper industry. Major gold strikes in resource-rich frontier areas like California, the Yukon Territories, Eastern Siberia, southern Australia, and later the Transvaal helped create large-scale mining camps in these once isolated regions. These diverse prospecting communities served not only to enrich the state but also to promote immigration into these often volatile frontier areas. These communities frequently served as the vanguard for further settlement and helped pave the way for more direct administrative control by the state.

By the mid-nineteenth century promoting immigration was a well-established aspect of Qing frontier policy. The Qing court was actively recruiting agricultural immigrants into frontier areas like Taiwan, Manchuria, Mongolia, and indeed Xinjiang, calling on them to open wasteland and settle these underpopulated areas. But for late Qing reformers, the imperialist threat to frontier areas prompted them to expand their definition of opening wasteland. No longer would the term refer specifically to agriculture and the process of putting once non-agricultural land to the plow. Instead, in Xinjiang at least, mining became another aspect of this project, as the term expanded to become more synonymous with a more generalized process of "settling" frontier areas.

The growing imperialist threat heightened the urgency of this task and led to the massive expansion of mining operations in frontier areas. Mining projects being proposed by prominent advocates of China's "self-strengthening" campaign were meant to assuage the worries of officials like Xinjiang's provincial governor Rao Yingqi, who worried in the late 1890s that, "every country envies Xinjiang's gold mines."[59] One prominent late Qing official who was a proponent of expanding mining operations argued that, "if we are careless [mineral resources] will be taken away, but if we manage them well they can definitely be used for profit."[60] This sentiment led to the unprecedented expansion of frontier mining operations throughout China during the second half of the nineteenth century. With regard to gold specifically, the latter years of the nineteenth century were notable for the number of frontier mines opened by local and provincial officials. New large-scale operations sprung up in areas ranging across the length of the Qing northern border, from Mohe in modern-day Heilongjiang to Kobdo and Urga in Mongolia to Tacheng on the farthest western edge of the empire.

By the last years of the nineteenth century, central investment and official oversight of frontier mining had become the norm. The new crop of mining enterprises that emerged was a critical outgrowth of the attempt by officials to profit off of mineral resources, while at the same time settling underpopulated stretches of the Qing border. The Tacheng Katu Gold Mining Company, established in 1899, was one such enterprise and is indicative of this broader shift. To more clearly understand the rapidly changing role of gold and gold miners in late Qing frontier areas, we will now turn and examine this particular enterprise more closely.

Converting Miners into Settlers

In Xinjiang, by the waning years of the nineteenth century, the need for a Qing border presence was acute. A Muslim rebellion, which began in 1864 and would not be put down until the mid 1870s, decimated the region's Han Chinese population and destroyed the Qing governmental infrastructure. In 1865, the sizable community of immigrant prospectors who had worked the gold veins of the Katu throughout the first half of the century "fled in the four directions," as rebels plundered and destroyed the mining camps.[61] For the next thirty years, the mines that once dotted the Katu Mountains sat largely abandoned; the mine shafts filled with water and the deserted mud dwellings crumbled in the face of the region's harsh elements.

Qing officials were faced with the daunting task of both populating this volatile, isolated corner of the Qing empire and the parallel process of filling the province's yawning treasury. In the 1890s gold emerged as a solution to both problems. It was no secret that in Xinjiang, "of the five metals, gold is the most plentiful."[62] Not only was it plentiful, it was also stable in value. This alone made it an attractive resource for provincial officials facing down the late Qing financial crisis and the commensurate decline in interprovincial financial assistance from Beijing. The value of silver—the Qing Empire's monetary base—plummeted; in Xinjiang, from 1887 to the mid 1890s its value was nearly halved. The dropping value was at least partly a response to the widespread global adoption of the gold standard in the latter half of the nineteenth century. The growing value of gold spawned renewed interest in the metal worldwide in the 1890s and 1900s and underwrote the unprecedented levels of gold production worldwide.[63] During the 1890s, these same economic forces, combined with a desire to populate frontier regions caused local and provincial officials throughout China to overlook the difficulties and risks and begin reexamining potential gold mining sites. In this context provincial governor Rao Yingqi and other officials in Xinjiang once again turned to Tacheng and its twisting maze of gold veins. They were driven by confidence that Xinjiang's "gold mines can be exploited for easy profit."[64]

Rao's confidence was linked to a surprising secret weapon he deployed in his campaign to unearth Tacheng's mineral resources. This weapon was none other than Russian capital and technology. In 1899 Rao and the Muscovite gold merchant A. G. Moskvin signed a nineteen-point agreement creating the joint Sino-Russian Tacheng Katu Gold Mining Company (*Tacheng Hatu Jinkuang Ju*). Inviting Russian participation was a choice rooted in desperation, a fact well illustrated by Rao's questionable decision to boldly redirect money out of the provincial military preparedness fund to meet the joint venture's initial outlay of 30,000 *taels*.[65] For Rao the risk was worth taking. The company not only promised huge profits that could be used to fund the skyrocketing administrative tab that the newly minted province was accumulating, it also would serve as the driving force for the establishment of a largely Han Chinese permanent mining community in the region.

Imbued with the ideals of the self-strengthening movement, provincial officials began recruiting immigrant miners from China-proper and organizing them into a state-funded and sponsored company. Facing down the Russian empire and an empty provincial treasury, immigrant miners were transformed in the eyes of Qing officials in Xinjiang. These officially sanctioned gold prospectors were no longer seen as a violent gang of bandits. As governor Rao noted in 1899, in the isolated, mountainous landscape around Tacheng it was up to local miners to "open the endless wasteland and ... develop the financial resources of the frontier."[66] No longer was it only agricultural settlers who were charged with opening the steppe—a transformation of the landscape that was seen by many Qing officials and elites as cultural, social, or political as much as it was physical. This vital act of claim and settlement would now be undertaken by the mining contingent of the Sino-Russian Tacheng Katu Gold Mining Company.

In January 1900 Moskvin and a Russian-speaking Manchu magistrate named Gui Rong, who represented the Chinese stake in the project as co-manager, led their mining contingent into the Katu Mountains. The Chinese administrative staff was made up of Gui Rong and his assistant mine manager Shi Zaimeng, who was the local vice magistrate, and two other officials who worked as secretary and treasurer of the enterprise. Aside from Gui Rong who was paid the highest monthly wage of fifty *taels* per month, each of the lower ranking officials was paid twenty-five *taels*. The mine also hired two clerks, two translators familiar with Kazakh and Mongolian respectively, one cook, nine guards, and eight grooms to man the four mounted courier posts that were to link the Katu site with the Tianshan North Road. The group's number would certainly have been swelled by a large number of Chinese laborers, people Rao must have felt were not worthy of mention in his otherwise minute accounting of the mine's administrative staff. He also failed to take note of an undetermined number of Russian administrators, mining technicians, and engineers who, with minor exceptions, received no mention in his memorials to the court.[67]

Marching into the low-lying Katu Mountains, it would have been impossible for the contingent to avoid the feeling that they were treading in the ghostly footsteps of the ill-fated mining enterprises of years past. The physical remains of the mining operations that had populated the region up until the 1864 rebellion, lay close to the surface, and the detritus continued to litter the Katu Mountains well into the twentieth century. The Russian mining engineer V. A. Obruchev detailed the extensive human footprint left on the region by the mining operations of the early 1800s. He described an area pocked with prospecting pits. The walls of local river valleys were often worked so intensely that they were terraced to accommodate the sizable number of tunnels following the region's quartz veins. In one pit, the prospecting crews charged with pumping out water discovered the body of a miner who had lain in the greenish water for more than forty years. They were surprised to find that he had been mummified by the high copper content of the water, "the only effect of time consisted in the blackening of the skin."[68] Other more subtle signs of humanity were the multitude of dilapidated, roofless mud huts that hollowly witnessed the return of mining enterprise to the region, a small shrine built into the side of a river valley wall, the long forgotten remains of granite quartz-crushing bowls and rollers, and most prevalent of all, mound after uncountable mound of off-white crushed quartz dust that sat heaped outside of nearly every one of the area's innumerable abandoned mining shafts.

For Qing officials hoping to establish a permanent presence in this uncultivatable "wasteland," the success of mining operations depended on the quick discovery of lucrative gold veins. And according to early reports submitted before the mine went into operation, the prospect for big profits was good. A Russian mining engineer named Matantsev who was hired by Moskvin to investigate the region's gold resources, reported his discovery of gold veins yielding nearly fifteen ounces of gold per ton and a half of ore.[69] On February 26, 1900, the production facility kicked into action and soon after, Rao was able to proudly boast that the enterprise "has already begun to see results."[70] Indeed, Rao's initial production figures suggest early success. After two days the mine had already produced around twelve ounces of gold. They produced three pounds the next month and during July/August produced the highest monthly total of gold—more than ten pounds. From February to September, the mine produced a total of nearly forty-four pounds of gold. The future seemed bright for the mine and Rao appeared cautiously sanguine as he informed the court that these early profits would be used to pay salaries. "If these days are signs of improvement, then we can hope to greatly reap the bounty of the earth," he proclaimed.[71]

By the beginning of 1901, however, Rao was beginning to show some concerns about the amount of profit being generated by the mine. The tone of his memorials to the court shifted as he aggressively argued for the need for additional operating funds above and beyond the initial investment. Rao laid out a risky new mining strategy, whereby the operations would be expanded heavily and the number of processing machines doubled. Altogether the changes would cost more than 66,000 *taels*, with new construction costs amounting to almost 43,000 *taels*. The expenditure, he argued was worth making on the grounds that "although we have received some gold, we still have not made up our investment." For his part, Rao acceded to the new financial demands by once again drawing money out of the provincial military budget. He tried to assuage any concerns from officials in Beijing, by confidently asserting that, "this belongs to the beginning phase, and there is still hope for a future with results."[72]

By December of 1901, a new sense of desperation pervaded Rao's communications. In a memorial to the court he fervently insisted on the urgent need for an increased financial commitment to mine activities. Instead of merely alluding to Tacheng's gilded future, a new impetus for mining began to creep into Rao's writings. He pointedly appealed to the patriotic sentiments of court officials and elites. Echoing the arguments of proponents of the Qing self-strengthening program, Rao suggested that Tacheng also should be regarded as part of China's broader push to self-strengthen and that abandoning the site would undermine the court's attempts to protect the country's sovereignty. He ominously warned that this weakness would not go unrecognized by the Western powers. "If we are not seeking to self-strengthen, and instead leave [this job] half finished, then we will be laughed at by the intelligent people of the world," Rao explained. He went on to emotionally argue, "The only strategy is determination and a hope for future success and striving for all that is humanly possible."[73]

In this context, the image that Rao paints of Russia changed as well. He began to describe it less as a partner and more as a threatening force seeking to monopolize the riches of Tacheng. Rationalizing his decision to draw more funds from the military budget and expand the increasingly costly enterprise, Rao wielded a long held image of Russia when he warned, "I worry that they want to monopolize the profits and therefore it is difficult to refuse their request."[74]

In October 1902, in the face of financial losses calculated at more than

81,000 *taels*, it was reported that "Moskvin formally insists he wants to dissolve the joint venture." By this time, Rao had already stepped down from his post as provincial governor. But his replacement Pan Xiaosu blamed the failure of the mine on a long list of factors. Provincial officials had employed "one hundred strategies," but in the end Pan asserted that the operation was derailed by machinery ill-suited to the local topography, a lack of skilled Chinese miners, and major strategic errors by the Russian engineers.[75] Other documents compiled after the fact suggest some different factors. One gazetteer noted that overly high salaries for the Russian engineers helped undermine profits while Obruchev argued that overconfidence in the site's wealth led to poor decisions about how to allocate the first year's investment.

In the end the Russians pulled out, the machinery was sold off, the provincial military funds went unrepaid, and at least for the time being, the land was once again deserted. One would think that this extraordinary failure would have shattered any illusions provincial officials still held about the region's gold wealth. But the prospect of once again abandoning this critical frontier region clearly troubled Qing officials. In an illustration of the power of gold and the high importance that Qing officials placed in opening this seemingly uncultivatable stretch of "wasteland," near the end of his final memorial on the joint venture, Pan innocently wrote, "Please allow me some time to investigate and I will report back on how to open a new [mine]."[76]

Conclusion

The desperate desire to populate the region and the parallel demand for resources overcame any pessimism that may have lingered in the hearts of local and provincial officials. In 1903 Governor Pan unveiled the fully Chinese Baoxin Company, which made use of the equipment and livestock left over from the Sino-Russian enterprise along with 20,000 *taels* of new official investment. But after losses of more than 18,000 *taels* this venture also failed. In the end, the logistical difficulties facing Qing officials in Xinjiang proved insurmountable and they could do little but throw up their hands in frustration. "Their spirit has been deflated and their minds are burdened, so they clamp their mouths closed, knot their tongues and do not dare to lightly suggest trying again," a 1906 gazetteer concluded in its section on the Katu Mountain gold fields.[77]

But it would be a mistake to glance at the spectacular failure of Qing gold mining enterprises in the Katu and dismiss Qing mining policy in the region as an insignificant blip on the historical radar. The miners marching into the Katu Mountains in 1899 were charged with the vital task of opening Xinjiang's vast wasteland not with plows but with picks, shovels, and quartz smashing hammers. Just as the process of pacification and settlement of this peripheral region on the margins of the Qing empire expanded to include these once violent immigrant miners with their "bandit hearts," it continued to expand throughout the Qing and Republican periods, as wave upon wave of new migrants broke upon Xinjiang's shores.

Over time, the concept of opening wasteland was irrevocably altered, as the diversity of twentieth-century settlement in China's border regions came to reflect a new socioeconomic reality. By the Republican period, despite the weakness of Chinese central government control in Xinjiang, the continued migration of a diverse group of settlers from China-proper into the northwest helped bolster not only Chinese territorial claims in the region, but also cultural and even historical ones (see Jacobs, Chapter 4).

The process of incorporation and settlement first undertaken by Qing officials in Xinjiang repeated itself following its "liberation" by the People's Liberation Army (PLA) in 1949. Rehabilitated Guomindang soldiers working on PLA farms played a critical role in laying the agricultural infrastructure for the incorporation of Xinjiang into the People's Republic (see Kardos, Chapter 7 by Kardos). This initial agricultural step was followed by an influx of nonagricultural workers sent to open factories, exploit oil fields (see Lim, Chapter 6), and indeed, once again begin mining gold in the Katu.[78]

In 1983 the Katu Mountain Gold Mine (*Hatu Jinkuang*) was formed with the stated intention of "renewing the shine of the ancient Daerdamutu gold mine's youth." By all accounts the mine appears to have succeeded where Qing mining enterprises failed.[79] But we should not be too overly dazzled by their economic success. Like the contingent that marched into the Katu in 1899, this new generation of miners working those same veins are also wrestling with the same task that was put to their predecessors. Despite more than a century of effort, Xinjiang as yet remains on the margins of China, or as Qing officials once put it, unopened; but these miners, along with wave after diverse wave of new settlers, have been charged with opening it.

Map 1. Tacheng and Katu Mountain Gold Fields

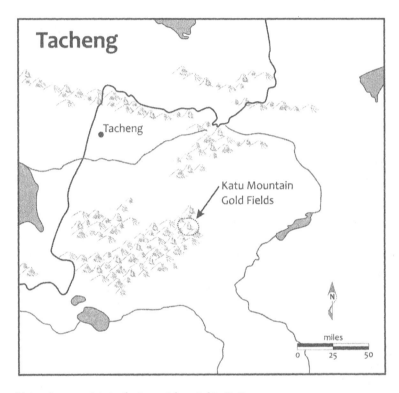

Note: Arrow points to the imperial capital in Beijing.
Cartography: Debbie Newell, 2010.

Map 2. Xinjiang Province

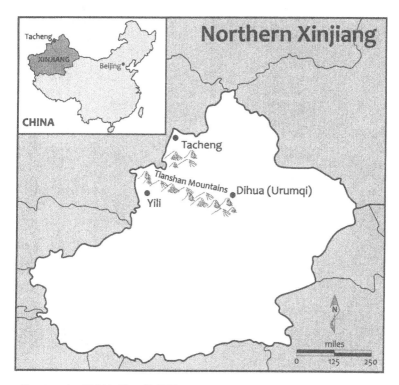

Cartography: Debbie Newell, 2010.

NOTES

Abbreviations used in the notes:

KWD   *Kuang wu dang* [Mining affairs documents] (Taipei: Zhongyang
        yanjiuyuan jindaishi yanjiusuo, 1960).

QDK   *Qingdai de kuangye* [The mining industry in the Qing dynasty]
        (Beijing: Zhonghua shuju, 1983).

QZEG *Qingdai Zhong-E guanxi dang'an shiliao xuanbian* [A collection of
        Qing dynasty documents on Chinese-Russian relations] (Beijing:
        Zhonghua shuju, 1979).

TZXZ "Tacheng zhiliting xiangtu zhi" [A gazetteer of local geography and
        history for Tacheng and its subordinate government offices], in
        Tacheng shi zhi (Urumqi: Xinjiang renmin chubanshe, 1995), 728–50.

XJTZ Yuan Dahua, ed., *Xinjiang tuzhi* [Xinjiang illustrated gazetteer]
        (Taipei: Wenhai chubanshe, 1906, 1923, 1965).

1. See "Zhalafentai deng zou chaban fen E maoyijuan an shimo zhe" [A memorial from Zhalafentai and others that investigates the case of the burning of the Russian trade concession from beginning to end], in QZEG, 185. See also *Tacheng diqu zhi* [Tacheng administrative area gazetteer] (Urumqi: Xinjiang renmin chubanshe, 1997) and An Changrong, "Guanyu Taerbahatai diming de kaozheng yu shae qinlue shiyao" [Regarding the name Tarbagatai and a short history of the czar's occupation], *Tacheng wenshi ziliao* (Tacheng: Zhongguo renmin zhengzhi xieshang huiyi, 1987), 63–65.

2. XJTZ, 1156.

3. The mountains were also known as the Hatu, Habutu, or Daerdamutu interchangeably. To eliminate confusion, I will refer to the mountain range as the Katu Mountains. The mountain range today is located in Tuoli county, Xinjiang, which is part of the Tacheng administrative district. During the Qing the site was administered as a part of the Tacheng subprefecture (*ting*).

4. TZXZ, 744.

5. Mildred Cable, "The Bazaars of Tangut and the Trade Routes of Dzungaria: The Fifth Asia Lecture, Read at the Evening Meeting of the Society 19 March 1934," *The Geographic Journal* 84.1 (1934): 17–31.

6. Song Yun, *Xichui zongtong shilue* [Imperial survey of the western frontier] (Taibei: Wenhai chubanshe, 1965; originally published in 1808), 624.

7. *Huangyu xiyu tuzhi* [Gazetteer of the imperial territory's western regions]. Quoted in *Tacheng diqu zhi*, 146.

8. *Taerbahatai shiyi* [Affairs of Tarbagatai] (Taipei: Chengwen chubanshe, 1969; originally published in 1805), 23–24.

9. Xie Lin, *Xinjiang youji* [Travel diary of Xinjiang] (Urumqi: Xinjiang chubanshe, 2001), 269.

10. XJTZ, 1156. Douglas Carruthers, "Exploration in Northwest Mongolia and Dzungaria," *The Geographic Journal* 39.6 (June 1912): 532.

11. He Ning, ed, *Sanzhou jilue* [Compiled records on three regions] (Taipei: Chengwen chubanshe, 1968; originally published in 1805), 340.

12. Ibid.

13. Su Beihai, *Xiyu lishi dili* [Historical geography of the western regions] (Urumqi: Xinjiang daxue chubanshe. 1993), 316. See also TZXZ, 744.

14. "Dizhi kuangchan zhi" [Geological and mining gazetteer] in *Xinjiang tongzhi 9* (Urumqi: Xinjiang renmin chubanshe, 1992), 1123.

15. Dang Tong, "Qingdai Taerbahatai kalun shezhi luetan" [A brief discussion on Qing dynasty guard posts in Tarbagatai], *Tacheng wenshi ziliao* (Tacheng: Zhongguo renmin zhengzhi xi shanghui, 1987), 65.

16. "Daerdamutushan, Jiaqing 6 nian, 2 yuechu, 2 ri, Bao Ning, Xiangchukezhabu, Song Yun zou" [Daerdamutu mountain, Jiaqing year 6, month 2, day 2, Bao Ning, Xiangchukezhabu, and Song Yun memorialize], in QDK, 540.

17. Reprinted from a Qianlong 60 edict in *Taerbahatai shiyi*, 36.

18. "Daerdamutushan, Jiaqing 16 nian, 6 yue, 21 ri, Xiangchukezhabu, Na Zhenbao, Bai Shun zou" [Daerdamutu mountain, Jiaqing year 16, month 6, day 21, Xiangchukezhabu, Na Zhenbo, Bai Shun memorialize], in QDK, 537.

19. Ibid. "Daerdamutushan, Jiaqing 15 nian, 4 yuechu, 5 ri, Xiang Bao zou" [Daerdamutu mountain, Jiaqing year 15, month 4, day 5, Xiang Bao memorializes], in QDK, 539.

20. "Daerdamutushan, Jiaqing 14 nian, 11 yue, 28 ri, Xiang Bao, Bai Shun zou" [Daerdamutu mountain Jiaqing year 14, month 11, day 28, Xiang Bao and Bai Shun memorialize], in QDK, 538.

21. Ibid.

22. E-tu Zen Sun, "Mining Labor in the Ch'ing Period," in Albert Feuerwerker, Rhodes Murphey, Mary Wright, eds., *Approaches to Chinese History* (Berkeley: University of California Press, 1967), 48. See also E-tu Zen Sun, "Ch'ing Government and the Mineral Industries Before 1800," *The Journal of Asian Studies* 27.4 (August 1968): 835–45 and William F. Collins, *Mineral Enterprise in China* (London: William Heinemann, 1918).

23. QDK, 539.

24. Ibid.

25. Ibid., 540. See also He Ning, ed., *San zhou jilue*, 341.

26. "Qing jie kuang jinwen, Jiaqing 19 nian, li bu shangshu Ying Heshu" [A document requesting the release of prohibition, Jiaqing year 19, ministry of personnel, Minister Ying Heshu], in QDK, 535. See also James A. Millward, *Beyond the Pass: Economy, Ethnicity, and Empire in Qing Central Asia, 1759–1864* (Stanford: Stanford University Press, 1998).

27. Millward, *Beyond the Pass*, 110.

28. Ibid.

29. "Daerdamutu shan, Jiaqing 19 nian, 7 yue, 24 ri, Song Yun zou" [Daerdamutu mountain, Jiaqing year 19, month 7, day 24, Song Yun memorializes], *Junjichulu fuzouzhe*, in QDK, 534.

30. He Ning, ed., *San zhou jilue*, 341.

31. "Daerdamutu Jiaqing 22 nian, 6 yuechu, 9 ri, Xiangchukezhabu zou" [Daerdamutu,, Jiaqing year 22, month 6, day 9, Xiangchukezhabu memorializes], in QDK, 532–33.

32. Ibid.

33. The court continued to hold some reservations about mining enterprise in these nomad-heavy areas and a Jiaqing era imperial rescript tersely warns provincial officials, "Where there is profit, there must be wickedness; it is your duty to strictly investigate" local mining operations. QDK, 534.

34. Ibid.

35. "Daerdamutushan, Jiaqing 24 nian, 4 yuechu, 8 ri, Xiangchukezhabu zou" [Daerdamutu mountain, Jiaqing year 24, month 4, day 8, Xiangchukezhabu memorializes], in QDK, 532.

36. XJTZ, 1157.

37. Millward, *Beyond the Pass*, 230–35.

38. Ibid.

39. QDK, 535.

40. "Zhalafentai deng zou bianmin mie fen E maoyijuan qiyin bing banli qingxingzhe" [Zhalafentai and others memorialize on the burning of the Russian trade concession by frontier people, the reason for the action and how to address it], in QZEG, 173.

41. "Ying Xiu deng zou Tacheng minren fen E maoyijuan yuanyou ji E fang shang wudongjing zhe" [Ying Xiu and others memorialize on the reason for the burning of the Russian trade concession by Tacheng citizens and also on the lack of a Russian response], in QZEG, 174.

42. Ibid.

43. Ibid.

44. Ibid., 177.

45. Ibid., 178.

46. Ibid.,172.

47. Ibid.,177.

48. Josephine Nailene Chou, *Frontier Studies and Changing Frontier Administration in Late Ch'ing China: The Case of Sinkiang, 1759–1911* (University of Washington, Ph.D. dissertation, 1976).

49. V. A. Obruchev, *The Minerals of Dzungaria* (Washington, D.C.: U.S. Joint Publications Research Service, 1961), 15.

50. Alison Dray, "Excerpts from E. P. Kovalevsky's *Journey to China*" *Papers on China*, 22A (Cambridge: East Asian Research Center, Harvard University, 1969), 53–88.

51. Quoted in Su Beihai, "Xiyu jinshan de lieshi he xianzhuang" [The history and current situation of western goldfield], *Xinjiang caijing xueyuan xuebao* 3 (1983): 64.

52. Mi Zhenbo, "1845 nian Ni Liubimofu de mimi kaocha yu Zhong-E Yili Taerbahatai Tongshang zhangcheng de qianding" [Ni Liubimofu's 1845 secret investigation and the Sino-Russian Yili Tacheng joint trade regulations], *Jindaishi yanjiu* 5 (May 1994): 26–31.

53. Xu Shuming, *Yili, Taerbahatai kaibu ji* [A record of the opening of ports in Yili and Tarbagatai] (Beijing: Zhongguo renmin daxue Qingshi yanjiusuo, 1986), 15.

54. N. Abramof, "Semipalatinsk," John Michell, trans., *Journal of the Royal Geographical Society of London* 32 (1862): 556.

55. Chou, *Frontier Studies and Changing Frontier Administration,* 153–67.

56. "Sheng Bao zou Zhong-E Yi Ta tongshang zhangcheng ying fangzhao Qiaketu zhangcheng banli pian" [Sheng Bao memorial on the Sino-Russian Yili Tacheng joint trade regulations and how they should emulate the Kyakhta regulations], in QZEG, 23.

57. Quoted in Chou, *Frontier Studies and Changing Frontier Administration*, 199.

58. XJTZ, 1157.

59. KWD, 2776, 4867.

60. The reformer was Xue Fucheng. Quoted in Zhao Fengtian, *Wanqing wushi nian jingji sixiang shi* [Economic thought during the last fifty years of the Ch'ing period] (Xianggang: Longman shudian, 1968), 42.

61. XJTZ, 1159.

62. KWD, 2773, 4865.

63. Pierre Vilar, *A History of Gold and Money 1450–1920* (Atlantic Highlands: Humanities Press, 1976), 331.

64. KWD, 2773, 4866.

65. Ibid., 4868.

66. Ibid., 4867.
67. Ibid., 4868.
68. Obruchev, *The Minerals of Dzungaria*, 29.
69. Ibid., 36. To put this in perspective, gold veins at Cripple Creek in Colorado, one of the most significant gold strikes of the late nineteenth century, typically yielded an average of nineteen ounces per ton of ore. Vilar, *A History of Gold and Money*, 328.
70. KWD, 2775, 4873.
71. Ibid., 4874.
72. Ibid., 2776, 4876.
73. Ibid.
74. Ibid.
75. Ibid., 2780, 4882.
76. Ibid.
77. XJTZ, 1156.
78. James Gao, "The Call of the Oases: The 'Peaceful Liberation' of Xinjiang, 1949–1953," in Jeremy Brown and Paul G. Pickowicz, eds., *Dilemmas of Victory: The Early Years of the People's Republic of China* (Cambridge: Harvard University Press, 2007), 184–204.
79. In 1985 alone the mine processed 1,500 pounds of gold. http://www.tczx.cc/yj/ReadNews.asp?NewsID=451.

3

CULTIVATING EMPIRE
Zuo Zongtang's Agriculture, Environment, and Reconstruction in the Late Qing

Peter Lavelle

Late in 1882, from one of the last official posts of his lengthy career, Zuo Zongtang (1812–1885) composed a memorial to the throne in which he lamented the environmental devastation of Nanjing. Almost wistfully recalling conditions in the city's eastern hills years earlier, before the chaos of the Taiping Tianguo uprising and its final defeat in 1864, Zuo described the plentiful resources of the land: "With sweet springs and rich earth, the area was known to be particularly fertile. In times past, the valleys were lushly verdant, with beautifully planted rows of timber." However, the intervening years of turmoil had drained the land of its vigor and had decimated its tree stock. This greatly concerned Zuo, the new governor-general of Liangjiang (Jiangsu, Anhui, and Jiangxi provinces), because city residents relied on the forest for their energy needs. These days, wrote Zuo, the hills "are all but denuded, there is no vitality (*shengqi suoran*)," and as a result, "folks have no way to obtain supplies of firewood for cooking. They all rely on reeds to cook their food."[1] Since reeds burned neither as long nor as vigorously as unaffordable coal or now-unavailable firewood, the poor households of Nanjing were suffering.

Zuo had come to his post as governor-general only months before. But even if the lack of timber in and around Nanjing posed a new, immediate concern, the degradation of postwar landscapes was hardly novel to him. An agent of central state power, Zuo had spent over twenty years fighting for the empire as a military general, devising strategies to defeat rebellions, and responding to the exigencies of postwar reconstruction in territories far and wide. He repeatedly approached the task of rebuilding with an agrarian model of political-economic renewal and drew upon his archive of agricultural knowledge to alter and ameliorate environmental conditions. Reconstruction proposals that he described in official memorials to Beijing used lands, water, trees, and people as strategic resources in the redevelopment or expansion of agriculture in a way that simultaneously structured a community's relationship to the environment and to the state.

In urban Nanjing, Zuo made the people's livelihood and local reconstruction an issue of trees. He judged that reinvesting the urban landscape with usable foliage would ameliorate the plight of residents who burned reeds by giving them a new source of firewood. According to the memorial, he had dispatched one of his staff to "purchase more than 374,000 pine and fir seedlings, disseminate them, and plant them in open spaces within the city."[2] Urban trees of these varieties would begin fulfilling the energy needs of residents, particularly when prices for oil and candles were constantly rising. But Zuo did not stop with firewood. The over two million mulberry tree saplings that he ordered another subordinate to purchase in Huzhou, Zhejiang, were to be ready for planting early the following spring to give a giant boost to the city's sericulture industry. Like rebuilding efforts earlier in his career, these seemingly simple orders for a massive urban sylvan program aimed to ease the dire predicament of residents, prop up local production, and, over the longer run, transform areas wrecked by warfare into governable, taxable communities.

Before ending up as governor-general in Nanjing, Zuo had gone great distances with his army to support the Qing state against rebels in the heartland province of Zhejiang, as well as in the frontier territory of Xinjiang, and had overseen reconstruction ventures in both corners of the empire. What makes his adherence to a central, essential vision for agrarian reconstruction all the more significant is that fact that this native of Hunan province traversed territories with vastly different natural environments, climates, and farming traditions, and with different geo-political relationships to the Qing center. Despite crossing these environmental and political boundaries and acknowledging the particularities of climate and the varying degrees of postwar calamity, he nonetheless stuck by a set repertoire of policies, agricultural techniques, and even certain types of plants that he favored, such that he seemed to deny any significant difference between the regions in which he served. And by using the same array of reconstruction techniques, Zuo initiated potential resemblances—in vegetation, agriculture, and economy—between the center and the northwestern margins of the empire. For the most politically and geographically distant of those margins, Xinjiang, Zuo's work triggered more than resemblance, as by the late 1870s he had begun to advocate the erasure of political distinctions between China proper and the territory by turning Xinjiang into a province.

Practical Learning and Zuo's Agriculture

As a young scholar, Zuo Zongtang initially learned about agriculture, land use, and governance through his preparations for the imperial examinations and his grooming as a future official within the Qing bureaucracy. His accumulation of knowledge about topics of so-called practical learning (*shixue*) is evidence of the influence of Hunan's intellectual climate and of prominent statecraft scholars who had studied in Changsha's Yuelu Academy and had benefited from its shift toward practical learning in the late eighteenth and early nineteenth centuries.[3] Proponents of the Hunan statecraft movement rejected what they perceived as ineffectual textual studies by focusing their scholarship on purportedly more practical matters like water control and geography. Statecraft scholars of the nineteenth century sought knowledge applicable to governance in order to strengthen the Qing state and deal with the problems particular to their times.[4] They not only had to confront social unrest and foreign incursion, but also troubling environmental and financial issues that challenged them to reconsider land use and wealth production.[5] In this intellectual and political context He Changling, a Yuelu graduate and editor of the well-known 1827 compendium of statecraft essays, encouraged Zuo to pursue practical learning, which the young scholar did under the guidance of He's brother in Changsha in 1831.[6]

Aspiring to the highest, metropolitan degree (*jinshi*) through the civil service examinations, Zuo prepared to write compositions regarding contemporary policy in addition to the requisite commentaries on classical texts. His commitment to a statecraft vision for agriculture is no more apparent than in one of his policy essays composed for the examination of 1838. In this essay, one of the last he would write as an ambitious bureaucratic hopeful, he articulated just how integral systems of crop and silk production were to social prosperity and state security. "For the whole realm under heaven," Zuo professed, "agriculture and sericulture are the tools to support life and the source of great benefit, while for the state, they are an inexhaustible treasury." As techniques for utilizing the productive capacities of land and human labor, agriculture and sericulture would not simply bring wealth, but also allow people and the state to autonomously enrich themselves without relying upon the other. Zuo continued: "Thus, those well able to nurture the people need not harm themselves to benefit the people, rather the people will benefit on their own (*ziyi*). Those well able to enrich the state need not impoverish the people to enrich the state, rather the state will be self-enriching (*zifu*)."[7] The examination candidate could hardly have asserted more strongly agriculture's direct connection to wealth production and accumulation. At the same time, he intimated that enrichment was a natural outcome of agriculture and sericulture, activities at the nexus of human labor, land, and environment.

Although Zuo began his essay with such terse assertions about agriculture and sericulture, shibboleths in the long tradition of Chinese statecraft, he proceeded to transcend the standard concern about agriculture as a model of political economy by ruminating on past agricultural knowledge and its deployment in contemporary governance. Zuo outlined a brief history of Chinese agricultural and related treatises, including Ming dynasty scholar Xu Guangqi's *Complete Book of Agriculture Policy* (*Nongzheng quanshu*), which he deemed worthy of great praise. Although it is difficult to assess to what extent Zuo's practical farming know-how came from treatises like these, his extensive familiarity with them shows how seriously he researched agriculture. They perhaps inspired him to write his own work under his style name, *Agricultural Treatise from the Pavilion of Pucun* (*Pucun ge nongshu*), in 1845.[8]

Zuo also discussed the complexities of implementing agricultural policy in diverse regions of the empire. That Qing officials governed lands and people with which they were not familiar struck Zuo as a troublesome obstacle to suitable agricultural policy and development. "Those who govern a locale," he wrote, "are not those familiar with the soil. As for the fertility or barrenness of the land, the timing of the seasons, the location of water sources, the suitability of particular plants to particular soils, and which instruments are most expedient, they are inferior to the people of the land who have long considered these things and know about them."[9] In other words, Zuo understood that for all the important aspects of agriculture, the knowledge of officials from distant locations could not match that of local residents.

Zuo's ensuing analysis of how Qing officials should be mindful of local particularities evinces a sensitivity to the problem of deploying agricultural knowledge across political and environmental boundaries, precisely the kind of boundaries he and his army would cross decades later. To emphasize regional discrepancies in the empire, Zuo employed a classic trope within Chinese agricultural writing of distinguishing dry northern or northwestern agriculture from its wet southern or southeastern counterpart. Implying that it would be foolhardy and damaging to local agriculture to devise policy without knowing local conditions, Zuo warned against trying to transform the northwest's arid fields into irrigated polders and the southeast's well-watered fields into dry land. He asserted that officials should "take advantage of the land in accordance with the land's benefits, for there is no need to force the northwest all to be paddy or the southeast all to be open fields. Benefit the people in accordance with what is advantageous to them, for there is no need to force the people of the southeast to eat wheat or the people of the northwest to eat rice." Advocating his own version of biological and economic diversity, Zuo suggested that certain regional crops and value-added products have their respective advantages and should not automatically be uprooted in favor of mulberry trees and silk cocoon production. Simply put, imperial officials ought to take local planting and production customs into account, along with all other particularities of the land. Doing so, Zuo concluded, would be the most advantageous policy: "If one were to rely on their seasons, tread through their wilderness, pass through their countryside, ask about what is beneficial for them, inquire about what is suitable, not working for one's own success or for official business, what benefits could not flourish!"[10] Officials needed to put themselves in relationship to the land—to get to know the seasons, the soils, water, and plants—and then learn from local inhabitants how to most effectively develop agriculture. Only then could they be sensitive enough to local customs and local environments and implement successful policy.

But many late imperial agricultural handbooks purveyed techniques applicable in a range of environments, and Zuo appears to have been enticed by at least some of them. Indeed, in the same year as his examination essay on agriculture, the young scholar penned a preface to a book about the area-field system (qutian zhi), a method for arranging cultivation on any given plot of land, regardless of location. As Zuo explained, farmers could grow robust crops able to withstand "tree-shaking winds," and without exhausting the soil or depleting its moisture content, by partitioning their land into small plots.[11] But to obtain rich yields, the primary payoff, farmers needed to be diligent and conscientious about their planting methods. Even the tiniest details were crucial. Zuo warned his readers that excessive transplanting would damage crops and derail the process. "Constantly moving a grain plant," wrote Zuo, "will make its vitality (yuanqi) dissipate time and again," leaving it incapable of production.[12] Fortunately, the area-field system not only minimized potential damage from transplanting, but could also, he claimed, boost yields to several times that of typical fields.

The area-field system also suited the needs of Qing political economy, especially insofar as it completely absorbed family labor into the process of production. Whereas work in the fields typically excluded all but able-bodied men, the system allowed for women, as well as old, young, or weak family members, to contribute to farm labor: "[N]o one is redundant, and no effort is insubstantial."[13] With labor fully engaged in production—just like the capacities of the soil—families would harvest an abundance from even small parcels of land, such that they could accumulate grain for themselves and survive years of famine. For Zuo, adoption of the area-field system augured prosperity, and he imagined that organizing agriculture in this way would enable families, towns, and the whole realm (tianxia) to become self-sufficient.[14] In other words, the area-field system, which Zuo held in high regard, was infinitely replicable throughout the empire regardless of differences in local custom or environment.

As a scholar, Zuo grappled with the functions and techniques of agriculture in his writing, while as a farmer, he tested crops and planting schemes. Frustrated yet again in 1838 by his failure in the metropolitan examinations, Zuo returned to live with his wife's family until 1843, when his financial situation had ameliorated enough to purchase a farm. Even before he had acquired some seventy mu of his own land, Zuo undertook experiments in agriculture, trying out the area-field system and different methods of cultivating mulberry trees.[15] Striving to increase his earnings and use the land to its capacity, he planted crops like tea and bamboo that other local farmers typically eschewed, but which could earn handsome returns on the commodity market.[16] But harvests were not always plentiful. Flooding that wiped out crops in his home district in 1849 forced him to observe and respond to the extensive devastation and disruption to cultivation in the community. He organized with other local notables to prepare stocks of grain to assist people in weathering the ensuing famine and he established a site for preparing medicines.[17] In this predicament, with disaster striking home in a familiar landscape, Zuo learned to coordinate relief efforts and look toward agriculture's revival, skills that would prove valuable in his service to the empire.

Reconstructing Agriculture in the Center and Along the Margins

Having failed to achieve a metropolitan degree and a high government post, Zuo nonetheless climbed in the bureaucracy beginning in late 1852, when he entered into service as a private advisor on military affairs to Hunan provincial governor Zhang Liangji. Through the growth of his reputation as a skilled military strategist and adept policy advisor among Qing bureaucrats in the later 1850s, Zuo was gradually awarded with accolades and positions, and then given his own army of Hunan recruits in 1860 and charged with helping wage battles against troops of the Taiping Tianguo rebellion.[18] Dispatched to undertake warfare, Zuo Zong-tang clung to his convictions about the utility of agriculture and his knowledge of cultivation practices. But as he found himself increasingly distant from Hunan and playing the role of the nonnative official determining agricultural policy—precisely what he had described in his 1838 exam essay—he did not consistently follow his own advice about localizing perspective and drawing on native knowledge. His missives from places as widely divergent as Zhejiang along the eastern seaboard and landlocked Xinjiang in the northwest detailed relatively similar blueprints for reviving agriculture. These projects consisted of encouraging resettlement among the local population, spurring productivity with donations of farming supplies or offers of tax breaks, and ordering his troops to undertake cultivation or refurbish irrigation and transportation infrastructure. When Zuo did describe the particularities of location, it was often in reference to the weather or the severity of the postwar crisis at hand: in his view, the extent of destruction and destitution in the northwest far surpassed that in eastern parts of the empire. And when he did tailor his reconstruction efforts to location, as when he encouraged cotton production in Gansu, his decisions were based not on local knowledge as much as his own judgments of what constituted expedient policy. So inasmuch as he chose various tactics and crops to suit the locale, Zuo responded to the climate and the terrain. But these special conditions generally did not change his program for remaking society around agriculture. He pursued reconstruction as an empire-wide project according to the same basic principles whether in rice fields in the east or surrounded by desert in the northwest.

Zuo's first substantial experience with reconstruction came with his appointment as governor of Zhejiang in 1862 and then his concurrent assignment as governor-general of Zhejiang and Fujian one year later. In a province where "white bones and yellow grass extend as far as one can see," where survivors slept on bare ground and subsisted on wild vegetables because fields had been abandoned for lack of farming tools, draft animals, and seeds, Zuo resolved to accelerate Zhejiang's recovery by purchasing basic necessities like grain seeds and plough oxen and recruiting farmers from neighboring provinces to move in and cultivate the land. He also emphasized that rich families had an obligation to contribute money for relief efforts so that officials could afford to purchase grain to aid war survivors and boost army provisions.[19]

The governor also realized that some farmers practiced sericulture to supplement income, but devising a straightforward policy for its revival was more complicated. In an 1864 sketch of the local political economy Zuo wrote, "Since field taxes are heavy for the people, they also rely on silkworms and mulberry trees for their livelihoods." Most prevalent in western Zhejiang, sericulture depended on controlling one particular natural resource: "Mulberry trees that the people manage are grown with irrigation, similar to managing paddy fields." But since the chaos of rebellion and warfare had passed through, Zuo lamented, the masonry of these irrigation systems had collapsed and fallen into disrepair. And given the current circumstances in which the population had all but dispersed, making "materials cheap but labor expensive," there was little hope for simple or swift repair. Unable to provide assurances to Beijing about the comprehensive reconstruction of Zhejiang's irrigation systems, Zuo instead reported on the completion of a pair of much smaller water projects near the provincial capital, Hangzhou. Nonetheless, news about the city's West Lake was less pleasant: "[S]ilt is already piled high, the roots of wild rice are long, and the water has dried up, but there is no spare time to discuss dredging it."[20] Reconstruction certainly was not his only concern as governor, but the tasks of rebuilding water systems, resettling refugees, and jump-starting crop production occupied an increasing proportion of his attention as his post shifted to the northwest a few years later.

Zuo found reconstruction in the northwest to be more difficult and more urgent than what he had experienced in Zhejiang. In an 1869 correspondence to his sons, the general described the unsettling abundance of death. "Since entering Gansu," Zuo recounted, "providing relief and protection has been most urgent. I did not at all desire to force my eyes to see a person who has starved to death, or listen with my own ears to death by starvation. The plight of Gansu is similar to conditions in Yanzhou, Zhejiang, but the desolation and barrenness surpass it, and not even one in a hundred people has survived. It's mostly wolves."[21] Three years before, in a letter to his older brother, Zuo had similarly noted the collapse of society and the consequent dilemmas for agricultural production: "Over half the people have died and departed. As for production among the Hui, there are already no people to plow [the fields] and tend [the animals]. As far as Han production goes, [the fields] have mostly gone out of cultivation."[22] The northwest's predicament was thus far more serious than what he had encountered in the southeast.

Zuo addressed the lack of a stable population base by making the labor of his soldiers a centerpiece of reconstruction projects. Even though he noted in his first year in the northwest that "southern recruits dread campaigning westward" into lands substantially different from home because they "cannot withstand the cold and are not accustomed to wheat-based foods,"[23] Zuo commanded them to undertake agricultural and infrastructural projects akin to those they had implemented several years before in Zhejiang. As he explained to Beijing in 1876, in the decimated towns of Gansu in which populations had shrunk by eighty or even ninety percent, the soldiers he left behind to guard the roadways and protect the people did much more than that. They plowed and sowed the land on behalf of absent farmers and rebuilt city walls to entice people back to their homes and back to agriculture. But not all of their projects were merely reconstructive in nature. They also dug wells and planted trees, the general boasted, and they "guide canals to irrigate the land, change the thirsty soil into fertile earth," as well as "pull out the demonic grasses and plant vegetable seedlings."[24] The duties of his soldiers, in other words, extended to altering the land by means of irrigation and plowing, not unlike their work in lush, coastal Zhejiang.

Proud of his soldiers' activities to entice peasants back to the land, Zuo bragged to other statesmen of their accomplishments. But despite the fact that his army engaged in reconstruction work when not fighting and did "not at all draw on the energies of the people," as he told Shaanxi governor Tan Zhonglin in 1875, there was more on his mind than reviving agriculture for the local people.[25] The more immediate challenge was how to create convenient sources of grain and supplies for the army, without which further warfare was not easily possible. As he asked his brother in an 1866 letter, "If we wait for provisions for people and hay and beans for the horses to be supplied from several hundred *li* or over one thousand *li*, how can war be waged? How can defense be maintained?"[26] The quandary of provisions, then, related directly to his army's geographic position within the empire, increasingly distant from the more fertile east. Disruptions to agricultural production caused by fighting and the headache of arranging financial disbursements from other provincial governments compounded the general's frustration over supplies.

In the northwest and without many provisions, Zuo resorted to using a form of agricultural military colony whose history dated as far back as the

Han dynasty. He indeed recognized the long record of the garrison cultivation (*tuntian*) system along the imperial margins, and his reflection on history, however brief, influenced his appropriation of this technology of rule. As he tersely stated in an 1866 missive to the capital, "From ancient times, soldiers have been used on the frontiers; military outposts (*tun*) must be established."[27] Based on his appraisal of the northwest's poor soil quality and its paucity of resources, Zuo determined that civilian agriculture alone could not support an army, particularly in times of warfare: "Northwestern land is mostly saline and its products are not plentiful. As soon as warfare breaks out, most of the rich lowlands that can be farmed or made into pasture, with water and grasses, will be ravaged. Attempts to purchase [supplies] are met with scenes of desolation; there is no way to buy grain." Zuo found grain transshipments to be equally useless, with horrendous road conditions making for exceedingly high transportation costs. Zuo therefore turned to agricultural colonies as the only solution, one that would allow his army to create supplies on the spot: "When garrison cultivation comes to fruition and prospers," Zuo surmised, "the army will not have the worry of suspended cauldrons [i.e., a lack of provisions] and civilians will have revived hopes."[28]

In another message to Beijing the same year, Zuo explained his logic and plan for utilizing agricultural colonies, something he had not readily done in Zhejiang. He envisioned the system as especially appropriate for arid regions like Gansu, where "the land is barren, for a thousand *li* grain is given as a gift, and even scholars have famished appearances." The "maladies of Gansu" also included the fact that Zuo was running out of remunerations and food for his soldiers. This concatenation of issues convinced him to adopt a policy of agricultural expansion via *tuntian* colonies. According to the plan, military reclamation units would be placed in strategic locations, along important thoroughfares, while civilian units he organized would be settled in out-of-the-way places. Both required initial outlays of farming tools and seeds, but Zuo concluded that preparatory expenditures were much preferable to soldiers without food.[29]

In choosing agricultural colonies as the solution to this predicament, Zuo considered his troops but rarely mentioned local customs or environments. He based his decision not so much on the landscape as on postwar deprivation, the condition for which his army was partially responsible but also had to survive. The reasons compelling him to choose agricultural colonies were not those of Gansu's environment, and he did not canvass experienced local farmers when ordering his soldiers to resettle civilians. Rather, the garrison cultivation system came from his historical and contemporary knowledge of techniques for ruling the northwest.

Zuo was perhaps somewhat more sensitive to Gansu's climate and terrain in electing to promote the cultivation of cotton. Noting in an 1874 communiqué to Tan Zhonglin that in Gansu "mountains are high and the air is cold," and so it would not be as suitable as Shaanxi for growing mulberry trees, Zuo ascertained that cotton could profitably be grown in both provinces. Especially on "sunny, rich, and warm land, and with proper cultivation, the benefits to be obtained [by growing cotton] have to be many." But the general's ruminations on cotton were not without an underlying motive. He not only hoped to encourage production in general, but also reach his objective of eradicating opium poppy cultivation. As Zuo explained, the strategy was to "first think of a kind [of plant] that can surpass the benefits [of the opium poppy] so people will know that growing opium is not as beneficial," and then reward farmers for growing it. He expected the advantages of cotton to be so evident, even after only one year of planting, that harsh, punitive measures to weed out opium poppies would be unnecessary.[30] From his perspective, making cotton flourish merely required educating the people, a process Zuo promoted by publishing two pamphlets about cotton for distribution among Gansu farmers.[31] Even though he would later advocate an empire-wide policy of levying high taxes on foreign and domestic opium in order to curb addiction, his attempts at crop substitution while in Gansu coincided with other Qing anti-opium campaigns aiming to expurgate the homegrown roots of the empire's opium problem and stamp out poppy cultivation.[32]

By 1878 the army had reached and reconquered the most distant territory of the empire's northwest, Xinjiang. If the peculiarities of landscape and weather were apparent to Zuo in Gansu, they had now become unavoidable. Relying on the input of his commanders in the field, the general recorded that the "food and drink as well as the seasons of places in the north [of Xinjiang] are vastly different from China proper (neidi)."[33] Despite the clear distinction of comestibles and climates, he did not make nearly as obvious a division between how he pursued reconstruction in the province of Gansu and in the imperial territory of Xinjiang. At the end of the 1870s, the latter region's remoteness from the east hampered military supplies even further, and the landscape's aridity posed major challenges for the swift revival of agriculture. Zuo tackled both of these distinctively northwestern problems with the same kinds of solutions he had employed elsewhere, namely by utilizing troops in agricultural projects and planning for the reconstruction of waterways.

Indeed, Zuo considered reconstruction of both places together as nearly a single project. One of his memorials in 1880, for instance, recorded the successes of planting trees, building schools, making the roads level, starting agricultural colonies, and fixing irrigation systems in Gansu and Xinjiang. Since his army by that time had already spent some years in Gansu, he provided statistical evidence for accomplishments there, but similar goals guided reconstruction efforts westward. He recounted how, after his army pacified Xinjiang, he had "ordered each defense battalion to work conjointly with each reconstruction bureau to dredge rivers and waterways, in order to promote the beneficial use of water; to build and repair city walls, for stern defenses; to level the roads, for the benefit of transport; and to build and repair official inns, to facilitate travel."[34] Zuo optimistically summarized these successes in both Gansu and Xinjiang, separating them rhetorically only by reference to their location in relationship to the western limit of the Great Wall: "inside the pass" (*neiguan*) or "outside the pass" (*waiguan*).

As in Gansu, dealing with water and land became crucial for controlling Xinjiang. Since the landscape was so arid, reviving agriculture presupposed that either troops or local people would repair irrigation systems to supply water to old fields and newly reclaimed land. In Turpan, his commanders and reconstruction bureau officials jointly promoted the repair of canals and *karez*—an irrigation system of underground channels and wells unique to Xinjiang—by borrowing grain to "supervise and encourage residents to dredge the *karez*, such that the year's harvest will have an autumn [i.e., be sufficient for the whole year]."[35] In another memorial on the same day, Zuo reported that aside from work on the canals of Turpan, *karez* had been dug in 185 locations—a success worth reporting to superiors in Beijing—in addition to the repair work on multiple waterways in seven other cities in Xinjiang.

Zuo also established agricultural colonies to spur production, supply grain to his army, and resettle refugees. As early as 1874 Zuo had dispatched one of his commanders, Zhang Yao, to the eastern Xinjiang oasis of Hami to establish colonies using the battalions under his purview. Zuo apparently expected to obviate the difficulty of grain transshipment, but it is unclear to what extent the agricultural output of Zhang's battalions satisfied the army's requirements or even if they expanded agricultural output in Hami.[36] However, after reconquering Xinjiang and with irrigation construction well underway, Zuo reported in 1880 that soldiers and civilians were participating together in developing farmland and agricultural colonies. Noting the increasing acreage and rising populations of five sites of reclamation in the north, he claimed that in the "eight cities from Turpan into southern Xinjiang, aside from desert, the barren land is gradually being reduced, and newly reclaimed land is all located along the banks of newly opened canals."[37] By putting his troops to work in organized colonies and by drawing on the labor of local people, Zuo intended to change the landscape enough to make agriculture a feasible undertaking in Xinjiang. As they had been in Gansu, *tuntian* colonies were simultaneously an agricultural measure and a means to control the region.

Transplanting from China Proper to the Margins

Having traveled thousands of miles across contrasting landscapes, Zuo recognized the expediency of choosing from the same set of reconstruction tactics with minimal regard for differences in terrain or environment, thus blurring the boundaries that marked one region from the next. But it was not only his convictions about agriculture and certain farming techniques that he imported to the northwestern margins. Zuo also planned to move plants from China proper into Xinjiang, a project with the potential to further diminish the distinctions between where Zuo and his army had started and where they had ended up. His plans opened up the possibility that environmental penetrations of Xinjiang could reproduce eastern landscapes in the far northwest.

One major transplantation within the blueprints for Xinjiang's reconstruction was Zuo's idea to import mulberry trees and sericulture experts all the way from Zhejiang. In this proposal the general looked ahead to the future of Xinjiang's development rather than to the region's immediate postwar needs. He envisioned the great expansion of mulberry cultivation, silkworm raising, and silk production as a means to satisfy the demands of a potentially growing silk market. He superciliously described how even though northern and southern Xinjiang already produced mulberries, the "natives (*turen*) substitute the mulberry fruit for grain, some call it medicinal material, and the benefits of silk textiles are not widespread."[38] Xinjiang already had mulberry trees—over 806,000 of them in all, according to the reports of Zuo's subordinates—but Zuo believed they were not being put to the best possible use. Rather, he argued that using mulberry trees to lift Xinjiang's silk production could help fulfill the demands of Russian merchants who otherwise traveled to Sichuan to obtain the precious cloth, as well as of Xinjiang's own nomadic population, which in the recent era had started consuming silks and woolens.

To vitalize the silk industry, Zuo drew on a model from what he considered the best tradition of silk production in the "central lands" (*zhongtu*), that of Huzhou, in Zhejiang. His plans indicate that he wanted to import the tradition wholesale from the east: he ordered one of his contacts to hire sixty Huzhou silk experts and send them to Xinjiang with mulberry seedlings, silkworm eggs, and appropriate tools. The experts were to teach local people all the techniques of silk production, from planting, grafting, and layering mulberry trees, to boiling the cocoons and spinning the thread. The resulting silk weaving would supplement agricultural production and the two together would comprise the household economy of "farming and weaving supporting each other" that Zuo and other statecraft scholars idealized.[39] With Zhejiang mulberries carpeting the landscape and eastern experts instructing Xinjiang people on the techniques of silk production, Zuo foresaw numerous advantages: the people would become rich, nomads would no longer need to travel afar to purchase silks, merchants could obtain what they wanted while Zuo would have greater opportunity to exert some control over them, tax revenues would rise, and new revenues would help relieve the urgent situation of army provisions. All of this would come from transplanting organisms and skills from Huzhou across the continent, or in Zuo's words, "spreading the benefits of Zhejiang into Xinjiang."[40]

To be sure, adopting production techniques from afar also meant transforming the local population of mulberry trees. Zuo failed to provide precise details of how many seedlings he had ordered or how they would survive the transcontinental journey to the margins of the empire, but he had a seemingly straightforward plan for them. Southern Xinjiang, where work would begin, already had many "wild" (*sheng*) mulberry trees, but "as soon as they are changed by grafting [new branches onto old trunks], then silkworms can be raised."[41] With new Zhejiang mulberry branches growing on their own trunks or grafted onto Xinjiang's trees, Muslims in the southern oases could expect to harvest large, round, plump mulberry leaves in abundance, a boon to silkworm raising. As sericulture manuals from the late 1870s and early 1880s testified, the empire abounded with mulberry varieties, the leaves of which produced various qualities of silk.[42] But if one wanted to produce high quality silk like Zhejiang, one needed the same type of mulberry leaves, grown from grafted branches, and Huzhou was known to have the best kind around.[43] Zuo's efforts to bring the most successful practices of sericulture therefore also necessitated and implied importing the best tree stock from the heartland of silk production.

Tree planting as an aspect of reconstruction was nothing new in Zuo's repertoire of postwar policy, as he had deployed his soldiers to sow willow, elm, and poplar saplings, in addition to mulberry, within towns and along the roads from Shaanxi province westward. One estimate puts the total number of trees planted by his soldiers in Shaanxi and Gansu at over half a million.[44] Zuo himself claimed that his soldiers had planted over 264,000 trees across 600 *li* from the county line of Changwu, Shaanxi, to outside the east gate of the Huining county seat in Gansu, as well as tens of thousands of trees elsewhere.[45] Some saplings planted along main highways had little productive value for local economies and functioned as part of the transportation infrastructure to shade and protect roadways. But mulberry trees like those for import into Xinjiang were a primary component of Zuo's push to combine sericulture with agriculture and boost the local economy. In his own words, the act of "moving mulberry trees from Zhejiang and planting them in the western regions (*xiyu*) pioneers miracles."[46] Whether or not it actually produced economic miracles, the transplanting scheme was a conscious attempt to spread one region's vegetation to another, thus drawing links of environment and economy, even if tenuous, between the two.

Zuo also envisioned importing vegetable seeds for cultivation and consumption by his troops, an attempt that likewise would have drawn subtle links between China proper and Xinjiang. In mid-summer of 1880, from his military encampment in Hami, he wrote a letter to his youngest son who planned to travel to the northwest the following month. Remarking on the extraordinary heat of Hami and Turpan, Zuo ended his letter with a request: "May your older brother please quickly purchase carrot and turnip seeds, as well as swan egg seeds, and send them, in order to distribute them to each military detachment; the more the better. In this place, the terrain conditions are extremely rich and planting vegetables would be most marvelous."[47] If Zuo was attentive to the large-scale problems of reconstruction and the need for provisions, in a request like this he also seemed sensitive to smaller aspects of living far removed from his home environment. Judging the suitability of the Hami soils to a few types of plants, Zuo requested seeds to improve the range of available vegetables. Whether the Hunanese general harbored an epicurean longing for tastes and foods not readily available in the northwest is difficult to prove, but receiving seeds might have reproduced home life in a small way, as other Chinese in Xinjiang in the late Qing era had done.[48] Had the seeds arrived and been planted, they may have also subtly increased the variety of vegetation in Hami. But there is no evidence the plans for vegetable cultivation ever came to fruition, as Zuo was recalled to Beijing several months later. Nonetheless, the request demonstrated his willingness to change the environment by transplanting organisms, in pursuit of his army's political goals.

Transplanting the Provincial System to Xinjiang

Zuo lost the ability to modify northwestern environments when he left the region for the last time in 1881. Direct influence in those local environments had depended on traveling, or temporarily transplanting himself into new lands. Yet perhaps the most significant legacy of his intervention in Xinjiang, the plan to make Xinjiang a province like those in China proper, did not require his presence. Zuo recognized the strategic value of claiming Xinjiang as a province, particularly at a time when imperial Russia had taken advantage of the preceding years of political turmoil in Xinjiang to occupy the historic military outpost of Ili. This action placed Russians in a better position to control regional commerce but caused great dismay among Chinese scholars about the loss of imperial authority and the potential forfeiture of the area's mineral resources (see Kinzley, Chapter 2). Zuo had also long studied the historical geography of the northwest and was familiar with previous scholars' proposals for reforming Xinjiang's political status within the empire.[49] His plan to transform Xinjiang from borderland into province did not reach fruition until several years after his departure, but it can still be considered one of the legacies of his presence in the northwest.

Zuo envisioned turning Xinjiang into a province as a logical extension of his army's reconstruction work. One of his 1878 missives to the imperial government, "Memorial Reporting the State of Affairs in Xinjiang," elucidated how Zuo closely matched the policies of reconstruction and provincialization. Even within a short period of time, argued the general, gathering refugees to resettle and farm had caused populations in northern oases to rebound. Southern cities like Kashgar and Hotan—"populous and rich" with "products aplenty"—were prosperous in comparison to their devastated northern counterparts but could also benefit from reconstruction. Given the momentum of postwar successes, Zuo argued, "the timing of heaven and human affairs both present an opportunity that can be made use of. If we let the present slip away without pursuing [provincialization], we would truly come to regret it."[50] To his mind, the immediate successes of reconquest and reconstruction provided the ideal chance to transform Xinjiang's political status.

Provincialization entailed the opportunity to standardize the territory's politics in a way that reconstruction alone could not. This primarily meant casting Xinjiang's administrative structures in the mold of the Chinese provincial system. Although regionalization within Xinjiang posed its own conundrums—for instance, how to formulate stable pecuniary policies for the territory without a united and easily convertible currency—Zuo focused on differences between the borderland and China proper (*neidi*). Since "political rule is carried out according to [local] custom" in Xinjiang, Zuo lamented, "one cannot do things together in the same fashion as China proper." Zuo considered the local custom of assessing taxes based on population, rather than on landholding as in the provinces of China, as a particularly pernicious problem of inequality, since poorer families often had many children. Owing to such discrepancies, Xinjiang "has long been generally seen as borderland."[51] Provincialization, however, would introduce new institutions and erode local customs, ushering in a standardized and, to Zuo, a more familiar system of politics, simultaneously solving quotidian administrative dilemmas while terminating Xinjiang's status as mere borderland.

Zuo also anticipated a wave of financial rationalization. According to his calculations, the Qing government could save huge amounts of money by streamlining troop deployments. Zuo reiterated a point made by the Qianlong emperor in the previous century, as well as by his fellow Hunan statecraft scholar Wei Yuan, that permanently settling troops in Xinjiang could reduce costs incurred in ruling the region.[52] "If a province is established for southern and northern Xinjiang," Zuo hypothesized, "the system of garrison rotation can stop permanently. It would also control the expense of rations for soldiers, and relieve each province of the great effort of assistance funds."[53] To Zuo's thinking, transforming Xinjiang into a province was not only a civil proposition, but had large ramifications for military deployment along the border and had the potential to reduce the expense of keeping the region within the empire.[54]

To prepare for and facilitate a policy of provincialization, the general also articulated nonagricultural projects during his last few years in the northwest. In his 1880 memorial summarizing the victories of postwar *tuntian* policy, he spelled out several of these measures. Carrying out a cadastral survey of cultivated land, for instance, became a priority, since tax assessments were made according to quantities and qualities of individual landholdings. Forging peaceful and stable relations between Chinese officials and Muslim subjects also required careful attention, especially since Zuo had judged that even though "Xinjiang has long been pacified, the Han and Hui are incompatible with each other, and there is misunderstanding between officials [the Han] and the people [the Hui], so government decrees are difficult to execute."[55] Given the misunderstanding, Zuo advocated inculcating non-Han students with Chinese knowledge in the Chinese language, as well as publishing and distributing basic texts used by students of the empire's civil service examinations. He planned to reformulate the relationship between officials and subjects by educating the latter to accept the Qing state and pursue its goals: "In the future, I hope to transform (hua) their special customs to make them like our Chinese (hua) practices." Doing so would require "establishing community schools and ordering Hui children to read and write and thoroughly understand [our] language."[56] Transforming Xinjiang politics therefore necessitated transplanting Chinese customs into the region, gradually eroding the distinction between the northwestern margins and China proper.

As the official from afar, Zuo again brought his own conceptions to bear on a region and its people thousands of kilometers distant from his home. In this case, Zuo pushed to minimize administrative and political distinctions, part of a process that has been termed the "domestication" or "internalization" of Xinjiang to the Qing empire.[57] Inasmuch as this process transformed the formal relationship between Xinjiang and the rest of the empire, it was a unique supplement to reconstruction. But the means by which the provincial administrative system entered Xinjiang did not altogether differ from Zuo's other imports into the northwest. Like Zhejiang mulberry trees, the system had originated in China proper. Zuo intentionally hoped to bring both westward to ameliorate conditions in Xinjiang and strengthen central government authority. Neither erased the particularities of place or environment in Xinjiang, but both made the territory somewhat less marginal to the center.

Agriculture, Environment, and
the Shifting Margins of the Qing Empire

Convincing the Qing court to transform Xinjiang's administrative system required several years of carefully crafted proposals. Even before the court accepted the plan and made Xinjiang a province in 1884, Zuo Zongtang had already returned from the margins of the empire to take up his post in Nanjing. Although he was back in the Yangzi valley without his army, he had not jettisoned familiar strategies of reconstruction. His late 1882 plans for reforesting Nanjing had included millions of mulberry trees from Huzhou, Zhejiang, just as he had devised for Xinjiang's renewal, thus opening the possibility for economic and environmental resemblances among the three locations. The trajectory of influence of this Hunan general seemed to arch from the heartlands toward to the margins and back again.

Yet Zuo recognized that imperial geography was changing, and that the center and margins were not quite static. With Xinjiang on the verge of becoming a province, new margins were emerging elsewhere. In late 1882, as Zuo considered how best to plan for Nanjing's regrowth, he perceived the significance of geopolitical changes along the eastern seaboard. Nearby Shanghai had once been "hinterland" (fudi), Zuo noted, but owing to the mixture of Chinese and foreigners in the treaty port, with its wharves and foreign concession zones, the "hinterland has already changed into frontier (bian)."[58] As far as Nanjing's energy problems were concerned, foreigners from the empire's coastal margins hawked oil to poor Nanjing residents, tantamount to "snatching away" (duo) the economic interests of the common folk, Zuo decried. But the governor-general had one more arboreal nostrum in the works. Common to the southeast, the Chinese tallow tree produced seeds whose oil could be extracted to fully satisfy all energy requirements provided by candles and other oils. Zuo complained that most people had gradually forgotten tallow tree oil in the shadow of valuable sesame, bean, and cottonseed oils. Even more upsetting, they could not remember that the foreign oil (yangyou) they purchased in larger and larger quantities was, in fact, "tallow tree oil natively produced in the central lands (zhongtu)." To reverse this foreign economic encroachment and reconstruct a robust domestic economy, the old general strongly asserted that officials everywhere should "widely encourage cultivation" of the tallow tree.[59]

As the margins of the empire shifted, just as when the center seemed to crumble into rebellion, Zuo devised ways to rebuild the Qing political-economic system, and he utilized the land, water, and plant resources available to him as tools to restore production. As he stated in an 1871 letter, "the benefits of nature (ziran) are ones that merely await humans themselves to obtain them."[60] During the twenty years of his campaigning, Zuo organized to use these natural resources to provide his army with crucial sources of supplies for carrying warfare and reconstruction westward, even if the output of their agricultural colonies did not always suffice. In other words, they utilized the environment for political ends, refashioning certain parts of the landscape to match their needs, cultivating crops to boost army provisions, and developing the land's productive capacity to aid their control.[61] In this sense, the legacy of the work of Zuo's army is visible in the efforts of their twentieth-century counterparts in Xinjiang, including post-1949 soldiers who settled and reclaimed agricultural land in the drive to ensure Xinjiang's place in socialist China (see Kardos, Chapter 7). As a scholar and examination candidate in the 1830s he had admitted that local farmers would always be more attuned than officials to seasons, soils, and plants in any given location, but as a general he relied on his own perspective and knowledge, accumulated as he traveled across the empire. The so-called benefits of nature were thus harnessed in attempts to reconstruct and propagate a political-economic order that Zuo and other Qing officials envisioned.

NOTES

1. Zuo Zongtang, "Guang chou zaizhong bing Galande tian she lingshi pian" [Brief on broadening plans for planting, and setting up additional consul in Galande], *Zuo Zongtang quanji* [Complete works of Zuo Zongtang], v. 8 (Changsha: Yuelu shushe, 1996), 161. (*Zuo Zongtang quanji* hereafter referred to as *ZZQJ*.)

2. Ibid., 161.

3. Daniel McMahon, "The Yuelu Academy and Hunan's Nineteenth-Century Turn Toward Statecraft," *Late Imperial China* 26.1 (June 2005): 94–95.

4. For a short discussion of nineteenth-century statecraft and scholarship, see Philip A. Kuhn and Susan Mann Jones, "Dynastic Decline and the Roots of Rebellion," *The Cambridge History of China* (Cambridge: Cambridge University Press, 1978), v. 10, 144–54.

5. Robert Marks has argued that an "environmental crisis" should be included in the list of problems that confronted Qing society in the nineteenth century. See his *Tigers, Rice, Silk, and Silt: Environment and Economy in Late Imperial South China* (Cambridge: Cambridge University Press, 1998), 333. Kenneth Pomeranz has coined the term "ecological bottleneck" to describe the environmental and resource limits to further economic development in the mid- to late Qing empire. See his book *The Great Divergence: China, Europe, and the Making of the Modern World Economy* (Princeton: Princeton University Press, 2000). The rising price of silver relative to copper cash and the growing financial crisis of the nineteenth century also vexed statecraft scholars with how to maintain the solvency of the empire without overburdening peasant taxpayers. According to the historian Man-houng Lin, aside from recognizing metal money as wealth, scholar-officials "also emphasized the common people's use of natural resources to produce goods as another form of wealth." See Man-houng Lin, *China Upside Down: Currency, Society, and Ideologies, 1808–1856* (Cambridge: Harvard University Press, 2006), 311.

6. Shen Chuanjing and Liu Yangyang, *Zuo Zongtang zhuan lun* [On the biography of Zuo Zongtang] (Chengdu: Sichuan daxue chubanshe, 2003), 27–28; Lanny B. Fields, *Tso Tsung-T'ang and the Muslims: Statecraft in Northwest China, 1868–1880* (Kingston: The Limestone Press, 1978), 8–9.

7. Zuo Zongtang, "Di si wen" [Fourth question], *ZZQJ*, v. 13, 446.

8. Tu Lien-chê, "Tso Tsung-t'ang," in Arthur Hummel, ed., *Eminent Chinese of the Ch'ing Period* (Washington, DC: U.S. Government Printing Office, 1943), 763.

9. Zuo Zongtang, "Di si wen" [Fourth question], *ZZQJ*, v. 13, 446.

10. Ibid., 447.

11. Although Zuo did not mention measurements in his preface, other Qing scholars

explained that the area-field system, properly arranged, would create small square plots with sides of about 1.5 *chi* (one half meter), with about 675 plots available for planting in one *mu* (one-sixth of an acre), leaving fallow plots between all cultivated plots. For example, see Li Yusun, *Qutian tu shuo* [Illustrated manual of the area-field system] (n.d.), 2a.

12. Zuo Zongtang, "Guang qutian zhi tu shuo xu" [Preface to the illustrated manual for spreading the area-field system], *ZZQJ*, v. 13, 244.

13. Ibid., 246.

14. Ibid., 247.

15. Li Enhan, "Zuo Zongtang de jingshi sixiang" [Zuo Zongtang's statecraft thought], *Jindai shi yanjiusuo jikan* 12 (June 1983): 3–4.

16. Gideon Chen, "Tso Tsung-t'ang: The Farmer of Hsiangshang," *Yenching Journal of Social Studies* 1.2 (January 1939): 214; Shen and Liu, *Zuo Zongtang zhuan lun*, 38.

17. Shen and Liu, *Zuo Zongtang zhuan lun*, 40.

18. For a timeline of events in this period of Zuo's life, see the chronology contained in *ZZQJ*, v. 15, 991–1001.

19. Zuo Zongtang, "Li chen Zhe sheng can li kun bi qingxing pian" [Detailed report on the hardships and misfortunes of the remaining masses in Zhejiang], *ZZQJ*, v. 1, 178.

20. Zuo Zongtang, "Jing chen Zhejiang ying ban shanhou shiyi pian" [Brief on what ought to be done about matters concerning reconstruction of Zhejiang, respectfully stated], *ZZQJ*, v. 1, 584.

21. Zuo Zongtang, "Yu Xiaowei deng" [To Xiaowei and others], *ZZQJ*, v. 13, 145.

22. Zuo Zongtang, "Yu Zhong xiong" [To elder brother Zhong], *ZZQJ*, v. 13, 117.

23. Zuo Zongtang, "Jiao Nian jiao Hui yi can yong chezhan tuntian pian" [Brief on the suitability of using cart warfare and *tuntian* in the suppression of the Nian and the Hui], *ZZQJ*, v. 3, 66.

24. Zuo Zongtang, "Guan Long suqing hui an bao jiang zhe" [Memorial related to mopping up Gansu, collecting records and defense honors], *ZZQJ*, v. 6, 379. See also Ma Xiao, "Zuo Zongtang yu Xibei jindai shengtai huanjing de zhili" [Zuo Zongtang and the management of the modern ecological environment in the northwest], *Xinjiang daxue xuebao (shehui kexue ban)* 32.2 (2004): 73.

25. Zuo Zongtang, "Da Tan Wenqing" [Response to Tan Wenqing], *ZZQJ*, v. 11, 557. See also Shi Jingren, "Tan Zuo Zongtang zai Xibei zhi shu zhong sang" [On Zuo Zongtang planting trees and mulberries in the northwest], *Xibei shidi* 2 (1994): 64.

26. Zuo Zongtang, "Yu Zhong xiong" [To elder brother Zhong], *ZZQJ*, v. 13, 117. One *li* equals one half of a kilometer.

27. Zuo Zongtang, "Jing chen chouban qingxing zhe" [Memorial on making preparations for the circumstances, respectfully stated], *ZZQJ*, v. 3, 373.

28. Zuo Zongtang, "Qing ba xi zheng de xiang yi zhi wei ju zhe" [Memorial on the request for raising funds for the Western expedition in order to prop up a desperate situation], *ZZQJ*, v. 3, 305.

29. Zuo Zongtang, "Jiao Nian jiao Hui yi can yong che zhan tuntian pian" [Brief on the suitability of using chariot battles and *tuntian* in suppressing the Nian and the Hui], *ZZQJ*, v. 3, 66.

30. Zuo Zongtang, "Da Tan Wenqing" [Response to Tan Wenqing], *ZZQJ*, v. 11, 444–45.

31. W. L. Bales, *Tso Tsungt'ang: Soldier and Statesman of Old China* (Shanghai: Kelly and Walsh, 1937), 335.

32. For the 1881 memorial containing Zuo's taxation plan, see Zuo Zongtang, "Yanjin yapian qing xian zeng yangyao tuyan shuijuan zhe" [Memorial about strictly prohibiting opium, requesting the prioritizing of raising foreign and domestic opium taxes], *ZZQJ*, v. 8, 30–33. For Zuo's work within the context of other Qing anti-opium campaigns, particularly crop substitution measures, see David A. Bello, *Opium and the Limits of Empire: Drug Prohibition in the Chinese Interior, 1729–1850* (Cambridge: Harvard University Asia Center, 2005), 290–92.

33. Zuo Zongtang, "Kefu Xinjiang beilu ge cheng an nei bu bo wu zhi ge yuan bian qing zhao yuan bao ji jiang zhe" [Memorial on recapturing each city in northern Xinjiang and a request to give honors according to original guarantee for each staff and officer within the case], *ZZQJ*, v. 7, 213.

34. Zuo Zongtang, "Fangying chengxiu ge gongcheng qing lai bu beian zhe" [Memorandum on defense battalions undertaking each project and request for imperial edict to put into the bureau record], *ZZQJ*, v. 7, 524.

35. Ibid., 524.

36. On the agricultural colony in Hami, see Qiu Zhanxiong, "Zuo Zongtang de zhongnong sixiang yu tuntian zhengce" [Zuo Zongtong's agricultural thinking and *tuntian* policy], in Hunan shida wenshi yanjiusuo, ed., *Zuo Zongtang yanjiu xueshu taolun hui lunwenji* [Collected papers from the academic conference on Zuo Zongtang research] (Changsha: Hunan shida wenshi yanjiusuo, 1987), 292–93; Bales, *Tso Tsungt'ang: Soldier and Statesman of Old China*, 331–32; Kwang-Ching Liu and Richard J. Smith, "The Military Challenge: The North-west and the Coast," *The Cambridge History of China* (Cambridge: Cambridge University Press, 1980), v. 11, 239.

37. Zuo Zongtang, "Banli Xinjiang shanhou shiyi zhe" [Memorial on matters dealing with reconstruction in Xinjiang], *ZZQJ*, v. 7, 518.

38. Ibid., 520–21.

39. See chapter 6 of Susan Mann, *Precious Records: Women in China's Long Eighteenth Century* (Stanford: Stanford University Press, 1997).

40. Zuo Zongtang, "Banli Xinjiang shanhou shiyi zhe" [Memorial on matters dealing with reconstruction in Xinjiang], *ZZQJ*, v. 7, 521.

41. Ibid., 521.

42. See Wang Yuezhen, *Hu can shu* [On Huzhou sericulture] (1880), *juan* 1, 11a–13a, in Xu xiu si ku quan shu bian zuan wei yuan hui, ed., *Xu xiu si ku quan shu* (Shanghai: Shanghai guji chubanshe, 1995), v. 978, 300–1; Ye Shizhuo, *Zeng ke sang can xu zhi* [Reprint of the essentials of sericulture] (1872), 16b–17b.

43. Henan can sang zhi wu ju, ed., *Can sang zhi wu ji yao* [Summary of silk textiles] (Henan can sang zhi wu ju, 1881), 19a.

44. Chen, "Tso Tsung-t'ang: The Farmer of Hsiangshang," 217.

45. Zuo Zongtang, "Fangying chengxiu ge gongcheng qing lai bu beian zhe" [Memorandum on defense battalions undertaking each project and request for imperial edict to put into the bureau record], *ZZQJ*, v. 7, 522–23.

46. Zuo Zongtang, *Zuo Wenxiang gong quanji: shudu*, v. 24, 17, quoted in Qiu, "Zuo Zongtang de zhongnong sixiang yu tuntian zhengce," 295.

47. Zuo Zongtang, "Yu Xiaotong" [To Xiaotong], *ZZQJ*, v. 13, 232.

48. Chinese travelers and exiles to Xinjiang in late imperial times, as Laura Newby has suggested, intended to bring their cuisines with them and reproduce a part of their home lives in a distant land. See L. J. Newby, "The Chinese Literary Conquest of Xinjiang," *Modern China* 25.4 (1999): 466–67.

49. Long before being dispatched by Beijing to the northwest, Zuo had begun to take an interest in historical geography and accumulate knowledge about the northwest. Alongside agriculture, geography was one of the main topics of Zuo's practical learning and it framed his conceptions of the empire's terrain and territorial composition. Zuo seems to have been particularly influenced by the historical geographies of seventeenth-century scholars Gu Yanwu and Gu Zuyu, which he read in 1829 (Tu, "Tso Tsung-t'ang," 762). He also had doubtless come across the essays of Gong Zizhen and Wei Yuan in the statecraft compilation of 1827 that advocated altering the relationship between China proper and Xinjiang by, for instance, encouraging large scale settlement of Chinese in the borderlands (James A. Millward, *Beyond the Pass: Economy, Ethnicity, and Empire in Qing Central Asia, 1759–1864* [Stanford: Stanford University Press, 1998], 241–45; Peter C. Perdue, *China Marches West: The Qing Conquest of Central Eurasia* [Cambridge: The Belknap Press of Harvard University Press, 2005], 497–501; Nailene Chou, "Frontier Studies and Changing Frontier Administration in Late Ch'ing China: The Case of Sinkiang, 1759–1911" [University of Washington, Ph.D. dissertation, 1976], 101-05). Like other scholars of the 1820s and 1830s, when studying the far northwest came into fashion, Zuo turned to official publications regarding Xinjiang compiled after Qianlong's conquest of the region in 1756 (Tu, "Tso Tsung-t'ang," 763; Perdue, *China Marches West*, 476–78). On the rise of interest in Xinjiang, see Newby, "The Chinese Literary Conquest of Xinjiang."

50. Zuo Zongtang, "Fu chen Xinjiang qingxing zhe" [Memorial reporting the state of affairs in Xinjiang], *ZZQJ*, v. 7, 193.

51. Ibid., 193.

52. Millward, *Beyond the Pass*, 41–42.

53. Zuo Zongtang, "Fu chen Xinjiang qingxing zhe" [Memorial reporting the state of affairs in Xinjiang], *ZZQJ*, v. 7, 193.

54. See also Zuo Zongtong, "Fu chen Xinjiang yi kaishe xing sheng qing xian jian dufu chen yi zhuan zecheng zhe" [Memorial reporting Xinjiang's suitability for establishing a province, and a request to first choose governor and inspector generals with special responsibilities for this matter], *ZZQJ*, v. 7, 528.

55. Zuo Zongtang, "Banli Xinjiang shanhou shiyi zhe" [Memorial on matters dealing with reconstruction in Xinjiang], *ZZQJ*, v. 7, 519.

56. Ibid.

57. The idea of domestication comes from Millward, *Beyond the Pass*, 232. Another scholar, Ho Ping-ti, has termed this process of incorporation "interiorization" and, in reference to the subsequent dominance of Chinese, "administrative sinicization." See his article, "In Defense of Sinicization: A Rebuttal of Evelyn Rawski's 'Reenvisioning the Qing,' " *The Journal of Asian Studies* 57.1 (February 1998): 148–149. Regarding the change in toponyms associated with the gradual incorporation of Xinjiang into the Qing empire, see James Millward, "'Coming onto the Map': 'Western Regions' Geography and Cartographic Nomenclature in the Making of Chinese Empire in Xinjiang," *Late Imperial China* 20.2 (1999): 86–87.

58. Zuo Zongtang, "Guang chou zaizhong bing Galande tian she lingshi pian" [Brief on broadening plans for planting, and setting up additional consul in Galande], *ZZQJ*, v. 8, 162.

59. Ibid.

60. Zuo Zongtang, "Zha Shaan Gan ge zhou xian shi zhong daogu sang mian" [Correspondence to each prefecture and county in Shaanxi and Gansu about trying to plant rice, mulberry, and cotton], *ZZQJ*, v. 14, 528.

61. Several Chinese scholars have assessed whether Zuo may be considered a proto-environmentalist by today's standards. His actions did involve conservation of lands and water inasmuch as he needed these resources to create stable agricultural systems. In addition, some of his efforts to plant elms, poplars, and willows along roadsides and between fields were aimed at forestalling drought and blocking wind and sand (Qiu, "Zuo Zongtang de zhongnong sixiang yu tuntian zhengce," 297). But as Zhao Zhen has suggested, Zuo worked with a short-term perspective to quickly develop agriculture and ameliorate economic conditions and neglected the degradation caused by reclaiming the desert (Zhao Zhen, "Qingdai Xibei diqu de nongye kenzhi zhengce yu shengtai huanjing bianqian" [The policy of agricultural reclamation in the northwest region during the Qing and changes in the ecological environment], *Qing shi yanjiu* 1 [2004]: 83). Another scholar, Ma Xiao, has characterized Zuo's changes to northwest environments as a "double-edged sword" which damaged local ecologies while at the same time helping local residents to use the environment to their benefit (Ma, "Zuo Zongtang yu Xibei jindai shengtai huanjing de zhili," 77).

4

CONFRONTING INDIANA JONES

Chinese Nationalism, Historical Imperialism, and the Criminalization of Aurel Stein and the Raiders of Dunhuang, 1899–1944

Justin Jacobs

On December 27, 1930, the Tianjin press boldly branded one of the world's foremost archaeologists an insatiable "thief" for the first time and demanded his immediate expulsion from the country. Unaware of the public besmirching of his name and newly arrived in the oasis outpost of Keriya nearly half a continent away, Marc Aurel Stein was far more concerned with an alarmingly persistent spew of bloody phlegm than with the vagaries of the Chinese press. The headline in the *L'Impartial (Dagongbao)*, however, was adamant: "Under Pretense of 'Travel,' Stein Plunders Xinjiang Antiquities; Outrageous Speeches in America Insult Chinese Nation; Immediate Expulsion Requested." According to the report, among Stein's many offenses were his "absurd claims" that the far northwestern province of Xinjiang "does not even count as part of Chinese territory" and that "the Chinese race is on the verge of extinction." By far his most unforgivable crime, however, was the "pilfering and permanent removal of Dunhuang's storehouse of treasures to a foreign land." This act alone constituted an "enormous loss to our country."[1]

Though several more months would pass before local obstruction efforts finally succeeded in driving Stein out of Xinjiang for good, the massive smear campaign directed against the diminutive Hungarian-born British citizen had now finally gone public, and the days of unchecked foreign archaeological expeditions in China were just about over. As Stein stubbornly pressed north toward the oases of Korla and Kucha in March 1931, Chen Yuan, a Chinese historian at the Nanjing-based Academia Sinica—the newly emergent vanguard of the professional Chinese intelligentsia—seized the opportunity to put the finishing touches on his monumental *Dunhuang jieyu lu*. Though discreetly translated into English as *An Analytical List of the Tun-huang Manuscripts in the National Library of Peiping*, anyone familiar with the Chinese language could not fail to miss the prominent position of the character for "plunder" (*jie*) smack dab in the middle of the title, and, if asked, could likely provide a more accurate translation: *An Index of the Dunhuang Manuscripts Remaining after the Plunder*.[2] Warned by friends and colleagues that the insertion of the character for "plunder" into the title itself was too "provocative" (*ciji*), Chen replied that, "on the contrary, this character is insufficient to express our full anger. I should use an even stronger character!"[3]

It had not always been like this. Three decades earlier (and in a much less afflicted state) Stein had been in the exact same place, wowing the local Qing officials of Chinese Turkestan (Xinjiang) with his erudite scholarship and indefatigable will. In 1899 Stein set out from India for the first of four expeditions to Xinjiang on funds obtained from the British Indian government for the express purpose of confirming "the large place which Indian language and culture must have occupied in the administration and daily life of this region during the early centuries of our era."[4] And the local Qing officials were only too glad to wine and dine him. On June 3, 1901, Han Yaoguang, prefect of Keriya county, filed a glowing report after his meeting with Stein. "In my opinion this traveler is quite genial and cultured, polite and refined. In fact, he is an outstanding individual in every respect." Han's many conversations with Stein were "exceedingly precious" and made the prefect "beam with joy."[5]

Yet by October 1930 the British consular officer in charge of securing Stein's Chinese visa felt compelled to alter both the tone and language of Stein's application. It had become prudent by this point to advertise Stein as a "truly good friend of the Chinese government" whose "aim in undertaking such archaeological activities within Xinjiang is nothing more than to uncover and extol the prestige of ancient China."[6] How did Stein plunge from "outstanding individual" to insatiable "thief" in the course of a single generation? Most Western accounts, parroting the exculpatory accounts of foreign adventurers unfamiliar with either the Chinese language or developments in Chinese intellectual circles, have been content to attribute Stein's fall to the vague "winds of nationalism" that swept across China during the 1920s. Such a fierce gale of "awakened nationalism," we are told, spurred "a new generation of indigenous archaeologists … [to seek] an early end to the days when Westerners, as if by writ, could uproot another nation's past."[7]

A fuller picture, however, can be reached through an examination of what Chinese diplomats, scholars, antiquarians, and journalists themselves were saying about Stein and his generation of controversial explorer-cum-archaeologists. The rise of a professional Chinese intelligentsia—a product of the Nanjing decade—in the late 1920s and early 1930s emboldened some Chinese scholars to re-evaluate the activities of the "haughty imperialists." And yet, at precisely the moment when chastened Western imperialists were fleeing the scene of the crime, the drive to implement what might be characterized as an unacknowledged policy of Chinese historical imperialism on the northwestern Central Asian frontiers reveals a less attractive—and heretofore unacknowledged—side to the effort to reach out to the geographic and cultural margins of the defunct Qing state.

A recent and laudable turn in the field of Chinese history, exemplified by the writings of scholars as diverse as James L. Hevia and Chen Jian,[8] has placed great stress on uncovering instances of "Chinese agency" within the context of China's long historical subjugation at the hands of Euro-American and Japanese imperialism. Yet it is of paramount importance that such scholarship goes one step further and makes at least a minimal effort to show how "Chinese agency" is not simply the benign opposite of passive victimization.[9] In our belated search for "Chinese agency" (often seen as anticipating or representative of Chinese nationalism), we must also begin to come to terms with the thin line separating nationalism from imperialism.[10] In his examination of the critique of the "barbarous" Western looting expeditions in the wake of the Boxer uprising in 1900–1901, Hevia raised the question of how Westerners, the self-proclaimed victims of Chinese "barbarism," could continue to "retain the moral high ground if they slavishly copied the behavior of savages?"[11] Throughout this chapter, we must ask precisely the same question of the bearers of Chinese agency, who not only "slavishly copied" the imperialist behavior of Western archaeologists,[12] but then almost immediately proceeded to suppress any discussion of their own imperialist actions by cloaking the historical record in an uncompromising discourse of criminalization.

Although the Dunhuang Thousand-Buddha Caves (*qianfodong*) ultimately yielded over 40,000 previously undiscovered ancient manuscripts, paintings, statuary, and ceramics dating from the fourth to eleventh centuries, ownership of the artifacts themselves was hardly all that was at stake. Rather, at issue were the fundamental historical and linguistic parameters within which China's northwestern frontiers would be framed and interpreted for generations to come. The Sino-Manchu-Mongolian ruling class that had administered local Qing authority in the northwestern frontiers for nearly two centuries prior to the arrival of Western archaeologists did not, for the most part, view the social integration of the peoples of Xinjiang ("New Dominions") into the greater Qing empire as a desirable end. Two hundred years of hands-off administration in the northwest allowed twentieth-century Western adventurist scholars the opportunity to stake their own unchallenged historical claims to the lands of "Chinese" Central Asia, much to the chagrin of their newly nationalist Chinese-educated counterparts.

As the archaeological heritage of Xinjiang and Dunhuang—and Stein's prominent lineage among the many raiders of Dunhuang—increasingly became an intellectual battleground for competing historical, linguistic, and ethnic narratives, many Chinese-educated scholars came to echo Qing statesman Duanfang's view that control over the Dunhuang manuscripts was "a matter of life and death for Chinese scholarship."[13] Anticipating the Nanjing decade and continuing throughout the 1930s and 1940s, the imposition of a muscular Han Chinese nationalist rhetoric on the historical margins of the northwestern territories was part and parcel of "largely unacknowledged twentieth-century modes of Chinese imperialist strategies in print and visual media," strategies that were "boldly and optimistically projected in anticipation of a time when the state would finally be able to back up such imperialist claims with credible military force."[14] The censure and ultimate "criminalization" of Western archaeologists spelled the death knell for any historical orientation that did not exalt and naturalize the primacy of the Chinese written word and the role of the Han peoples.

First Contact: Antiquarian Officials React to Stein and Dunhuang, 1900–1910

As word filtered up through the local yamens in Xinjiang in the summer of 1901 that a "casual foreign traveler" (*youlizhe*) had unearthed "wooden tablets, fragments of leather plaitings ... [and] quite a bit of tattered paper with tracings of writing visible," the Chinese-educated officials serving on the Qing frontier apparently assumed that such writings would be in their own language.[15] How else to account for the naïve bureaucratic request mechanically forwarded to Pan Zhen, district magistrate of Khotan, that he "transcribe" an additional file copy of several 2,000-year-old Sanskrit documents that Stein had produced for his inspection? The awkward position in which Pan found himself as he carefully crafted his May 17, 1901, reply is evident. "Insofar as I cannot make out the style of calligraphy used in this script," he admitted sheepishly, "any attempt to trace a copy by hand would ultimately prove futile."

Much to Pan's surprise, however, the foreign traveler "does appear to be able to make sense of the majority of the writings in this script, and reports that they are letters and correspondences between local chiefs and princes from the kingdoms of this region in earlier times and the Indians who ran errands back and forth among them."[16] Two weeks later Keriya prefect Han Yaoguang also had to rely upon Stein's linguistic skills in order to report that "these are all ancient Indian characters, not of the sort still in use today. They are perhaps 2,800 years old, a date [Stein] verified by reference to an annotated English version of Xuanzang's account of his trip to the Western Regions."[17]

Stein's well-known penchant for casting himself in the role of a modern-day Xuanzang—the celebrated Chinese-educated monk who traveled to India during the seventh century and brought back thousands of Buddhist Sanskrit scriptures for translation into Chinese—resonated repeatedly with literate officials and religious monks stationed in Xinjiang who were familiar with the many tales that had grown up around this venerated historical figure. Frequently invoking Xuanzang's perilous journey in search of original Sanskrit versions of "lost" Buddhist sutras in northern India, Stein cloaked his efforts as those of one who is "performing a pious act in rescuing for Western scholarship all those relics of ancient Buddhist literature and art which were otherwise bound to get lost earlier or later through local indifference."[18]

In fact, Chinese-educated officials did not fret over the loss of manuscripts not in Chinese. Ye Changchi, the provincial education commissioner for Gansu province from 1902 to 1906, maintained copious diary entries regarding the specific contents of Chinese-language documents and steles that had begun to trickle out of Dunhuang's Thousand-Buddha Caves during his tenure in Gansu. In his entry for September 28, 1904, however, Ye made only a terse remark regarding the receipt of a gift of "31 leaves of a manuscript sutra ... all in Sanskrit," whose strange script he derisively characterized as a "flurry of raindrops in a windy storm, with letters puny as flies." In December 1909, however, three years after retiring to his home in Zhejiang province, Ye deeply mourned reports that the French sinologist Paul Pelliot had carted off a great many Chinese "Tang-Song manuscripts and paintings" from the Dunhuang cave library.[19]

The linguistic preferences of Western and Chinese scholars were also evident within the northwestern manuscript forgery business, whose proprietors staked their very livelihood on the profitable exploitation of wealthy scholars. From 1895 to 1901 Islam Akhun and his band of Khotanese accomplices ran a highly lucrative business forging manuscripts in "unknown languages" and selling them to European "sahibs" in Kashgar. According to Stein, "a certain Ibrahim Mulla ... made it his special business to cultivate the Russian demand for 'old books,' while Islam Akhun attended chiefly to the requirements of British officers and other collectors." The scam was so successful that by 1896 the forgers no longer copied everything by hand but rather started to produce fake books by means of "repeated impressions from a series of wooden blocks."[20]

What sort of person would prove most likely to exchange large sums of silver for a short length of Chinese-scripted hemp, silk, or paper? Zhao Weixi, a Qing official traveling through Gansu and Xinjiang during 1910–1911, provides a classic character profile of an interested buyer of Chinese-language Dunhuang manuscripts. Zhao's sojourn through the northwest on his way to Dihua, the provincial capital of Xinjiang, occurred at precisely the same time that Luo Zhenyu had begun to agitate (successfully) for the Ministry of Education to begin the excruciating process of shipping to Beijing the remaining 9,000 or so Dunhuang manuscripts not taken by Stein or Pelliot.

When on October 23, 1910, Zhao decided to rest his weary limbs at a wayside inn near Gansu province's Jiayu Pass, perched on the northwestern precipice of what could only tenuously be referred to as "China proper," he prepared himself for his imminent entry into Chinese Turkestan by penning a lengthy colophon on the backside of a *Mahā-parinirvāna* sutra from Dunhuang (given to him the previous year by one-time Gansu garrison commander Chai Hongshan). "The paper and ink appear to be brand new, while the characters are vibrant and smooth, tender yet muscular," Zhao observed. "The structure is tight and orderly. Bursting with latent vitality, in form and appearance the characters succeed in harmonizing elegance and grace with a firm, robust bearing." Such a feat, Zhao believed, "can only flow from the brush of an early Tang genius."

After tabulating each and every one of the sutra's 7,788 characters individually, Zhao triumphantly declared that "every character is worth a pearl, and if placed in a *hu*-vessel these pearls would burst out over the side."[21] Zhao's passion for the abstruse minutiae of the Chinese calligraphic art—more than one-third of the entire colophon is taken up with such purple prose—was not atypical. When the famous calligrapher Wang Shubo gazed for the first time upon the mesmerizing strokes of the *lishu* script on a manuscript brought from Turpan in 1914, he dreamily described the sight as "an elegant flow interspersed with rich splashes of recklessly bold ink dashes that achieve intensity through a refined grace. The entire page," Wang continued breathlessly, "is overcome with a mesmerizing beauty. No one has seen such a thing for over a thousand years." This time mere pearls were insufficient to gauge the worth of each character, for these exquisite specimens were deemed worthy of "a thousand pieces of gold each, enough to cure one's hunger."[22]

Antiquarian officials and calligraphers such as Zhao Weixi and Wang Shubo tended to divide their colophon commentaries between two subjects: aesthetic particularities of the Chinese calligraphic craft as evinced on the manuscript in their possession, followed by a brief speculation on the implications of Stein's and Pelliot's removal of the greater portion of manuscripts from the Thousand-Buddha Caves. But in contrast to the uncompromising polemics hurled at these foreign explorers in later decades, these initial reactions were mild, often even approving. Much like the friendly cooperation evident in the establishment of the Sino-Russian joint mining operations (see Kinzley, Chapter 2) in Tacheng in 1899—the same year that Stein began his first expedition—Chinese-educated scholar-officials in the first decade of the twentieth century encouraged, approved, and even collaborated with Stein's archaeological endeavors.

On October 30, 1908, Zhu Ruichi, prefect of Pishan county in Xinjiang, wrote a personal letter to Stein in which he expressed concern at the latter's encounter with "snowcapped mountain peaks and winter gales so fierce that they pierce the human body and severely chap the hands and feet." When Zhu heard of Stein's plight in the fearsome outdoors, he immediately "mourned" for the archaeologist's welfare. After further consideration, however, the prefect's mourning turned to admiration. "What I mourn," Zhu clarified, "is the thought of you scaling mountain cliffs, fording bodies of water, and enduring all sorts of strenuous obstacles. What I admire is your stern fortitude and stoutness of heart." For Zhu and other antiquarian officials unaccustomed to ever leaving the comfort of their study, Stein's activities on the frontier "confer glory upon the desert sands of the Gobi and add luster to the mountain peaks of the Kunlun."[23]

In stark contrast to the creative tongue-lashings that later generations of nationalist Chinese scholars would broadcast, in this early period Stein's and Pelliot's relocation of archaeological artifacts to Europe was consistently mediated via decidedly neutral verbs such as "obtained" (*huoqu*), "transported" (*yunsong*), "carried away" (*xiedai*), and "sent back" (*jihui*).[24] As late as 1925, Cai Yuanpei, president of Beijing University, maintained a nonaccusatory tone while stating matter-of-factly that "ever since the discovery of Dunhuang's stone caverns, the majority of important materials has been shipped (*yunwang*) to Europe by the English scholar Stein and the French scholar Pelliot." Though it was certainly a "pity" that "scholars wishing to read such manuscripts have no choice but to travel to Europe," no erudite Chinese-educated scholar or high official in these early decades thought that Stein and his ilk were "criminals" for taking Chinese manuscripts to libraries and museums across Europe.[25]

Even when Zhao Weixi called the removal to Paris of ten thousand of the most exquisite manuscripts "a deep humiliation for our people," he did not condemn the remover. And while Luo Zhenyu confessed to a "troubled state of mind" and yearned to "accompany Dr. Pelliot on his journey back to the West," he also immediately stated his "appreciation for Dr. Pelliot's generosity and warm-heartedness," calling him a "dear friend of high moral integrity."[26] On the contrary, these antiquarians consistently blamed Abbot Wang—the hapless Daoist guardian of the Dunhuang caves who repeatedly sold manuscripts and relics to raise money for temple repairs—and the many local officials who pecked away like scavengers at the poorly secured stash of Dunhuang manuscripts that were transported to Beijing in 1910.

Certainly the purported desire of eccentric antiquarian official Duanfang to "buy back" (*gouhui*) a portion of those Dunhuang manuscripts in Pelliot's posses-sion indicates some sense of entitlement to the Chinese-language documents. Yet Pelliot—who refused Duanfang's request—continued to stay in the good graces of Chinese scholars, largely because he cooperated with them and read classical Chinese fluently. The facilitation of Pelliot's considerable contributions toward the field of classical Chinese learning were deemed to be of far greater priority than petty—and decidedly ungentlemanly—quibblings over who got there first.[27] Indeed, to the first dirt-encrusted man of learning to arrive on the scene went the spoils, and not a single scholar writing in Chinese would ever dispute this tacit agreement during the early decades.

Buttressing the Classics: Luo Zhenyu and the Antiquarian Scholars, 1911–1924

The first serious Chinese scholar to arrive on the scene of Dunhuang studies was the antiquarian Luo Zhenyu. In stark contrast to such Holy Grail–seeking antiquarian officials as Zhao Weixi and Duanfang, Luo and his young protégé Wang Guowei did more during the sixteen years from 1909 to 1925 than anyone else to collect, copy, publish, analyze, and propagate knowledge of the Chinese-language archaeological finds that had begun to emerge in increasing numbers from Xinjiang and Gansu. Luo and Wang's painstaking efforts to search out and translate speeches given by Stein and Pelliot and printed in such forums as the London-based *Geographical Journal* finally alerted the broader Chinese scholarly community on the eastern seaboard to the activities of foreign explorers along the northwestern frontier.

A mere two years following Stein's first visit to Dunhuang in May 1907, Luo published a collection of speeches by English, French, German, and Japanese explorers in which the latest finds and archaeological discoveries were elaborated upon in detail. Translated into respectable classical Chinese by even more respectable scholars such as Wang Guowei and Fan Bingqing, *Visiting the Ancients among the Shifting Sands (Liusha fanggu ji)* served as a crash-course introduction to the considerable head start foreign archaeologists had attained over their Chinese counterparts in the excavation—and reclamation—of the history of a land still caught between the competing toponyms of "Eastern" and "Chinese" Turkestan. To borrow Stein's characterization, antiquarian scholars cast in the mould of Luo and Wang were notoriously uninterested in the politics of "new China's" struggle to claim historical and political sovereignty over the northwestern frontiers. Wang's translation of Stein's March 8, 1909, speech before the Royal Geographical Society, in which Stein first disclosed the details of the "discovery" of Dunhuang's Thousand-Buddha Caves, freely interchanges the toponyms "Turkestan," "Xinjiang," "Eastern Turkestan," and "Chinese Turkestan," on one occasion even omitting the "Chinese" half of the original document's "Chinese Turkestan."[28]

Antiquarians like Luo and Wang used Chinese-language materials from Dunhuang and Xinjiang mainly to confirm the activities of the same Chinese social and political elite groups "that are also documented in the textual sources." As Lothar von Falkenhausen has observed, because Chinese researchers "have been led to believe that they already knew what happened ... the goal of archaeology was merely to demonstrate the correctness of an already-accepted view." This outlook reduced archaeological finds to "useful supplier[s] of evidence" for the venerated Confucian classics, and subjected historical materials to become the "virtual handmaiden of antiquarianist historiography." Studies of Chinese-language antiquities unearthed from the desert sands throughout Stein's lifetime are without exception prefaced with determinist introductory phrases in the mould of "According to the History of the Han Dynasty ..." Wang Guowei's most celebrated scholarly achievement was a "path-breaking reconstruction of Shang royal genealogy, which, gratifying to those who believed in the accuracy of the transmitted texts, demonstrated the essential correctness of the genealogy presented by Sima Qian" nearly two millennia prior.[29]

Despite the self-imposed straitjacket of a determinist agenda based largely on the Chinese classics, however, the date of February 16, 1925, ushered in a new era in Dunhuang studies. For on that day, Luo Zhenyu was one of several prominent intellectuals who gathered to see 33-year-old Chen Wanli off at the Beijing train station. Chen's final destination was Dunhuang. And though this marked the first time ever that a Chinese scholar had made the arduous journey to the distant Thousand-Buddha Caves since its "opening" nearly three decades earlier, what Chen encountered along the way would shake the very foundations of the Chinese scholarly community.

Chen Wanli and the Criminalization of Langdon Warner, 1925–1926

Chen Wanli was a doctor by training whose experiences on the Langdon Warner expedition would inspire him to become one of China's foremost historians of ceramics. His fascinating account of American art historian Langdon Warner's ill-fated Harvard-sponsored expedition to Dunhuang in early 1925 is a surprisingly sympathetic eyewitness record of the shock and frustration experienced by all members of the party—both American and Chinese—upon encountering xenophobic, poverty-stricken peasants who had finally learned how to turn crumbling bodhisattva debris into ready cash. The real Chen Wanli was neither the heroic anti-imperialist Chinese scholars have come to venerate nor the saboteur extraordinaire of Western lore. In fact, he seems to have had little inkling of the powerful forces plotting around him.

According to William Hung (Hong Ye), newly appointed dean of Yanjing University in Beijing, the Chinese interpreter from Langdon Warner's first expedition in 1923–1924 came to him one night in early 1925 and confessed with tears and on bended knee that he had witnessed Warner removing several frescoes from the walls of the Thousand-Buddha Caves the previous year yet had never reported the matter. Because word was now circulating that the same Americans had returned to China with an even larger quantity of fresco-loosening glycerin and cheesecloth in preparation for a second expedition, Hung made up his mind to notify Vice Minister of Education Qin Fen, who in turn "instructed local authorities to provide these friends with ample protection and courteous treatment, but on no account allow them to touch any historical relics."[30]

The ensuing course of events is significant precisely because it showcases the highly sympathetic outlook—indeed, outright mimickry—of the professional Chinese intelligentsia toward the sort of invasive archaeological reconnaissance procedures that had characterized nearly every foreign expedition prior to 1925. Chen must have known that the expedition would encounter polite resistance from local yamens and a few staged protests from the local people—that was all an expected part of William Hung's original plan. Never in their wildest dreams, however, did Chen's Beijing sponsors imagine that Chen himself—an official Chinese representative of Beijing University who was merely intent on replicating what foreigners had already been doing for decades—would be hounded like a criminal and subjected to a humiliating inquisition backed up by the threat of violence. After more than three decades of idly standing by while cartloads of irreplaceable artifacts had poured out of the country, the Chinese scholarly community—as represented by Chen—was now finally able to carry out its own on-site archaeological research missions. Yet the unwelcome realization that Gansu peasants saw no difference between the "looting" of foreign Americans and the "excavations" of Chinese scholars would lead directly to the criminalization of the foreigners.

On March 24, 1925, little more than a month after setting out from Beijing and still eight weeks shy of Dunhuang, approximately twenty local peasants from a tiny village known as Jingchuan cornered Chen along with several members of the American expedition outside of the Luohan Caves in southeastern Gansu. Amidst a flurry of accusations the villagers "grabbed the reins of the horses firmly and would not let us leave." Soon more villagers arrived, "making a big ruckus," and "accused Jayne [one of the Americans] of breaking some Buddhist statues." According to Chen's diary, one villager "grabbed onto Jayne's sleeve and told him that … if they did not make arrangements for the compensation of the Buddhist statues they would not release him." In the end an unruly throng composed of residents from six neighboring villages succeeded in detaining the expedition's members (both Chen and the Americans) for more than two hours before a cash settlement was reached—two dollars apiece for eighteen small statues and thirty dollars for one large statue.[31]

Not long after the agreed sum had been handed over, however, the local magistrate arrived on the scene, followed soon after by his security guard, who returned the money and reported that the "representative for the villagers had been intimidated and threatened, and that he was no longer willing to accept the payment." (One does not have to read too much between the lines here to understand that the intervention of the local official was almost certainly the catalyst for the return of the money.) During his negotiations with the villagers, Chen had placated them with repeated promises of how he would hold off "bothering the government officials" as long as they could reach a peaceful settlement among themselves. Circumventing the often corrupt local officials, Chen believed, "would ensure the welfare of the villagers," who in the eyes of the magistrate had clearly gone too far on their own initiative in confronting the formidably connected foreign and Beijing scholars.[32]

If Chen's goal had been to tarnish the image of the Americans, he could have simply framed this dispute as justified peasant wrath toward the haughty incursions of foreign "archaeologists," and omitted his own role in the fiasco. Yet Chen's own avowed marching orders—that he advance the nascent discipline of Chinese archaeology—dictated that he himself also enthusiastically participate in the Americans' "plunder." Recalling his discovery the previous day of a broken-off portion of an inscribed stele, Chen lambasted the Jingchuan villagers for "not understanding that they are supposed to cherish things like this." Even more difficult to stomach, however, was the realization that when the local officials "moved the [main base of the] stele to Wen Temple, they too neglected to move this portion along with it." Why had the stele been haphazardly broken in two and moved about recklessly? The banal, decidedly unscholarly catalyst of "a dispute concerning the temple's foundations" clearly exasperated Chen. "In light of this I resolved to transport the remaining portion to Beijing so that the university's archaeology department could study it. Otherwise, how could the fate of this stele remnant be anything other than eventual destruction?"[33] Much like Stein's earlier invocation of the preservationist mission of the monk Xuanzang, here the wholesale internalization and imitation by Chinese scholars of the Western methodological and moral approach to archaeology is nowhere more evident.

When the quarrel with the Jingchuan villagers broke out Chen fretted over his possession of the stele. "If the villagers stopped me then they would have wanted to unwrap it and take a look, and the dispute would have escalated quickly." When Chen first spotted the stele in the eastern grotto ten villagers had already been stationed in the cave to supervise his movements, continually pestering Chen with such inquiries as, "Are you going to leave this piece here? What about that one, are you taking it?" Rather than informing Chen that ancient relics of the village's local and religious heritage were not to be tampered with, these hard-luck peasants seemed to be far more concerned with determining the proper price to be paid for their ancestors' wares—all of which were clearly for sale. In cloaking their desire for hard cash within a discourse of "plunder," the villagers made no distinction between Americans from Cambridge and Chinese from Beijing. In the eyes of the peasants, both were outsiders and both would have to pay. Fortunately for Chen's pocketbook, the "ten workers who had been supervising my work in the grotto never appeared during the debate. How fortunate was I!"[34]

Chen's barely concealed disdain for (in the words of recent Chinese scholarship) these peasant "organic protectors of China's national heritage" ultimately got the better of him, and he initially made no attempt to hide his complicity with his American "friends." "Though our removal of Buddhist statues ... was Alan [Priest]'s idea, I wholeheartedly believe that it was the correct thing to do for the sake of research, and I assisted in the process." Because this was Chen's "first time traveling in the northwest ... I was not able to anticipate such problems. For burdening my friends with several hours of terror," Chen expressed "deep remorse."[35]

Yet this account is not the widely accepted version of the expedition's troubles as currently told among Chinese and Western historians. The current consensus completely omits the incident at Jingchuan, and instead inexplicably jumps ahead to the expedition's arrival in Dunhuang nearly two months later, where "an angry mob forced the Americans to retreat without photographs and frescoes."[36] Recent Chinese historians, aware of William Hung's backstage machinations yet still attracted to the tantalizing possibility that proto-nationalist peasants were the first to stand up and confront the heinous deeds of foreign "archaeologists," have taken this miscalculation even further. "The common Chinese peasant masses were the chief reason why Warner's expedition packed up and fled without any success," maintains one recent mainstream account. "These Chinese peasants, in obstructing the route of would-be thieves of our cultural artifacts, became the organic protectors of China's ancient heritage."[37]

The sudden emergence of officially orchestrated "anti-foreign" mobs that the party encountered at Dunhuang—the second public disturbance of the expedition—has been explained away by suggesting that the "May 30 incident," the day on which British-employed Sikh and Chinese policemen fired on Chinese labor protesters in Shanghai and ignited a wave of antiforeign sentiment in several urban centers, was largely responsible for "harassment at every step by the local authorities, as well as by a hostile populace."[38] Such an explanation, however, flies in the face of logic: Not only were the Americans confined to a three-day visit to Dunhuang a full week before the events of May 30 unfolded over a thousand miles away, but there is no evidence that the post–May 30 industrial worker protest movement (largely confined to the major urban centers of the eastern seaboard) ever reached the isolated rural villages that Warner's expedition visited in northwestern Gansu.[39] A crucial distinction needs to be made here. The staged mobs of Dunhuang were part of a pre–May 30 plot orchestrated by an elite Chinese nationalist (William Hung) based in Beijing. By contrast, the reason that Chen was so unnerved by the brouhaha at Jingchuan was precisely due to the fact that it was a local, unscripted "organic" peasant protest that opportunistically exploited for financial gain not only the the "imperialist" greed of the Americans, but also the "nationalist" greed of their Chinese understudy.

A year after the expedition's demise, Beijing University published Chen's original manuscript as A Diary of Westward Travels (Xixing riji). Following the lead of Warner himself, who was unable to read Chinese, Western scholarship has dismissively described this work as a "slanderous book" in which Chen supposedly claimed "that he had joined the Americans for the express purpose of keeping track of their actions and preventing them from marauding."[40] This is only partially true. As he clearly indicates throughout his diary, Chen himself was highly sympathetic to the archaeological mission of his American colleagues, and nowhere in his original notes does he reveal any insider knowledge of Hung's plans.[41] It was Chen's superiors back in Beijing, attuned to the rising nationalistic public outcry over the May 30 incident in Shanghai, who seized upon Chen's diary as a golden opportunity to "criminalize" the foreigners and marginalize Chen's sympathetic complicity. "Criminalization" emerged as the only plausible face-saving measure for those Chinese scholars who had absolutely no intention of relinquishing their newfound academic territory, regardless of how many extortionary roadblocks the "ignorant peasant masses" might erect. Thus it passed that Chen's *A Diary of Westward Travels* underwent the interpretive prism of a whopping three prefaces authored by some of the biggest names in Chinese academia. Ma Heng and Shen Jianshi, prominent members of the university's Archaeological Society, fully subscribed to historian Gu Jiegang's carefully selective sentiment that "the malice (*e'gan*) of the locals toward Westerners" was an "enormous cause for regret" insomuch as it prevented Chen from dallying longer at many of the sites. In order to extricate Chen from the "crimes" of the foreigners, Gu determined that the ignorant peasants of Jingchuan had "misconstrued" Chen's actions at the Luohan Caves, mistaking "preservation" for "destruction," or even "as theft for our own monetary gain!" On the contrary, Gu pointed out significantly, the illiterate Abbot Wang—who "unlawfully profited from the sale of Dunhuang's ancient relics" to foreigners for over a decade—was a prime example of a real "thief."[42]

The *coup de grâce* against the Americans was delivered in a tardily appended supplement to the diary, written *after* Chen had already returned to Beijing and was apparently debriefed regarding the delicacies of the new political line. In a striking shift in tone from the body of the original diary, Chen suddenly and suspiciously laid the blame squarely on the foreign presence. This post-expedition supplement marks the only place throughout the entire published diary where Langdon Warner is blamed for the expedition's ignomious departure from Dunhuang (despite the fact that Warner was detained long before he could reach the caves). Chen then goes even further by embellishing Warner's moral culpability, ignoring his earlier admission of "friendship" with the Americans, and portraying Warner's peeling of the Dunhuang frescoes in 1924 as every bit as odious as the mass vandalism carried out by hundreds of White Russians who had sought refuge in the caves for nine months during 1920–1921.[43]

The published diary of Chen Wanli encouraged the dispatch of a series of "scholar-spies" who "fatally compromised" Sven Hedin's Sino-Swedish expedition of 1927–1930 and capably undermined Aurel Stein's fourth and last expedition to Chinese Turkestan in 1930. The much publicized fiasco that was Stein's final expedition signaled the triumphant arrival of a nationalist, professional Chinese intelligentsia financed by government support, united in aims, and eager to pick up where the criminalized imperialists had left off: staking a claim on the marginal lands beyond the pass.

Translating Stein: Fu Sinian and the
Chinese Intelligentsia, 1927–1936

As the criminalization of every non-Chinese person who had ever taken so much as a Buddha's ear out of China gained steam following Warner's departure in late 1925, the formerly unspoken bias toward sinocentric interpretations of history relying solely upon Chinese-language documents now became blatantly overt. The report of the National Commission for the Preservation of Antiquities, reprinted in the Chinese press in December 1930, slammed Stein for stealing Chinese manuscripts despite "not knowing a word of Chinese," while a review of Stein's book *On Central-Asian Tracks* criticized him for "not including a single Chinese character" within its pages.[44] In his 1931 preface to *An Index of the Dunhuang Manuscripts Remaining after the Plunder*, Chen Yuan boldly staked out the rigid linguistic parameters within which Chinese Dunhuang studies would now proceed. "Manuscripts written not in Chinese but rather in one of the ancient Central Asian languages are not worth much to us," Chen bluntly declared. "What the Chinese people value are ancient manuscripts written in Chinese." Chen's index bears out this claim: Of the 8,679 manuscripts that he chose to catalogue, only one is in a language other than Chinese.[45]

The implications of such a bias reach far beyond the Dunhuang manuscripts. When the first generation of homegrown Chinese archaeologists embarked on their maiden voyage to Xinjiang as part of Sven Hedin's joint Sino-Swedish expedition in 1927, the Chinese members of the expedition were incapable of interpreting any inscribed artifact other than those that painted the history of Xinjiang via the Chinese script. When Xu Bingxu discovered a "pile of rocks" displaying various non-Chinese inscriptions, the response among his colleagues was telling. "The pictures look as though they have something to do with measurements of the sun," Xu hypothesized. "The writing contains ten letters, the last four of which are '1700,' but we don't know what language the letters are written in." One person suggested Russian, "but that can't be right." Huang Wenbi declared "somewhat arbitrarily" that it was written in Tibetan, "but we really just don't know, and I harbor my own doubts."[46]

The fact that some of the most preeminent Chinese archaeologists of the twentieth century could not even distinguish—much less read—Russian from Tibetan in a land where so much of the region's history had been recorded in one or the other was apparently troubling even to such old-school antiquarians as Wang Guowei. Shortly before his suicide, and at about the same time that Huang and Xu were struggling to differentiate the Tibetan and Cyrillic scripts, Wang deemed it a "pity that Chinese scholars have not yet conducted any research on these ancient [non-Chinese] languages." As a result, Wang lamented, "even if we actually did desire to conduct such research, we would have no choice but to apply for the assistance of English, French, and German scholars."[47] The battle for historical sovereignty over the northwestern frontiers was also a battle of linguistic orientations. And nationalist Chinese scholars, who lacked proficiency in all but one of the region's twenty or so recorded languages, were about to emerge victorious.

In place of the neutral verbs employed by the previous generation of antiquarian scholars and officials, newly nationalist Chinese scholars belonging to the professional intelligentsia in Beijing and Nanjing now proceeded to substitute more damning terminology, words such as "loot" (*daozou*), "steal" (*qiequ*), "plunder" (*qiangjie*), and "pillage" (*duoqu*). One translator of Stein's works expressed his "indignation" at Stein's "wanton bundling" (*dasi soukuo*) of the Dunhuang manuscripts, while another was repulsed by reports that Stein's Chinese translator and collaborator at Dunhuang "was actually later awarded a gold medal by the British Indian government!"[48] As translations of Stein's works grew more and more popular, however, general audiences unburdened with the nationalist agenda of the Beijing and Nanjing scholarly worlds began to offer unorthodox perspectives. A 1929 article in the *Eastern Miscellany* praised Stein's "amazing accomplishments" and "historical authority," with nary a single reference to "theft."[49] A prominent book review of Stein's *On Central-Asian Tracks*, while acknowledging that Stein had indeed "looted" China's national treasures, nevertheless contended that "all those Chinese antiquities that Stein shipped to London have in fact been preserved in perfect condition." If not for the measures taken by Stein and Pelliot, these priceless treasures "may very well have been lost forever at the hands of the stupid local peasants, who in their ignorance would have burned the manuscripts and idols in order to cure a disease."[50]

With such a diversity of popular views and inflammatory labels circulating in the mainstream press, Fu Sinian, director of the Nanjing-based Academia Sinica and one of the most powerful scholars in China, suddenly stepped in and attempted to impose a single orthodox interpretation. According to Fu, the only Western sinologists worthy of praise were those who "acknowledge and propagate the contributions of Chinese scholars." Such a man Stein certainly was not. Because Stein—unlike Pelliot—had never at any point evinced the slightest interest in sharing his finds with Chinese scholars, instead jealously hoarding up his obscenely large stash of Central Asian antiquities at the British Museum in London, Fu admonished against "recklessly mixing the names of Stein and Pelliot together." In an influential 1935 article published in the Tianjin *L'Impartial*, Fu insisted on the rehabilitation of Paul Pelliot's scholarly reputation while at the same time condemning Stein to the purgatory of Chinese public opinion. "In discussing the matter of Pelliot's connection to the Dunhuang manuscripts," Fu opined, "we must carefully examine the course of events at that time as well as issues of morality." Because Pelliot—who, unlike Stein, evinced a remarkable fluency in spoken, written, and classical Chinese—utilized his cache of manuscripts to "make new contributions to the field of sinology (*hanxue*), he naturally deserves the respect of the people of our great nation."[51]

Stein, on the other hand, once gave a speech at Harvard during which William Hung (the mastermind behind Langdon Warner's downfall) overheard Stein claiming that the Chinese "lack scholarship." Supposedly uttered at a 1929 fundraising event designed to raise contributions for his fourth and final expedition to Chinese Central Asia, Stein's public speeches brazenly encouraged donations on the explicit premise that only he had cultivated the erudition necessary to properly examine and interpret what he was likely to uncover in Xinjiang. Stein, whose callous admission that he "only knew Old China" could not help but ruffle the feathers of the scholars of "New China," cared little for the present-day political tapestry of East Asia.[52]

Pelliot was far more sympathetic to the plight of his Chinese scholar friends. When Fu asked him whether he intended to visit friends in Japan during his 1934 East Asian tour, Pelliot vented his "dissatisfaction" with Japan's recent behavior and said that he had cancelled his planned trip to Japan. Also off-limits was Luo Zhenyu, the disgraced antiquarian scholar of early Dunhuang studies who had recently collaborated with the Japanese in Manchuria. Pelliot again successfully treaded the treacherous political waters, claiming "no desire to meet with him." And what about Pelliot's by now undeniable "theft" at the Thousand-Buddha Caves in 1908? In the eyes of an approving Fu, Pelliot had apparently shown considerable progress toward reforming himself, this time around only purchasing "ordinary books along with recently published periodicals ... it is clear [this time] that he has not taken a single rare manuscript out of the country."[53]

In laying down the official line of the largest research institute in China, Fu Sinian defined the political positions and cultural sympathies to which all foreigners wishing to gain access to historical materials within China's borders would have to adhere. A mere three months after Fu's article, *L'Impartial* published a series of nineteen scholarly reports over a ten-month span that were authored by Beijing-based scholar Wang Chongmin. What Wang chose to publish in Tianjin's *L'Impartial*, however, effectively essentialized the manuscripts of Dunhuang into a miniscule, highly selective collection of well-known "Confucian classics" that in no way reflected the diversity of peoples, histories, and languages to which the authors of the original manuscripts belonged. On the contrary, a representative selection from the first two months reads like a bestseller's list of the most venerable and oft-quoted of the Chinese-language classics: the *Spring and Autumn Annals, Book of Rites, Analects of Confucius*, and the *Zhuangzi*, to name just a few.[54]

In light of the fact that the Dunhuang manuscripts were composed overwhelmingly of Buddhist monastic literature (approximately 90 percent, less than half of which were written in Chinese), Wang's "representative selection" was actually a narrowly rigid lens focused on less than 5 percent of the entire collection.[55] Thus at precisely the same time that Fu Sinian and his cadre of nationalist Chinese scholars were attempting to distance themselves from the taint of antiquarianism as typified in "traitors" such as Luo Zhenyu, Wang Chongmin's selective reports from London and Paris revealed the profound debt that the new generation of scholars owed their forbears.

Revitalizing the Han: Dunhuang as a National Resource, 1937–1944

It is perhaps one of the great ironies of twentieth-century Chinese history that the loss of the ancient Chinese heartland to the Japanese in 1937 resulted in the symbolic relocation of China's "national essence" to the decidedly non-Chinese northwestern frontier in Dunhuang. The westward exodus of Chinese scholars to the wartime capital of Chongqing in October 1938 transformed the relationship between Dunhuang and the academic centers of Beijing and Nanjing. Once distant cousins barely on speaking terms, all these focal points of historical scholarship suddenly found themselves intimate neighbors closely connected through blood and kinship ties forged during wartime.

Xiang Da—Stein's Chinese translator—even suggested that Dunhuang could now serve as a hallowed stand-in for the lost homelands of Confucius. "Much like Qufu in Shandong, which is not the private property of the Kong lineage," Xiang wrote from the Thousand-Buddha Caves in 1942, Dunhuang similarly is not the private reserve of the people of Gansu. When Xiang wrote that Dunhuang was a representative of "Chinese culture as a whole" (*Zhongguo zheng ge wenhua*) on par with the ancient sage-king himself, he was applying the same essentialized interpretive framework that Wang Chongmin had foisted upon the threatening mass of unmediated manuscripts in Europe.[56]

Xiang Da was in Dunhuang as part of one of the now frequent delegations of Chinese scholars to the neglected caves, which suddenly seemed much closer to the wartime base of the ultra-nationalist Chinese intelligentsia in Chongqing. Confronted with the grandeur of the caves for the first time in person (incredibly no Chinese scholar had visited the caves in the seventeen years since Chen Wanli had first made the trip in 1925), Xiang struggled to give voice to his innermost feelings. "Thinking back on the spirit of our people, I could not help but shed tears out there," he admitted. Marveling at the "surpassing genius of those early frontier engineers," Xiang deplored the loss of "the spirit of our Han and Tang ancestors."[57] The Han and Tang dynasties were often regarded by Chinese scholars as the two most glorious "Han

Chinese" dynasties, which succeeded in extending the colonial reach of the Chinese empire farther west than had any other "Han Chinese" dynasty. Thus any concrete souvenir from Han and Tang times—be it wooden tablets from a frontier garrison in Xinjiang or a Tang-era manuscript from Dunhuang—became a potential salve for intellectuals coping with the depressing ebb of wartime China's international prestige.

Yet even the reclamation of ancient Han-Tang relics was insufficient to satisfy Xiang's wounded national pride. For too long "we have watched while foreign scholars conduct their archaeological excavations, extolling and lamenting the passing of that remarkable fortitude of our garrison soldiers and the unlimited genius of those architects of the Great Wall." Instead of building upon Chen Wanli's maiden voyage to Dunhuang seventeen years prior, "we just stand off to the side and stir up an empty uproar." In a moment of candid self-criticism for a man who spent the better part of his adult life translating the literary works of a foreigner he believed to be a thief, Xiang suddenly expressed a sense of profound jealousy toward his alter ego. "When we examine the archaeological work that Stein conducted up here and all the maps that he charted, we suddenly realize that what he accomplished is quite simply the dream of every one of us today who merely talks about establishing infrastructure along the Hexi corridor."[58]

When Xiang Da wrote the foregoing exhortatory words he was lobbying for the Nationalist government in Chongqing to extend official state protection to the Dunhuang grottos. Yet when the world-renowned painter Zhang Daqian made a three-year pilgrimage to the Thousand-Buddha Caves from 1941 to 1943, politics were the last thing on his mind. Zhang took advantage of wartime Chongqing's proximity to Dunhuang by preparing a series of hand-painted, on-site copies of the Dunhuang frescoes for exhibition in Lanzhou and Chengdu in late 1943 and early 1944. A pamphlet for the Chengdu exhibition characterizes Zhang's sojourn in Dunhuang as an opportunity "to reminisce on the past so as to shake the present." According to Zhang, the Dunhuang frescoes "are the forerunners of the six methods of Chinese painting" that dated from a supposed golden age when "the four barbarians all yearned to adopt and imitate Chinese ways."[59]

By closely scrutinizing the features of the people depicted in the Dunhuang frescoes and other Tang paintings, Zhang was able to conclude triumphantly that "the moustache and hair resemble those of western Europeans." The implication was that Tang Chinese "clothing and cultural trappings ... had once spread all the way to western Europe," such was the strength of ancient China back in the day.[60] Because the Dunhuang murals preserved intact the spirit of those vigorous and admirable Chinese who flourished during the Tang, the fine art connoisseurs who crowded Lanzhou and Chengdu's exhibition halls during 1943–1944 could gaze upon Zhang's lifelike copies and silently intuit the long-lost cure—the cosmopolitan Tang imperial spirit—for China's current malaise.

Wide-eyed pilgrims fleeing the depressing hell of wartime Chongqing had to make room for one last group of unabashed admirers. On September 30, 1943, Joseph Needham, a 42-year-old British biochemist from Cambridge University, arrived on horseback with an eclectic team of Chinese graduate students, reporters, and artists. As the chief representative of the British-financed Sino-British Science Co-operation Office, ostensibly formed "to break the Japanese intellectual and technical blockade round China," Needham was drawn to Dunhuang as a potential "gold-mine" for his upcoming *Science and Civilisation in China* series.[61] Conceived as a means of proving to the wider world that "the achievements of ancient and mediaeval Chinese science could be shown to be dazzling," Needham fully subscribed to Fu Sinian's stipulations binding any legitimate foreign research expedition within China: active collaboration with Chinese scholars, overt sympathy for the tragic plight of modern China, and above all, a research agenda that aimed to extol and publicize the timeless genius of the Han Chinese people.[62]

Armed with the official blessing of Fu and the Academia Sinica, under whose auspices Needham's research was conducted, Needham repaid such privileged access and support by utilizing materials found at Dunhuang to praise what he referred to as the "Chinese race" as possessing "the only other great body of thought of equal complexity and depth to our own," if not more so.[63] "Inventions and technological discoveries were made in China which changed the course of Western civilization, and indeed that of the whole world," Needham boldly declared in a widely publicized 1947 lecture that all but ensured a lifetime Chinese visa stamp on his passport. In fact, Needham continued reverently, "the more you know about Chinese civilization, the more odd it seems that modern science and technology did not develop there" instead of in the West.[64] So different from the likes of Stein, Joseph Needham was a sympathetic foreign scholar that Fu Sinian could deal with. And by the time Needham left China in 1947, the strict entrance criteria for foreign scholars hoping to conduct research in China had become clear: The Needhams of the world were embraced as the "good friends of the Chinese people." By contrast, the Steins—and even the Pelliots—had become "criminals."

Whose Margin?

In February 1944 the central government in Chongqing finally extended state protection to the Dunhuang caves.[65] Nearly forty-four years had passed since the unassuming Abbot Wang first discovered Dunhuang's hidden library cave by accident in June 1900, a mere year after the Qing government—in an acknowledgment of the link among territorial sovereignty, mineral resources, and the role they play in modern states—had established the Tacheng Katu Gold

Mining Company in 1899 (see Kinzley, Chapter 2). The tantalizing riches of the Katu mines had once required no less than the "point of a sword" to push wide-eyed "gold digging 'bandits'" back within the borders of the Qing empire. Yet the early twentieth-century discovery of Chinese-inscribed relics beneath the sands of the northwest prompted Chinese nationalists to invoke the powerful cultural myth of a geographically vast Chinese scriptural imperium of yore as a pretext to "reclaim" Chinese prestige along a borderland increasingly bereft of Chinese authority.

Much like their Egyptian counterparts during the same time period, Republican Chinese scholars also recognized the "vital role archaeology could play in shaping their modern national identity" as well as the role archaeology can play in the construction of a legitimate claim to sovereignty over the lands within the ethnically and linguistically diverse margins of the modern state. Yet whereas Donald Malcolm Reid has presented Egyptian "nationalist challenges ... to Western imperialists' interpretations of its history" as a liberating phenomena revealing colonial agency, this study suggests that Chinese nationalist challenges to Western imperialist histories can be just as imperialist in nature as the dethroned imperialist himself.[66] Scant attention has been paid to the many historical and linguistic doors that were slammed shut by the Chinese scholars who followed in Stein's footsteps—doors shut by the same Chinese scholars and intellectuals who often singled out in the historical record for their pivotal roles in exhibiting Chinese agency during the "good fight" against Western imperialism.

Yet it is now clear that they also followed a Chinese historical imperialist agenda that denied legitimacy to non-Han residents of the northwestern regions and silenced any scholarly approach that complicated the historical primacy of the Chinese written word and the role of the Han Chinese peoples. The uncovering of extensive Chinese writings in the northwest played into the nationalist desire to naturalize a Chinese-language pedigree for the region. By 1943, Chinese Dunhuang scholars scarcely batted an eye at the prospect of publishing a serious scholarly examination of a bilingual Brahmi-Chinese Dunhuang stele that not only entirely ignored the non-Chinese portion of the stele, but actually went so far as to whitewash into historical oblivion any trace of the rival foreign language on the stele's surface (see figure, p. 85). Nothing can better illustrate the means by which the putative purveyors of Chinese civilization managed to prosecute the battle with Western scholars for historical and linguistic sovereignty over a region situated on the geographic margins of both European and Asian empires.

Unlike the large-scale protests undertaken in 1947 by Shanghai barbers dissatisfied with their representation in the public sphere (see Iovene, Chapter 12), the long-vanished speakers of Central Asia's dead languages could scarcely mount an alternative vision to the Chinese interpretation of the history of the region. Likewise, living twentieth-century descendants of two other amply represented historical languages in the Dunhuang manuscripts—Tibetan and Uyghur, both of which lacked ethnocultural association with an internationally recognized state—were not yet in a position to advocate for the historical importance of their linguistic heritage. In reaching out to the margins of the northwest and painting over its still malleable historical canvas in brilliant Chinese strokes, Chinese scholars of the Republican era ensured that the "northwestern margins" of the East would never again become the "far eastern margins" of the West.

Figure 1. Whitewashed Brahmi-Chinese Dunhuang Stele Fragment

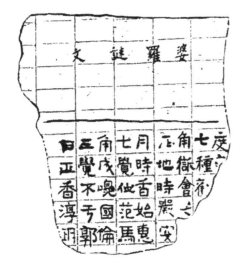

Note: In this 1943 reproduction of a Dunhuang stele for inclusion in an edited volume, the lower half reproduces the Chinese characters as originally inscribed on the stele. The Brahmi script that was originally inscribed on the upper half of the stele has not been reproduced. In its place are four Chinese characters that read: "Brahmi script" (*poluomi wen*).

Source: Dan Tu and Su Yinghui, "Dunhuang shike kao" [Examination of Dunhuang steles], in *Zhongguo xibei wenxian congshu xubian: Dunhuangxue wenxian juan* [Edited collection of documents pertaining to China's northwest: Dunhuang studies documents], ed. Feng Zhiwen, vol. 21 (Lanzhou: Gansu wenhua chubanshe, 1999), 297.

Hevia has suggested that the wanton Euro-American and Japanese plundering of Chinese works of art in the immediate aftermath of the Boxer debacle severely challenged the contemporary moral discourse of European civilization at the dawn of the twentieth century: "Could one be civilized, or claim the superiority of European nations, if one looted?"[67] The unsettling answer, as suggested by the findings of this chapter, is not that transcultural looting expeditions preclude claims to civilizational superiority, but rather that they *enable* such claims, and eventually pave the way for the consolidation of transnational rhetorical hegemony. "When will our countrymen measure up to the Stein and Pelliot spirit," asked one envious 1930s Chinese pundit writing in a Buddhist venue, "and venture out into the world, unearth and gather up exquisite cultural treasures, and bring them back to our country, all for the greater glory of our nation?"[68] There is now little doubt that the bearers of "Chinese agency" in early twentieth-century interactions with foreign imperialists traced a familiar historical path, duly cultivating the imperialist ambitions of the nationalism that originally nurtured their anti-imperialist struggle for sovereignty.

NOTES

1. For a day-by-day account of Stein's location and activities during these months, see Wang Jiqing, *Sitanyin di si ci Zhongguo kaogu riji kaoshi: Yingguo Niujin daxue cang Sitanyin di si ci Zhongya kaocha lüxing riji shougao zhengli yanjiu baogao* [Examination of Stein's diary during his fourth archaeological expedition in China: research compiled on the draft of the diary used on Stein's fourth archaeological expedition to Central Asia and stored at England's Oxford University] (Lanzhou: Gansu jiaoyu chubanshe, 2004), 330–31. For the Chinese press account of his transgressions, see "Guwu baoguan hui cheng fuyuan qing quzhu Sitanyin chujing, jiaming youli qiequ wo Xinjiang guwu, zai Mei fufa kuanglun wu-ru woguoren" [Under pretense of "travel," Stein plunders Xinjiang antiquities; outrageous speeches in America insult Chinese nation; Antiquities Preservation Committee requests immediate expulsion of Stein], *Tianjin dagongbao* (December 27–28, 1930).

2. Chen Yuan, *Dunhuang jieyulu* [An index of the Dunhuang manuscripts remaining after the plunder], *Guoli zhongyang yanjiuyuan lishi yuyan yanjiu suo zhuankan* 4 (March 1931).

3. Liu Naihe, *Liyun shuwu wen xue ji* [Scholarly inquiries from the desk of Liyun] (Beijing: Shenghuo, dushu, xinzhi sanlian shudian chuban, 1982), 153–54.

4. M. Aurel Stein, *Ancient Khotan: Detailed Report of Archaeological Explorations in Chinese Turkestan* (New York: Hacker Art Books, 1975; originally published in 1907), viii.

5. "Han Yaoguang wei bao Sitanyin ruchu Yutian xian riqi ji suo huo guwu shi gei Li Zisen de shenwen" [Han Yaoguang's document submitted to Li Zisen about Stein's entry and exit dates at Yutian county and acquisition of antiques], in Zhongguo Xinjiang Weiwuer zizhiqu dang'an guan and Riben fojiao daxue Niya yizhi xueshu yanjiu jigou, eds., *Jindai waiguo tanxianjia Xinjiang kaogu dang'an shiliao* [Modern historical material about foreign explorers in Xinjiang] (Wulumuqi: Xinjiang meishu sheying chubanshe, 2001), 108–9.

6. "Shilifu wei qingzhun Sitanyin dao shamo kaogu shi gei Jin Shuren de dianwen" [Sheriff's telegraph sent to Jin Shuren for permitting Stein to make an archaeological tour in the desert], in *Jindai waiguo tanxianjia Xinjiang kaogu dang'an shiliao*, 136.

7. Karl Ernest Meyer and Shareen Blair Brysac, *Tournament of Shadows: The Great Game and the Race for Empire in Central Asia* (Washington, D.C.: Counterpoint, 1999), 383.

8. See, for example, James L. Hevia's *Cherishing Men from Afar: Qing Guest Ritual and the Macartney Embassy of 1793* (Durham: Duke University Press, 1995) and *English Lessons: The Pedagogy of Imperialism in Nineteenth-Century China* (Durham: Duke University Press, 2003), 14; also Chen Jian, *Mao's China and the Cold War* (Chapel Hill: University of North Carolina Press, 2001).

9. John W. Garver has critiqued Chen's account of Mao's Cold War foreign policies as emblematic of a recent vein of China-related scholarship that has "forego[ne] critical analysis in favour of understanding how China's leaders viewed the world." See Garver, "The Opportunity Costs of Mao's Foreign Policy Choices," *China Journal* 49 (January 2003): 127.

10. In his *Sovereignty and Authenticity: Manchukuo and the East Asian Modern* (Lanham: Rowman and Littlefield, 2003), Prasenjit Duara writes that nationalist projects, by their very nature, carry within them the oft realized potential to be "deployed for imperialist ends or with imperialist consequences" (13).

11. James L. Hevia, "Looting and Its Discontents: Moral Discourse and the Plunder of Beijing, 1900–1901," in Robert Bickers and R. G. Tiedemann, eds., *The Boxers, China, and the World* (Lanham: Rowman and Littlefield, 2007), 102.

12. I do not mean to suggest that these Chinese figures re-enacted the violent slaughter of Western armies who invaded China in 1900. Rather, I use this description in exclusive reference to ethnocultural looting projects enacted by Euro-American, Japanese, and Chinese imperialists during the first half of the twentieth century.

13. Luo Zhenyu, *Liusha fanggu ji* [Visiting the ancients among the shifting sands] (Shangyu: Songfen shi, 1909), 37.

14. Justin Jacobs, "How Chinese Turkestan Became Chinese: Visualizing Zhang Zhizhong's *Tianshan Pictorial* and Xinjiang Youth Song and Dance Troupe," *Journal of Asian Studies* 67.2 (May 2008): 587.

15. Additional characterizations used for other foreign archaeologists included "traveling official" (*youliguan*), "scholar" (*shiren*), and "explorer" (*youlishi*). See Cordula Gumbrecht, "Chinese Passports for the German Turfan Expedition," in Desmond Durkin-Meisterernst et al., *Turfan Revisited—The First Century of Research into the Arts and Cultures of the Silk Road* (Berlin: Dietrich Reimer Verlag, 2004), 114.

16. See "Pan Zhen wei Sitanyin zai Hetian youli, xunwa guji ji ruchu jing riqi shi gei Li Zisen de shenwen" [Pan Zhen's document submitted to Li Zisen about Stein's trip in Hotan, excavation of ancient remains and entry as well as exit dates], in *Jindai waiguo tanxianjia Xinjiang kaogu dang'an shiliao*, 107–8.

17. "Han Yaoguang wei bao Sitanyin," in *Jindai waiguo tanxianjia Xinjiang kaogu dang'an shiliao*, 108.

18. M. Aurel Stein, "Explorations in Central Asia, 1906–8 (Continued)," *Geographical Journal* 34.3 (September 1909): 248.

19. Li Jianhong, "Lun Dunhuang shibao ji Ye Changchi 'Yuandu Lu riji chao'" [Concerning the loss of Dunhuang's treasures and Ye Changchi's "Diary of Mr. Lu Yuandu"], *Dunhuang yanjiu* 64 (2000): 36; and Rong Xinjiang, "Ye Changchi: Pioneer of Dunhuang Studies," *IDP Newsletter* 7 (Spring 1997).

20. Stein, *Ancient Khotan*, 510–12.

21. "*Da banniepan* jingjuan di shisi (tiba 8–1)" [*Mahā-parinirvāna* sutra no. 14 (colophon 8–1)], in Beijing daxue tushuguan and Shanghai guji chubanshe, eds., *Beijing*

daxue tushuguan cang Dunhuang wenxian [Dunhuang manuscripts collected in the Peking University Library] (Shanghai: Shanghai guji chubanshe, 1995), v. 1, 124.

22. "Foshuo shou lengyan sanmei jingjuan xia (tiba)" [*Foshuo shou lengyan sanmei* sutra (colophon)]," in Shanghai guji chubanshe and Shanghai bowuguan, eds., *Shanghai bowuguan cang Dunhuang Tulufan wenxian* [Dunhuang-Turfan manuscripts collected in Shanghai museum] (Shanghai: Shanghai guji chubanshe, 1993), v. 1, 113.

23. Wang Jiqing, "Sitanyin di er ci Zhongya kaocha qijian suochi Zhongguo huzhao jianxi" [Brief analysis of the passport obtained by Stein for his second Central Asian expedition], *Zhongguo bianjiang shidi yanjiu* 4 (1998): 74.

24. Other verbal phrases used to describe the activities of foreign archaeologists include "to admire ancient relics" (*zhanwang guji*), "to search for ancient relics" (*kaocha guji*), "to search and dig for ancient relics" (*xunwa guji*), "to inquire about ancient relics" (*chafang guji*), and "to dig for ancient relics on a large scale" (*kaiwa guji*). Gumbrecht, "Chinese Passports for the German Turfan Expedition," *Turfan Revisited*, 114.

25. Cai Yuanpei, "Dunhuang duosuo xu" [Preface to the Dunhuang manuscripts], in Liu Fu, ed., *Dunhuang duosuo* [Selections from the Dunhuang manuscripts in Paris], *Guoli zhongyang yanjiuyuan lishi yuyan yanjiu suo zhuankan* 2 (October 1925): 1. Though it is certainly possible that some Qing officials felt that China's numerous unequal treaties with Western powers constrained them to treat representatives of these countries with unusual restraint and obsequious courtesy, just as many politically unencumbered scholars expressed similar sentiments. Stein himself purposely avoided beginning his expeditions on the east coast, preferring to make arrangements through the British consulate at Kashgar and entering Xinjiang through the Central Asian passes. The one time he was forced to go through Chinese officialdom in Nanjing in preparation for his fourth and final dig in 1929, the expedition ended in failure.

26. For Zhao Weixi's comments, see "*Da banniepan* jingjuan di shisi (tiba 8–2)" [*Mahā-parinirvāna* sutra no. 14 (colophon 8–2)], in *Beijing daxue tushuguan cang Dunhuang wenxian*, 125. For the reaction of Luo Zhenyu, see his "Dunhuang shishi shumu ji fajian zhi yuanshi" [Index of the Dunhuang stone cavern and account of its discovery], *Dongfang zazhi* 6.12 (January 1910): 87.

27. Luo Zhenyu, *Liusha fanggu ji*, 37–38.

28. For the original English version, see Mr. McCartney et al., "Explorations in Central Asia, 1906–8: Discussion," *Geographical Journal* 34.3 (September 1909): 264. For Wang's subsequent translation into Chinese, see Luo Zhenyu, *Liusha fanggu ji*, 23.

29. Lothar von Falkenhausen, "On the Historiographical Orientation of Chinese Archaeology," *Antiquity* 67.257 (December 1993): 839–49.

30. Susan Chan Egan, *A Latterday Confucian: Reminiscences of William Hung (1893–1980)* (Cambridge: Harvard University Council on East Asian Studies, 1987), 114–15.

31. This account is taken from Chen Wanli, *Xixing riji* [A diary of westward travels] (Lanzhou: Gansu renmin chubanshe, 2000), 43–44.

32. Ibid.

33. Ibid., 44–45.

34. Ibid.

35. Ibid., 44.

36. Meyer and Brysac, *Tournament of Shadows*, 384.

37. Liu Shiping and Meng Xianshi, *Dunhuang bainian: yi ge minzu de xinling licheng* [Dunhuang centennial: the spiritual journey of a nation] (Guangzhou: Guangdong jiaoyu chubanshe, 2000), 119.

38. Peter Hopkirk, *Foreign Devils on the Silk Road: The Search for the Lost Cities and Treasures of Chinese Central Asia* (Amherst: University of Massachusetts Press, 1980), 223–24.

39. See Richard W. Rigby, *The May 30 Movement: Events and Themes* (Canberra: Australian National University Press, 1980); and Nicholas R. Clifford, *Shanghai, 1925: Urban Nationalism and the Defense of Foreign Privilege* (Ann Arbor: Center for Chinese Studies, 1979).

40. Theodore Bowie, ed., *Langdon Warner through His Letters* (Bloomington: Indiana University Press, 1966), 129.

41. In light of the fact that the diary was published well after the nationalistic fervor of the May 30 incident had spread throughout the country, there was little incentive for Chen to conceal any insider knowledge to which he may have been privy. Quite the contrary, he probably could have benefited immensely from a retroactively jingoistic narrative of the expedition and his supposed role in its sabotage.

42. Chen, *Xixing riji*, 8.

43. See Chen's supplement to the main body of the diary, "Dunhuang Qianfodong san ri jian suo de zhi yinxiang" [Impressions gleaned from a three-day visit to Dunhuang's Thousand-Buddha Caves], *Xixing riji*, 119.

44. See Meyer and Brysac, *Tournament of Shadows*, 374; and "Sitanyin xiyu kaocha ji," *Tianjin dagongbao tushu fukan* 175 (April 1, 1937).

45. See Chen Yuan's preface in the *Dunhuang jieyulu*, 3–4. The lone non-Chinese standout was a Tibetan copy of the "Foshuo wuliang shou" sutra. See *Dunhuang jieyulu*, 9.

46. From a diary entry dated November 16, 1927. See Xu Bingxu, *Xu Xusheng riji* [Diary of Xu Xusheng] (Beiping: Zhongguo xueshu tuanti xiehui xibei kexue kaochatuan lishihui yinxing, 1930), 57.

47. Wang Guowei, "Zuijin er sanshi nian zhong Zhongguo xin faxian zhi xuewen [New discoveries in Chinese scholarship over the past twenty to thirty years]," in Feng Zhiwen and Yang Jiping, eds., *Zhongguo Dunhuangxue bainian wenku: zongshu juan* [One hundred years of documents from Chinese Dunhuang studies: summary documents volume] (Lanzhou: Gansu wenhua chubanshe, 1999), 52. This article was published posthumously three years after Wang's suicide in 1927.

48. See translations by Xiang Da, "Sitanyin Dunhuang huoshu ji" [A record of Stein's acquisition of Dunhuang manuscripts], *Tushuguanxue jikan* 4.3-4 (1930): 429–38; and He Changqun, "Dunhuang qujing ji" [An account of the acquisition of Dunhuang's manuscripts], *Xiaoshuo yuebao* 22.5 (May 1931): 621–41.

49. Zhe Sheng, "Zhong yaxiya kaogu tanxianzhe Sitanyin" [Stein: Central Asia's adventurer archaeologist], *Dongfang zazhi* 26.17 (September 10, 1929).

50. Hua Yi, "Ping Xiang yi Sitanyin *Xiyu kaogu ji*" [Review of Xiang Da's translation of Aurel Stein's *On Central-Asian Tracks*], *Tianjin yishibao dushu zhoukan* 86 (February 4, 1937).

51. Fu Sinian, "Lun Boxihe jiaoshou" [Concerning Professor Pelliot], *Tianjin dagongbao* (Februrary 21, 1935).

52. See Egan, *A Latterday Confucian*, 122.

53. Fu, "Lun Boxihe jiaoshou."

54. I was able to locate nineteen installments of Wang's intermittent series of reports, all of which were published in *L'Impartial*'s weekly literary supplement from May 30, 1935 to March 12, 1936. Other Chinese classics featured by Wang include the *Chuci*, *Wenxuan*, *Shiji*, and *Hanshu*.

55. For specific details concerning the overall composition of the original Dunhuang

manuscript collection, see Fujieda Akira, "The Tunhuang Manuscripts: A General Description," *Zinbun* 9 (1966): 1–32 and 10 (1969): 17–39.

56. Xiang Da, "Lun Dunhuang Qianfodong de guanli yanjiu yiji qita liandai de ji ge wenti" [On the management of Dunhuang's Thousand-Buddha Caves and other related matters], *Chongqing dagongbao* (December 27, 28, 30, 1942).

57. Ibid.

58. Ibid.

59. "Zhang Daqian suo mo Dunhuang bihua xu" [Preface to the exhibition of Zhang Daqian's Dunhuang mural copies] in Lin Sijin, *Qing Jitang ji* [Collected writings of Lin Sijin] (Chengdu: Bashu shudianshe chuban, 1989), 624–25.

60. Ibid.

61. Joseph Needham and Dorothy Needham, eds. *Science Outpost: Papers of the Sino-British Science Co-operation Office (British Council Scientific Office in China): 1942–1946* (London: Pilot Press, 1948), 13.

62. See Joseph Needham's foreword in Pan Jixing, ed., *Li Yuese wenji: Li Yuese boshi youguan Zhongguo kexue jishu shi de lunwen he yanjiang ji (1944–1984)* [Collected writings of Joseph Needham: A collection of Dr. Needham's speeches and essays related to the history of science and technology in China (1944–1984)] (Shenyang: Liaoning kexue jishu chubanshe, 1986), 3.

63. Excerpted from Needham's May 12, 1947 Conway Memorial Lecture in London, later published in book form. See Joseph Needham, *Science and Society in Ancient China* (London: C. A. Watts and Co., 1947), 19.

64. Needham, *Science and Society in Ancient China*, 5.

65. Xiang, "Lun Dunhuang Qianfodong."

66. Donald Malcolm Reid, *Whose Pharaohs? Archaeology, Museums, and Egyptian National Identity from Napoleon to World War I* (Berkeley: University of California Press, 2002), 2.

67. Hevia, "Looting and Its Discontents," 102.

68. Yi Tuo, "Du 'Dunhuang shishi fangshu ji' ji 'Sitanyin qianfodong qujing shimo ji'' hou" [After reading "An account of a visit to the library of the stone caverns of Dunhuang" and "A complete account of Stein's acquisition of manuscripts at the Thousand-Buddha Caves], *Haichao yin* 17, no. 12 (December 1936): 50.

5

"A DREAM DEFERRED"

Obstacles to Legal Reform and Rights Reclamation in Early Republican China

Jeremy Murray

The early years of the Chinese republic, from the fall of the Qing in 1911 until the Nationalist Northern Expedition of 1926–1928, remain, as Andrew Nathan referred to them thirty years ago, "perhaps the darkest corner of twentieth-century Chinese history."[1] We think of this "warlord era" as dark both because of the paucity of studies on that topic, and because of its frequent conflicts, regressive policies, and militarist rulers.[2] The popularity of Darwin and Spencer led intellectuals of that time to raise the specter of Chinese national extinction resulting from external threats and internal disunity. This ignominious possibility, in the view of a nationalist historian, makes the period the most shameful of China's "century of shame."

In the nearly two decades since the crushing of the Beijing Spring movement of 1989, historians have looked to the late Qing and republican periods for political and cultural resonances, precedents, explanations, and even predictions or prescriptions for China's political future. Reform and political activism during earlier periods of history are central topics in such studies and discussions. While many of the early republican rulers have been assumed to have simply stifled or ignored cries for reform from the May Fourth Movement to the Nationalist revolution, recent work, including Xu Xiaoqun's, suggests that this view is unsound. It seems increasingly likely that our view of the early republican period as an age of darkness has been influenced by the Whiggish, nationalistic depictions of the period by both Nationalist and Communist narratives. In the case of judicial independence, Xu finds that the Nationalist conquest completed in 1928 represented, for legal reformers, a closing down of the relative dynamism and optimism of extensive reforms that had been implemented prior to the Northern Expedition.[3]

The publication in 2004 of the collected writings of one prominent reformer, Zhang Yaozeng, reflects a revived interest in reform and civilian governance in the warlord period. Zhang represented, and often led, a group of legal reformers that expanded and thrived in the early republican period, before being thwarted in its attempts at reform by a combination of foreign duplicity and the Leninist party discipline of Nationalist and Communist revolutionaries. Zhang's career began both at and beyond the geographical margins of China, as a student in Japan advocating for the people of his home province of Yunnan on China's southern border. His pragmatism, expertise, and political connections led him to the post of a cabinet minister and prominent political activist in the early republic. His career came to an abrupt halt on the eve of the Northern Expedition, when the Nationalist government implemented policies that pushed the agendas of legal professionals like Zhang off the new government's list of priorities. The new class of legal professionals was sapped of its autonomy by a Nationalist policy that required membership in the ruling party for all judicial officials.[4] Disenchanted with work at the political center, Zhang later sidestepped an opportunity to serve in the new regime, after receiving a personal invitation from Jiang Jieshi (Chiang Kai-shek).[5]

Concerns about unequal treaty rights for foreigners, domestic judicial independence, and constitutionalism defined the interests of the group of legal reformers that grew in early republican China. They generally favored the decentralization of power, from federalism at the national level, to a nonpartisan and independent judiciary represented in every local court. The abolition of extraterritoriality—or the jurisdiction of foreign governments over their nationals on Chinese soil—was a goal of the reformers, and many of their proposed reforms coincided with the prerequisites for abolition put forward by the foreign powers. Extraterritoriality represented an inward creep of China's legal margins. Some of the humiliations of extraterritoriality were visible in the metropolitan centers of China, even while the legal practice symbolized the encroaching outer limits of China's ability to control its own territory.[6]

Twice debased, the Chinese worldview had fallen far, first from that of the cultural center of the world to simply being a nation among nations, and second, to the realization that China was in fact a rather weak nation among strong ones. The claims of foreign sovereignty on Chinese legal soil represented the further shrinking and embarrassment of the once-great empire. Pragmatic legal reformers like Zhang Yaozeng sought to lead the reclamation of China's legal sovereignty, to fight at China's legal margins, using the rhetoric of those they opposed, in an attempt to rise at least to the status of equality among other nations.

Some official representatives of foreign powers in China apparently shared this agenda of legal reform, and their gestures and statements of goodwill caused considerable optimism among China's legal reformers. But hopes sagged as the foreign powers proved reluctant to support anything beyond short-term regime stability and the maintenance of their special treaty rights.

Beginning with Zhang Yaozeng and moving on to broader issues of reform and rights reclamation, this chapter urges a reconsideration of the work of reformers of the early republican period who have been marginalized by studies that simply see the "warlord period" as the darkness out of which emerged the ideological sprouts of two subsequent Chinese regimes. In addition to the celebrated radicals of the May Fourth Movement, there were other activists who struggled with the task of reform, sometimes opposed by stingy military leaders, and finally stopped by a combination of foreign duplicity and partisan revolutionary urgency.

Early Activism

In 1904, at age nineteen, Zhang Yaozeng left Beijing to study law and political administration in Tokyo. He was the first student to be sent abroad by his home institution, the forerunner of Beijing University.[7] Reformers and radicals alike found refuge in Japan from persecution by the Qing government. These exiles had a strong influence on Zhang. For instance, he was one of the earliest members of Sun Yat-sen's Revolutionary Alliance (Tongmenghui). But even in this early period, Zhang defied the conventional distinction between radical revolutionary and moderate reformer. Though he was a member of the revolutionary Tongmenghui, Zhang did not call for the violent overthrow of the Qing dynasty in his writings. Still, on substantive issues from educational reform to boycotts, he criticized Qing policies.

Following the 1895 Treaty of Shimonoseki and the rush by the treaty powers to claim sovereign outposts and increased realms of special privilege in China, Zhang's main concern was not reforming or toppling the atrophied Qing court but rather the external threat of division and conquest and national extinction. Zhang was one of the founders of *Yunnan Magazine* [*Yunnan zazhi*], a journal published by Yunnanese students in Japan about the affairs of their native province.[8] Under Zhang's editorship, *Yunnan Magazine* dealt with such problems as improving the educational infrastructure of Yunnan and encouraging resistance to what the editors perceived to be exploitative mining and industrial activities led by foreign firms. Most of the articles dealt with issues related to the home province of fellow Yunnanese students in Japan. When Zhang wrote about larger national reformist and revolutionary trends, he counseled for pragmatism, not ideological passion, as the foundation of the work to be done. He obliquely criticized the vagaries of revolutionary rhetoric, and what he saw as pointless quibbling over philosophical details: "What do we mean when we discuss 'national character' anyway? What do we call good and bad character? Today I do not care about what a good or bad national character is. All I am asking is how we will strengthen our resolve, hold fast to our rights, and resist the power of foreigners."[9]

In *Yunnan Magazine* Zhang advocated broadening access to education by opening more public schools. He acknowledged the efforts of Qing reformers, but he lamented the corruption and decadence of the Yunnan school system.[10] "In Yunnan schools today, there are students quitting school, going on strike from classes, manipulating records, and there is even opium-smoking."[11] Considering Zhang's career as a pragmatic reformer, this is one of the most revealing pronouncements of his early years. Zhang so valued education as a means of personal and national self-strengthening and cultivation, that he lumped together the most revolutionary activity of the day—student strikes—with the most counter-productive and pathetic—opium smoking. He condemned any obstruction to education, whether it was reactionary dope or revolutionary strikes.[12]

Driven in large part by the distribution within Yunnan of *Yunnan Magazine*, popular dissent played a central role in local resistance to the transfer of Yunnanese mining rights to foreign firms. This was a significant regional accomplishment, considering much of Qing and later republican China's infrastructure had been essentially mortgaged to foreign firms and governments. To Zhang, the protests that led to the successful removal of Yunnan officials who collaborated with the foreign firms represented an informal and rudimentary form of participatory government, and he drew parallels to the power of contemporary popular protest in Europe.[13]

Li Genyuan, a Yunnanese student in a Japanese military academy and Zhang's coeditor of *Yunnan Magazine*, took a more radical view than his friend when it came to confronting the Qing empire. After completing a year-long course of military study and training with a Japanese regiment, he returned to Yunnan in 1909 to serve as superintendent in a military school. When the 1911 revolution began, Li helped plan the overthrow of the loyalist Yunnan authorities, becoming the head of the military branch of the new Yunnan government.[14] Shortly after Li's success, Zhang received an invitation to serve as Yunnan's representative in the provisional National Assembly in Nanjing. In 1912, at age twenty-six, Zhang accepted the post and returned to China. His legal training in Japan also qualified him to serve as an advisor to the drafters of the constitution of 1912.

The failures of the early republic and its fall to Yuan Shikai prevented the immediate realization of the ideals of both revolutionaries and reformers.[15] For most of Zhang's earlier and later life he was a prolific writer, but in 1913 he published only one brief open letter, which he sent to *Shenbao*, a prominent Shanghai newspaper. It was titled, "A Letter upon Departing for the East." In it he noted the optimism he had felt in abandoning his study of law at Imperial University in Tokyo to return and serve the republic at the invitation of the provisional government of his home province. But after watching the failure of the young republic, he said, "one year later, we have above us a government monopolizing power, while below the people waste away in a state of chaos. I am in the middle, trying to mediate between them, and my heart is sick with the task."[16] In the letter, Zhang announced his plan to return to Tokyo to complete the legal training that he had cut short two years earlier.

After quickly completing his studies in 1914, Zhang returned to his alma mater, Beijing University, as a law professor. He was there to witness some of the significant political and cultural ferment that led to the New Culture and May Fourth Movements. Though it seems he did not publish any writings while he was teaching, there is some evidence that the Beijing government considered him a significant critic of the increasingly conservative northern regime of Yuan Shikai.[17] His work in this period as an organizer of the Political Science Group (Zheng xuehui) allowed for the survival of a northern parliamentary faction sympathetic to, and overlapping in membership with, the southern Nationalist Party, which had descended in turn from the Tongmenghui.[18] Zhang became an early member of the Nationalist Party, and his loyalties were stretched between Beijing and Guangzhou, the home of the *de facto* regime based in the south.[19] Hope for peace and unification came with the death of Yuan Shikai in 1916. This brought about the first brief presidency of Li Yuanhong, who favored constitutionalism, a strong legislature and judiciary, and reconciliation between north and south. Zhang returned to public office in the northern regime when he accepted an invitation to serve as minister of justice in Li's cabinet.[20] Throughout this period, Zhang's teaching and political organizing contributed to the emergence of a growing class of legal professionals. As minister of justice, serving in 1916, and again in 1922 and 1924, Zhang was the sometime leader of this group.

The Sphere of Legal Professionals

Two primary factors drove the development and actions of the growing community of legal professionals in early republican China under Zhang's leadership: anti-imperialism and democratization.[21] Zhang and other legal experts taught in universities, published journals, and worked within the national and provincial governments to draw attention to both the inequity of foreign legal privilege in China and domestic autocratic abuses of power. Anti-imperialism and democratization were parallel concerns for many May Fourth leaders, and Chinese legal reformers considered their work to be combating both foreign imperialism and the self-destructive policies of any comprador or autocratic Chinese regime that would mortgage its assets while repressing popular uprisings. Certain groups within the foreign community favored the abolition of extraterritoriality and gave reformers like Zhang a platform for expressing their views in foreign language journals.[22]

For legal reformers, extraterritoriality was both a symbolically and substantively important matter. It was a relic of the treaties that symbolized China's "century of shame" and military weakness. The rapid expansion of the foreign population in China in the late nineteenth and early twentieth centuries from a handful of merchants and adventurers to thousands of European, American, and Japanese soldiers, entrepreneurs, missionaries, and diplomats had made the extraterritorial system a conspicuous affront to China's territorial and legal sovereignty. Chinese efforts to prove that the anachronism of extraterritoriality was no longer necessary to protect the lives and property of foreigners living in China came in attempts at reform of the legal system. In the opening years of the twentieth century, most of the powers had signed treaties that expressed agreement that extraterritoriality ought to be abolished, pending reforms of the Chinese legal infrastructure.[23] Extraterritoriality became one of China's legal margins—the symbolic front lines of China's struggle for reform and equal treatment in the family of nations. Sometimes these legal margins overlapped with geographical margins, as Zhang found earlier in his work to defend industry and resources from foreign exploitation in Yunnan; but with the enforcement of extraterritorial rights for all nationals of the powers living in China, the new wave of missionaries, for example, wore those margins effectively on their own bodies, as they marched the cross deep into the Chinese heartland.

The emergence of a class of legal professionals in China was, as it had been in Japan, a central aspect of the reforms implemented in the effort to show an international audience the justice in reclaiming China's legal sovereignty. As Alison W. Conner notes in an essay on this emerging profession, "Lawyers were a necessary evil, introduced as part of the modern judicial system adopted to end extraterritorial privilege."[24] The legal profession grew in numbers, as Conner notes, but also in ideological coherence, a development that is apparent in the publication of journals by and for the legal community. Zhang Yaozeng served as the head of several prominent committees of legal scholars, and as minister of justice his work was essential to the creation and unity of the nascent community of Chinese lawyers and legal scholars.

Inspired by Jurgen Habermas's theoretical work on the public sphere, and the rise and fall of the Beijing Spring movement in 1989, some historians became interested in late Qing political precedents for spherelike divisions of people with shared political concerns.[25] In the case of the growing class of legal professionals in early republican China, however, the dichotomy of official (*guan*) and private (*si*), with the all important public (*gong*) between the two, appears too tidy, especially if actors are assumed to behave, along Marxist lines, according to the interests of their social group. Zhang Yaozeng led an important class of legal professionals, many of whom were employed by the central state in Beijing, and thus decidedly "*guan*." His attempted reforms, however, which would expand citizens' access to power, especially in relation to arbitrary state power, and his push to establish an independent judiciary, suggest a role more like such non-state "public sphere" actors as merchants, journalists, and professional guilds. There were powerful lawyers who were not necessarily employed by the state, but their professional leaders were mostly involved with state-mandated committees and legal societies, people like Zhang Yaozeng, Wang Chonghui, and Gu Weijun. These figures sat near the center of China's power structure in the early republic, fighting to hold the line and eventually extend China's legal margins in response to encroaching imperialistic powers; and domestically, they sought to extend legal margins by increasing popular access to the law as a tool of social justice for all.

As minister of justice, Zhang sought to broaden popular access to the law as a means of combating and weakening the state's arbitrary power, but this was not simply a zero-sum equation of state and citizen power. His reforms were also intended to have a clear impact at the international level. The improvement of China's legal infrastructure would strengthen the new and fragile republican government by abolishing foreign infringements on Chinese legal sovereignty. Legal reforms would lead to the abolition of extraterritoriality and hence the international empowerment of the republic, even while strengthening the power of the Chinese people to challenge state power.

But the development of China's legal professionals as a class was a frustrating undertaking. It was hindered both by the unstable political climate of the warlord era as well as by the sympathetic words but uncooperative actions of official and nonofficial foreign interests in China. Zhang complained often of the lack of adequate funding for his reforms, but I will attempt to sketch out some of the obstacles faced by legal reformers in their campaign to abolish extraterritoriality as a way of demonstrating that the greater obstacle to legal reform was the duplicity of foreign diplomats.[26] This was part of the time-honored and ongoing imperial tradition in foreign relations of supporting stability over meaningful democratization.

"The Keystone of Foreign Privilege"

The China scholar H. G. W. Woodhead was no friend of revolution or reform in China. Referring to the surge of anti-imperialist opinion among Chinese intellectuals in the 1910s and 1920s, Woodhead suggested that these rabble-rousers deployed inflammatory terms like "unequal treaties" and "national humiliation" as a means of inciting to violence the most ignorant elements of the population. In 1920s China, Woodhead's opinions on this and other matters were well noted within the foreign community, for he served as editor of the *China Yearbook*, as well as the English-language papers, the *Peking Times* (which published the *Yearbook*) and the *Tientsin Times*. In the pages of these papers, he further declared that using the phrase "Opium Wars" to refer to the lopsided nineteenth-century military conflicts between the Qing and British empires was also Chinese nationalist propaganda. According to Woodhead, these wars had been nothing more than "the struggle[s] to vindicate the principle of equality of the Western nations with China."[27] In his view, extraterritoriality was "the keystone to all foreign privileges in China. Once it is removed, the whole elaborate fabric, the result of nearly a century of constructive effort, must collapse."[28] His view was typical of those who defended extraterritoriality. So crucial was foreign privilege to the imperium that he euphemistically called "the whole elaborate fabric" that it had to be defended in spite of any actions taken by Chinese reformers.

Throughout the 1910s and early 1920s, extraterritoriality had indeed been at the very epicenter of Chinese national and international politics. Legal reformers claimed that foreign courts inhibited and confused the proper functioning of China's legal system. The paradoxical though flexible counterargument from opponents of abolition like Woodhead was that Chinese law was either nonexistent or excessively punitive, or (somehow) both simultaneously.

The case against the abolition of extraterritoriality boiled down to the protection of the lives and property of foreign nationals in China. Merchant interests emphasized trade rights, and Christian missionaries sought the ability to proselytize freely and safely in China's interior.[29] Following World War I, German concessions on the Shandong peninsula were not returned to the Chinese, and instead the European and American victors of the "Great War for Civilization" turned over the concessions to the Japanese in the face of vehement Chinese protest. The senior Japanese delegate at Versailles tried to calm the resulting furor in Chinese cities by issuing a statement indicating that it was his government's policy shortly to "return the [Shandong] peninsula in full sovereignty to China, retaining only the economic rights and privileges [that had formerly been] granted to Germany and the right to establish a settlement under the usual conditions at [Qingdao]."[30] This statement was issued on May 5, 1919, a day after the student protests that both reflected and accelerated anti-imperialist sentiment throughout Chinese cities.

The Japanese statement was not successful in quelling outrage in China, which was expressed in urban marches and some acts of violence directed toward Chinese officials whom the protesters deemed responsible for this diplomatic disaster. The promise to return nominal sovereignty to China was not enough to calm the protests, for the protesters would not be satisfied as long as special "rights and privileges" were maintained on Chinese soil. The stakes were high for Chinese legal reformers. They could not accept nominal control of a territory if it fell short of complete judicial sovereignty, or the abolition of extraterritoriality.

Most foreign portrayals of Chinese law in the 1910s and 1920s by people such as Woodhead did not acknowledge the significant professional growth underway in the legal community. Rather, foreign accounts—both in the press and from official sources—dwelled on anecdotes of lawlessness throughout the country's vast territory, invoking the specter of unpunished and unpunishable "Boxerism." Foreigners in the cities were terrified by stories of kidnapping and violence against European and American missionaries in rural China. The number of missionaries in China grew steadily in spite of the anti-Christian Boxer Uprising. From the fanatic who sought martyrdom at the end of a Boxer's halberd to the altruist who set out to educate or heal a community of peasants, Christian missionaries acted upon their recently exacted treaty rights to live, work, and own land throughout the Chinese interior. For example, from 1890 to 1925 the number of American Protestant missionaries in China rose from 500 to 5,000, and the Chinese central government was held responsible for the safety of every one.[31]

"Boxerism" was condemned among the same groups of Chinese intellectuals who railed against foreign privilege in China. This type of random anti-foreign violence, they said, was grounded in ignorance and antiquated religious superstition, and it was not an articulation of anti-imperialist or nationalist sentiment.[32] In taking this view, Chen Duxiu was correct in asserting that little of this mob violence could be equated to modern nationalism. But even though the motivation for the violence was not national in scope, foreign advocates of extraterritorial privilege took this violence as something for which the entire Chinese nation was responsible. Foreign diplomats thus felt justified in meting out collective punishment upon the Chinese government and people by maintaining their extraterritorial privileges and exacting heavy indemnities for every outrage. Ultimately, leaders of the foreign communities in China interpreted acts of "Boxerism" as an indication of Chinese racism and a general nation-wide prejudice against all foreigners: "The great influence for good which Christianity has exerted in China cannot be controverted. Nevertheless, the zealous promulgation of missionary teachings has at times been looked upon as an encroachment by *the great mass of the people.*"[33]

Strictly in terms of custom and treaty agreements signed by China and the treaty powers, such incidents of individual anti-foreign violence did not in fact provide just cause for advocating the perpetuation of extraterritoriality. Still, this was one of the most often-cited components of the case against abolition. In one pamphlet, Woodhead listed the recent crimes committed against foreigners in China, from British Inspector L. H. Gabb ("Captured by Chinese soldiery at Changteh, Hunan, wounded by a spearthrust, and tied up to a post naked without food or drink for 18 hours") to the murder of priests and ministers, and acts of piracy committed against Japanese vessels. His list of eighteen "individual outrages" in the span of six months is significant at an individual level, but policing the Chinese interior was simply not provided for in the treaty agreements. This type of thumb-on-the-scale diplomacy frustrated the efforts of Chinese legal reformers who obviously did not have the power to reform the policing and protection of every village in which the Christian god had stationed a missionary, whether it was at the margins of the Qing empire or the Chinese republic.

The conventions and practices of extraterritoriality as ratified in earlier treaties noted that the plaintiff (the foreign victim) would follow the defendant (the Chinese accused) into the Chinese court.[34] They protected a foreign *defendant* from being called before a Chinese court or magistrate, but they did not provide for the right of a foreigner to bring charges against a Chinese defendant in a foreign consular court. Not surprisingly, raw power politics meant that foreign lawyers were less than vigilant in observing this legal distinction, and the settlement of cases of violence against foreigners was generally conducted through diplomatic rather than judicial channels.[35] If there was a disagreement between the Chinese and foreign parties with respect to a blatant violation of treaty and convention, a foreign gunboat was usually close enough to steam into a nearby harbor and clarify the path forward.

I found only one acknowledgment of this contradiction by a foreign writer, in a chapter entitled "Attacks on Foreigners" contained in G. W. Keeton's two-volume study of extraterritoriality in China: "There was another class of mixed cases, however, which was left untouched by the first treaties, and which was, indeed, *never directly dealt with in the extraterritorial arrangements.* These were the cases in which a Chinese subject committed a crime against a foreigner." Keeton cited his concerns about a "lack of faith and perversion of justice" on the part of Chinese magistrates for the long list of cases he cited in which gunboat-enforced punishment was exacted for crimes against foreigners that ranged from murder to being "hooted, pursued, and pelted with stones." In a British parliamentary debate on whether such cases should prompt the consular representative to press for the decapitation of the alleged Chinese offenders, one British observer noted simply that, "For the making of an omelet, Asiatic rulers know only one method, the breaking of eggs."[36] Never mind that the punishment of execution for the crime of "pelting with stones" was carried out on the orders of, and often under the watchful eye of, British consuls, and not "Asiatic rulers." Detailing the hypocrisies of empire may be old news, but it is significant to note that the high-minded proponents of international law in a family of equal nations continued consciously and deliberately to carry on such extralegal practices in the postwar era. Another point of frustration for some of the more liberal-minded missionaries of the early twentieth century was that they were not given the choice of waiving punishment for any crime against them, no matter how petty or grievous, so long as they had not officially renounced their citizenship.[37] Only outright expatriation would have precluded extralegal but routine punishments of Chinese people, implemented on the foreigners' behalf by home governments. In the American example, "whether residing temporarily or permanently, [a U.S. citizen] remains as much under the jurisdiction of his government as if he were residing at home."[38]

While foreign legal experts ignored such disparities between practice and treaty agreement (except for Keeton's passing reference), Chinese legal reformers criticized the hypocrisy. In an interview with the English-language *China Weekly Review* in December 1922, Zhang Yaozeng spoke directly to the treaty-port community on the issue of crimes committed by Chinese individuals against foreigners on Chinese soil. To cite violence against missionaries as a means of defending extraterritoriality, said Zhang, was dubious at best because "there is no legal system in the world which can put a check to unexpected occurrences that will endanger lives and property." It was a simple distinction between the policing and the prosecution or adjudication of a crime. Zhang referred to a recent case of kidnapping, suggesting that "no legal code could make forewarning and forearming possible."[39] The sensationalism of anti-foreign violence overshadowed both the foreign treaty violations of exacting punishment for these crimes as well as the ongoing efforts at legal reform that naturally did not—and feasibly could not—include assigning outfits of bodyguards to every meandering missionary.

Shortly after Li Yuanhong ascended to the presidency and invited Zhang to serve as his minister of justice in 1916, a conservative faction led by his own premier pushed Li out of office. From 1917 through 1928, Beijing and the national mantle changed hands often as the prize of factional and regional fighting. In 1922, one of these victorious military leaders invited Li back to Beijing to serve as president once more, and once more, Zhang was summoned to serve as minister of justice. Though his tenure was again very brief, Zhang acted quickly to combat the domestic and international inertia that had slowed Chinese legal reforms and prevented the abolition of extraterritoriality. As a persistent affront to Chinese sovereignty, extraterritoriality served to rally the efforts of legal reformers.

Optimism Following the Washington Conference

In the early 1920s, in addition to his post as minister of justice, Zhang Yaozeng served as chair of the "Society for the Discussion of Judicial Rights," to which Beijing deputed the task of assessing weaknesses in the legal infrastructure and implementing reforms. He also acted as an advisor at the Washington Conference in winter 1921–1922, a peace conference organized especially to focus on postwar issues in Asia at which the Chinese delegation achieved results that appeared more favorable than those of Versailles.

In early 1921 Zhang was a central figure among Chinese intellectuals and reformers who targeted the extraterritorial system as a debilitating and outdated relic of imperialism. So vociferous was their campaign that an American journalist in Shanghai noted that there was a "feeling in the air that the days of foreign extraterritorial rights in China are numbered."[40] This palpable "sense of danger" was seized upon a few months later when the peace conference convened in Washington, and the delegates addressed this and other issues that had rankled since Paris. The Chinese delegation sent to Washington represented the most sophisticated of foreign-educated Chinese, all of them fluent in the languages, customs, and most importantly, the legal traditions of their Western and Japanese counterparts.[41]

The Chinese delegation was challenged at the outset. Could it be accepted at the conference as a representative of all China considering the tenuous condition of the republican government?[42] But the Chinese representatives satisfied such questions, which were likely intended to weaken the Chinese bargaining position. Led by Wang Chonghui, the Chinese delegation went on to impress the representatives with its case for the abolition of extraterritoriality and the prospect of genuine adherence to a doctrine of equality among the "family of nations." It was, after all, the rhetoric of Versailles that the Chinese delegates employed in an appeal for respect for the doctrine of mutual sovereignty. In addition to rhetoric, however, these legal scholars cited extraterritoriality as a hindrance to Chinese legal reform and the domestic legitimacy of the Beijing government, asserting that this outdated and embarrassing practice was far from an inspiring example of judicial rationality, as some opponents of abolition still claimed.

Chief delegate Wang explained the history of extraterritoriality in China and went on to list the reasons for its abolition. The checklist of causes for abolition ranged from the intangible and emotional to the most pragmatic. "[Extraterritoriality] is a derogation of China's sovereign rights, and is regarded by the Chinese people as a national humiliation," argued Wang. He continued in a more mundane way, citing the confusion resulting from a "multiplicity of courts in one and the same locality," as was the case especially in large cities when a Chinese court and a foreign consular court claimed jurisdiction over the same territory or individuals. In a very different sort of situation, when there was no consular court nearby and a case involved a foreigner or a foreign interest, the extreme distance to such a court made it difficult or impossible to transport witnesses and evidence. Further, Wang noted the tendency of some foreigners, "under the cover of extraterritoriality, [to] claim immunity from local taxes and excises which the Chinese themselves are required to pay."[43]

Wang's appeal was cogent, and his advocacy of abolition was received warmly by most of the assembled delegates. A resolution relating specifically to the extraterritorial problem in China was adopted at the conclusion of the conference. "Being sympathetically disposed towards furthering in this regard the aspirations to which the Chinese Delegation gave expression," it was resolved by all delegations that an international commission would be established, with representatives from each country that continued to operate extraterritorial courts in China plus a Chinese representative. The commission would survey in person the Chinese legal infrastructure and attempt to determine an appropriate course of action that would resolve the extraterritoriality issue in a way satisfactory to all parties. The resolution stated that the commission would be convened within three months of the conference's conclusion. In the meantime, the powers agreed to "give every assistance towards the attainment by the Chinese Government of its expressed desire to reform its judicial system and to bring it in accord with that of Western nations." Further, they were "prepared to relinquish extraterritorial rights when satisfied that the state of the Chinese laws, the arrangement of their administration, and other considerations warrant them in so doing."[44] Perhaps this language was welcome, though it differed little from the twenty-year-old treaties between the Qing government and the powers.

The need for reform in the Chinese legal system was undisputed, even by the Chinese delegation, so this was the task confronting China's community of legal experts. While warfare continued to frustrate the adoption of a constitution and a stable government that could claim a truly national mandate, the Washington Conference concluded on an optimistic note. The international commission was scheduled to begin its work almost immediately, functioning as both a diagnostic team and an assistant to reform.

Reform and Reclamation

In anticipation of the international commission's arrival, Zhang Yaozeng planned his own survey tour of China's legal infrastructure. On the tour, Zhang spoke to several gatherings of legal societies. "It will not fall to the foreigners [to end extraterritoriality]. We Chinese must do this, and it will not be done through government action alone, but through the participation of all citizens of China."[45] Zhang sought to mobilize support for the comprehensive legal reforms that were necessary before the powers would agree to the abrogation of their extraterritorial rights. Early signs of Zhang's disenchantment with the good will and good faith of the foreign representatives were apparent in remarks such as the one above. After the Washington Conference, the convention of the international Commission on Extraterritoriality was repeatedly delayed. If the foreign powers could not be trusted to keep a date for a commission, what were the chances they would act in good faith in later negotiations or indeed provide any of the promised help in the prerequisite reform process?

It was not a matter of weeks, but three *years* later that the commission held its first meeting in Shanghai in 1926. Then Chinese minister to the United States, Sao-ke Alfred Sze (Shi Zhaoji), did not mince words: "Since China has been improperly blamed for the postponement of the first session of the Commission until January 1926, it is of interest to state the essential facts." Sze then listed the "extraneous" and unnecessary delaying tactics, especially on the part of the Americans and the French. "For nearly a century now," he continued, "the Chinese people have labored under the fiscal and jurisdictional limitations upon their freedom of action, limitations which weaken the powers and efficiency of their government, lower the respect and authority of that government in the eyes of those who should support it ... and which ... give the alien residents in China rights and immunities which the Chinese themselves are not permitted to enjoy." Sze spoke for the Chinese legal community, and after four years of delays his impatience was apparent: "China asks that affirmative steps be taken to restore to her the jurisdictional and fiscal rights which should never have been taken from her."[46] Sze's frustration was a result of the extraterritoriality issue being only one of a multitude of issues about which the powers had not acted in good faith, and plagued the Beijing regime by sapping its domestic credibility during the long crisis of internal disunity.

Four years earlier, in 1922, even before the extent of the stalling was apparent,

Zhang Yaozeng had emphasized the importance of not waiting for the foreigners in China willingly to surrender their extraterritorial privileges. He conducted an extensive survey of China's legal system and submitted a report as an internal government document in February 1923, which was then published in 1924.[47] In addition to conducting this survey, Zhang and other legal professionals were also active in publishing articles that amounted to status reports of the progress being made in reforming the legal infrastructure. The methods of reform were also common to both Zhang's survey and the journal articles. Because the content and expressed purpose of the Beijing and Shanghai journal articles and Zhang's survey overlapped in purpose, I will outline them together here as representative of an essentially united legal community in the midst of reform projects.

The Law Weekly (Falü zhoukan) published in Chinese, and The Law Weekly Review (Falü pinglun) published in both Chinese and English, provided accounts of the reforms and persistent problems in the legal system. They also included advocacy of reform by Chinese and foreign supporters. During 1922 and 1923, the tone of both journals was quite optimistic. The reports emphasized progress and criticized those forces that obstructed the reforms.

The journal reports and Zhang's survey were not unrealistic or falsified reports of China's legal infrastructure. They were often sobering and critical accounts of shortcomings and areas that needed improvement. In the winter of 1922–1923, the international Commission's initial convention had only been delayed about a year, and apparently some believed that it would begin its work soon. In a speech made in December 1922, Zhang declared, "In May of the coming year, representatives of the powers will come here to China to determine whether they will abrogate their extraterritorial rights." Rather than lament the delays that were already apparent (and which would continue for another three years) Zhang used the supposed imminence of the visit to strengthen his case for implementing urgent reforms: "I therefore see this as a good opportunity, and I must make a determined effort to visit every province and conduct a thorough survey."[48]

One visible improvement in many regions involved relieving local magistrates of their judicial duties in order to focus exclusively on administrative matters. Legal specialists were appointed as judges for the provincial and local courts. An independent judiciary was considered essential to a modern legal system in China, and many examples of the establishment of this parallel post are noted in these journals. This type of fundamental and critical reform was building on the recommendations of legal reformers in the last decade of the Qing. All that was required was the funding initiative and an active and growing community of Chinese legal experts to fill the posts, both of which were adequate for meaningful progress to be made.[49]

One journal article referred to the work of Shan Yusheng, whom the Beijing ministry of justice had appointed chief justice in Fengtian in 1920. After less than three years in office, the Falü pinglun honored him with an essay entitled "A Few Good Records of the Judicial Reorganization in [Fengtian]." "Formerly there were over ten districts in [Fengtian], where no trial judge could be found," the journal proclaimed. "Now all these districts have been provided for, while in those districts which are crowded with litigation, special judicial offices have been created paving the way for the establishment of Branch Courts."[50]

Published both in English and Chinese, these journals were probably read by foreign lawyers in China, if not by the general foreign public. For this reason, the journal was not used simply to celebrate progress and report shortcomings but also to confront the international readership with examples of blatant violations of the treaty agreements that favored foreign commercial and political interests. In one editorial, following a report of substantial progress in the improvements of facilities in Jiangsu, a complaint was made about the lack of access for Chinese defendants and plaintiffs in the Hankou magistrate's courts. It should be noted that the court in question was a Chinese one and not under the consular or extraterritorial jurisdiction of any foreign power. "According to present regulations governing civil and criminal cases involving Chinese and foreigners ... the [magistrate] has specially granted permission to four lawyers to practice in his court. All of these four lawyers, with [one] exception ... are foreigners introduced by the Shanghai Mixed Court."[51] This article reflected the journal's role as an oversight mechanism of the Chinese legal community, exposing such practices as the illegal staffing of courts with foreign lawyers. This was a result of local corruption according to the article, and it had doubtless been initiated by the powerful foreign legal establishment that connected Hankou with Shanghai.[52]

The work of Zhang's survey committee, the "Society for the Discussion of Judicial Rights," sparked an increase in this type of legal oversight, and the journals became a combination of progress report and legal watchdog. The exemplary Chief Justice Shan in Fengtian had managed to implement his reforms with only limited help from the central government. In one port town he raised ten thousand yuan to construct a modern courthouse and prison. By late summer 1923 political instability in Beijing had made funding unavailable outside of surrounding Zhili, as the threat of further warfare between rival factions loomed. Shan was resourceful and brilliant in his work, especially in his ability to raise a further two hundred thousand yuan, relying only on the civil government of his home province, for the construction of modern courthouses and prisons in several other key districts. Justice Shan won the praise of one journalist when it was noted that he had reserved a portion of the legal budget for the construction of a clubhouse, a "profitable place for the law officers to repair to" after a day in court.[53] During Zhang's survey tour, in his meetings with the legal societies throughout the provinces, and in the pages of these legal journals, there was an increased collective professional awareness within the legal community, both in the coherence of views on critical issues of reform or the more light-hearted prospect of a shared leisure space for a newly respected calling.

While only limited funding was forthcoming, one thing the central government could provide was approval and encouragement. In October 1923 a presidential mandate was published in *Falü pinglun* on the need to construct more modern prisons and to reform old penal practices. "The people are the backbone of the country ... Therefore every convict should be taught a trade during his term of sentence ... Order is hereby given that ... new prisons providing instructive courses for prisoners should be set up ... " The proclamation went on to specify that fundraising for this project would be assigned to "local authorities," as was the case in the Fengtian example.[54]

The financial and military weakness of the central government suggests that such a proclamation carried little weight at China's margins—margins that sometimes crept close to the capital of the fragile republic. This may be true, but these reforms were already being implemented and had been underway for some time. Shortly after the publication of the presidential mandate, in direct and enthusiastic response, reports came back of ongoing projects that involved expanding prisons to more humanely accommodate inmates, as well as providing prisoners with workshops in which they might learn a vocation before their release.[55] This emphasis on the prison as a site of reformatory education was relatively new, leading one historian to term the prison the "cathedral of modernity" in China.[56] The spread of information about the urgency of prison reform and the publication of recommended courses of action led to a "remarkable degree of convergence ... between different penologists in republican China."[57] Frank Dikotter's observation about a kind of professional "convergence" further reinforces the idea of horizontal awareness and interaction of legal and criminal specialists throughout China.

In a study of later reformers, Christian Hess cites the late 1910s and the early 1920s as "the most successful period for education and moral guidance" in some areas of prison reform. These improvements came especially in the implementation of such institutions as vocational education in prisons, and the "confessional speech" in which a convict shared his story with his inmates, often to a rousing and sympathetic response.[58] This period of progress in prison reform suggests that in spite of a lack of ample central funds, local legal societies were energized in this period and their reforms were far-reaching and effective. Again, the instability of the central government highlights the contributions and active participation of local legal societies throughout the provinces. During his survey tour, Zhang was welcomed in each location by a local group of legal scholars, posing for commemorative photographs with them, seated prominently in the center of each with his secretaries. The increase in uniformity of prisons and prison reform reflects local initiative that was a result of the integrative work that included the publication of legal journals as well as the lectures and the survey tour taken by Zhang in 1922.

During inspection of prisons, Chinese legal experts also examined those located in foreign concession areas, including the French Concession in Shanghai. While improvements of educational facilities in Chinese prisons noted by

Hess impressed contemporary legal scholars, Chinese surveyors of the French Concession prisons were disappointed. In assessing the French prison, a surveyor noted the following with respect to the area of education and rehabilitation: "Education. No attention is paid to this matter, the prison having neither school rooms nor teachers." This was undoubtedly a painful evaluation for the French, if they were paying attention, for they were among the powers that continued to claim that their courts served as an example of modern jurisprudence and enlightened judicial practice for Chinese emulation. After criticizing the failings of the prison in the realm of education, this surveyor went on to remark on other problems. "Blankets are issued to prisoners at night time and collected back in the day time. No bed is provided and prisoners sleep on the floors. For foreign prisoners, beds, tables and chairs as well as clothing are provided. There is a vast difference between treatment of foreign prisoners and Chinese prisoners."[59]

In an inspection of another foreign-run prison, this one in the International Settlement of Shanghai, the surveyor provided a taciturn remark on the high death rate in that prison: "Death. The press reports that last year there were about 800 cases of death in the prison, or more than half the number of prisoners. The strictness of the prison regulations and not the lack of sanitary methods or proper medical attendance is said to be the cause." No more explanation or argument is provided here, but the inclusion of this statistic and the brief explanation seemed to say quite bluntly that the prisons in the International Concession were brutal and strictly punitive institutions. In the final remarks on the "reformatory" for minors, the surveyor notes that there are currently fifty prisoners being held in two bedrooms, with those prisoners who are "under fifteen separated from those under twelve."[60]

This type of journalism exposed the assumed enlightenment of Western legal ideals as a smoke-and-mirrors job to maintain a broad range of privileges on Chinese soil. In addition to legal privileges, Western control of China's tariff economy was a crucial way of influencing the politics of fragile Beijing regimes, and in this, stability was favored over political and social reform. Decades later, Hu Shi reviewed an American study of extraterritoriality in China—Wesley R. Fishel's—and it was clear that his frustration lingered with the reliance on the symbolic issue of extraterritoriality as an excuse to perpetuate foreign privileges: "[E]xtraterritoriality did not come to China as an isolated thing, nor was it modified and finally abolished [in 1943] as an isolated thing … [Fishel's work] has deliberately ignored such related 'facets' as the tariff and the foreign settlements and concessions."[61] For legal reformers, after having surveyed both Chinese and foreign courts and prisons on Chinese soil and found that the foreign courts were not exemplars of judicial and punitive enlightenment, the legitimacy of foreign claims was undermined. When the international commission finally arrived, it predictably decided that China could not yet be trusted to try foreign nationals in its courts.

Legacy of Professionalism, Pragmatism, and Reform

Zhang Yaozeng's work for legal reform in early republican China did not bring an end to extraterritoriality in his own lifetime. The wars between the Nationalists and Communists overlapped with warlord conflicts, and the Japanese invasion starting in the early 1930s prevented anything more than a sporadic reform of China's legal infrastructure. The passage of a Chinese civil code in 1930, and the 1943 abrogation of extraterritoriality by the British and American governments appear to be watersheds in China's legal reform and rights reclamation. But Philip Huang has shown that the Chinese legal code of the Qing, especially in its statutes and substatutes, covered many of the areas of law that would ultimately be incorporated in the civil code, making the 1930 date less of a key milestone of legal reform than the formalization of legal practice that had been underway for centuries in China. As for the 1943 abrogation of extraterritoriality, this wartime gesture was little more than political expedience—an attempt to compete with the appeal of anti-imperialism in the Japanese Greater East Asian Co-Prosperity Sphere.[62]

More than the hollow dates of 1930 or 1943, the early 1920s saw a dynamic period of legal reform and growth of the legal profession in China. But Zhang Yaozeng never claimed to have pulled these reforms out of thin air. "[D]uring the declining years of the Manchu Dynasty," he stated, "foreign legal principles were incorporated into the Chinese legal system by the adaptation of the laws of the Continental system such as those enforced in France and Germany."[63] While late Qing reformers like Shen Jiaben proposed extensive changes, it was in the early 1920s that a burgeoning class of legal professionals spearheaded the effort to implement them. Philip Huang states that by the late Qing, when implementing the legal code in China, "the courts acted consistently to protect and uphold legitimate ownership, land transactions, lending contracts, marital agreements, and succession and inheritance agreements."[64]

Ultimately, Zhang's goals were more ambitious than merely abolishing extraterritoriality. In 1922 he told a crowd of legal experts that educating the populace would increase its access to the legal system as well as opening its eyes to the need for removing foreign courts.[65] He believed that legal reform, education, and increased access to the law could be an effective remedy for many of China's problems of weakness and disunity in the republican era.

While his goals of complete sovereignty, national unity, and broad political mobilization were in line with some of the goals of the Nationalists in the south, Zhang saw that the plodding daily work toward those goals would itself lead to the steady expansion of the numbers involved in the reform movement. This mobilization push would be the foundation of the effort to achieve the goals of unity and rights reclamation. Mobilization would come through participation in reforms; nationalism would come through broader education; unity would come through broader legal participation; and China's sovereignty would finally be realized when the reforms progressed and prison and courthouse conditions improved, ending the need for extraterritoriality. Reforms implemented along the way would hopefully become self-sustaining improvements to the legal system, and they would make permanent the tenuous proposals for legal reform in the late Qing period. While the abolition of extraterritoriality was not the only measure of victory or defeat, Zhang's failure in the drive for abolition defined the limits of his reforms. They also define his legacy, for many of the obstacles to his work have persisted over the years, continuing even now to frustrate and constrict reform in China.

Persistent Obstacles: Foreign Duplicity and Party Discipline

The reluctance of foreign powers to abrogate their extraterritorial powers was a consistent obstacle to Zhang Yaozeng's reforms and his attempts to reclaim judicial sovereignty for China. Though Zhang was schooled in several legal traditions, it did not take a legal expert to perceive that the "potent fiction" of the "rule of law" did not extend far beyond the coasts of the lands in which those ideas originated.[66] The merchants, missionaries, and official envoys of the foreign lands that boasted a rich tradition of the rule of law did not seem to have any compunction about leaving that cherished tradition behind when they stepped onto Chinese soil.[67] Zhang spent much of his career working to reform the Chinese legal system in a way that would satisfy the demands of foreign powers. But satisfying foreign standards was clearly not his only concern. More importantly, the duplicitous behavior of foreign powers in China does not define or negate the importance of Zhang's work. Beyond the issue of extraterritoriality in China, a nonissue today, foreign obstructions to reform work continues to be important in the power politics that define international legality.

International law was and is a powerful weapon in the hands of those who back up rhetoric with real or implied military force.[68] In Peru and Venezuela during the 1920s and 1930s, for example, the more powerful United States obtained its objectives with little difficulty when third-party conflicts emerged between American companies and the governments of Latin American countries. Referring to the U.S. government's "right" to overrule any contracts made between American companies and foreign governments, one American legal expert wrote, "It seems unnecessary to cite any legal authority to support an assertion that international law recognizes the right of a nation to intervene to protect its nationals in foreign countries."[69] The United States and other powers could easily shrug off the claims to territorial sovereignty made by weaker nations, and they continued to do so in Latin America, as in China, because "international law of the family of nations must be observed in the treatment of foreigners."[70]

These harsh realities put Zhang Yaozeng and the Chinese republic in a helpless position. It was in response to profound mistrust of the entire American and Eurocentric international system that the southern revolutionaries sought guidance from Soviet Russia, which had staked out the moral high ground by offering to abrogate its extraterritorial privileges.[71] Perhaps Zhang allowed himself a sardonic grin as he addressed a crowd of legal experts at a survey stop in Anqing, Anhui: "I am eager to [take the foreigners at their word and] help them cast aside their special extraterritorial privileges in China." After outlining the history of unequal treaties and exactions by foreign powers in China, Zhang returned as always to his straight-forward message of self-strengthening: "In reforming the legal system, the responsibilities rests with the people of our own nation."[72]

The inconsistencies and illegalities associated with foreign legal practices did not paralyze Zhang, nor did he attempt to mobilize antiforeign violence with xenophobic diatribes, though he was in an ideal position to do so during the speech-and-survey tour. While Zhang acknowledged that the foreign powers continued to violate international law through the operation of their courts in China, he also understood that the legal traditions and practices that were currently being taught in Europe, Japan, and the United States were important models for Chinese reform. Education of Chinese legal experts in foreign universities was an essential element in his plan for legal reform in China. Upon returning to Beijing after completing the survey, an upgrade of the education required of Chinese legal experts was one of the most prominent and concrete recommendations that he put forward.[73] The inadequacy of China's educational institutions led him to advocate sending more scholars abroad to study law as he had, and also to improve the Chinese educational system.

Zhang's education had shown him the best of these foreign legal traditions, though his work had revealed the worst. Still he did not resort to demagoguery when frustrated about his work, and in this, he was exceptional. Even the most cosmopolitan and politically moderate of China's republican reformers, Gu Weijun (V. K. Wellington Koo), ran out of patience when he was forced to deal with the outrageous hypocrisy of the foreign powers on Chinese soil in this period.

In spring 1923, in what was later called the "Lincheng incident," a train was robbed and its passengers taken hostage. Of the twenty-five foreign passengers, most were Americans, and they were held for several weeks before being released unharmed. The incident became thrilling global news, and the foreign governments involved began discussing a strong response directed at the Chinese government for failing to secure its rails, in the familiar and illegal pattern of similar incidents discussed earlier in this chapter. The measures included paying an indemnity and increasing the number of foreign troops stationed in China. Gu Weijun, an American-educated lawyer, was minister of foreign affairs at this time. Throughout his life Gu was personally and professionally close to British and American interests in China, even to the point of being accused of betraying his own country for the benefit of the Americans. But the foreign response to the Lincheng hostage crisis was, in Gu's estimation, far too harsh a punishment. In a recent biography of Gu, Stephen Kraft recounts the decision of the Chinese foreign ministry to leak the indemnity demands as well as notes on discussions about organizing the railroad police under foreign control. In Kraft's estimation, there seems little doubt that Gu had been involved in leaking these plans, and further that Gu was responsible for writing a series of articles under a pseudonym to condemn the foreign response to the incident.[74]

For Zhang, the road to "national renewal" was not through violence or hostility directed at either foreigners or weak Chinese regimes that bent to their demands. Revolution would leave the new leadership with the same problems of inadequate legal infrastructure and international weakness. "What is the path to self-respect and self-renewal? I would say, the answer is to establish a transparent legal system, an independent judiciary, and to maintain law and order in such a way that politics remains within the confines of law."[75] Considering the reaction of the ever-moderate Gu Weijun to the outrages of foreign duplicity in a context of blunt hegemony, one might reasonably consider Zhang to have been too trusting of his Western counterparts. Finally, with the Japanese invasion, Zhang supported military defense, though in his writings, he still focused on means other than military in resisting the Japanese.[76]

The turn to Leninism—to revolution, party discipline, and political tutelage— taken by both Communists and Nationalists was a turn away both from warlordism, and from Western and Japanese imperialist betrayal in the wake of World War I. This shift led to the Northern Expedition and Nationalist military success, which is the epilogue to this study of reform in the early republican period. Under both the Nationalist and Communist regimes, the "dream of constitutionalism" was indefinitely postponed. Zhang's emphasis on nonmilitary solutions to the problems facing China was a reaction to the failures of the militaristic "warlord era" in which he worked for reform. But ultimately it was not warlords, but first a lack of foreign cooperation, and second the urgency of partisan discipline and its political power, that deferred the dream of Zhang's reforms. Today, these two remain central obstacles to work for legal reform in China.

Ultimately, the energetic work of Zhang and his supporters represented a brief period of hope for peaceful change that would lead to national sovereignty, stability, and legal reform. While today an observer might say that two out of three is pretty good, Zhang also aimed for the third. Today many continue to work for reform, inside and outside of the government, though the din of prosperity and international glory often drowns out any reportage on their promising work. Legal reforms under Zhang's leadership actually represent one of the brightest moments of potential for reform in the twentieth century, even in the "darkest corner of twentieth-century Chinese history." Thirty years ago, in another period of optimism for reform in China, Jerome Alan Cohen reminded his Western audience that, "Although the Chinese political-legal tradition is very different from that of western industrial democracies, it turns out that Chinese—not only intellectuals but also many less well-educated people—share with the outside world a common sense of injustice and would like their government to observe minimum standards of fundamental decency in dealing with them."[77]

NOTES

1. Andrew J. Nathan, *Peking Politics, 1918–23: Factionalism and the Failure of Constitutionalism* (Berkeley: University of California Press, 1976), 2. My title, "A Dream Deferred," is taken from the Langston Hughes poem, "Harlem," first published in *Montage of a Dream Deferred* (New York: Henry Holt, 1951). Zhang Yaozeng, who is central in this study, described his hopes for constitutional and judicial reform in China's future as a dream.

2. Diana Lary's 1980 article, "Warlord Studies" in *Modern China* 6.4 (October 1980): 439–70, also considered this the "darkest period of [China's] modern history" (439). Since Lary's article, considerable work has been done by Arthur Waldron, Edward McCord, Hans van de Ven, Lary, and others to improve our understanding of the period. One of the few suggestions Lary puts forth for future work that is not related to the military history of the period is "the civilian arm of warlordism, and the fate of bureaucratic government" (468). My study aims in this direction, but without the assumption that the reformers and bureaucrats of this period were merely the atrophied "civilian arm" of the warlords, doomed to fail under the heavy hand of militarism. The recent works of Xu Xiaoqun have been an inspiring move in this direction.

3. Xu Xiaoqun, "The Fate of Judicial Independence in Republican China, 1912–1937," *China Quarterly* 149 (March 1997): 1–28; "The Rule of Law Without Due Process: Punishing Robbers and Bandits in Early-Twentieth-Century China," *Modern China* 33.2 (April 2007): 230–57.

4. Xu, "Fate of Judicial Independence," 10.

5. Zhang Yaozeng, in a letter to Jiang Jieshi, June 10, 1933, reprinted in *Xianzheng jiuguo zhi meng: Zhang Yaozeng xiansheng wencun* [A dream of saving the nation through constitutional governance: the collected works of Mr. Zhang Yaozeng] (Beijing: Falü chubanshe, 2004), 183; hereafter this volume is cited as *XJZM*.

6. See Elya Zhang's chapter in this volume and her treatment of the Shanghai *Subao* case.

7. Yang Hu, "Zhang Yaozeng xiansheng zhuan" [Biography of Mr. Zhang Yaozeng], in *XJZM*, 1–2.

8. Ibid., 1–2.

9. Zhang Yaozeng, "Shuo quanli" [Speaking of rights], *Yunnan zazhi* 8 (August 15, 1907), reprinted in *XJZM*, 18.

10. Zhang Yaozeng, "Diansheng yi ji xing gongxue" [Yunnan province should urgently promote public education], *Yunnan zazhi* 14 (June 30, 1908), reprinted in *XJZM*, 22.

11. Ibid., 22. Donald S. Sutton, *Provincial Militarism and the Chinese Republic: The Yunnan Army, 1905–25* (Ann Arbor: University of Michigan Press, 1980), 36.

12. Zhang also was early in advocating equal educational opportunities for women. Zhang Yaozeng, "Lun Diansheng dang xing nü xue" [On the recent beginnings of women's education in Yunnan], *Yunnan zazhi* 15 (November 10, 1908), reprinted in *XJZM*, 25–28.

13. Zhang Yaozeng, "Guomin nengli guojia jinbu zhi guanxi" [The relationship between the strength of the citizenry and national progress], *Yunnan zazhi* 18 (November 24, 1909), reprinted in *XJZM*, 28–30. "It is significant that the students in Japan initiated the movement ... [as] the first organized expression of public opinion by Yunnanese" (Sutton, *Provincial Militarism*, 40).

14. Howard L. Boorman, *Biographical Dictionary of Republican China* (New York: Columbia University Press, 1967–1979), 305–7.

15. Ch'ien Tuan-sheng, *The Government and Politics of China* (Cambridge: Harvard University Press, 1961), 61–93; and Li Chien-nung, *The Political History of China, 1840–1928* (Stanford: Stanford University Press, 1967), 274–303.

16. Zhang Yaozeng, "Dongdu zhi gaobie shu" [A letter upon departing for the East], *Shenbao* (November 9, 1913), reprinted in *XJZM*, 31.

17. In 1915, Zhang's only sibling, younger brother Huizeng, died of pneumonia while studying in Edinburgh. Zhang commissioned a memorial shrine to summon his brother's soul back from Scotland, where the faculty members of the economics department at the University of Edinburgh had attended to his burial there. But Yuan's harassment forced Zhang to cut short his mourning and flee Beijing. Finally, when Zhang wrote a memorial for his brother in 1920, he remained bitter about the ritual indignity he and his brother had suffered at the hands of "Mr. Yuan." Zhang Yaozeng, "Wang di Kuanxi shilüe" [A short biographical account of my departed younger brother, Kuanxi], reprinted in *XJZM*, 35–37.

18. Nathan, *Peking Politics*, 253–57.

19. Being a moderate reformer or federalist in the late 1910s often meant trying to work in the shifting sands of Beijing politics while representing the interests of the southern Nationalists. Li Chien-nung, *The Political History of China*, 361, 401.

20. According to Li Chien-nung, Li Yuanhong was also a "simple-minded" man, or at least seemed one in the world of Beijing politics, but his weak presidencies also brought national focus to the issues of federalism and constitutionalism. See Li Chien-nung, *The Political History of China*, 362.

21. I use the term democratization here in its broadest political sense as a broadening of participation in political power, expanded suffrage and equal protection before the law.

22. See Chang Yao-tseng (Zhang Yaozeng), "The Present Condition of the Chinese Judiciary and Its Future," *The Chinese Social and Political Science Review* 10.1 (1926): 163–82.

23. Perception was important. In Japan, as in China, penal reforms "were intimately linked to [the] struggle to escape ... the inferior status [Japan] was assigned within the imperial world order." See Daniel V. Botsman, *Punishment and Power in the Making of Modern Japan* (Princeton: Princeton University Press, 2005), 140. Reforms perhaps had some relevance to decisions by the powers to abrogate extraterritorial privileges, but there is little proof of this. The 1895 date of abrogation in Japan marked Meiji Japan's defeat of the Qing empire. Many of the Japanese reforms had been promulgated and implemented for some years by 1895. Turan Kayaoglu maintains in *Sovereignty, State-Building, and the Abolition of Extraterritoriality* (University of Washington, Ph.D. dissertation, 2006) that reforms led to unilateral abrogation. But the 1943 abrogation in China came in the midst of a war. It did not follow a period of legal reform like the one in the early 1920s, but rather the *curbing* of judicial independence by the Nationalists in the late 1920s and 1930s, as Xu Xiaoqun's work shows.

24. Alison W. Conner, "Lawyers and the Legal Profession During the Republican Period,"

in Philip C. C. Huang and Kathryn Bernhardt, eds., *Civil Law in Qing and Republican China* (Stanford: Stanford University Press, 1999), 246.

25. Jurgen Habermas, *The Structural Transformation of the Public Sphere: An Inquiry into a Category of Bourgeois Society* (Cambridge: Polity, 1989).

26. Chang Yao-tseng, "The Present Condition of the Chinese Judiciary and Its Future," 181.

27. H. G. W. Woodhead, *Extraterritoriality in China: The Case Against Abolition* (Tianjin: Tientsin Press, 1929), 1–3.

28. Woodhead, *Extraterritoriality in China*, 8.

29. "Foreign" interests here are primarily British, American, Japanese, and French. Russian and German relations with China were in flux during this period. See Bruce A. Elleman, *Diplomacy and Deception: The Secret History of Sino-Soviet Diplomatic Relations, 1917–1927* (Armonk: M.E. Sharpe, 1997), 23, 182; and William C. Kirby, *Germany and Republican China* (Stanford: Stanford University Press, 1984).

30. Ge-Zay Wood, *The Shantung Question: A Study in Diplomacy and World Politics* (London: Fleming H. Revell, 1922), 150–51.

31. Lian Xi, *The Conversion of Missionaries: Liberalism in American Protestant Missions in China, 1907–1932* (University Park: Pennsylvania State University Press, 1997), 4–6; Kathleen L. Lodwick, *The Widow's Quest: The Byer's Extraterritorial Case in Hainan, China, 1924–1925* (Bethlehem: Lehigh University Press, 2003).

32. Paul Cohen, *History in Three Keys: The Boxers as Event, Myth, and Experience* (New York: Columbia University Press, 1997), 227–30.

33. Benj. H. Williams, "The Protection of American Citizens in China: Cases of Lawlessness," *The American Journal of International Law*, 17.3 (July 1923): 489.

34. Shih Shun Liu, *Extraterritoriality: Its Rise and Decline* (New York: Columbia University Press, 1925), 96.

35. Lodwick's exhaustive study, *The Widow's Quest*, is an excellent example.

36. George W. Keeton, *The Development of Extraterritoriality in China* (New York: Howard Fertig, 1969), v. 1, 250, 255 (my emphasis).

37. Lodwick, *The Widow's Quest*, 38; Westel W. Willoughby, *Foreign Rights and Interests in China* (Baltimore: Johns Hopkins Press, 1927), 634–35.

38. Willoughby, *Foreign Rights and Interests in China*, 635.

39. Frances Zia, "A Chinese Jurist's Views on Extraterritoriality," *China Weekly Review* 23.5 (December 30, 1922): 168.

40. Rodney Gilbert, "The Foreigner's Rights in China," *North China Daily News* (March 24, 1921).

41. For Gu Weijun, see Stephen G. Craft, *V. K. Wellington Koo and the Making of Modern China* (Lexington: University Press of Kentucky, 2004), 16–21. For Wang Chonghui, see Boorman, *Biographical Dictionary of Republican China*, 377.

42. Wesley R. Fishel, *The End of Extraterritoriality in China* (Berkeley: University of California Press, 1952), 59.

43. Westel W. Willoughby, *China at the Conference: A Report* (Baltimore: Johns Hopkins Press, 1922), 114–15.

44. Ibid., 118–20.

45. Faquan taolun weiyuanhui, ed., *Kaocha sifa ji* [Record of the legal administration survey] (Beijing: Beijing ribao guan, 1924), 9. See David Chang's chapter in this volume for a thorough examination of the inclusive and pragmatic reforms that extended political and legal margins over a decade earlier. Zhang Yaozeng frequently alluded to reforms

of the late Qing. He praised not only the efforts, but the solid accomplishments of late Qing reform—a foundation that hasty revolutionaries should not have lightly discarded or underestimated.

46. "Extraterritoriality: A Detailed Analysis of the Subject, Giving Foreign and Chinese Views with Suggested Plans for Solving the Problem," supplement to *China Weekly Review* (June 19, 1926), 66–67.

47. Faquan taolun weiyuanhui, ed., *Kaocha sifa ji*.

48. "Jinnan fajie huanyinhui yanci" [Speech before the Jinnan legal society welcome committee], *Kaocha sifa ji*, reprinted in *XJZM*, 48–49.

49. *Falü pinglun* 9 (August 26, 1923): 6; 11 (September 9, 1923): 4; 13 (September 23, 1923): 4. As Xu Xiaoqun points out in "The Fate of Judicial Independence," these reforms were built upon the Qing reforms.

50. *Falü pinglun* 9 (August 26, 1923): 3.

51. *Falü pinglun* 7 (August 12, 1923): 6.

52. The article goes on: "[M]ost of the cases involving Chinese and foreigners at [Hankou] are fictitious ones, that is, the foreign parties are only fictitiously concerned in them." Ibid. Foreign involvement would allow for legal interference.

53. *Falü pinglun* 9 (August 26, 1923): 3–4.

54. *Falü pinglun* 15 (October 7, 1923): 1–2.

55. *Falü pinglun* 18 (October 28, 1923): 4.

56. Borge Bakken, "Introduction: Crime, Control, and Modernity in China," in Bakken, ed., *Crime, Punishment, and Policing in China* (Lanham: Rowman and Littlefield, 2005), 3.

57. Frank Dikotter, "Penology and Reformation in Modern China," in Bakken, ed., *Crime, Punishment, and Policing in China*, 45.

58. Christian A. Hess, "Unlikely Spaces of Liberal Hope: Yan Jingyue and the Model Prison in Republican China," manuscript (cited with permission of the author), 27.

59. *Falü pinglun* 3 (July 15, 1923): 2.

60. *Falü pinglun* 1 (July 1, 1923): 6.

61. Hu Shih [Hu Shi], "The End of Extraterritoriality in China," *American Historical Review* 58.1 (October 1952): 122.

62. Chiang Kai-shek bluntly threatened capitulation to the Japanese if not given unconditional military aid. Abrogation by the U.S. and Great Britain was intended to bolster the Generalissimo's domestic popularity, but in the chaos of wartime China, there was little more than symbolic relevance of the legal nuance of jurisdictional claims.

63. "A Chinese Jurist's Views of Extraterritoriality," *China Weekly Review* (December 20, 1922): 168.

64. Philip C. C. Huang, *Code, Custom, and Legal Practice in China: The Qing and the Republic Compared* (Stanford: Stanford University Press, 2001), 15–27.

65. "Speech to Hangzhou Legal Society," from *Kaocha sifa ji*, reprinted in *XJZM*, 45–47; "Faxue yinggai tongsuhua" [The study of law should be popularized], *Zhongguo gongxue san rikan* (November 1929), reprinted in *XJZM*, 56–58.

66. Eileen Paula Scully, "Crime, Punishment, and Empire: The United States District Court for China, 1906–1943" (Georgetown University, Ph.D. dissertation, 1994), iv.

67. "Since the colonial enterprise itself was founded legally upon the Crown's exercise of its prerogative power—the formal erection of an *imperium*—it was this exercise of the ultimate public authority that set the parameters of legality within the colonial polity." P. G. McHugh, *Aboriginal Societies and the Common Law: A History of Sovereignty, Status, and Self-Determination* (New York: Oxford University Press, 2004), 33.

68. For a more recent manifestation, see Jeremy Scahill, *Blackwater: The Rise of the World's Most Powerful Mercenary Army* (New York: Avalon, 2007).

69. Samuel R. Howell, "Effects of Acts of Private Individuals on a Nation's Right to Protect Them Abroad" (Georgetown University, thesis, 1930), 6.

70. Ibid., 38, 39.

71. See Li Chien-nung, *The Political History of China*, 442–43.

72. "Speech to Anqing Legal Society," from *Kaocha sifa ji*, reprinted in *XJZM*, 44.

73. Faquan taolun weiyuanhui, ed., *Kaocha sifa ji*, 584.

74. Craft, *V. K. Wellington Koo*, 76–79.

75. Zhang Yaozeng, "Lieguo zai Hua lingshi canpanquan zhiyao" [Summary of the powers' extraterritorial privileges in China] (1923), reprinted in *XJZM*, 51–52.

76. Zhang Yaozeng, "Wuli wai zhidi fanglüe guanjian" [A general plan for fighting the enemy in ways other than with military strength] (September 4, 1937), reprinted in *XJZM*, 88–94. In 1933, during the Nationalist extermination campaigns against the Communists, Zhang was invited to serve in the Nanjing regime. He responded in a letter to Chiang Kai-shek in a noncommittal tone, and in his discussion of "internal" matters Zhang subtly conveyed his disapproval of Chiang's policies: "Do not rely exclusively on military force, for these internal caprices will eventually be resolved." (Zhang Yaozeng, in a letter to Chiang Kai-shek, June 10, 1933, reprinted in *XJZM*, 183.)

77. Jerome Alan Cohen, "China's Changing Constitution," *China Quarterly* 76 (December 1978): 840.

6

OIL FOR THE CENTER FROM THE MARGINS

Tai Wei Lim

When the Japanese blockaded the Chinese coast in 1938, Chinese leaders in Chiang Kai-shek's Nationalist government became acutely aware of their loss of access to foreign petroleum and oil extraction equipment. As a Chinese historian has remarked, the blockade marked the "fundamental end to the inflow of Western oil."[1] Cut off from imported oil, the Nationalist government intensified its search for indigenous sources of oil. This task was made all the more difficult by wartime conditions because by 1938 Chiang's government had retreated from cities well positioned for transporting oil (Shanghai and Nanjing) and had set up its wartime capital in Chongqing, an inland city 900 miles west of Shanghai. Chongqing was relatively isolated because it was at the headwaters of the Yangzi River hundreds of miles from the nearest railway lines. Thus marginalized, how could the Nationalist government meet its wartime needs by finding, extracting, and transporting oil?

Discovery and Extraction

The Japanese wartime naval embargo and the invasion of mainland China provided a sense of urgency to sustain oil industry developmental efforts, opening the way for the eventual discovery and drilling of an oilfield in Gansu province by the Nationalist government's National Resources Commission. More than a mere project to tide over China's temporary wartime oil shortage, the search for an indigenous oilfield was further motivated by "circumstances of daily increasing cries for oil within the country."[2] Energy resources from the margins were needed to keep the war machine going.

On December 23, 1938, geologist Sun Jianchu and seven others set off from Jiuquan (Gansu province) for Yumen, which was near the border of Xinjiang, 865 miles northwest of Chongqing. In the last leg of their arduous journey, they traveled on twenty-two camels' backs, the only available form of transportation. On December 26, 1938, Sun and his team of surveyors set up tents at Laojunmiao and met a small child whose body was drenched in crude oil and whose face was blackened by the soot from burning crude with only his eyes visible. Upon further investigation, Sun and his team learned that this boy, whose nickname was "oil doll" (*youwa*), was hired by a local entrepreneur to collect oil at a leak found in the river bank and transport the liquid in a wagon to faraway farming communities for sale.[3] This leak eventually led Sun and his team to set up an oilfield in Yumen.

The next step was to extract Yumen's oil in previously uncharted marginal territory. Sun Jianchu mapped out Yumen's geological makeup as a blueprint for technological exploitation. Although Sun's expedition was sponsored by the Nationalist government, he dug the first wells in 1938 using Communist drills from Yanchang that were originally old American drills for Japanese steam engines dating back to 1906.

The Nationalist government secretly arranged to borrow the drills from Communists at Yanchang through the National Resources Commission with Zhou Enlai approving the request.[4] The Communists delivered to Sun the two drills along with twenty oil workers to aid in the drilling.[5] The Communists authorized the loan in the name of "unity and overall interest of anti-Japanese war" (*tuanjie kangri de daju*).[6]

Sun Jianchu used the two borrowed Communist drills from Yanchang to investigate sites in Yumen in 1939, finally hitting oil in August 1939 at a depth of 88 meters at Laojunmiao.[7] The two drills excavated sixty large-scale shallow oil wells, which were the source of Yumen's first oil output.[8] When the drill reached the oil strata, it drew out 10.5 tons of oil on the first day.[9] This event was unprecedented. Earlier foreign-led expeditions had discovered and extracted oil in China,[10] but this was the first all-Chinese drilling team that successfully drilled for oil in a location that was also surveyed by an all-Chinese exploratory team. And it was done in a cooperative effort—as part of the United Front between Nationalist and Communist personnel.

After the first drilling, the well at Laojunmiao churned out approximately one ton of oil per day.[11] Further drilling revealed a few more oil deposits. Yumen personnel dug three more wells, Shiyougu, Baiyanghe, and Yarxia. Oil was struck at Baiyanghe in April 1940 and it quickly became Yumen's main oil source. In total, Yumen's production for the year 1939 was 418.85 tons and 1,346.756 tons for 1940.[12] During wartime, the locations of these four oil wells were kept a secret within the China Information Committee of the Chongqing government, referring to them only as a "district."[13]

In Chongqing, the Nationalist government instituted a self-reliance policy based on shifting heavy industries away from China's coastal areas and into its interior as a "new economic center" so that it could have the industrial capacity to fight a modern war from a self-contained defensible military-industrial base.[14] The government created a bureau, the Gansu Oil Field Administration (Gansu youkuangju) in March 1941 within the National Resources Commission to take charge of the Yumen oilfield in Gansu province.

Sun Yueqi (1893–1995), a Beijing University graduate who furthered his studies and conducted research in the U.S. before receiving training at Los Angeles and Texas oil fields, became the general manager of the Gansu Oil Field

Administration, which oversaw the development of China's largest wartime oil reserve. Despite the long distances involved, he shuttled between his obligations at the wartime capital Chongqing during winter and spring, and Yumen, where he was based for summer and autumn. As an agent of the Nationalist government, Sun worked closely with the government in Chongqing through a branch of the Gansu Oil administration at the wartime capital. As he later recalled:

> As such, we placed the Gansu oil mine office at Chongqing in charge of finance and purchase of machinery and established the transport department at Gelesan, located in between Chongqing and Yumen. Various stations along this route were also set up to facilitate the transportation of machinery to Yumen continuously. Otherwise, the construction and production of oil wells in Yumen would not have been possible. Besides supplying oil to northwest line unit, the transport department also moved the stock of oil to Lanzhou and Chongqing. In this way, the Chongqing office was not only in charge of Yumen but also provided the products and services associated with the oil industry. This is why Yumen's oil products became successful in such a short time.[15]

Sun Yueqi recalled that he and his team had to depend on components supplied by only 100–200 Chinese factories that had been moved by the Nationalist government to the wartime capital Chongqing from Shanghai in the wake of the Japanese invasion.[16] Cut off from coastal supplies of oil, the Nationalist government established factories in Chongqing to produce materials needed to drill for oil. It also tried to import equipment from the United States, but the Japanese attack on China prevented much of the American equipment and supplies from reaching China. Out of twelve rotating drills, only four made it safely to China.[17] Consequently, pooling together their own existing resources, the Communist and the Nationalist governments formed a United Front to get two drills from Communist Yanchang to Nationalist Yumen. In general, Nationalist government planners had great difficulties with underdeveloped Yumen as it was deficient in food supply, manpower and communication for Nationalist forces. The terrain was so rugged that the Allies were not able to transport refinery equipment and new machinery for drilling after the fall of Burma.

Once the locations of the oil wells were ascertained, Sun Yueqi directed the use of indigenously developed cement for construction:

> Chongqing has only one supplier for cement, something needed in the process of digging oil wells. It was transported to Yumen by car. The spar that is used for oil mining can only be found in the Pei Lin area. It was first transported through water routes and then by car. We used the

self-made rolling mill to break the big pieces of spar into small pieces and then used the ball mill to grind those pieces to powder. The powder had to go through the sieve. When the oil well drill reached the oil level, this powder was mixed into the mud at the bottom of the well to prevent the petroleum from blowing up in the well.[18]

Despite the limited availability of cement and the great efforts needed to transport cement to Yumen, the process was a testimony to Chinese dependence on their own wartime resources in producing materiel necessary for the construction of the Yumen oilfield.

In 1941, wells in Gansu were producing about 60,000 gallons of crude oil a month[19] and they were expected to boost production to 450,000 gallons per month or 5.4 million gallons annually with the addition of new machinery.[20] The Chinese economist D. K. Lieu noted that "a single mine in Gansu (Yumen), operated by the National Resources Commission, produces as much petroleum as was usually imported into China before the war, which is several thousand times the 1934 figure for that province."[21]

According to figures released by the Chongqing government's Ministry of Information in 1942, Yumen's production in 1941 was 3,000,630 gallons of crude oil with a part of this converted to gasoline.[22] By 1943, fourteen productive oil wells were dug[23] and, between 1939 and 1945, twenty-six oil wells were dug in Laojunmiao producing 52,830 tons of various grades and types of oils, becoming an important wartime industrial oil source for the Nationalist government.[24] Gansu, including Yumen, became China's main domestic oil source contributing a significant amount to the Nationalists' total oil production between 1939 to 1944, which came up to 1.0568 million gallons, including 200,900 gallons of petroleum and 87,500 gallons of aviation fuel.[25] Petroleum varieties included mostly gasoline with some amount of kerosene and diesel oil.

Refining, Transportation, and Consumption

After drilling, the next step was to refine the extracted oil. The Nationalist government found its own wartime refineries at Yumen wanting due to limited capacity and inefficiency. Liu Mo's memoirs on his experiences at wartime Yumen noted the lack of refinery equipment and storage facilities, resulting in gasoline evaporation under the hot sun in the Gobi Desert.[26] The solution was to order from the United States a 1,500-barrel refinery with distillation, thermal-cracking and polymerization plants able to produce 64 percent gasoline.[27] Most of the machinery was successfully shipped to the Nationalist government's facilities but, due to the loss of Burma to the Japanese military and the shut down of the Burma Road by the Japanese government, a component of the refinery was lost at Bhamo and Wanting and never reached Chongqing or Yumen. The fatal loss meant that the Nationalist government had to rely fully on indigenous refining capability and had to depend on Chongqing's water utilities company to put together twenty-four makeshift distillation and refining ovens for Yumen.[28] But this was only a temporary solution.

Consequently, the Gansu Oil Bureau decided to institute a domestic program of creating an oil refinery on its own. The Bureau made this decision despite the lack of imported refining machinery due to the ongoing war situation and set a target of 1,800,000 tons of gasoline by 1942.[29] Gansu Oil Bureau was able to find the machinery needed within China. The Nationalist government accumulated the raw materials necessary for the construction from various parts of China (including Luyang, Guilin, Guiyang, Kunming, Chongqing, Xian, etc.), according to official records, because it was "forced by circumstances to be self-reliant and nondependent on outsiders (*bide zhiligengsheng, buzai yilai wairen*)."[30] This assertion might sound like empty rhetoric, but in fact the Chinese oil expedition was very resourceful and even creative. In this sense, the Chongqing government in the wartime center collected resources from the margins to help develop the Yumen oilfield, itself in the margins.

Jin Kaiying, the Nationalist government official placed in charge of early Yumen's oil-refining function, constructed a makeshift refinery in 1939 by using a large wok heated underneath with a distillation tower covering it. The wok was made by welding two big oil barrels together and was able to process over 1,000 kilograms of oil per day, which was gradually increased to more than 2,000 kilograms near the end of World War II.[31] Fortunately, this oil required little processing because it was sufficiently sulphur-free to be usable even without much refining.

In 1940, the makeshift refinery was replaced by the newly completed refining facility at nearby Shiyouhepan. Subsequently, in April 1941, Gansu Oil Bureau constructed another refinery at Yumen's largest oilfield at Laojunmiao. During wartime, two refineries were then functioning: one was in the oilfield itself and was equipped with three sets of shell stills to produce straight distillates and the other with semicracking capability was located to the east of the oilfield.[32]

Although the oil men at Yumen set precedents for Chinese exploration and refining, they still needed to find ways to store and deliver the products to the end-users. Sun Yueqi later recalled the tremendous challenge that he had faced in designing and building storage facilities:

> Because of the continuous day and night drilling, oil continually flowed out to an oil pool. From here, oil was transported to the refinery to produce petrol, kerosene, diesel, petrol residual oil, candles, etc. But the transportation of oil could only be done in daytime and not at night so we had to store the oil in a big tank. Previously, we had transferred two oil tanks from Changsha here for oil storage but this was still not enough

to meet the supply requirements so this became a big problem for us. We were not able to make the steel plates needed for manufacturing oil tanks. I once requested the finance committee to collect three-gallon oil drums but it was in vain, so we had to make a decision whether to continue producing oil day and night continuously.[33]

To make up for the shortage of oil tanks, trucks and the problem of distance, the Yumen planners thought of a novel way in November 1942 to stitch up large rafts made up of 360 pieces of goat skin using wooden and bamboo poles that could accommodate 168 barrels of oil each (24 tons). Each of these rafts required a crew of four for transportation to the refinery to be topped up with oil before being shipped over water instead of land to Chongqing over a distance in excess of 940 kilometers.

The final and perhaps the most important step was delivering Yumen oil supplies to their destinations. The challenges here again required the creative and innovative use of makeshift technologies. Sun Yueqi later described the various forms of transportation that were used to convey oil on the arduous journey of 2,500 kilometers from Yumen to Chongqing.

> Because there was no railway transporting oil from Yumen to Chongqing, we only relied on a few lorries to transport oil through this 2,500-kilometer road journey. Since this also wasted a lot of petrol, we later moved some oil on rafts made of goat skin on the Jialingjiang (Jialing River). Now oil could be transported from Yumen to Guangyuan, Sichuan, first and then the oil tanks could be transported on rafts by river to Chongqing. This shortened the journey by 800 kilometers and solved the problem of high petrol consumption too. The goat skin raft could be flattened and returned to Guangyuan along with the empty oil tanks for reuse. This saved costs too.[34]

Sun sent these river rafts of oil down the river this way eight times a year.[35] He thus minimized the dependence on overland transportation and economized on vehicular use.

The creative but primitive goat skin technology did the job until the Nationalist government provided additional support with transportable used oil tanks for containing oil. Sun was thankful for the Nationalist government's support:

> The army committee provided 30,000 oil tanks. Although most of the oil tanks supplied were worn out, they could still be used after repair. This solved our problem, and the oil refinery factory was able to produce oil continuously in three shifts thereafter. When all units of the military arrived to collect oil, they brought along empty oil tanks

that had a capacity of 53 gallons each, so that we could exchange our filled-up oil tanks for their empty oil tanks. This process made oil transportation faster and facilitated convenience for the oil end users.[36]

Sun's description of the Nationalist government's support in providing 30,000 oil tanks highlights the limitations of makeshift technologies even when they were used creatively. While goat skin rafts were able to support logistical needs under wartime exigencies, Sun eventually needed the institutional support to upgrade the productivity of the oilfield.

Yumen was a pioneering model in the state-run military-industrial complex (or "national defense industry" in Nationalist terminology). The oilfield was also the Nationalist government's first integrated complex (*zhonghexing qiye*), a self-contained unit with its own sub-units for geological exploration, drilling, extraction, civil engineering and refining. It is also the first indigenously constructed Chinese oilfield with complete communications and transportation networks. In 1939, the oilfield's management and the Nationalist government's military engineers constructed a highway and connected the phones lines between the oilfield and Jiuquan in Gansu.

The result of Yumen personnel's creativity, technology, and pioneering hard work in the margins should not be discounted. In 1941, wells in Gansu were producing about 60,000 gallons of crude oil a month.[37] Figures released by the Chongqing government's Ministry of Information in 1942 indicated that Yumen production in 1941 was 3,000,630 gallons of crude oil with a part of this converted to gasoline.[38] By 1943, fourteen productive oil wells were dug.[39] Laojumiao also became the first oilfield to be developed under the National Resources Commission.

All in all, Yumen was pre–1949 China's most prolific oilfield, generating nearly 500,000 tons of crude oil between 1938 and 1949 which made up 90 per-cent of China's total oil output and over 70 percent of forty-five years' worth of pre-1949 oil.[40] Yumen also produced twelve varieties of oil, including gasoline, kerosene, lubricants. Yumen oilfield supplied oil for both military and civilian uses. In terms of military application, Yumen's gasoline supplied Nationalist troops in China's Northwest (*Xibeijun*), including the military administration, wartime transport and the Eighth Regional Command. In terms of civilian usage, Yumen oil supplied the Northwest and Xinjiang traffic bureaus. The Nationalist government's National Resource Commission prioritized the distribution of Yumen oil, allocating most of it to its departments of military administration, public transportation aviation, Chongqing military organs, American troops stationed in China and the Gansu provincial government.[41] No statistical records have been found of the actual quantities allocated to each of these units.

The Nationalist government was also aware of the high yield of aviation-grade kerosene in the Laojunmiao oil field and augmented its oil production facilities to better separate out this grade of oil from the rest in that oil field. Aviation fuel was particularly vital to the survival of the Nationalist regime in Chongqing as its strategy of withdrawing to the interior meant that it was dependent on aviation gasoline to fly the allied planes that brought supplies to China from India.

According to accounts written in 1945, Yumen crude oil was converted into gasoline locally and used in the northwest to fuel traffic on the road to Russia. Since the Northwest was dominated by the Communists and Yumen provided the only domestic source of aviation fuel for the Nationalists, Yumen benefited both parties. At the time, the Chinese Ministry of Information noted that "enough is produced to service trucks taking wool and tungsten to Soviet Russia via Sinkiang and returning from the border with Soviet barter goods."[42]

In this account, Yumen was only vaguely referred to as being "in the Northwest where promising oil wells have been and are being worked."[43] During this era of the United Front, the Nationalists and Communists were allies and both considered the Soviet Union to be friendly to their causes. Postwar accounts published in Nationalist government-controlled Taiwan continue to corroborate this observation. Yumen was able to refine crude to gasoline for use in trucks and its refined gasoline was only 20 yuan per gallon as compared to 500 yuan per gallon in Chongqing at the time according to the findings of D. K. Lieu.[44]

Management

Yumen's staff members who served under Sun Yueqi were basically categorized into technicians and workers. Technicians included engineers, gravimetric surveyors or cartographers, and workers who held jobs as truck drivers, drillers, and other members of the oilfield labor force. The difference in salary between management and workers was as much as a factor of ten[45] and salaries were probably dispensed by the Gansu oil mine branch office at Chongqing that was placed in charge of finance[46] and under the charge of Sun as the general manager of the Gansu Oil Field Administration. Other than technicians and workers, others present in the oilfield were security forces in artillery, infantry, armored and engineers divisions and the mine's own security guards. At the end of World War II, the information recorded of Yumen's manpower categorizations and strength showed that in 1945 it employed 589 technicians and 5,903 workers.[47]

Recruiting and training workers was difficult under wartime conditions and required considerable expense and time to produce personnel capable of "sustaining large-scale industrial undertakings."[48] China only had an estimated two million-strong industrial labor force before the Pacific War and even fewer during the war due to conscription. In the Nationalist government's wartime heavy industries, workers were recruited by managers of state-supported wartime industries. Competition for workers was so keen that the Nationalist government warned these managers not to poach workers from other industries.[49]

Most of the early Yumen oilmen recruited by the managers were first-timers with only a little experience in coal mining. Japanese sources claimed that laborers drawn from various locations in China were brought there by recruiters using strong-arm methods.[50] Recruiters and managers backed up by the Nationalist government used its powers to round up able-bodied men and farmers (many of whom were bankrupt) to work at Yumen. Accounts more sympathetic to the Nationalist government noted that other sources of recruits came from displaced populations whose homelands were invaded by the Japanese and youths in need of jobs.[51]

Once recruited, each Yumen worker acted as a guarantor for another, a measure instituted in 1942 to reduce incidents of crime and theft.[52] Workers were issued labor registration cards with photographs attached.[53] From postwar accounts, we have a glimpse of how the workers at the Yumen oilfield were organized. For example, when the Nationalist Yumen oilfield transitioned to Communist control after the civil war, Xue Guobang led over twenty workers under his supervision to a new People's Republic of China (PRC) oilfield and settled there,[54] indicating that a possible ratio of a foreman to his team of subordinates was around 1:20.

The Nationalist government was also aware of the value of engineers, paying tribute to a small band of chemical engineers who succeeded in distilling mineral oil. In Yumen, Sun Yueqi noted a dearth of specialists.

> Due to the shortage of technicians on the staff, we had no choice but to train more of them. At that time, Yumen had officially become an oilfield. Other than those people who had worked at Yanchang oilfield earlier, nobody else in our country had any experience in opening up oilfields ... At that time, the chairman in charge of oilfields Yan Shuang had graduated from Beijing University's department of mineral mining and he had been trained in the U.S. Geologist Wen Wenbo had studied in England and was later trained in Poland's oil fields. Director of refineries Jin Kaiying had studied in the U.S. and became factory director of Chongqing automated oil factory. He was later transferred to work at the oilfields. Only four of us had ever come across an actual oilfield and even we had not obtained practical work experience in operating them. There were no oil experts in the universities and no university graduates had ever come across an oilfield before.[55]

The training and expansion of skilled personnel could not be entirely dependent on a marginal periphery like Yumen. They had to be recruited and cultivated from major training centers. Before the war, the Nationalist government funded mining and refinery departments in Chinese universities like Beiyang University in Tianjin that offered courses on oil extraction. These departments churned out China's first corps of indigenously educated oil technocrats. When recruiting, the National Resources Commission placed a premium on scholarly qualifications and consultations with leading Chinese technical universities.

After the war broke out, because of the importance of technical personnel to the wartime economy, the Nationalist government decided to concentrate its limited resources on cultivating engineering skills by restricting the option of doing graduate work overseas to students in the sciences (especially those related to national defense). In addition, science students already in overseas universities who had financial difficulties in paying their school fees were automatically given government funding to continue their education.

To make up for the shortage in skilled manpower, the Nationalist government turned to experienced American personnel and sent their own Chinese personnel to the United States to pick up the skills of using preventive technologies for stopping gas leaks. During wartime, the Nationalist government dispatched three batches of seventeen-member teams to study and apprentice in the United States and Iran and three additional people to undergo on-the-job-training in the United States after the war ended.[56]

A gradual technocratization and bureaucratization of labor occurred within Yumen as workers began to specialize in different tasks. When the Yumen oilfield became operational, except for a few members who were transferred from the Sichuan and Xibei oilfields and the Chongqing automated oil factory or other units, most came from Xibei Industrial College (Xibei gongye xueyuan) and other universities.[57]

Labor Relations

In the area of labor relations and workers' welfare, there are two accounts by historian Shen Lisheng and Yumen eyewitness Liu Mo which offer valuable contrasting perspectives. Their accounts also reflect the extent of central control (Nationalist government in Chongqing) over the marginal periphery (Yumen oilfield). In Shen's account, the Nationalist government was able to assert its control over the Yumen oilfield through its ability to maximize profits to the detriment of the workers and for the benefit of the wartime power center in Chongqing. In other words, his analysis focused on central control by the Nationalist government from Chongqing and how its policies were implemented.

Shen accused the Nationalist government of manipulating the economy by raising the prices of goods only after salaries were dispensed. Salaries were so low that workers were said to be unable to buy clothing after deducting living expenses from their salaries and after taking inflation into account during their first year on the job. Harsh financial punitive measures were also in place for workers who broke the rules. In one example, when a Type 525 truck driver disappeared, a fine of 33,660 yuan was imposed on his guarantors in addition to salary cuts. The high costs of spare parts and the severity of the monetary penalties imposed officially often caused the drivers to run away whenever parts were lost from the trucks in their course of work.[58]

In addition, the government was said to have maximized profits through cost-savings measures and minimal or, in some cases, nonexistent infrastructural welfare. In his account Shen is highly critical of the Nationalist government and claims that workers lived in caverns and pits, wore sheepskin and some were even forced to sell their daughters for income. One worker by the name of An Guangxue sold his seven-year old daughter to a "capitalist," and she was then abused, doused with kerosene, and burned alive. Capitalism was also denounced for squeezing its profits out of the workers and benefiting only a small group of people at the management level.

According to Shen, an emphasis on profit-making also resulted in higher rates of accidents and casualties in the oilfield. A jingle circulated among the workers lamented the low salaries and long working hours at Yumen. Workers worked ten- to twelve-hour shifts, resulting in accidents due to fatigue. Serious accidents resulted in deaths; eight people died in a collapsed mine at Shiyouhepan in Yumen in August 1942 and another eight lost their lives in an oil drum explosion on May 17, 1943. There was also apparently one recorded incident of the management's delay in dispensing salaries for twenty days, prompting a general strike, which lasted over thirty hours. According to Shen, the management only grudgingly gave in to the striking workers and ordered the police and military at the oilfield to monitor those who participated in the strikes thereafter.[59]

Shen's account is contradicted by Liu Mo's account which also emphasized the financial power of the wartime center (Nationalist government in Chongqing) but gives a favorable portrayal of the exercise of that power. The personal involvement of the top leadership of the Nationalist Party and the support of the Nationalist government is seen as an advantage for the Yumen oilfield because of the government's ability in securing finances for building community infrastructure for the workers at Yumen. Yumen had a primary and secondary school, a hostel with an area of 45,264 square meters that included 31,900 square meters of living space, a 760–square meter hospital with thirty-three beds and two bathing facilities.[60]

Besides the central government's dispensation of funds for basic infrastructure, Liu also highlighted the existence of welfare, such as entertainment programs and recreational facilities. Choices for entertainment included a cinema with two small projectors and films rented from wartime Shanghai, a library, dramatic/operatic troupes, and a daily newspaper that was started in Nationalist Yumen in 1940 known as the *Saishang ribao*.[61] In describing these activities, Liu's account suggests the existence of greater local autonomy for workers at the Yumen oilfield.

While Liu claimed to have observed autonomy for workers at Yumen, Shen emphasized that regulatory power at Yumen was imposed from the center at

Chongqing. According to Shen's account, Nationalist government-run Yumen had an oppressive management system, specifically its guarantor system instituted in 1942. The practice of using guarantors was continued in the postwar years by the Nationalist government-sponsored Zhongguo Shiyou Youxian Gongsi (Chinese Petroleum Corporation) with each individual covered by three, four, or ten guarantors upon entering the mine. The management meted out punitive measures in case of violations by any of the guarantors; for example, a worker by the name of Li Xingcai was captured and interrogated by the mine police when his guarantor ran away from Yumen.

Torture was also carried out using electricity and water. Between 1943 and 1945, nine people were said to have been beaten or tortured to death by the mine authorities. Such practices prompted a strike in the summer of 1944, and workers surrounded the administration office while the authorities retaliated by using armed military police to seal off the exits and declare a curfew at Yumen.

In another incident on August 23, 1942, oil from the No. 8 well breached its perimeters and flowed with the water currents to the workers' housing area. An oil slick on the water caught fire, engulfing the entire oilfield, including the workers' housing area, in a blaze. The incident started another general strike as well as the departure of 450 workers from Yumen, prompting the authorities to send out paramilitary personnel to capture the escapees. Notices were dispatched to the surrounding counties for these wanted men, and their families were rounded up for questioning. Three hundred seventy of them were eventually captured and later tortured back in the camp, while eighty were killed in this manhunt.

Shen accused Chiang of devaluating the Nationalist currency, sending prices sky-high. Workers under detention by the Yumen authorities were not given salaries. Instead, the money was used to invest in silver dollars. At the same time, the market was manipulated by the Nationalist government causing the workers great losses. The workers' thirty-three representatives sent to negotiate with management were arrested under curfew restrictions after a representative fought with the management and the arrested workers were allegedly tortured by the authorities.

The prisoners continued their struggles even in the prison, apparently drawing the sympathies of other workers in Yumen who raised a couple of hundred silver dollars to financially support those in prison. According to Shen's history of Yumen, these workers were released on the eve of the Communist victory. The "1945 Incident" was seen as the foundations for the eventual workers' takeover of Yumen on the eve of the People's Liberation Army (PLA) entry into the facility.[62]

The oppressive conditions in Shen's portrayal of Yumen are again contradicted by Liu's account. Liu Mo's autobiographical book on Yumen describes far more pleasant lifestyles in Yumen. After the welfare department was set up in Yumen, workers began to enjoy amenities, including provision and grocery shops, a shoe shop, tailor, tofu house, soy sauce and sesame seed oil factories, an oil dispenser, snack shop, public bath, barber, hotel, entertainment centers including several forms of theater, plays, cross talk comedy (*xiangsheng*) and a unique "*chechehui* (a gathering of people for casual talk)." Guesthouses like *Shamozhigong* (a palace of the desert) could accommodate parties up to five tables serving a specialty dish called *yinpinguo* and a delivery system for goods to be brought to the doorstep of a worker's accommodations.[63]

In terms of food supply, Liu Mo's biographical account of Yumen noted that the Nationalist government management at Yumen hired experts to upgrade soil conditions for growing vegetables and feeding farm animals (ox, goats and pigs) on a large-scale. In terms of medical facilities, Yumen's Laojumiao oilfield had to call on medical manpower from Lanzhou hospital though it did have in residence a well-known surgeon, a pediatrician, pharmacists, nurses, and a Chinese medicine shop.

A special commissioner was sent by the Ministry of Social Affairs to Gansu Oil Mining Bureau to "direct and supervise welfare work."[64] The Ministry of Social Welfare was an organ created by the National General Mobilization Act of 1942 to recruit wartime manpower and regulate issues of promotion and salaries. In other words, the central government not only took care of welfare but made it a point to monitor local conditions with special care to make sure that welfare remained at a high standard.

In the name of welfare, facilities were provided for families within Yumen. This included a primary and secondary school, a hostel with an area of 45,264 square meters including 31,900 square meters of living space, a 760–square meter hospital with thirty-three beds and two bathing facilities.[65] Concerned about single males workers being lonely and having problems getting married, the authorities at Yumen under the personal direction of Sun Yueqi[66] decided to hire a group of female students to work at Yumen, encouraging them to settle down, form their families with the male workers there and "work at the facility with a peace of mind (*anxin kuangqu gongzuo*)."[67]

The contrasting accounts between industrial historian Shen Lisheng and Yumen observer Liu Mo may be attributable to the fact that Liu was reconstructing the oilfield mainly from memory and describing it as he had left it in the pre-1949 period and may not have had the opportunity to revisit the oilfield thereafter. On the other hand, Shen had the benefit of hindsight and was able to compare and contrast the development of the oilfield before and after 1949, leading to his critique of the Nationalist government's shortcomings in Yumen's development. Ultimately, both may be equally valid and valuable accounts of the same oilfield and, pieced together, they give a fuller picture of its development.

The Nationalist Government's Control

While Shen and Liu disagree about social welfare at Yumen, they and all other
available sources agree that Chiang Kai-shek's Nationalist government exercised
power over the Yumen oilfield. On the eve of Yumen's discovery on August 7,
1935, Chiang Kai-shek personally sent a telegram to the relevant departments
involved in Yumen, saying they "must use Chinese capital in exploitation."[68] In the
war years, between October 1941 and August 1942, Gansu's Yumen mineral oil
reserve was designated as a national reserve and subjected to the Chinese Mining
Law, which had first been promulgated on May 26, 1930, and revised for the third
time on July 22, 1938, to meet wartime demands. The most important feature of
the law was its nationalization of mineral resources and exclusion of foreigners
from ownership of those resources by requiring more than half of the directors in
any mining company to be Chinese citizens with the chairperson and the manager
Chinese as well.

In addition, the involvement in Yumen of the Nationalist government's
military, which was under the firm control of Chiang Kai-shek, indicated the
important stake that the Nationalist government and Chiang himself had in
the development of Chinese oil resources. Through the armed forces, Chiang
and the Nationalist military positioned police, paramilitary, special intelligence
and military units at Yumen with powers to search and detain. Nationalist Party
branches were also set up in Yumen with the purpose of monitoring the workers
and their political thought.[69]

Chiang Kai-shek also indicated the importance of Yumen by showing a
personal interest in it. He promulgated an official policy in October 1939 that
"ordered" employers at Yumen not to poach workers from other industries and
for workers not to change jobs "without the consent of the employers" and not
to "resort to sabotage under any condition." To enforce these rules, workers
had to submit labor registration cards with photographs attached; workers'
handbook was rather candid about the penalties: "[L]aborers are *forced* to go
back to their original factories in case they leave without the consent of their
employers."[70]

Power exercised from the wartime center, however, was contested. The
Nationalist Party's influence over heavy industrial projects like Yumen
caused tensions between the Party and the Nationalist government's National
Resources Commission. The Nationalist government's bureaucrats who
believed in the superiority of the controlled economy rallied strongly around
the head of the National Resources Commission, Weng Wenhao, who had
gained power and prestige at the expense of Chen Lifu in the Nationalist Party.
Both had to try to resolve their differences and collaborate in a series of major
planning conferences, the most important of which lasted ten days in April

1943 to review a National Resources Commission plan for postwar China.[71] Compromise eventually led to a consolidated schedule for the development of key industries, including the fuel sector.

In fact, the top Nationalist government leadership, including Chiang Kai-shek, acknowledged that oil specialists like Sun Yueqi were in charge of the site in Yumen. Chiang delegated authority to Sun because he had to rely on him to manage the oilfield. Power in this sense was shared between a political leader in the wartime center who had overall authority (over security and finances) and a technocratic leader who had local and working knowledge (in operations and recruitment) of the facility on the margins.

In one prominent instance, according to Sun, when Nationalist leader Chiang Kai-shek personally visited the Yumen oilfield in August 1942, he told Sun that he understood the difficulties of developing an oilfield in a desolate location like Yumen and assured Sun that if he needed support to solve any problems at the oilfield, he would have the backing of the Nationalist government. Sun Yueqi did take up Chiang's offer and asked for help with obtaining empty oil barrels for transporting Yumen's output and his request was granted by the Nationalist government as Chiang had promised.[72] The symbiotic relationship between the two is demonstrated here.

The Nationalist government dealt from the center with both political and technical issues and concerns that occurred on the geographic margins. Such an approach could only succeed because of the flexibility of the Nationalist government, the cooperation of the Communist Party, and the pragmatism of technocratic management. First, local pioneering work such as the first Yumen drilling was made possible under an overarching framework of political cooperation between the Nationalist government in Chongqing and the Chinese Communist Party at Yan'an. When help from the center was not possible, the dynamics shifted to the margins as Yumen's oilmen constructed makeshift refineries and transportation containers. But, in other aspects, when Yumen was short of resources on the margins, technocratic management on the margins turned back to the center for vital help with the recruitment of engineers and training of technicians and workers.

In all of these respects, the central government in Chongqing was involved from the top down, and the engineers, staff, and workers had a degree of autonomy in Yumen at a distance from Chongqing. This indicated that, though the wartime Nationalist government was strong and centralized, neither the Chongqing center nor the Yumen periphery had total control and their mutual accommodation provided supplies and financing from Chongqing while leaving room for the oilmen at Yumen to solve their technical and managerial problems imaginatively. The Nationalist government and its oilmen met the wartime needs for oil by establishing a dynamic tension between Chongqing at the center and Yumen on the margins.

NOTES

1. Zhang Shuyan, *Yumen youkuang shi 1939–1949* [A history of Yumen oil field: 1939–1949] (Xi'an: Xibei daxue chubanshe, 1988), 1.

2. *Zhongguo lianyou gongye* [China oil-refining industry] (Zhongguo: Shiyou gongye chubanshe, 1989), 30.

3. Zhang Shuyan, *Yumen youkuang shi*, 24.

4. Yumen shi difang zhibian zuanweihui, ed., *Yumen shi zhi* [A gazetteer of Yumen City] (Beijing: Xinhua, 1991), 163.

5. Zhongguo lianyou gongye, ed., *Zhongguo lianyou gongye*, 31.

6. Shen Lisheng, *Zhongguo shiyou gongye fazhan shi* [The developmental history of China's petroleum industry] (Beijing: Shiyou gongye chubanshe, 1988), 85.

7. Shen Lisheng, *Zhongguo shiyou gongye fazhan shi*, 33–34.

8. Zhang Shuyan, *Yumen youkuang shi*, 13.

9. Shi Baohang, *Zhongguo shiyou tianranqi zhiyuan* [China's oil and natural gas resources] (Beijing: Shiyou gongye chubanshe, 1999), 10.

10. Lim Tai Wei, "Oil in China: The Quest for Self-Reliance" (Cornell University, Ph.D. dissertation, 2007).

11. Kanbara Tatsu, *Chugoku no sekiyu sangyo* [Petroleum industry in China] (Tokyo: Ajia Keizai Kenkyujo, 1991), 5.

12. Wen Houwen, Wang Zhujun, Zhang Jiangyi, Guan Xiaohong, Liu Minxing, Chen Zhuohua, Dai Na, Nan Yongsheng, Wu Qiwei, Zhang Shuyan and Wang Shuyong, *Bainian shiyou 1878–2000* [100 years of petroleum: 1878–2000] (Beijing: Dangdai Zhongguo chubanshe, 2002), 29.

13. Hubert Freyn, *China's Progress in 1940* (Chungking: The China Information Committee, 1940), 20.

14. William Kirby, "The Chinese War Economy," in James C. Hsuing and Steven I. Levine, eds., *China's Bitter Victory: The War with Japan, 1937–1945* (Armonk: M.E. Sharpe, 1992), 187–88.

15. Sun Yueqi, "Ji Yumen youkuang de chuangjian he jiefang" [Recording the establishment and liberation of the Yumen Oilfield] in Zhang Wenzhao, ed., *Dangdai Zhongguo youqi kantan zhongda faxian* [The important discoveries of contemporary China's oil and gas exploration] (Beijing: Shiyou gongye chubanshe, 1999), 153.

16. Ibid.

17. Zhang Shuyan, *Yumen youkuangs hi*, 44.

18. Sun Yueqi, "Ji Yumen youkuang de chuangjian he jiefang," 151–60.

19. David Nelson Rowe, *China Among the Powers* (New York: Harcourt, Brace and Company, 1945), 61.

20. Freyn, *China's Progress in 1940*, 20.

21. D. K. Lieu, *China's Economic Stabilization and Reconstruction* (New Brunswick: Rutgers University Press, 1948), 10.

22. Ministry of Information of the Republic of China, *China After Five Years of War* (New York: Chinese News Service, 1942), 96.

23. The Chinese Ministry of Information, *China Handbook 1937–1943: A Comprehensive Survey of Major Developments in China in Six Years of War* (New York: The MacMillan Company, 1943), 483.

24. Shen Lisheng, *Zhongguo shiyou gongye fazhan shi*, 11–12. The Nationalist govern-

ment dated the opening of the Yumen oil field as 1941. See Xingzhengyuan xinwenju yinhang, ed., *Shiyou* [Oil] (Zhongguo: Xingzhengyuan Xinwenju, n.d.), 2.

25. Shen Lisheng, *Zhongguo shiyou gongye fazhan shi*, 12.

26. Liu Mo, *Laojunmiao de gushi* [The story of Laojunmiao] (Taibei: Huaqiao wenhua chubanshe, 1979), 20.

27. The Chinese Ministry of Information, *China Handbook 1937–1943*, 484.

28. Sun Yueqi, "Ji Yumen youkuang de chuangjian he jiefang," 153.

29. Zhang Shuyan, *Yumen youkuangshi*, 101.

30. Ibid., 102.

31. Wang Yangzhi, *Zhongguo shiyou shihua* [About the history of China's oil industry] (Beijing: Shiyou gongye chubanshe, 1992), 58.

32. The Chinese Ministry of Information, *China Handbook 1937–1943*, 484.

33. Sun Yueqi, "Ji Yumen youkuang de chuangjian he jiefang," 154.

34. Ibid.

35. Zhang Shuyan, *Yumen youkuang shi*. 130.

36. Sun Yueqi, "Ji Yumen youkuang de chuangjian he jiefang," 154.

37. Rowe, *China Among the Powers*, 61.

38. Ministry of Information of the Republic of China, *China After Five Years of War*, 96.

39. The Chinese Ministry of Information, *China Handbook 1937–1943*, 483.

40. Zhang Shuyan, *Yumen youkuang shi*, 2. In the eleven years from 1939 at the first drill to 1949, Yumen produced a total of 524,000 tons of oil or 90.6 percent of China's total production from 1939 to 1949 or 73.2 percent if Fushun and other historical extraction were taken into consideration starting from the year 1904. Shi Baohang, *Zhongguo shiyou tianranqi zhiyuan*, 10.

41. Shen Lisheng, *Zhongguo shiyou gongye fazhan shi*, 264–65.

42. The Chinese Ministry of Information, *China Handbook 1937–1943*, 247.

43. Ibid.

44. Lieu, *China's Economic Stabilization and Reconstruction*, 70.

45. Shen Lisheng, *Zhongguo shiyou gongye fazhan*, 316.

46. Sun Yueqi, "Ji Yumen youkuang de chuangjian he jiefang," 153.

47. Shen Lisheng, *Zhongguo shiyou gongye fazhan shi*, 300.

48. H. D. Fong, *The Postwar Industrialization of China* (Washington, D.C.: National Planning Association, 1942), 13.

49. The Chinese Ministry of Information, *China Handbook 1937–1943*, 469.

50. Kanbara Tatsu, *Chugoku no sekiyu sangyo*, 132.

51. Zhang Shuyan, *Yumen youkuang shi*, 153.

52. Shen Lisheng, *Zhongguo shiyou gongye fazhan shi*, 313.

53. The Chinese Ministry of Information, *China Handbook 1937–1943*, 469.

54. Wen Houwen, et al., *Bainian shiyou*, 114.

55. Sun Yueqi, "Ji Yumen youkuang de chuangjian he jiefang," 155.

56. Zhang Shuyan, *Yumen youkuang shi*, 161.

57. Sun Yueqi, "Ji Yumen youkuang de chuangjian he jiefang," 156.

58. Shen Lisheng, *Zhongguo shiyou gongye fazhan shi*, 311–22.

59. Ibid., 15–16 and 321.

60. Zhang Shuyan, *Yumen youkuang shi*, 145.

61. Liu Mo, *Laojunmiao de gushi*, 86.

62. Shen Lisheng, *Zhongguo shiyou gongye fazhan shi*, 322–23.

63. Liu Mo, *Laojunmiao de gushi*, 46.

64. The Chinese Ministry of Information, *China Handbook 1937–1943*, 468.
65. Zhang Shuyan, *Yumen youkuang shi*, 145.
66. Wang Yangzhi, *Zhongguo shiyou shihua*, 42.
67. Zhang Shuyan, *Yumen youkuang shi*, 153.
68. Yumen shi difang zhibian zuanweihui, ed., *Yumen shi zhi*, 162.
79. Shen Lisheng, *Zhongguo shiyou gongye fazhan shi*, 314.
70. The Chinese Ministry of Information, *China Handbook 1937–1943*, 469.
71. Kirby, "The Chinese War Economy," 199.
72. Sun Yueqi, "Ji Yumen youkuang de chuangjian he jiefang," 154.

7

A ROCK AND A HARD PLACE

Chinese Soldiers in Xinjiang Caught between Center and Periphery after 1949

Amy Kardos

When the Chinese Communist Party (CCP) entered Xinjiang as its new ruling party in late 1949, the People's Liberation Army began a process of building and expanding a base of Chinese settlers on military farms in the northwest borderland. General Wang Zhen took the leading role in managing these military farms for the newly created Xinjiang Military District and populating them with Chinese citizens from the center of China. According to a story that one of his close associates told, Wang Zhen and his roommate were discussing what they would do to build up the country now that the CCP had come to power. His roommate said, "I will beat a hammer!" while Wang Zhen responded by saying, "I will carry a hoe."[1] This hagiographic portrayal of Wang Zhen as an agriculturalist concerned with the economic build-up of China's state farms is frequently cited in Chinese-language literature published in the People's Republic. Wang Zhen was the 359th Brigade commander of the 8th Route Army during the Chinese Civil War when he received the order to go to Naniwan and open up uncultivated land for production. According to his biography, Wang Zhen once said about his career: "My individual revolutionary career goes from opening up uncultivated land in Nanniwan to national agricultural reclamation, [where I am] still opening up uncultivated land."[2]

However, this characterization of Wang Zhen is misleading. His most effective tools for building "New China" were not agricultural but human. As a hardline military man and loyal Communist Party member since 1927, Wang Zhen was first and foremost a commander. He oversaw the transfer of millions of people to work on state farms throughout China in the first few decades of the People's Republic. The policy to reclaim uncultivated land and turn it into productive farmland in large state farms focused primarily on the areas of Xinjiang, Heilongjiang, Yunnan, and Guangdong. Of these areas, Wang Zhen had a special relationship to Xinjiang. He led his troops into Xinjiang at the end of 1949, was active in the Xinjiang Military District, and retained a special relationship with Xinjiang when he took over as the first minister of the

National Ministry of State Farms and Land Reclamation. If viewed from his perspective and the perspective of Mao Zedong and other top-level decision makers in Beijing, the process of incorporating Xinjiang into the newly formed People's Republic might well have seemed linear and peaceful.[3] But if viewed from the perspective of the approximately 200,000 soldiers of the People's Liberation Army (PLA) who implemented the policies of the Xinjiang Military District in the first few years of the People's Republic, this process was much more complicated and far from smooth. What were the experiences of these soldiers, who lived in the harsh conditions of military farms far from their hometowns under the orders of hardline military men such as Wang Zhen? To what extent were they marginalized or privileged in the process of the CCP's incorporation of Xinjiang? Did some groups of Chinese soldiers have greater flexibility or the advantage of what Philip Kuhn refers to as "cultural capital"[4] in Xinjiang? If so, why? An examination of the experiences of these Chinese soldiers complicates our understanding of Xinjiang's relationship to the People's Republic, a relationship that created both constraints and opportunities for those caught in the middle.

The soldiers who worked on the military farms included former Nationalist Army troops, former troops of the East Turkestan Republic (1944–1949), and Wang Zhen's PLA troops who marched with him into Xinjiang in the winter of 1949–1950. The groups who constituted the majority of the workers on military farms were the former Nationalist Army troops who were twice-marginalized: first geographically in their assignment to live in Xinjiang far from their home provinces, and second, institutionally, in terms of their position in relation to the PLA and the CCP. In this complex dynamic, the former Nationalist troops supported the rest of the army, mainly composed of Wang Zhen's original troops, while taking instruction from the Turkic-speaking soldiers of the former East Turkestan Republic (ETR), the independent multi-ethnic Turkic state formed in northern Xinjiang in the mid-1940s. In the meantime, these former Nationalist Army troops were serving as the main instruments for the implementation of CCP policy in Xinjiang and charged with "assisting" the supposedly more backward Uyghur and Kazakh peasants.

By examining the attitudes and perceptions of these three groups of soldiers—former Nationalists, PLA, and ETR—in the Chinese Communist settlement of Xinjiang, this chapter will show the differences between the intentions of high-level PLA officers and the experiences of the soldiers on the ground. Under the authority of their commanders, what choices were available to these marginalized soldiers? What decisions did they make and why? Were they prisoners, restricted by their role as new soldiers in the People's Liberation Army, or were they complicit colonists, tools for hammering or hoeing Wang Zhen's and Mao's New China into shape in the borderland?

A Hard Place:
Former Nationalist Army Troops in Xinjiang

After attending two months of political study, former Nationalist soldiers entered the Shihezi area for a different kind of political education—this one learned through hard labor and suffering under harsh conditions on military farms. For example, the advance team, which was composed of fourteen people who lived outside for two nights in the middle of winter, had to rely on wild fires for heat. Soldiers of the Seventy-sixth Regiment had to wade into freezing water while building canals, and they had to eat raw wheat for food. A special company of the Seventy-eighth Regiment cut down trees in the snow-covered mountains in order to get wood for construction.[5] The Xinjiang newspaper praised this endurance of hardships at the time as a great achievement—a willing sacrifice made for the benefit of the nation. Yet the soldiers in the military farms of the Manas River Valley reclamation area were not voluntary PLA troops but were members of the former Nationalist Army who had been reorganized into the PLA and put to work on military farms. How should scholars understand their experience? Were they soldiers who were voluntarily liberated from the Nationalist regime and willingly served the Chinese Communist Party? Or, were they prisoners of war, forced into surrender and then conscripted into the PLA? The answers to these questions first necessitate an examination of the process of surrender, their transfer into the PLA, and their work on military farms.

When Mao and other CCP leaders were meeting in March 1949 to decide when and how to march into Xinjiang, the region was ruled by two armies, one of which was the army of the Nationalist government based in the capital city of Dihua (later renamed Urumqi), where Burhan Shähidi had recently been named to serve as provincial governor. The northernmost parts of Xinjiang were ruled by the ETR, under multi-ethnic Turkic leaders who were then closely allied with the Soviet Union. In 1946, the Nationalist governor Zhang Zhizhong, who possessed a remarkable degree of diplomacy and sensitivity to all parties involved, was able to negotiate an agreement between the two opposing forces for a coalition government. Yet, this coalition did not last. Zhang Zhizhong relinquished his post to a Turkic nationalist whose anti-Soviet position threatened those in the ETR leadership. Over the next several years, relations between the two governments remained hostile and, in 1949, the 12,000 men of the ETR army were engaging the 80,000 troops of the Nationalist Army. It is important to note that neither government represented local vs. imperial interests. As James Millward points out, what makes this period so complex is that different groups of Xinjiang Turkic nationalists joined both the Chinese Nationalist government and Soviet sides with a variety of ideas about how to best obtain autonomy for the Turkic peoples of the region.[6]

Gao Rujie was a lower-level officer of the Nationalist army stationed in the Manas River area in northern Xinjiang. He received an urgent telegram in late September 1949 requesting him to meet with the Nationalist army's commander in Xinjiang, General Tao Zhiyue. Gao had been frantically searching for days for transportation to Dihua, but transportation was difficult to come by in the fall of 1949. The area was considered a frontline for conflicts between the Nationalist army soldiers and those of the Soviet-supported ETR stationed across the river.

Eventually Gao found transportation to the capital city but was told that General Tao Zhiyue had already left for Beijing to meet with PLA officers to negotiate Xinjiang's surrender. Unable to see Tao, Gao was given an audience with Tao's cousin, Tao Jinchu. During the course of several meetings in early October, Tao Jinchu enlisted Gao in a mission to deliver Soviet arms to incoming PLA troops. He was instructed not to inform his fellow Nationalist army soldiers of his role in what later would be termed the "peaceful uprising" of Xinjiang. Gao's recounting indicates that, though the terms of the Nationalist army's surrender were negotiated by the leadership of the Xinjiang garrison by the end of September 1949, Xinjiang's incorporation into the People's Republic was a longer and more complex process, involving a diverse group of actors working for different purposes than the desire to join in the Chinese Communist Party's vision of New China. Gao began a covert assignment to support the PLA's march into Xinjiang primarily to avoid a fight that he felt he could not win. Facing two hostile armies, one in the north in the form of the ETR, and the other the PLA, which was making plans to approach from the south, Gao felt that the outcome was predetermined. He also mentions that the Xinjiang garrison was staffed with soldiers who were not willing to die for a government that was no longer able to feed or pay them. For better or worse, their best chance for survival was to cooperate with the PLA, a common experience during World War II.[7]

Later, Gao and the approximately 60,000 other soldiers of the Xinjiang garrison were absorbed into the PLA and put to work as farmers on military state farms throughout Xinjiang where they would be required to stay for the rest of their lives. Most of these soldiers had only recently come from China to the northwest borderland in the mid-to-late 1940s and had not intended to remain after the end of the China's Civil War. Contrary to their expectations, the former Nationalist army soldiers began a new long-term Chinese settlement in Xinjiang that was intended to allow China to achieve cultural and political dominance of a region over which it had previously held only marginal control. They were not allowed to return to their native places and instead were conscripted into the PLA as part of their surrender. Their compulsory service to the new government served a purpose similar to that of political exiles in the Qing empire—bolstering the

Chinese administrative control of the new territory while also marginalizing and controlling politically unreliable segments of the Chinese population.[8]

As historians in China have recently observed, the new mission of the former Nationalist army soldiers was to "Settle Down, Take Root, and Build a New Xinjiang for the long-term."[9] They built roads, repaired ditches and canals, irrigated fields, turned semidesert into farmland, and even constructed a new city meant for future Chinese immigrants. Without this initial group of soldiers, there would have been little infrastructure to support a long-term settlement since much of the previous infrastructure had been damaged during the political instability of the decades preceding 1949. Without new infrastructure, the government could not have supported the future Chinese settlers who today comprise the majority of Han in Xinjiang. Without the future settlers, Xinjiang would have remained a distant Central Asian territory. The recruitment and work of former Nationalist soldiers in Xinjiang's People's Liberation Army from 1949 to 1955 laid the foundation for Beijing's integration of Xinjiang. Wang Zhen and other PLA leaders saw this work as an explicit continuation of a process of integration begun during the late Qing, some examples of which are discussed by Lavelle and Kinzley in this volume. This process of integration, however, was fraught with difficulties and resistance among the settlers who were the link between the center and periphery, largely due to their position as former soldiers of the Nationalist army during the Civil War before 1949. An examination of their experience in relation to other groups of soldiers reveals the extent to which their situation was more restrictive than other conscripts into the PLA after 1949.

Gao Rujie recalls the skepticism on the face of the Soviet envoy when he saw that he would be relying on a Nationalist soldier to deliver Soviet supplies to the PLA.[10] But this case was not unique. The existence of multiple and shifting allegiances among soldiers was not unusual during and after the Chinese Civil War.[11] In twentieth century Xinjiang, it was almost commonplace. Xinjiang has long operated as a meeting place of Central Asian, South Asian, and Chinese cultures and a field in which competing polities battled for control. However, many of the Nationalist army soldiers were newcomers to the dynamics of this twentieth-century great game. Gao, for example, only came to Xinjiang in 1948, though he had graduated from Nationalist Army officer school in 1939. The surrender of the Nationalist government in Xinjiang was conditioned by pressure from outside forces, such as that of the Soviet Union and the Chinese Communist Party, as well as by forces resulting from the Nationalist government's inability to logistically support the soldiers in the face of rampant inflation and shortages caused by war. In addition, many soldiers who were not as fortunate as Gao to serve as officers had ended up in Xinjiang because they were captured by or sold to the Nationalist army in western China in places such as Gansu province.[12] Whether they had positive sentiments about their employer, many of the soldiers had definite negative views of the soldiers who would become their compatriots after 1949, those of the East Turkestan Republic. The relations between the Nationalist army and the ETR troops had been tense for several years, and in 1949, they were again on the brink of full-scale war. Only after negotiations between representatives of both governments were the tensions around the Manas River area defused enough to avoid military conflict.[13]

Although facing this threat from the ETR before the arrival of Communist troops, the former Nationalist troops were still unsure of their position in the new government of the People's Republic, and the Communist leadership remained skeptical of the Nationalist soldiers' political loyalty. Following their incorporation into the PLA, they were required to take pledges renouncing their former thinking. On March 2, 1950, the Seventy-fifth Regiment commander of the Twenty-fifth Division of the newly formed Twenty-second Army, a division that was among the first to engage in land reclamation work in the Manas River area, gave a speech outlining the pledge to be taken by all officers and soldiers of the regiment, which had formerly been the 382nd regiment of the Nationalist army.[14] Among the ten-point pledge was that they would resolutely relinquish the standpoint of the Nationalist counterrevolutionary faction and reform their thinking, not fear difficulty, hardship, fatigue or hard work, and plain living.[15] The reference to hard labor and difficulty was not theoretical.

Working long hours in harsh conditions with little food to sustain them, these soldiers began the arduous task of turning semidesert into farmland through clearing brush, repairing and building canals, and plowing fields. References to "ideological" problems and incorrect thinking among the soldiers reflect the degree of hardship and discontent. In retrospect, they most remembered the hunger. According to the division commander, in the spring of 1950 in Pao Tai, conditions were extremely difficult and equipment was scarce. At that time the newly formed PLA Twenty-fifth Division had been reorganized from former Nationalist army troops, who were given three months of "class contrast education" and the "suku" movement in which soldiers were encouraged to complain of their sufferings under the previous regime.[16] The commander of the division recalled, "At that time there still were people who had not been reformed, who spoke cynically against these conditions: Eat wheat with bran, shit wheat with bran, why bother to farm wheat? Also, some people say [about the military farm at Xiao Guai, northwest of Shihezi], 'Xiao Guai is good, Xiao Guai is good ... There, people have no food; horses have no grass; hurry, [liberate] your feet and flee.'"[17]

A critical reading of April 1950 directives given to the Twenty-sixth Division exposes not just the awareness among the leadership of problems in the implementation of production goals but also the attitudes of the soldiers. An emphasis on achieving a certain kind of thinking was not grounded in the desire to create a new man but rather the desire to boost morale. The need to convince the troops of the importance of working as farmers even though they were technically now PLA soldiers implies that soldiers were not content with their new position in Xinjiang. The PLA leadership wanted to meet certain production goals, which meant the reclamation and cultivation of farmland in the Manas River Valley area. The directives indicate that the thinking and attitudes of the soldiers, now largely relegated to serve as farmers, were hindering production.[18]

The directives also included holding conferences that addressed the problems of laziness and the use of competitions to improve "enthusiasm and efficiency." These suggest that the soldiers were less than model workers.[19] These directives also concede that progress would be slow, admitting that shortcomings and mistakes would occur, with the majority of shortcomings being those of the resistance and discontentment in the attitudes of the individual soldiers.[20] Much of this discontent expressed itself, in the words of the directives, as "adopting the attitude of compliance in public but opposition in private."[21] In the words of James Scott, the soldiers resorted to using the weapons of passive resistance.[22]

Difficult conditions continued to exacerbate discontentment. The soldiers dug caves into the ground when they first entered the area in the spring of 1950. The shortage of building materials such as wood and stones was exacerbated by transportation difficulties. At that time, in the early spring, the snow had not yet melted and the ground was frozen, so they burned various types of trees and reeds to be able to dig into the ground.[23] There were a few single tents available that provided effective cover from the wind and rain, but they could not keep out the cold. Most people dug shallow holes, which were relatively warmer than the tents. Every night it snowed, so each morning people would frequently be buried in snow. Although every farm built more houses every year, new farms continuously increased as well. People who originally had already moved out of caves that they had dug were transferred to a new farm to do guidance work because they had mastered technology on their own farm. These new farms did not have barracks built yet, so the soldiers again had to live in the underground housing.[24]

Does confinement to military state farms and harsh working conditions in Xinjiang mean that the former Nationalist army soldiers were essentially prisoners of war, though they worked outside of the official prison system? Although work within the PLA teams was similar for both Wang Zhen's PLA troops and those of the former Nationalist army, the former Nationalist army soldiers were not afforded primary positions in the border defense mentioned above by Wang Zhen as being exempt from the production movement. They were collectively transferred into work teams and then in 1953 and 1954, collectively demobilized into the paramilitary and economic organization, the Xinjiang Production and Construction Army Group (Bingtuan). Furthermore, former Nationalist army soldiers continued to occupy secondary positions in the military hierarchy, not just as members of the Bingtuan, but even among the leadership of the Xinjiang Military District. In their new role as unwilling farmer-soldiers on Xinjiang's state farms, they were practically and ideologically disadvantaged in relation to Wang Zhen's PLA troops. This disadvantage was reflected in the focus on "ideological" training among the Twenty-second Army.

The former Nationalist army soldiers, in particular the departmental leaders and staff of the Twenty-second Army, were ordered by the Xinjiang Military District in May of 1950 to study the "Historical Development of Society." For almost one month, two hours a day, 270 soldiers studied this text. The high rate of illiteracy among the former Nationalist troops explains why this particular form of reeducation was restricted to the leadership of the Twenty-second Army. Interviews in newspaper reports reflect the kind of thinking that was required of the officers, one of whom said, "In the past, I believed that high quality civilizations in the world were created by a small number of scientists; having studied the history of the development of society, I finally believe they were created by workers." Another soldier said, "Now I finally know that in society there are classes and there is class struggle." "In the past, I believed professionals should control people, [and] workers should be controlled by professional people."[25] Despite these proclamations, there remained problems in the "ideological education" of the former Nationalist army soldiers. Some of the complaints were that the soldiers did not take the courses seriously, only doing enough to complete the lesson while not actually learning or internalizing the lessons. Other related complaints are that they were not able to apply the concepts and were only concerned with selfish personal interests.[26] Despite reports that efforts were made to incorporate them into the party structure,[27] these reports are unwittingly contradicted by Tao Zhiyue's autobiographical account, the former Nationalist army officer who occupied the highest positions of authority of any Twenty-second Army member in the PLA, the Bingtuan, and the Xinjiang Military District. He did not become a party member until September 1982. He received an invitation by Zhang Zhonghan in 1965, but the Cultural Revolution began soon after, which made party entry for someone with his background as a former Nationalist Party officer nearly impossible.[28] Even the most privileged of officers were denied party membership.

However, if the former Nationalist army soldiers were politically marginalized within the PLA, can they be considered prisoners of war? How did they fare in comparison to the other groups of the new Xinjiang army?

Leaders of the Revolution?
Wang Zhen's PLA Troops in Xinjiang

As soldiers who were supposedly more politically reliable, did the attitudes and perceptions of Wang Zhen's lower-level PLA soldiers reflect those of the upper-level officers who were writing policy for the new Xinjiang? To fulfill the mission to march into Xinjiang, Wang Zhen took the Sixth and Ninth Armies of the First Army Group from the First Field Army. These soldiers, who were longtime veterans that had been involved in many successful battles, were not at all excited about the prospect of marching into Xinjiang. According to Wang Enmao, a Long March veteran who would come to occupy the highest positions of power in Xinjiang, "some comrades said 'the Second Army are old troops that have several times defended Yan'an; Mao will transfer us to Beijing to protect the Party Central committee.'"[29] Wang Enmao also reported that others said, "Now that we have already come to Baoji, possibly [they] will let us go south to Sichuan to live a happy life!"[30] When the news was spread that the army's mission would be to "Liberate the Great Northwest [and] Go to Xinjiang," there were many leading cadres who did not want to go because they knew that although Xinjiang was very large, it had an inhospitable landscape with many semidesert and desert areas. They also considered Xinjiang's economy and transportation conditions to be backward.[31] Many of the later groups that would be sent to Xinjiang were essentially exiled for being politically unreliable. Xinjiang was more than a place far from home or just another military assignment. Even these first PLA soldiers who had been Communist Party members for a considerable period of time viewed being sent to Xinjiang as a kind of exile or banishment. These sentiments were not much different than those of the former Nationalist army soldiers who were sent to Xinjiang in the 1940s. It seems that the idea of Xinjiang as a place of exile crossed party lines, class divisions, and even time periods of political rule in the middle of the twentieth century, which is not to say that Xinjiang has not also been viewed by some as a land of potential economic opportunity.

Throughout Xinjiang, soldiers implemented the nationwide production movement, launched by Mao's order on December 5, 1949, that the PLA should participate in productive work.[32] Once they arrived in the Shihezi area, these PLA soldiers in 1950 worked alongside the former Nationalist army soldiers. The Seventy-third Regiment of the Twenty-fifth Division of the Ninth Army marched into the Shihezi area on March 17, dug holes in the ground to serve as housing, and began preparing to plant seeds. They were not afforded better technology; instead they were given plows that had to be pulled by several men. Newspaper reports highlighted the hundreds of thousands of Chinese acres that were opened up for cultivation by the PLA Sixth and Ninth Armies alongside reports of the acreage that was opened up by the former Nationalist army soldiers of the newly formed Twenty-second Army.[33]

The political departments of the PLA divisions fought against discontentment, particularly in response to the difficulty of the labor, among both PLA and former Nationalist army soldiers. Such efforts included focusing on the ideological benefits of hard labor, with comments such as, "I have blisters on my hands, but there are no blisters in my thinking."[34] Ten years later, Zhang Zhonghan, a PLA officer in charge of the work teams, who played a large role in the building of Shihezi city and the management of the Bingtuan, reiterated the same sentiment, saying that although the situation was difficult for the soldiers, the hard work benefited them mentally.

He conceded that ordinary people would not have been willing or able to do the work, so it had to be done by soldiers, commenting also that it was good for them to obey directives.[35]

In describing the work of the PLA troops in the first six months after arriving in Xinjiang, one newspaper notes that the PLA was implementing the policy of long-term build-up by cultivating land.[36] The work of the PLA before its official reorganization into production armies was largely concentrated on cultivating the semidesert and grassland north and south of the Tianshan mountain range, which also involved building and repairing canals for irrigation. Once the weeds and brush were cleared and the soil was loosened, the freshly planted land needed water, which was the biggest challenge in successfully turning uncultivated land into productive farmland. Reports mention the importance of building canals if agricultural production is to be improved.[37] These descriptions are almost identical to those of the work of the Twenty-second Army in the Shihezi area, which suggests that Wang Zhen's initial PLA troops that were reorganized into the "production armies" worked on military farms and experienced conditions similar to those of the former Nationalist army.

In April 1952, Wang Enmao stated that although Wang Zhen had already reorganized the PLA into land reclamation armies (*tunken jun*) and worker armies in order to build-up the economy, this order was not well understood or implemented. He noted much hesitation to implement the order and sought to diminish the resistance. Much of the resistance came from soldiers who expressed sentiments such as "Serving in a defense army is an honor; Serving in a land reclamation army is not an honor," "[I am] willing to serve in the defense army; [I am] not willing to serve in the *tunken* army," and "It would be better to return home to produce rather than being in the *tunken* army and produce in Xinjiang."[38] These sentiments were probably more likely to have come from Wang Zhen's PLA troops, who felt that even temporarily marching into Xinjiang was a form of banishment, let alone being told to become farmers in Xinjiang. But, it also marked a psychological shift from short-term goals to long-term settlement, whether the soldiers were Wang Zhen's original troops or former Nationalist troops. Though the leadership may have intended to create a long-term Chinese settlement, the rhetoric to "settle down for the long-term in Xinjiang" was actively promoted at this time in the *tunken* armies and worker armies.[39] In 1952 for the first time the soldiers knew that they would be required to live out their lives in Xinjiang. Their exile had been made official. However, these soldiers were also provided opportunities for party membership and mobility within the military hierarchy that were denied to former Nationalist army soldiers. Though they were also caught in a hard place, the pressure exerted by the center in the form of the PLA was more fluid and permeable.

Turkic Soldiers in the New PLA:
The "Nationality Army"

Uyghurs and Kazakhs served as advisors to military farms in the first few years of the People's Republic in Xinjiang, which implies that nationality was not always in indicator of ideological or institutional privilege. Ill-prepared to live and farm in Xinjiang, the former Nationalist army soldiers and Wang Zhen's troops relied on local Uyghurs and Kazakhs for assistance. Each production team recruited someone local to provide technical guidance, which was limited to the use of old fashioned plows and a Uyghur mattock used for loosening soil called the *kantuman*. So, while they had to hurry to get the irrigation system working and do the sowing and plowing for the spring, they also had to learn as they went along. In the Manas River area, the former Nationalist soldiers were sent to the new city of Shihezi for training classes as short as eight to ten days and some even as short as three to five days. The people who went through the classes immediately became the teachers of new classes in their work units.[40]

The relationship between the former Nationalist soldiers and Uyghurs and Kazakhs, particularly the soldiers of the former ETR, required much "political education." The Nationalist troops were required to learn the new nationality policy, in which they were the previous oppressors of the non-Chinese ethnicities in Xinjiang and therefore they themselves were backward. Instead of viewing the soldiers whom they were fighting the previous year as enemies or rivals, they were instructed to view them as brothers united by class. As one Nationalist soldier stated in 1950, "Whether or not relations are good is a test of whether or not our class consciousness is high or low."[41] This relationship was important because the Fifth Army composed of former ETR troops took a leading role in helping the Twenty-second Army, particularly in using Soviet technology. One report stated that a company of the Fifth Army provided 33 soldiers, 112 horses, and 14 plows in helping the Seventy-seventh Regiment for an entire day.[42] The PLA intended the political education to better the relationship between two former rival armies so that they could both meet the production goals of the Xinjiang Military District.

Relations between the Twenty-second Army and the Fifth Army still remained problematic though, for both parties. One newspaper report in 1950 indicates that the former Nationalist army soldiers who had just undergone the "suku" movement had shown an improvement in their thinking, but they were still "confused" about Nationality policy.[43] The report attributes this to "Great-Han chauvinism" (*Da Han zhuyi*), which was a Marxist-Leninist term for the belief that Han Chinese were culturally superior to other ethnic groups. The former Nationalist army soldiers were required to convene meetings to discuss Nationality policy and carry out self-criticisms. They were encouraged to acknowledge that the Nationalist Party attitude had been a mistake and that the nationality question was a class question. An important part of this political education was also the emphasis on historical roles in the Chinese revolution. The former Nationalist army soldiers learned that the Fifth Army soldiers as members of the ETR had helped the poor people's revolution while "we, on the other hand, made counter-revolutionary tools."[44] Statements also indicate that the relationship was not just about ending up on different sides of historical political movements, but was fundamentally about attitudes based on ethnicity—Chinese attitudes about the Turkic people of Xinjiang and their attitudes toward the Chinese. For example, one soldier reported that they believed that the members of the ETR army in the past did not understand reason.[45] A report about the activities of the troops in the Shihezi reclamation area stated that one of its main shortcomings was that the soldiers do not clearly understand the policies, and in particular, do not respect the lifestyles and customs of non-Chinese ethnic groups.[46]

The Turkic members of the Fifth Army also expressed discontentment toward Chinese soldiers of the former Nationalist army. Alternatives to Xinjiang's status as an autonomous region of the People's Republic of China were considered at that time by different groups, though the CCP had already decided on that course. Wang Enmao outlined and evaluated four different viewpoints concerning Xinjiang's future: an independent Xinjiang; Xinjiang as part of the Soviet Union; Xinjiang as a republic of China similar to the republics of the Soviet Union; and Xinjiang as a region with autonomy for ethnic minorities. He stated that the first scenario was reactionary, the second two scenarios were mistakes, and the final scenario was the correct one.[47] His speech is interesting not as an affirmation of the CCP's intentions but rather as an acknowledgment that three other scenarios had a strong enough footing in popular consciousness to be worth repudiating by one of the highest-leading officials of the PLA in Xinjiang. The Fifth Army was at the center of many of these discussions, particularly the ones that including Xinjiang as either part of or similar to the republics of the Soviet Union. Wang Enmao praised the Fifth Army's former ETR soldiers for opposing the Nationalist government before 1949, for being Marxists, for having a strict military institution, and for advancing in class consciousness. Yet, he also mentioned shortcomings that involved anti-Han Chinese sentiment, noting that some people express the belief that "Before it was the Han people who ruled us, now it is also Han people who govern."[48]

Not long after the establishment of the military-state farms, the party intended that the logistical relationship should change. Instead of advising the soldiers on farming techniques, Uyghurs and Kazakhs were then ordered to study and emulate the methods of the military state-run farms. Within a few years, the small farming settlements that had only recently been able to produce a decent harvest were touted as models for the peasant-run farms among the local minorities. Propaganda issued in the mid-1950s claimed the local inhabitants, that is, Uyghurs and Kazakhs living in the Manas River area, frequently went to examine the state-run farms where soldiers would show them the various production processes that they had developed. It stated that they wanted to try the machines, and having tried them, they all went back to their communities convinced that they had to collectivize, because only if they organized could they purchase machines. Instead of a local farmer attached to an army production unit, propaganda described encountering soldiers attached to local Kazakh communities engaged in agricultural production. It also described an elderly Kazakh woman's excitement at her seeing a female soldier driving a tractor. The descriptions all follow the same pattern: When the local inhabitants first saw the soldiers, the soldiers had practically nothing, and they knew nothing about farming. Within a few years, they had advanced so quickly that the local inhabitants wanted to begin learning from the PLA-run farms, the implication of which was that local peasants desired to form collectives.[49] The commander of the 26th Division also reiterated the same story of the PLA production teams being the impetus for the collectivization of local minority peasants, including using the example of Kazakh women being impressed with female soldiers who drove tractors and operated mechanical harvesters.[50] The soldiers themselves were considered labor models, and examples of their work ethic were publicized both locally and nationally.[51]

Even before the more ideological campaigns later in the decade, the shift that began in 1953 in the characterization of the relationship between the soldiers and masses was likely due to the official promotion of collectivization. The military farms were instructed to take the lead in the collectivization of Xinjiang. In spearheading the collectivization movement as model workers, despite their ironic position as having considerably less experience farming successfully in Xinjiang, the PLA and former Nationalist army soldiers were viewed as outsiders and, even according to some reports, colonists.[52] Other scholars have also indicated that these soldiers fared relatively better during political campaigns launched later that decade, such as the Anti-Rightist Movement and the Great Leap Forward, than the Uyghurs, Kazakhs, and other non-Han ethnicities of the former Yili National army.[53] In this sense, though the options of former Nationalist soldiers were limited within the administrative structure of the Xinjiang Military District, they were at least given a place within that structure that allowed them to avoid the more violent and oppressive consequences suffered by their non-Han counterparts, many of whom were purged for their Soviet connections when Sino-Soviet relations deteriorated later in the decade. Their role as the fathers of a future generation of Chinese children in Xinjiang is likely one of the reasons why former Nationalist army soldiers avoided the worst effects of the Chinese Communist Party's political campaigns. The former Nationalist army soldiers, though not categorized as such, were treated similar to prisoners of war within the PLA, which contradicts the assertion by the CCP that the settlement of Xinjiang was a linear and peaceful integration process that was worked out through high-level negotiations between a few key military and political leaders. Their negotiated surrender did not actually involve "liberation." However, they were not treated as counterrevolutionaries and, in that sense, remained prisoners who needed to undergo "reform" rather than prisoners who needed to be purged or executed.

Marriage Migrants or Female Soldiers?

These three groups of soldiers, Wang Zhen's PLA troops, the former Nationalist army soldiers, and the former ETR soldiers, worked alongside one other important group of new PLA members: recently recruited women from innerland China (neidi). From the perspective of the men in the borderland, the shortage of women was a considerable problem, which was discussed by PLA leaders as a contributor to low morale.[54] To solve this problem, soldiers who were already married were allowed to bring their wives and those who had fiancées could return home to marry them. However, the former Nationalist soldiers were in a particularly difficult situation because they had been in Xinjiang for quite a bit of time before the CCP came. According to Wang Enmao, the scarcity of potential wives had become the most important issue after 1952 for the new tunken armies. Once the tunken armies were told that they would be settling down in Xinjiang for the long-term, the issue of wives became paramount and was not easily resolved. Even in the mid-1950s reports indicate widespread discontentment about the lack of available women.[55] Not having wives was part of a larger complaint of not wanting to live in Xinjiang. Wang Enmao observed that an overemphasis on the wives issue in order to solve discontentment would be wrong: "Although some people want a wife, because their thinking still has problems, they do not want to settle down for the long-term in Xinjiang."[56] Married or not, the PLA soldiers did not want to live in Xinjiang. So why did women sign up to migrate to Xinjiang when it seemed almost no Han Chinese person wanted to? How did they react to their new situation once they arrived?

    Although top party officials such as Wang Zhen instituted a plan to mobilize women for the explicit purpose of creating a population of potential wives for the male soldiers in Xinjiang, most of these women did not know that they were coming to marry soldiers or veterans; they thought they were coming to be soldiers themselves. In a recent documentary produced by the Bingtuan, one woman recounts a meeting with former Nationalist army and later Bingtuan Commander Tao Zhiyue in which he asked them if they had come to Xinjiang for the long-term or for the short-term. She says that they replied that they had come to Xinjiang to construct the borderland for three years and that after they had done it well, they would return to their hometowns. Tao Zhiyue then responded that this situation was not acceptable; three years of building would not be good enough. He said that Xinjiang needed them, the borderland needed them, and they were needed to participate in the construction of the borderland for a long period of time.[57] Another female soldier recounts going to school after arriving in Xinjiang and receiving a notebook. Printed on the cover of the notebook was the slogan, "Settle down, Plant roots, Build a new Xinjiang for the long-term." She recalled thinking, "'Plant down roots?' Are we not going to be able to go home?"[58]

Besides deception, desperation was another contributing factor to the recruitment of women into the Xinjiang army. Stories of women interviewed by bingtuan researchers in Shihezi reveal several common elements in the CCP's mobilization strategies. They describe the recruitment organization coming to their hometown in China announcing that they were looking for women ages sixteen to twenty-two to join the Xinjiang army. Some of the women say they and their families were unwilling but were pressured to fulfill the quota set for each county. Other young women's parents wanted them to go and they reluctantly agreed. In some cases, the women describe wanting to sign up to escape their situation at home. In one such case, the now elderly woman recalled that she rejected her grandfather's proposal that she should marry an older man who was thirty-five years old. She described the beatings that she received from her father for her rebellion. In her case, she defied her parents by signing up, and local leaders had to pressure her parents into letting her go. She said that she did not know where Xinjiang was or what kind of place it would be, only that she wanted to leave her hometown.

Although the circumstances made the decision to enlist sometimes compulsory and sometimes voluntary, the women were told the same terms: that there was good work in Xinjiang and that they could return to their hometown after three years. These terms of their recruitment were later changed when they were told that the party needed them to stay in Xinjiang. As mentioned earlier, from the beginning the party leaders intended that these women would be wives to the soldiers already in Xinjiang and thereby be part of a new group of permanent settlers.

To further entice women, work teams promised bright opportunities such as going to the Soviet Union to study or become actresses in the PLA.[59] However, not everyone was deceived. Some received more accurate non-official information. One woman, Liu Yuxia, went with her neighbor to town to listen to the recruiting cadre. The recruiting cadre told her that Xinjiang had electricity and telephones and huge fields of white rice so that she would be able to eat whenever she wanted. Both she and her neighbor decided to enlist. Her neighbor's father, however, objected. He said that in Xinjiang people ride camels all day, and there are snakes all over the ground. Also, people in Xinjiang eat camel meat. Liu Yuxia recounts that she was afraid to eat such meat because she feared she would throw up after one bite. However, she thought that she could avoid eating it if only she could eat the plentiful white rice. She remembers that her neighbor's father also said that they would not be allowed to be soldiers. Instead, they would be given to others to be wives. He told her that one female soldier would be divided among six crippled army men. Liu Yuxia says that she did not know from where he was getting his information, but his daughter did not dare go. In her village, only two people went, Liu Yuxia and a widow.[60]

Why did she decide to go when she was pressured not to enlist? The reason she gave was that her family was poor and did not have enough to eat, particularly since her father and grandfather had passed away. Many women who decided to go had similar situations. They describe large families with not enough to eat and unstable work. Liu Yuxia also mentions that when her neighbor told her about the recruitment process, she wanted to go because being a soldier was a great honor.[61] Several women also mentioned the honor of being a soldier as an incentive.

Another woman named Liu Kuizhen claims that she enlisted because she did not think the matter through. Both her parents were CCP members and had four daughters and one son. Liu Kuizhen says that at that time, their situation was not that bad. They had enough to eat and she even attended elementary school. In 1952, the recruitment organization came to Shandong. They left a notice in her county that said they were recruiting unmarried young women ages 16 to 22 and that the standards of eligibility were very strict. At that time, her mother was a cadre and asked Kuizhen if she would go. Kuizhen said she would. In reflecting on her response, Kuizhen says, "At that time, people's thinking was all very simple; we did not consider it very much."[62] Her mother told her to find a companion to accompany her. She found a friend who did not hesitate to go because her family had eight young children and was very poor.

Other women were pressured to go through their school even though they were not willing. One woman recounted that if someone went to Xinjiang, a place that she says people in the south describe as being at the end of an 8,000-mile road, that person would be considered a real adventurer. She says that of those young students who went, neither their families, friends, nor their classmates were willing to give consent or approval.[63] Still, they were required to go.

These stories are generally consistent with three groups identified by James Gao as those who responded to these recruitment techniques. The first were students who were middle school or college graduates. Although he states that these students went largely for ideological reasons, many of them did not want to go at all but were pressured by family or school officials. The second were young women from large, poor families who had few opportunities for education and decent work, which indicates that in some cases Xinjiang was a place of escape and, possibly, self-reinvention. The third group of women came from families of landlords, rich peasants, the Nationalist Party military, or other family backgrounds that were considered shameful,[64] reinforcing the longstanding image of Xinjiang as a place of political exile. Although Gao does not mention it, most were pressured by local institutions or deceived by the terms offered by recruiters. Most of the migrants who went to Xinjiang after 1949 were met with circumstances that went beyond their expectations. These new female PLA soldiers not only found a harsh climate, foreign local culture, and difficult work conditions, they also were placed in an unexpected role as new spouses and given the responsibility of creating the future generations of settlers.

Though women had separate underground housing, they worked alongside men in the fields as part of the implementation of the production movement. In a published interview in the Shihezi area, a female soldier mentioned a production song called "Build a Garden on the Gobi." Despite an overly romanticized view of their role in the production movement, the song is notable for its characterization of their situation as completely lacking in basic necessities and resources, from tools, housing, and food to even arable land:

> No tools, we make them by ourselves; No farmland, we reclaim uncultivated land; No houses, we build them ourselves; No vegetables, we hunt wild sheep! Two hands that are working are sufficient to reverse heaven and earth, On the shore of the Gobi [we] build a garden. Build irrigation canals, make embankments, 3 days and 3 nights we never close our eyes, freedom is spread, the spring of happiness never ceases to flow. Two hands that are working are sufficient to reverse heaven and earth, On the shore of the Gobi [we] build a garden.[65]

The author did not arrive in Xinjiang until 1954, meaning that the conditions had not improved much by that time in contrast to official reports that portray all problems as having been solved after a first few years of suffering. Even if written before 1954, the female soldier presents the song as descriptive of her experience. In reflecting on the work, Liu Kuizhen mentioned the arduous tasks that they performed. They burned uncultivated grassland, plowed soil, and fertilized it. In addition to their work in reclaiming uncultivated land alongside the former Nationalist army troops, they were also expected to find husbands among them and to fulfill their main purpose as stated by Wang Zhen in 1951: to serve as good wives and mothers for the sons and grandsons who would be the future generations of Han settlers in the New Xinjiang.

The following stories reveal a different layer of authority and control as it was exercised over these women by Party cadres in their companies. After two years of working, Kuizhen's friend, Cuixiang, was very unhappy. She had many suitors but they were much older, and she pined for a handsome young singing instructor whose name she did not even know; she had only caught a glimpse of him on the train ride to Xi'an. Kuizhen recalled that one night in the room that they shared, Cuixiang was despairing about her situation, telling Kuizhen that she never sees the singing instructor and that she misses her family. The next day, Cuixiang was gone. Kuizhen was so distraught that she could not eat or sleep. A group of people organized a search but could not find her. Finally, one day, a male soldier had trouble drawing water from a well and, upon investigating the problem, he found the body of Cuixiang. The recommendation of the group leader to Kuizhen after her friend's tragic death was that Kuizhen should marry.

Marriage was arranged by local company leaders. In a published account, one woman from Shandong, Wang Qiaoling, described her Hunan friend and fellow worker, Tang Meizi, sneaking over to the Fourth Company to find fellow Hunan people. Wang Qiaoling heard that Tang Meizi and the Fourth Company commander were romantically involved. Unfortunately, their company's assistant commander, who was over thirty years old and was physically described by Qiaoling in an unflattering manner, had taken an interest in Tang Meizi and repeatedly, with the help of the party leader, tried to convince her to marry him. She ended up marrying the assistant company leader; Wang Qiaoling was transferred to the Fifth Company.

In discussing her own marriage, Wang Qiaoling says that she was unable to escape the same fate of Tang Meizi. She was introduced by the political leader to a man who was thirteen years older, whom she describes as having an unclean beard. She was unwilling and angrily shouted, "I'll curse anyone who dares to introduce me to a lover!" [66] She ran out, but in the following days people in her organization tried to get her to see that she was mistaken. She was called in for another meeting with the political leader, who left her alone with the man who she was supposed to marry. She asked the man, "I don't know you, how can I have an opinion toward you?" [67] After that, they did not speak. When the political leader finally returned, he told her to place her handprint on a form. Confused, she did as he suggested, later finding out it was a marriage registration form. She explains that her company decided that she would marry on May 1 along with four other couples whom she did not know. The night after her wedding, she sneaked off to the fields to cry. Her marriage was an unhappy one. She gave birth to two daughters, after which her husband beat her, denied her food, and treated her poorly because he wanted a boy. After she finally gave birth to a son, she says that he no longer abused her and that her marriage became better. She tried to divorce him in 1961 because of the physical abuse but he would not agree to it.

In published collections of their stories, this initial group of women is often said to have been forced into undesirable marriages with men who were older, less educated, and/or from different native places. Some women developed relationships that grew out of mutual affection but that was a privilege that most did not experience until the initial group of older former Nationalist army soldiers had been married off. Before the settlements had above-ground housing, the newly married couples would spend one or several nights in a special room for the purpose of procreation and then return to their separate living quarters. The local party organization's goal was the creation of families—a second generation of Chinese settlers that would live on the land that they were transforming. These women signed up for temporary jobs as soldiers in the Xinjiang military and ended up experiencing two different kinds of arduous labor: agricultural work on military farms and reproductive work in arranged, if not forced, marriages.

Conclusion

Decisions about who would serve as the primary labor force on military farms and what their position would be within the PLA was not arbitrary. Wang Zhen placed former Nationalist army troops in the early People's Republic in Xinjiang in an ideological position below incoming PLA troops, who often exercised authority over the former Nationalist army soldiers. This ideological privilege revealed itself in the general institutional division between "production armies" for the former Nationalist troops and "defense armies" for the PLA soldiers.

Wang Zhen also required that the former Nationalist soldiers learn about politics and practical matters from local Uyghurs and Kazakhs, particularly those of the former ETR. Former Nationalist soldiers were therefore twice-marginalized: both in terms of their geographic location in a distant borderland and within the administration of the region. Geographic marginalization in China was not simple, but rather particularly profound in the case of Xinjiang when one's hometown was so culturally and ecologically different from one's new location. In many ways, the geographic marginalization of these soldiers caused more resentment and personal hardship than political marginalization.

While former Nationalist soldiers were conscripted into the PLA after the surrender, their leadership was placed in secondary positions of power. They were disarmed and put to work on military farms that functioned as labor camps meant to support the regular PLA, and most were continually denied party membership. Not until several years later were these marginalized Han Chinese soldiers of the former Nationalist army placed in positions of leadership during the collectivization movement over local Uyghurs and Kazakhs, many of whom viewed them as colonists. Their continued denial of positions of authority and power within the new hierarchy in Mao's China, combined with their placement on military farms working under the harshest of conditions at that time, demonstrate that they were treated similar to prisoners of war.

Wang Zhen's original troops, female soldiers, and the Turkic soldiers of the former ETR also had restrictions on location and work, but individuals among each of these latter groups became party members and were presented with opportunities in "New China" that were never available to the former Nationalist army soldiers consigned to state farms. Wang Zhen, despite his assertions to the contrary, entered Xinjiang wielding a hammer, first in conscripting the former Nationalist army soldiers into PLA work teams, and then in using them to form military-agricultural settlements that would allow the CCP to control Xinjiang's natural resources. Ironically, the Nationalist soldiers' undesired placement in military farms allowed them in the post-Mao era to become models of patriotic sacrifice and hard work in the CCP's promotion of the Bingtuan's economic development of the region.

It is also important to note that two other groups, Wang Zhen's PLA soldiers who entered Xinjiang in the winter of 1950 and the Turkic soldiers of the East Turkestan Republic were considered more politically reliable, at least initially, but their perspectives and attitudes still reflected degrees of resistance to their intended position in the new Xinjiang branch of the People's Liberation Army. The experiences of these soldiers in the new Xinjiang People's Liberation Army and their degree of marginalization in the PLA in Xinjiang depended on pre-1949 political alliances. This, rather than nationality, became the capital upon which new opportunities were created or denied, though the Han Chinese soldiers, whether members of the PLA or the Nationalist army before 1949, seemed united in their view of their life in Xinjiang as a form of exile. All four groups were among the first generation of soldier-farmers who were charged with implementing the majority of CCP policies in Shihezi, Xinjiang after 1949, and their experiences reveal that the settlement of Xinjiang and its integration into the People's Republic involved more than just top-level negotiations among different political elites. Many of the first generation of "military-reclamation people" (*junken ren*) now celebrated for their hard work and sacrifice resisted the project from its inception, viewing the orders from the center as a pressing and immovable force pushing them against the harsh landscape of Xinjiang's military farms.

NOTES

1. Wang Enmao, "Jin Xinjiang de jueding" [The decision to enter Xinjiang] in Yuan Guoxiang, ed., *Nan wang zheng cheng: jin jun Xinjiang de gu shi* [Unforgettable expedition: Stories of marching into Xinjiang] (Urumqi: Xinjiang renmin chubanshe, 2000), 7–10.

2. Zhang Yong, *Wang Zhen zhuan* [Biography of Wang Zhen] (Beijing: Dangdai Zhongguo chubanshe, 2001), v. 2, 1.

3. See James Z. Gao, "The Call of the Oases," in Jeremy Brown and Paul G. Pickowicz, eds., *Dilemmas of Victory: The Early Years of the People's Republic of China* (Cambridge: Harvard University Press, 2007).

4. Philip Kuhn, *Chinese among Others: Emigration in Modern Times* (Lanham: Rowman and Littlefield, 2008), 2.

5. "Er shi liu shi de xin sheng" [The Twenty-sixth Division in a new life), *Xinjiang ribao* (June 20, 1950), 2.

6. James Millward, *Eurasian Crossroads: A History of Xinjiang* (New York: Columbia University Press, 2007), 230.

7. Gao Rujie, "Women zou de qiyi de lu shi mei cuo de: Xinjiang heping qiyi huiyi" [We walked correctly the road to uprising: A recollection of Xinjiang's peaceful uprising] *Shihezi wenshi ziliao* 1 (1988): 18–35.

8. Joanna Waley-Cohen refers to this strategy as the Qing policy of achieving multiple ends by a single means (*yi ju liang de*). See Waley-Cohen's *Exile in Mid-Qing China: Banishment to Xinjiang, 1758–1820* (New Haven: Yale University Press, 1991).

9. Li Fusheng and Fang Yingkai, *Xinjiang bingtuan tunken subian lishi* [History of the Xinjiang Army Group reclaiming and garrisoning the borderland] (Urumqi: Xinjiang keji weisheng chubanshe, 1997), v. 1, 190.

10. Gao Rujie, "Women zou de qiyi de lu shi mei cuo de," 21.

11. See Jeremy Brown, "From Resisting Communists to Resisting America," in Jeremy Brown and Paul G. Pickowicz, eds. *Dilemmas of Victory*.

12. One informant whose father was a former Nationalist Army soldier in the Shihezi area who was incorporated into the PLA and then later into the Bingtuan related his father's journey to Xinjiang. He was originally from Gansu, but was sold to the Nationalist Army by his father at the age of 15. Interview by author, Shihezi, Xinjiang: October 2005.

13. Burhan Shähidi, "Manasi he huitan" [Manas River talk], in Yuan Guoxiang, ed., *20 shiji Xinjiang tupian jishi* [Twentieth-century Xinjiang photographic record: A look into the past] (Urumqi: Xinjiang meishu zheying chubanshe), v. 2, 26–27.

14. *121 tuan chang zhi* [121st Regiment farm gazetteer] (Urumqi: Xinjiang renmin chubanshe, 1999), 551.

15. Ibid., 551–52.

16. Liu Zhenshi, "Pao Tai shengchan" [Production in Pao Tai], in *121 tuan chang zhi,* 562.

17. *121 tuan chang zhi,* 565.

18. *Nong ba shi ken qu Shihezi shi zhi* [The Eighth Agricultural Division reclamation district Shihezi city gazetteer] (Urumqi: Xinjiang renmin chubanshe, 1994), 822.

19. Ibid.

20. Ibid.

21. Ibid.

22. James C. Scott, *Weapons of the Weak: Everyday Forms of Peasant Resistance* (New Haven: Yale University Press, 1987).

23. Chu Anping, *Manasi he kenqu* [The Manas River reclamation district] (Beijing: Zhongguo nianqing chubanshe, 1956), 90.

24. Liu Zhenshi, "Pao Tai shengchan," 564.

25. "Er shi er bingtuan shude ganbu renyuan zai xuexi cunzai qiedian cuowu" [The existing shortcomings and errors in the study being undertaken by the cadres and staff directly subordinate to the Twenty-second Army Group), *Xinjiang ribao* (July 11, 1950), 2.

26. Ibid.

27. "Tongguo jiaoyu gongzuo gaizao de liu yue, er shi liu shi bu dui qingxu tigao le: liu bai duo ren guangrong de jin dang jin tuan" [Having passed through six months of education and labor reform, the Twenty-sixth Division soldiers' sentiments increased: more than 600

people gloriously entered the party and the youth league] *Xinjiang ribao* (July 15, 1950), 2.

28. Tao Zhiyue, *Tao Zhiyue zishu* [Autobiography of Tao Zhiyue] (Changsha: Hunan renmin chubanshe, 1985), 211.

29. Historians such as Donald McMillen have portrayed Wang Enmao as a regional middleman, adapting the central directives of the national government in Beijing with the unique conditions of Xinjiang, though he was least successful during periods of increased inflexibility such as the years of the Great Leap Forward and the Cultural Revolution. See Donald McMillen, *Chinese Communist Power and Policy in Xinjiang, 1949-1977* (Boulder: Westview Press, 1979).

30. Wang Enmao, "Jin Xinjiang de jueding," 10.

31. Ibid.

32. "Er shi wu shi qi shi san tuan bu dui quanxin quanyi di xuexi li de gaijin" [The Twenty-fifth Division Seventy-third Regiment soldiers wholeheartedly study improvements in plows], *Xinjiang ribao* (April 26, 1950), 2. See also Tao Zhiyue, *Tao Zhiyue zishu*.

33. "Er shi er bingtuan chaoguo wancheng shengchan renwu, zhong zhi er shi er wan yu mu" [The Twenty-second Army Group over-fulfills production tasks, planting more than 220,000 mu of agricultural crops], *Xinjiang ribao* (July 15, 1950), 1. For analysis of yearly production figures, see Li Fusheng and Fang Yingkai, *Xinjiang bingtuan tunken subian shi* [History of the Xinjiang Army Group reclaiming and garrisoning the borderland] (Urumqi: Xinjiang keji weisheng chubanshe, 1997), v. 1-2.

34. "Si shi he er shi li shi shude bu dui zai shengchan yundong jian dang jian tuan, zhujian di jiaqiang bu dui de zhongyang lingdao" [The troops subordinate to the Fourth Division and Twenty-sixth Division build the party and build the youth league in the production movement, gradually strengthening the central leadership of the troops], *Xinjiang ribao* (May 28, 1950), 4.

35. Huang Keqi, "Xinjiang bingtuan de zongde qingkuang [The general situation of the Xinjiang Army Group], in Zhongguo dalu wenti yanjiusuo, ed., *Xinjiang shengchan jianshe bingtuan diaocha baogao* [Xinjiang Production and Construction Army Group survey report] (Xianggang: Xianggang Zhongwen shugan gong yinshe, 1970), 3-4.

36. "Zhongguo renmin jiefang jun zai shengchan jianshe guangrong chengji de ban yue" [Half a year of glorious achievements in production and construction by the Chinese People's Liberation Army], *Xinjiang ribao* (July 31, 1950), 1.

37. "Wang Zhen qinzi dao Wusu qu diaocha shuili gongcheng" [Wang Zhen personally travels to Wusu to inspect water conservancy engineering] *Xinjiang ribao* (October 26, 1950), 1.

38. Wang Enmao, *Wang Enmao wenji* [The collected works of Wang Enmao] (Beijing: Zhongyang wenxian chubanshe, 1997), 124.

39. Ibid., 126-27.

40. Chu Anping, *Manasi he kenqu*, 90.

41. "Er shi liu shi zai xin sheng," 2.

42. Ibid.

43. "Er shi liu shi qi shi qi tuan jinjun shengchan diqu hou, xuexi dang he zhengfu de minzu zhengce, xiaomie guoqu minzu diyi de cuowu" [After the Seventy-seventh Regiment of the Twenty-sixth Division marched into the production district, it studied party and government nationality policy, eliminating past nationality hostility mistakes], *Xinjiang ribao* (May 16, 1950), 2.

44. Ibid.

45. Ibid.

46. "Er shi wu he er shi liu zhengzhi gongzuo huiyi jiesu" [The Twenty-fifth and Twenty-sixth Divisions' political work conference satisfactorily concludes], *Xinjiang ribao* (August 14, 1950), 1.

47. Wang Enmao, *Wang Enmao wenji*, 82–84.

48. Ibid., 86.

49. Chu Anping, *Manasi he kenqu*, 92.

50. Liu Zhenshi, "Pao Tai shengchan," 564.

51. *121 tuan chang zhi*, 565.

52. Party members addressed such criticisms that surfaced during the Hundred Flowers movement.

53. Millward, *Eurasian Crossroads*, 239.

54. Chu Anping, *Manasi he kenqu*, 99.

55. See Chu Anping, *Manasi he kenqu*.

56. Wang Enmao, *Wang Enmao wen ji*, 126–27.

57. The interview was published in the script for a documentary film. See Hou Youquan and Yu Wensheng, "Dianji xibu" [Settling the west] (Urumqi: Xinjiang dianzi yinxiang chubanshe, 2004).

58. Zhu Qiude, et. al, *Xibu nüren shiqing: Fu Xinjiang nübing rensheng mingyun gushi koushu shilu* [The experiences of western women: Oral record of stories of the lives of Xinjiang's female soldiers] (Beijing: Jiefang jun wenyi chubanshe, 2001), 362.

59. See Gao, "Call of the Oases."

60. Zhu Qiude, et al, *Xibu nüren shiqing*, 194.

61. Ibid.

62. Ibid., 66.

63. Hou Youquan and Yu Wensheng, 35.

64. See Gao, "Call of the Oases."

65. Zhu Qiude, et al, *Xibu nüren shiqin*, 69.

66. Ibid., 233.

67. Ibid., 234.

II

Margins in Relation to Centers

8

REFORM IS A BONUS

The Networking of Upper-Level Officials in the Last Decade of the Qing Dynasty

Elya J. Zhang

Center and margins are usually interpreted in a spatial sense in Chinese studies, with the center referring to the capital (seat of the central government) and the margins referring to the frontiers (e.g., Xinjiang). Many of the chapters in this volume reflect this orientation. I would like to take a slightly different approach to the center-margins relationship by applying it to political relationships.

The literal meanings of center and margins are sometimes conceived in terms of the important and the peripheral. These are relative terms that reflect one's research priorities. Center and margins thus most often find form in relationships such as capital-province, province-locality, or metropole-colony. If, for example, the central government is established as one pole (the center), another pole or margin within this political system can be conceived as the body of the personal activities and priorities of provincial governors.

This chapter focuses on provincial-level interaction, which is the basis of my research on the last decade of the Qing dynasty (1900–1911). The literature on this decade often emphasizes two things. First, reform is identified as the indispensable and general trend. Reform is the center around which all other activities revolve. The New Policy (Xinzheng) period as a whole is cast as an exciting decade when the whole country earnestly carried out reform under the leadership of the Qing court and radical institutional changes took place in arenas like education, finance, and culture. This period is reconsidered in the first part of this chapter.

Second, in terms of identifying the concentration of political power, either the central government or the local government is identified as the axis of decision-making and political life in Qing China. The first is the purview of court-centered history; the latter is the purview of local history. But could there have been an alternative core of political life that was not local, yet could affect both local-level decisions and national affairs? The second part of this chapter examines this possibility by exploring the cross-provincial networks that enabled, in this case, a viceroy hundreds of miles away to manipulate a dispute in a treaty port, thus mediating and ultimately controlling the flow of information between the capital, the treaty port, and even foreigners. Might there have been an alternative center that was rooted in what otherwise appears marginal—that is, in the personal activities of provincial governors?

In short, what has been considered central (or most important) up to now has been institutional change, and what is marginal (or less important) is the organization of personal relationships, such as relationships between governors. The existence of the institutional agenda is not disputed, but it is argued here that networks were more important than institutions in the Chinese political system in the early twentieth century and should therefore be at the center of this analysis.

Reform as a Bonus

Toward the end of the Qing, governors and viceroys had concentrated the control of finance, personnel, law and the army in their hands, and had made provincial treasurers and judges merely their subordinates, a subject taken up in many biographies.[1] Their interactions with each other, the court, subordinates and the urban elites were vital for any reform project. A look at scholarly articles and books often reveals that a section on "reform" is almost a matter of course. Such sections invariably note an official's contributions in setting up schools, building railway lines, promoting trade, etc.

However, was commitment to reform really a necessary credential for provincial officials? How central a part did reform play in their roles as governors, or in their ability to gain and keep office? To answer these questions, we should begin with the basic facts of political life and examine how a high official managed to hold his position in the first place. The rise to a first- or second-rank position required years of effort, careful networking, and a lot of luck. Several unique characteristics of the provincial positions emerged from a close reading of the list of metropolitan officials and provincial high officials during the late Qing period. To some extent, a seat in the upper echelon of the government was a tenured position. There was no term limit for officials at or above the second rank, whereas there was a two- to three-year limit for the lower officials. Those ranked governor or higher were rotated less frequently than those below them, barring personal or professional misdeeds. As R. Kent Guy points out in his research on how provincial governors were indicted during the Qing, "The Chinese government's treatment of the misdeeds of its provincial governors had to be both exemplary and publicly proclaimed," and "in a real sense the dynasty's survival depended on its maintaining the appearance of a regular and exemplary treatment of civil servants."[2] In general, the higher the position, the less frequently one was replaced.

However, great advantages also led to high stakes. In not a single case was a first- or second-rank official guilty of wrongdoing punished by demotion. He was simply fired outright. Some managed to get reinstated within a few years but there was not much middle ground between high official and commoner. Members of the upper echelon of the government could not afford to commit wrongdoings that would lead to dismissal.

Table 1 presents a list of dismissed high-ranking officials along with the written and unwritten reasons behind these dismissals. The high officials here include the grand councilors, viceroys, and governors. From the personnel roster of all the governors, viceroys, and grand councilors during the last thirty years of the Qing (1880–1910), only those who met the following criteria were selected: (1) this was their last position, and (2) they did not die in office. This left 131 officials. Among these, excluded were those who were honorably retired because of age—as shown by the award of a temple name. Also excluded were officials who were honorably retired due to health failure (i.e., those who died of illness within two years of their retirement date). The final list of sixty-two officials is shown in the Appendix. Table 1 is a statistical tally of the Appendix.

Table 1. Statistical Tally of the Dismissed Governors, Viceroys, and Grand Councilors from 1881 to 1910

Reason for Dismissal	People	%	Reason for Dismissal	People	%
Boxers	8	12.9%	Expendable	2	3.2%
Power struggle	7	11.3%	Fiscal shortfall	2	3.2%
Riot/Uprising/Bandits	7	11.3%	Offended Cixi	2	3.2%
1884–1885 Sino-French war	6	9.7%	1895 Sino-Japanese war	2	3.2%
1898 Hundred Day Reform	5	8.1%	Forging documents	1	1.6%
Natural disaster	5	8.1%	Judiciary complaints	1	1.6%
Death of missionaries	3	4.8%	Tax complaints	1	1.6%
Corruption	2	3.2%	Unspecified	8	12.9%

Sources:
1. Zhao Erxun et al., *Qing shigao* [Draft of Qing history] (Beijing: Zhonghua shuju, 2006).
2. Zhongyang yanjiuyuan lishi yuyan yanjiusuo et al., *Qing shilu* [Veritable records of the Qing dynasty] (Taipei: Zhongyang yanjiuyuan jisuan zhongxin, 2000], http://nrs.harvard.edu/urn-3:hul.eresource:qingshil.

As we can see from the table there were fifteen general categories of wrongdoing that led to dismissal. Yet the inability to carry out reform was not one of them. A total of 33.87 percent of the dismissals were caused by four major events: the Sino-French war in 1885; the Sino-Japanese war in 1895; the Hundred Days Reform in 1898; and the Boxer debacle in 1900. In the first two cases, when a war was lost, heads rolled. No matter what roles those dismissed officials had actually played in the war, the official records were full of justifications, such as "poor leadership," "unauthorized absence," and "cowardice." These officials were not necessarily incompetent; they just had the misfortune of being at the wrong place at the wrong time. As for the Hundred Days Reform, since the emperor was excluded from the accountability picture, it is not surprising that five high-ranking officials were sacked. The Boxer debacle directly led to the biggest political reshuffle in late Qing history. For these dismissed officials, events like the four mentioned above were not developments they could have expected or prepared for. The remaining eleven situations were much more common, even though mismanagement of them could lead to dismissal.

The governors and viceroys were aware of these eleven pitfalls. To maintain their positions, they would have had to commit a large fraction of their available resources to prevent these problems from getting out of control. Providing security for missionaries required close monitoring; the same went for dike quality. With several millions of people under one's jurisdiction, legal appeals, tax complaints, and potential riots had to be dealt with quickly since they could happen at any time. To make a reform agenda more important than these basic concerns was unwise in terms of maintaining one's position. Furthermore, due to its high-cost, reform often increased the likelihood of corruption, fiscal shortfall, and tax complaints.

The first challenge of reform for governors was the extra demand it placed on revenues, a demand that impinged on normal expenses. This was even harder during the last decade of the Qing because the Boxer Indemnity alone had cut a huge share out of provincial revenues. On average each province paid a million taels of silver out of its treasury for reparations. Some provinces paid more than two million. Table 2, originally composed by Chinese scholar Shen Xuefeng, shows the percentage of Boxer reparation payment and foreign debts in provincial revenues in 1910. In Anhui, Fujian, Jiangsu, and Jiangxi, the payment amounted to one-third of total provincial revenues.

Reform projects were no less costly than the payment of reparations and foreign debts. In Hubei, under Zhang Zhidong's jurisdiction, as early as 1900 the expense of the Hubei arsenal had already reached 839,170 taels of silver.[3] The cost of building schools totaled 700,000 taels in 1905. In Zhili, under Yuan Shikai's jurisdiction, the Beiyang arsenal cost 2,020,244 taels in the five years

Table 2. Percentage of Boxer Reparations and Foreign Debts in Provincial Revenue in 1910 (unit: tael of silver)

Province	A: Total Revenue (in taels)	B: Boxer Reparation and Foreign Debts (in taels)	B/A (%)
Anhui	4,997,800	1,805,930	36.1
Fujian	5,061,163	1,611,854	31.8
Gansu	3,805,956	355,637	9.3
Guangdong	23,201,957	4,771,768	20.6
Guangxi	4,470,000	610,250	13.7
Henan	9,741,000	1,865.,655	19.2
Hubei	1,3545,147	2,567,739	19.0
Hunan	7,661,153	1,430,651	18.7
Jiangsu (Ning part)	25,741,937	4,444,697	17.3
Jiangsu (Su part)	9,834.,751	3,424,991	34.8
Jiangxi	7,432,925	2,955,967	39.8
Shaanxi	4,213,510	996,592	23.7
Shanxi	8,188,561	1,327,421	16.2
Sichuan	23,676,100	3,885,972	16.4
Zhejiang	14,289,452	3,451,590	24.2
Zhili	25,335,170	1,036,559	4.1

Source: Shen Xuefeng, *Wanqing caizheng zhichu zhengce yanjiu* [Study on the expense policies of the late Qing government] (Beijing: Zhongguo renmin daxue chubanshe, 2006), 96.

from 1903 to 1907.[4] In Jiangxi, under Duanfang's jurisdiction, exploration of the Ganzhou bronze mine alone cost 400,000 taels from 1905 to 1907.[5] Meanwhile, around five to seven hundred students were sent to study abroad. Students who incurred the least expenses—those sent to Japan—cost 700 taels each, and the ones in the United States and Europe cost double or even triple that amount. Table 3 shows the deficits in several provinces in 1908. The provinces with the most reform projects, such as Hubei and Zhili, also showed the biggest deficits.

Table 3. Fiscal Deficit in the Provinces in 1908 (unit: tael of silver)

Province	Revenue	Expense	Deficit
Anhui	6,,006,000	6,741,000	735,000
Gansu	3,121,000	3,290,000	169,000
Guangxi	4,890,000	4,992,000	102,000
Hubei	16,545,000	18,521,000	1,976,000
Hunan	6,028,000	6,424,000	396,000
Jiangxi	7,569,000	7,895,000	326,000
Jilin	4,858,000	5,355,000	497,000
Xinjiang	3,172,000	3,340,000	174,000
Yunnan	6,011,000	6,983,000	972,000
Zhili	21,658,000	23,574,000	1,916,000

Source: Shen, *Wanqing caizheng zhichu zhengce yanjiu*, 46.

Fiscal shortfalls of this sort could have justified the dismissal of a governor. The increasing tax demand associated with reform projects also aggravated social instabilities. To prevent their grand designs from being undermined by meager funding, provincial governors like Zhang Zhidong and Duanfang generated new sources of revenues, including bronze coin making and interprovincial opium customs.[6] For instance, Hubei earned 14 million taels from bronze minting during 1902–1903 and 12 million taels from opium customs during 1903–1905.[7] These innovations did alleviate the financial pressure to a certain degree but also brought about another type of tension when the court tried to take its cut.

Two examples will illustrate this tension. One was Duanfang's confrontation with Tieliang in 1904. To subsidize its central military project with estimated costs up to 960 million taels of silver, the court sent Tieliang on an imperial mission to audit the treasuries of affluent southern provinces. When Tieliang proposed that the court receive a share of the newly created revenues, including bronze and interprovincial customs, Duanfang vetoed this idea and impeached Tieliang. They held a personal grudge against each other from then on.

The other is the long-term feud between Zhang Zhidong and Grand Councilor Weng Tonghe. It all started in 1894. There was an unwritten rule that for every one million taels the province received from the Board of Revenue, the province would "contribute" 4 percent (40,000 taels) of it to the board for the officials there to share as a bonus. To fund his reform projects, Zhang Zhidong, then governor of Guangdong, cut this routine kickback to 2 percent and thus seriously offended Weng Tonghe, then head of the Board of Revenue. Weng retaliated in early 1898 by undermining Zhang Zhidong's chances of becoming a grand councilor.[8] If Weng had not been dismissed during the Hundred Days Reform, it is almost certain that Zhang would have suffered even more from this feud.

Reform was a bonus, not a job requirement. It not only increased the risks of one's dismissal, as shown above, but also did not appear to be a necessary credential for one's promotion. Of a hundred governors, viceroys, and grand councilors in office from 1900 to 1911, Li Hongzhang, Zhang Zhidong, Yuan Shikai, and Duanfang remain the most memorable names in both academia and popular culture due to their grand visions and innovative moves. However, century-long fame should not be confused with the contemporary requirements for power and fortune. The major actors on the late Qing political stage were a much bigger group than what we now remember. Let us look at the experiences of four high-ranking officials—two grand councilors and two viceroys.

Grand councilor Wang Wenshao (1830–1908) started his career by passing the highest level of the civil service exam in 1851 and gradually rose up to become a grand councilor in 1898. He remained there for almost the rest of his life. Having served under three emperors (Xianfeng, Tongzhi, and Guangxu) for fifty-six years, Wang was never once dismissed or demoted and was known colloquially as "the slickest of the slick" (lit. "loquat seed soaked in oil"). He did not even seem concerned about violent attacks from the revolutionaries. Every morning on his way to the Forbidden City, his sedan chair was accompanied by a huge, bright lantern marked with his surname "Wang." When his subordinates urged him to take the character off to protect him from bombings or shootings, he explained that he intended to make himself easily identifiable so that the rebels would not mistake him for other officials and hurt him.[9] While some of his colleagues suffered the consequences of their office in innovative ways—Weng Tonghe was dismissed outright, Li Hongzhang was shot in the cheek, and Xu Tong committed suicide—Wang Wenshao held his position until he retired honorably in 1907. The official who held the position of grand councilor for the second longest period in the last decade was Rongqing (1859–1917). Like Wang, Rongqing neither actively supported reform nor stubbornly rejected it—he never initiated the court policies, only sometimes executing them.

At the provincial level, Chen Kuilong (1857–1948) shot upward as Governor of Henan, Governor of Jiangsu, Viceroy of Sichuan, and Viceroy of Huguang, before finally assuming the most prestigious position outside the capital—Viceroy of Zhili. Throughout his career he had been calling himself a "conservative" (baoshou yipai) and avoided interacting with three groups of people: scholars of new learning (xinxuejia), overseas students (liuxuesheng), and phony literati (jia mingshi).[10] He remained the last Viceroy of Zhili under the Qing dynasty. Chen's self-evaluation could just as well apply to Zhang Renjun (1846–1917), the famous "retrograde" viceroy who never changed his stand against constitutional reform.

Like Chen, Zhang's underachievement as a reformer did not seem to hinder his career. He variously held the governorships of Shandong, Henan, Guangdong, and Shanxi. He rose to Viceroy of Liangguang and later assumed the second most prestigious position outside of the capital—the Viceroy of Liangjiang—before his retirement.[11]

Officials such as these four, though powerful in their day, are often now criticized today as "non-reform-minded," "underachieving," "enjoying the emolument of office without merit," or even "retrograde." But let us not assume that these men were doing nothing. On the contrary, they might have done plenty to make sure that nothing happened. With the rapid changes occurring around them in the first decade of the 1900s, maintaining peace was a challenge requiring the mastery of many variables. First, there was the hard fact of population pressure on all existing resources. Second, handling affairs related to foreigners had become more important than ever. A murdered missionary could get half of the officials in a province punished. Third, the court's increasing demand for taxes was pushing the masses into a corner. Even a petty clash could trigger an uprising. Fourth, the burgeoning merchant and other elite groups continued to clamor for more rights and constantly mobilized the press for support.

Here we can try to draw a comparison between a "competent placeman" and a "reformer." "Competent placemen" refer to officials who did the job but were not prone to proposing innovations. They excelled not so much in the skill of solving problems as in preventing problems from developing. The classic example was Shen Shixing, the Ming grand-secretary in Ray Huang's *1587: A Year of No Significance*: "If little could be said about his management of his office, this meant that he had kept things as they should be."[12] Such achievements were accomplished through a subtle balance of personnel and resources.

If China was like a very large house and each governor was responsible for maintaining a constant temperature in his chamber, then we could say that the chief resource at his disposal was the bureaucratic machine that acted like an air conditioner. In his chamber, there might be an oven on, a broken window, and holes in the roof; meanwhile, outside elements like wind and rain and even hail occasionally blew in to disturb the equilibrium. Thus maintaining the temperature required a huge expenditure of energy. The most passive of governors might simply leave the air conditioner running all day, using up all available energy resources. Another with more initiative might devote himself to patching the holes in the roof. It would be rare for a governor to put the remodeling projects into action without in some way jeopardizing his primary role as one who controls the temperature. Fine balancing was not impossible, but it required exceptional ability.

On the other hand, a reformer holds a vision and is visible in the forefront of his contemporaries. Late Qing reformers included Zhang Zhidong, Yuan Shikai, and Duanfang. Based on their stories and those of Martin Luther (the greatest reformer in early modern Europe) and Wang Anshi (the most famous reformer in imperial China), we can compare several characteristics shared by reformers. Martin Luther was disillusioned by the corruption of the Church as much as his fellow Europeans but it was he who undertook the decisive move to send his *Ninety-Five Theses* to an archbishop and nailed another copy to the door of the Castle Church in Wittenberg in 1517. Wang Anshi proposed the concepts of the welfare state and the planned economy in the eleventh century. Duanfang and Yuan Shikai petitioned for constitutional reform. These were the characters who set the train in motion, not the ones who followed its movement.

While a lonely visionary is a philosopher, a reformer must be able to cultivate some kind of group consensus. Zhang Zhidong's thousand-member *mufu* was one such example. Further, a reformer is not necessarily able to generate good results or achieve success in the short term. In many cases the high demand of initiating reform on existing resources may lead to brutality and economic chaos. Yuan Shikai once earned a reputation as "Butcher Yuan" for both his suppression of the Boxers in Shandong and his brutal tax levying in Zhili. Fourth, and most importantly, a reformer faces a high risk of destroying his career. Wang Anshi was permanently exiled in 1085 and died in depression the year after. Martin Luther's final statement, "We are beggars," was a mournful note on his accomplishment of Protestant Reformation. Duanfang's sudden dismissal in 1909 was also related to his push for assembling a national parliament.

The Networking Factor

The key to understanding the exceptional ability of a reformer is to comprehend the concept of networking skills. A reformer is different from a thinker—he cannot be alone with his thoughts. To realize his ideas about progress, he has to convince others, find companions, and draw from around him a consensus of opinion. Among the viceroys and provincial governors in the last decade, those with broader vision and political ambition had to have the power of networking in order to incorporate a critical mass within their reform efforts.

Network operation stands between policy and institutional change. In the case of a powerful governor or viceroy, the web of his connections could spread across the country and dominate the flow of information and the power relationships among Beijing, the provinces, and the international settlements. Duanfang's handling of the Subao case in 1903 illustrates how a networker managed to seize control of a national trial.

The *Subao* incident in 1903 was the first time in Chinese history that the government (as a legal party) confronted individuals in court. When a group of Chinese students in Tokyo organized the National Military Education Society to oppose the government, the *Subao* newspaper in the Shanghai International Settlement printed the "unusually violent and uncompromising material," which made "other radical journals of the day seem relatively tame."[13] The *Subao* articles, written mainly by Zhang Taiyan and Zou Rong, not only directly advocated the killing of Manchus but denied any possibility of reformist compromise with the government. The sincerity of reformers such as Kang Youwei was impugned as "slave identity," and "one article even hinted that if Kang assumed office, he might be in danger of assassination." Furthermore, words and phrases such as "revolution" and "oppose the Manchus" were intentionally printed in boldface, thus enhancing the provocative contents of the articles.[14] Such activity hinted at a rising radical trend in China that simultaneously targeted the Manchu ruling group and the Qing imperial system.

Upon the request of the Qing government, in June 1903 the Shanghai Municipal Police arrested six *Subao* contributors (including Zhang Taiyan and Zou Rong). The Qing government then tried to have the prisoners extradited so that they could be tried under Chinese law. The negotiation lasted five months and Chinese officials from grand councilors to the consuls of five countries—Britain, America, France, Germany and Russia— became involved. In the end the trial was held in the Shanghai Municipal Court in January 1904 with two Qing officials sitting in as assistant judges. Zhang Taiyan was sentenced to three years of labor and Zou to two years. Zou died in prison at the age of twenty and became one of the most famous martyrs of twentieth-century China. Zhang Taiyan served out his term and was welcomed as a revolutionary hero upon his release.

In 1986 the History Association of China published a collection of 198 telegrams exchanged among Qing officials on the *Subao* case.[15] A chart based on these telegrams (see Chart 1) shows Duanfang, the acting Viceroy of Huguang, as the central figure out of thirteen parties and institutions to whom 192 of the total 198 were directed.

Of the thirteen people and institutions appearing in the chart, the one who sent or received the most telegrams was not Wei Guangtao (Viceroy of Liangjiang), not Yuan Shuxun (Circuit Intendant of Shanghai), nor Enshou (Governor of Jiangsu), but rather Duanfang, acting Viceroy of Huguang. He is no doubt the central figure in this correspondence map, since 192 of the total 198 telegrams were related to him.

As a provincial governor far from Shanghai, Duanfang's "official" task was to limit the impact of this case in his own province. He did it well. Students in Beijing and Anhui had been inspired by the bold articles in *Subao* to boycott classes in a show of moral support.[16] They also sent emotional letters to students in Hubei, exhorting them to join in their cause.[17] Duanfang sabotaged this attempt at mobilization. The students in Hubei public schools boycotted classes for only one morning and were persuaded by Duanfang to resume normal class schedules. As for the students in private schools, there was almost no response to the boycott.[18]

Chart 1. Telegram Correspondences of the *Subao* Case, 1903

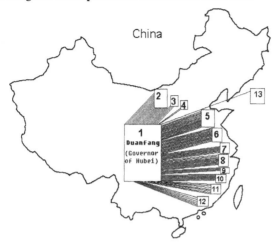

Table 4. List of *Subao* Correspondents

	People/Institution	Residence	Official Title	Telegram
1	Duanfang	Hubei	Governor of Hubei	Sent 107, received 85
2	Zhang Zhidong	Beijing	Grand Councilor	Sent 5, received 31
3	The Grand Council	Beijing		Sent 1, received 3
4	Liang Dunyan	Beijing	Assistant Controller of the Ministry of Foreign Affairs	Sent 1, received 1
5	Wei Guangtao	Shanghai	Viceroy of Liangjiang	Sent 14, received 27
6	Yuan Shuxun	Shanghai	Circuit Intendant of Shanghai	Sent 25, received 15
7	Enshou	Shanghai	Governor of Jiangsu	Sent 3, received 5
8	J. R. Ferguson	Shanghai	Owner of *Xinwenbao* (a national newspaper)	Sent 13, received 12
9	Zhao Binyan	Shanghai	Senior	Sent 4, received 4
10	Zhao Zhujun	Shanghai	Zhang Zhidong's key coordinator in Shanghai	Sent 4, received 4
11	Jin Ding	Shanghai	Expectant magistrate, sent by Duanfang to Shanghai	Sent 12, received 9
12	Zhi Zanxi	Shanghai	Inspector, sent by Duanfang to Shanghai	Sent 4, received 3
13	Cai Jun	Tokyo	Ambassador to Japan	Received 1

Source: Zhongguo shixuehui, ed., *Xinhai geming* [The 1911 Revolution] (Beijing: Zhonghua shuju, 1986), v. 1, 408–80.

Duanfang himself seemed determined to take a personal role in the counter-attack on *Subao* and its inflammatory articles. Duanfang reported the *Subao* activities to the Grand Council and made accusations against Zhang Taiyan and Zou Rong quicker than his colleagues in Jiangnan did. In just four days he had sent nine telegrams to the Circuit Intendant of Shanghai, Viceroy of Liangjiang, and Governor of Jiangsu, pressing for the immediate arrest of the radicals. And it was his foreign connections (e.g., J. R. Ferguson) that made the arrest possible. Dissatisfied with the rather lenient and indifferent attitudes of his colleagues in Shanghai and Jiangsu toward the case, Duanfang managed to pressure them into adopting a hard line through his patron in the Grand Council. Furthermore, he gathered a group of eyes and ears on the scene that included one Shanghai Arsenal official, one expectant magistrate, two investigators, and one member of the Shanghai Chamber of Commerce (see Table 4).[19] Just three weeks after his first mention of the case to the Grand Council, Duanfang's efforts resulted in his becoming the intermediary between the central court and those who should have been in charge of the *Subao* case. At the provincial and municipal levels, from Shanghai officials to the viceroy of Liangjiang, all of them deferred to Duanfang before making a decision. By directly consulting with the grand councilors, exerting pressure on Jiangnan officials, pacifying overseas students, sending aides to monitor Shanghai officials, and manipulating the media, Duanfang did not just push the case; he made the case into his own stage.

As we can see, to get the *Subao* radicals punished, Duanfang drew on all the resources at his disposal. His vast network, which enabled him to be the prime mover of a case outside his jurisdiction, consisted of thirteen acquaintances (see Chart 1). How did Duanfang manage to connect with all these people and to intervene within the jurisdiction of the officials in Shanghai and Jiangsu? The main factor that enabled him to do so was the existence of his strong patron Zhang Zhidong in the Grand Council. Duanfang surely understood this ultra important node in his network. As the sworn brother of Zhang's eldest son, Duanfang had always posed himself as Zhang's young disciple and had been following Zhang's lead loyally and devotedly for the previous three years. Support from the high court was not the only bonus Duanfang received from his mentor; he also partly inherited Zhang's connections. Two of his acquaintances—Zhao Zhujun and Liang Dunyan—became involved in the *Subao* case for Zhang Zhidong's sake. Zhao Zhujun had been one of Zhang Zhidong's top aides since the 1880s. The two had been close comrades for a long time. In 1896 when Zhang's enemies pressed a severe charge against Zhang for "selling government positions," Zhao took all the blame and left Zhang's career intact. After that Zhang kept Zhao on the payroll of the Hubei Telegram Bureau and made Zhao his key coordinator in Shanghai. From 1896 to 1903, Zhao cultivated a friendship with his fellow townsman Zhang Jian who had become a prominent member of the Shanghai Chamber of Commerce. Through Zhang Zhidong Duanfang met Liang Dunyan. When Liang returned from studying in the United States in 1881, Zhang Zhidong had offered him his first job as the director of the Hanyang Customs, the most profitable customs in inland China—a very high level position for a fresh college graduate. Duanfang's network was not just a simplified version of Zhang's. He had his own unique nodes. The first one was J. R. Ferguson, an American who had been in China since the 1870s who was also founder of Jinling University (Nanjing University), owner of *Xinwenbao* (The News), and a senior advisor to the Chinese Ministry of Commerce. Ferguson's friendship with Duanfang was a rarity among Chinese officials and foreigners in China at that time. Most officials could not speak English at all and at best had some occasional business relations with foreigners. But Duanfang and Ferguson were drawn together by their shared interests in antiques. Both of them were well-known connoisseurs of Shang dynasty bronzes. London *Times* journalist G. E. Morrison once praised Duanfang as "the greatest authority living on Chinese antiquities" and whose collection was "the finest in the empire."[20] In 1997 Thomas Lawton of the Smithsonian Museum wrote a book entitled *Two Collectors of Chinese Art*, which featured Duanfang and Ferguson's bonding and their antique exchanges. John Ferguson later reminisced about their meetings: "He left in his *T'ao Chai Chi Chin Lu* (*Duanfang Collection of Antiques*) a complete record of his great collection, but, when looking through his valuable book, I always miss the flashing eyes and nervous movements of the great connoisseur as I can remember him while handling his wonderful bronzes."[21] We might imagine Qing politics as a game of bridge. One player's hand might not be strong in all suits but it might contain a particular combination of cards or one or two suits that can change the dynamics of the game. In Duanfang's case, this was the antique card. It provided him with a solid foreign connection, causing even super elites like Zhang Zhidong to turn to him for help on foreign affairs.

Another noteworthy aspect of Duanfang's *Subao* network was the fact that several of his own nodes had developed through the Hubei governorship. Jin Ding was Duanfang's subordinate-turned-friend. With Cai Jun, the Chinese ambassador to Japan, their bonds were solidified since 1901 when Duanfang made Cai business coordinator of the Hubei Central Mint in Japan. Every year after that Cai handled orders amounting to 200,000 taels of silver and earned huge sums in commissions. Furthermore, Duanfang never trusted anybody to finish the job completely, so he made further plans within his original plans: he asked Ferguson to monitor Yuan Shuxun and then assigned Jin Ding to monitor Ferguson.[22]

Duanfang's handling of the *Subao* case provides us with an opportunity to visualize how personal networking replaced institutional operations as the central force in managing a political crisis. The *Subao* trial was far more than a case of the Qing government versus revolutionaries. Through Duanfang, a large number of parties—grand councilors, Chinese and foreign diplomats, an American entrepreneur, a British journalist, lawyers, private investigators, students educated abroad, and Chinese entrepreneurs—were pulled into this incident. Duanfang did not just act as the intermediary between the central government and its Shanghai branch. Although he resided in Hubei away from the Beijing or Shanghai circles, he made himself the central figure and marginalized the officials in both Beijing and Shanghai in the *Subao* case, and his manipulation of personal connections marginalized the institutional operations that one might otherwise expect to predominate in such a mixed trial.

Greasing the Wheels: The Position-Centered Favor Exchange System

However, no matter how significant it was, a case like this was still only one incident in a governor's busy working schedule, which included building dams, balancing the deficit, maintaining social order, and so forth. A governor's network was many times larger and more complicated than what we were able to see from the *Subao* correspondences alone. In other words, a networker's strength lay in the vast pool of coordinators (nodes) that he had spent years cultivating. And when an emergency like the *Subao* case came up, he activated some nodes from the pool and spread out his influence. Moreover, as the coordinators built up connections among themselves, the initial patron-client (governor-associate) webs were likely to spawn resilient horizontal connections. Such lower networks could even survive the dismissal of the network originator, just as in some cases of severe brain traumas neural networks can continue functioning and even grow alternate connections.

How did provincial officials like Duanfang develop such extensive networks in the first place? The last part of this chapter explores the central pillar that held up one's network—that is, the exchange of favors. Other parallels such as a common political stand and common native places though important functioned more as supplemental or balancing pillars. One's political stand, as we saw from chapter one, often shifted in line with political circumstances. And, for two reasons, the native place factor mattered little in an official's daily operation when he rose to the provincial level and above: first, his peers—governors, viceroys, and grand councilors—came from a broad range of geographic areas; second, due to the avoidance system (imperial officials were in principle not assigned to posts in their native counties or provinces), his jurisdiction would be distant from his hometown and for his own convenience he often needed to create alliances with locals in order to get things done.[23] The exchange of favors made use of the immediate resources at one's disposal and enabled connections that could be carried on despite the change of time and place.

The major "favor" that a provincial official could exchange with others was not money, which would have been too blatant. It was his official position, which could naturally lead to securing control, acquiring material benefits, and achieving reputation. The trading of positions could also be perfectly disguised as an appointment based on merit and virtue. Offering of positions was widely practiced and was different from selling positions directly for money. A governor or viceroy in the last decade of Qing usually had at least 1,500 official positions under his jurisdiction at his disposal. Hu Sijing, provincial censor of Guangdong in the 1900s, noted in his memoir that in the last several decades of the Qing, with the exception of the provincial treasurer, judge, and censor positions, almost all other offices within a province were appointed by or at least needed to be approved by the governor or viceroy.[24]

A close look at the channels of the appointments of in-province officials may help us better understand Hu's comments. The total number of civil offices in the late Qing was around 20,000 and 60 percent of them—about 12,000—were in the provinces.[25] Whenever one of those positions became available due to dismissal, retirement, promotion, transfer, death of parents, or health problems, the protocol was that the governor or viceroy would be the one to name a candidate, memorialize the Grand Council or Board of Civil Appointments, wait twenty to thirty days for approval from Beijing, and then arrange for the candidate to assume the position. However, as Hu Sijing and many other scholars point out, starting from the 1870s this procedure had been shortened due to the increasing power of provincial officials. After sending out the memorials about the candidate, the governor/ viceroy no longer waited for approval from the capital but usually went ahead and allowed the candidate to take office.[26] In this way a provincial official became both the recommender and arbiter of the appointments of most in-province officials.

From how big a pool did a governor or viceroy draw the candidate and by what standards? This was the dimension with the greatest leeway. There were four ways to get into the pool of the qualified—passing the civil service exam, winning military honors, becoming a renowned senior scholar, or contributing a considerable amount of money to the court. The last one was called *juan'na* (donation-contribution), which started from the Kangxi reign when the emperor needed this extra revenue to fund his war with the Three Feudatories, and was carried on until the end of the dynasty. Besides a few key positions such as grand councilor, minister, deputy minister, governor, viceroy, provincial treasurer, judge, censor, commander-in-chief, and general, almost all the other offices had a price. For instance, in Jiangsu province in 1899, the office of a Circuit Intendant (*daoyuan*) cost 4,723.2 taels of silver; Prefect (*zhifu*), 3,830.4 taels; and magistrate (*zhixian*), 648 taels.[27] In other words, by paying the price, a clean-record civilian could join the same candidate pool with those who scored high in the civil service exam, performed well in battles, or held exceptional literary reputations. According to court regulations, such a contributor-donor would be treated equally in this pool.[28] For wealthy commoners, the *juan'na* channel, which could save them many years of mental labor and physical risk, appeared to be much more attractive than the other three. Thus their determination to "buy an office" never stopped. In the budget chart compiled by the Ministry of Revenue in 1910, the income from *juanna* amounted to 5,650,000 taels of silver nationwide.[29]

But one thing needs to be clarified. What money bought was not an actual position but rather the credentials for a position. The popular *juanna* practice naturally resulted in an explosion in the number of "expectant officials" (*houbu guan*). As the saying went at the time, "There were as many expectant officials as hairs on an ox."[30] In Jiangsu in 1874, seventy "expectant circuit intendants" (*houbu dao*) competed for two vacancies.[31] In Sichuan in 1905, a total of fifty-nine available offices, from prefect to magistrate, was confronted with more than one thousand "expectant officials" in line. Of these 10 percent were degree holders, 30 percent military achievers, and the rest paid for their candidacies.[32] The turnover of the in-province offices was usually every two to three years, and it was fairly common for an expectant official to wait more than ten years to get an actual position.[33]

Under these circumstances, the governor or viceroy became the arbiter who selected the lucky candidate from the large pool. The chances of getting a position without cultivating connections with the governor or his acquaintances were not zero but were still very small. Take the position of "circuit" (*dao*), for instance. From 1890 to 1910, there were about 180 *dao*-level positions in the twenty-three provinces in China, and they rotated every three years, meaning that there were around eight hundred opportunities for the expectant *dao* officials to become incumbent somewhere. However, Hu Sijing recalled that in those twenty years, only one person, Zhang Lüchun, obtained a position without recommendations from either grand councilors or provincial officials.[34] The odds of such an occurrence were 0.125 percent.

The governor or viceroy did not just play a crucial role in the appointment of new officials but also in the promotion of incumbent ones. The official handbook identified only two general requirements for the promotion of a local official: first, he had to have served in his current position for at least three years; second, he should have been impeached less than ten times. Since more than half of the incumbent officials could meet these requirements, the governor or viceroy was left with significant leeway to select their candidates. Furthermore, toward the end of one's term (usually two to three years), an evaluation would be drafted by one's supervisors and later sent to the court by the governor or viceroy. An official with negative or plain comments would be automatically dismissed in order to open up a space for the expectant ones. Thus, just in order to maintain one's position, cultivating a favorable impression from the provincial officials was essential.[35]

Besides the positions listed on the regular payroll of the provincial administration, a governor or viceroy also controlled two other major employment avenues for expectant officials: the governor's or viceroy's private administration (*mufu* and *yamen*) and newly created reform-related institutions. Ch'ü T'ung-tsu

Table 5. Zhang Zhidong's Private Administration (*mufu* and *yamen*) from 1882 to 1909

Time Period	Jan 1882 to May 1884	June 1884 to Nov 1889	Dec 1889 to Sept 1907	Sept 1907 to Oct 1909
Zhang's Position	Shanxi Governor	Viceroy of Liangguang	Viceroy of Huguang	Grand Councilor
Number of People in *Mufu and Yamen*	40–50	130–160	More than 400	5–7

Source: Li Renkai, *Zhang Zhidong mufu* [Zhang Zhidong's private administration] (Beijing: Zhongguo guangbo dianshi chubanshe, 2005), 300.

and Bradley Reed have both described the "one-man" government at the county level, meaning that the magistrate was the only one in his *yamen* listed as a formal official.[36] The same description can also be applied to the governor or viceroy. One interesting aspect of the provincial administration of the Qing dynasty was that the provincial treasurer and provincial judge both had their own bureaus, but a governor or viceroy did not have a regular quota of posts for employees in his *yamen* or *mufu*. These employees, hired through a private agreement, existed entirely outside the formal networks of official posts and jobs. Different from a governor's bureaucratic subordinates, they were usually addressed as "clerks" (*li*) rather than "officials."

Employment in a governor's or viceroy's private administration provided considerable opportunities for expectant officials. First, being managed exclusively by the governor or viceroy himself, the hiring was very flexible.[37] Second, the number of positions available was not small. Take the case of Zhang Zhidong: Li Renkai's monograph on Zhang's *mufu* lists the names and backgrounds of 398 Chinese and 239 foreigners who once served as Zhang's private subordinates.[38] Table 5 shows the size of Zhang's private administration in several different periods.

As we can see, Zhang Zhidong's private administration offered more than four hundred positions in Hubei and Hunan provinces during the last decade of the Qing. A look at his subordinate list shows that one-third of them were filled by expectant officials. Zhang was not the only one. Yuan Shikai, Tao Mo, and Zhao Erxun had also held sizable private administrations (see Table 6, originally composed by Chinese scholar Guan Xiaohong).

Table 6. The Structure of the Viceroy's Private Administration in the Liangguang and Huguang regions in the 1900s

Year	Official	No. of Units	No. of Staff
1901	Yuan Shikai—Governor of Shandong	44	430
1901/1902	Tao Mo—Viceroy of Liangguang	24	Unspecified
1908	Zhao Erxun—Viceroy of Huguang	24	Unspecified

Source: Guan Xiaohong, "Wanqing dufu yamen fangke jiegou guankui" [A glance at the private bureau of governors and viceroys during the late Qing], *Zhongshan daxue xuebao* 3 (2006): 58–59.

The third major opportunity for employment controlled by the governor or viceroy was those institutions newly established in the provinces related to military, economic, and educational reform programs. Table 7 (originally composed by Shen Xuefeng) presents an extensive list of the names of these institutions in the provinces and provides a sense of the burgeoning of these institutions in a rather short period of time. Just like the governor's or viceroy's private administration, these institutions were outside the formal court and provincial bureaus and were funded solely by provincial revenues. The sources do not give an exact number regarding the total number of positions in these institutions, but based on the number of institutions we can estimate that their employees could easily exceed a thousand in each province.

In light of a governor's or viceroy's strong influence on the employment patterns of the provincial bureau, reform-related institutions, and his private administration, we can see how he could have thousands of positions at his disposal. These positions served as the major source of favor-trading that he used to cultivate political connections.

In order to develop this idea further, we look at the parties with whom a governor/viceroy usually exchanged favors. Records on exchange of favors can only be found in personal letters or secret documents and are usually rare. Fortunately, the Duanfang Archives, housed in the First Historical Archives of China, collected a number of Duanfang's personal papers. From volumes 15, 19, and 29 of this collection, I have found twenty-eight letters that explicitly asked Duanfang for a favor during the first month of his terms as governor of Hubei, Jiangsu, and Hunan. They are listed in Table 8.

Table 7. Newly Established Institutions in the Provinces during the Last Two Decades of the Qing Dynasty

Type	Name of Institutions	Number
Military Supply 军需	Supreme Board of Reorganization 善后總局 and its sub-branches (12~15), Supreme Military Board 軍需總局, Bureau of Transport of Troops 转运局采运局, etc.	> 35
Foreign Affairs 洋务	Office of Foreign Affairs 洋务局, Telegraph Office 电报局, Telephone Station 電話局, etc.	> 7
Education 教育	Normal School 師范學堂, Primary School 小学堂, Elementary School 蒙学堂, Professional School 實業學堂, etc.	> 36
Local 地方	Government Newspaper Office 官報局; Sanitary Office 衛生局; Building Office 工程局; Branches of the Central Mint 造幣分廠, etc.	> 21
Various Duties 厘卡	Likin Station 釐捐局, etc.	> 40
Total		**> 139**

Sources:
1. Shen, *Wanqing caizheng zhichu zhidu yanjiu*, 191.
2. Liu Ziyang, *Qingdai difang guanzhi kao* (A study on the local administration of the Qing dynasty] (Beijing: Zijincheng chubanshe, 1988), 459–523.

Table 9. Selected Favor-related Letters Duanfang Received in Three Months in 1901, 1904, and 1905

Time	People	Position	Favor asked from Duanfang	Result
March to April 1901 (First month of Duanfang's term as Governor of Hubei)	Cai Naihuang 蔡乃煌	Circuit Intendant of Su-Song-Tai of Jiangsu Province	Duanfang's support for Cai's own promotion	Done
	Dai Hongci 戴鴻慈	Senior Vice-President of the Ministry of Revenue	Position for Dai's acquaintance Gao Zhen, expectant magistrate	Done
	Dexin 德馨	Former Governor of Jiangxi	Position for Dexin's acquaintance Luo Tingzhen	Unspecified
	Feng Xu 馮煦	Provincial Treasurer of Sichuan	Position for Feng's acquaintance Liu Qijia	Unspecified
	Huang Changnian 黄昌年	Court Censor	Position Huang's younger brother Huang Lüyi	Done
	Huang Shaochun 黄少春	General-in-Chief of Marine Forces of Yangzi River	Position for Huang's son in the Hubei Customs	Done
	Qian Junxiang 錢俊祥	Eminent merchant in Haining county, Zhejiang Province	Position for Qian's acquaintance Tan Risen	Done
	Shen Yiqing 沈翊清	Lieutenant-Colonel of Ministry of War	Position for Shen's acquaintance Lin Zijing, expectant prefect	Done
	Sun Jianai 孫家鼐	Grand Councilor	Position for Sun's acquaintance Lu Yuren	Done
	Wang Yanwei 王彥威	Secretary of the Grand Council	Position for Wang's acquaintance Jin Mengsong, expect magistrate	Done
	Wei Guangtao 魏光燾	Viceroy of Liangjiang	Position for Wei's acquaintance Benkui, expectant magistrate	Done
	Wu Zhaotai 吳兆泰	Court Censor	Position for Wu's son Wu Bao	Done
	Xilun 錫綸	Tartar General Military Governor of Ili	Position for Xilun's acquaintance Sun Rong, expectant magistrate	Done

Time	People	Position	Favor asked from Duanfang	Result
March to April 1901 (First month of Duanfang's term as Governor of Hubei)	Yi Shunding 易順鼎	Provincial Censor of Guangdong	Position for Yi's acquaintance Hu Shurong, expectant magistrate	Unspecified
	Yun Yuding 惲毓鼎	Chancellors of the National Academy	Position for Yun's former servant Yang Ming	Done
	Zhang Baixi 張百熙	Minister of Civil Appointments	Position for Zhang's acquaintance Zhang, expectant Lieutenant	Done
	Zhang Xunhe 張荀鶴	Provincial Censor of Shandong	Position for Zhang's younger brother Zhang Yinzha	Done
	Zhang Yinglin 張英麟	Junior Vice-President of the Ministry of Civil Appointments	Position for Zhang's acquaintance Zeng, expectant magistrate	Done
	Long Dianyang 龍殿揚	General of the Ministry of War	Position for Long's acquaintance Wang Zhiping.	Done
May to June 1904 (First month of Duanfang's term as the Governor of Jiangsu)	Ding Zhenduo 丁振鐸	Governor of Shanxi	Position for Ding's acquaintance Feng Yingshu, expectant magistrate	Done
	Kungang 昆岡	Grand Councilor	Position for Kungang's acquaintance Zhang Shouyong, expectant magistrate	Done
	Lü Peifen 呂佩芬	Compiler of the First Class of the National Academy	Position for Lü's brother-in-law Lü Qianji	Unspecified
	Yang Zonglian 楊宗濂	Director of Zhili Arsenal	Position for Yang's nephew Yang Qichang	Done
	Zeng Guanghan 曾廣漢	Senior Vice-President of the Board of Rites	Position for Zeng's younger brother Zeng Guangjun	Done
	Zhang Renjun 張人駿	Governor of Guangdong	Position for Zhang's disciple Wang Wanzhen, expectant circuit intendant	Done

Time	People	Position	Favor asked from Duanfang	Result
Dec 1904 to Jan 1905 (First month of Duanfang's term as the Governor of Hunan)	Cheng Wenbing 程文炳	General-in-Chief, Marine Forces of Yangzi River	Position for Cheng's acquaintance Lin Zhaoxiong	Done
	Chuo Habu 綽哈布	General-in-Chief, Hubei Brigade	To send a join-memorial for the promotion of Liang Dingfen, expectant circuit intendant	Unspecified
	Lü Haihuan 呂海寰	Minister of Works	Petition to let Lü's former teacher Li Shiying stay in his current prefect position for another term	Done

Source: Dunfang Archives, Collection IV, *Han* (Correspondences), vols. 15, 19, and 29.

As we can see, these letters were sent by a broad range of officials, from grand councilor, minister, court censor, lieutenant-colonel, and national academy scholar in Beijing, to the viceroy, governor, general-in-chief, and financial commissioner in the provinces. The main theme running through these letters was "to find someone a job." Readers might ask why those powerful officials in the central bureau, some of them as high up as a grand councilor, chose to ask Duanfang for help instead of finding a position for their acquaintance or relative in Beijing. The truth of the matter is that officials in Beijing, no matter how high their rank, quite simply did not have as much direct access to the appointment process as provincial officials. Table 5 also shows that when Zhang Zhidong was transferred back to Beijing, the number of his subordinates dropped from more than four hundred to five because Zhang could no longer allocate provincial revenue to pay his personal staffs. Further, it was widely known that the income of officials in Beijing, especially that of the lower officials, was much less than the income of their counterparts in the provinces. They were often in desperate need of "bestowals" from officials in the provinces in order to make a living.[39] Due to this material reality, most expectant officials wanted to begin their careers in the provinces. This also helps explain why high-ranking officials in the court needed to ask governors such as Duanfang for help in appointing their acquaintances. Another noteworthy point was that Duanfang received more requests for favors when he was Governor of Hubei than when he governed Jiangsu and Hunan. This is related to the fact that Hubei, where Zhang Zhidong had been working for a decade, was at the forefront of every reform program. Consequently, there were more job opportunities in Hubei both in the governor's private administration and in the reform-related institutions.

On each letter listed in Table 8, Duanfang, or possibly his secretaries, had written the comment, "important letter" (*yaohan*). All but four of the people recommended in these letters obtained positions within a short period, a fact evident in later correspondence. For the four who were not immediately appointed, Duanfang sent letters to their recommenders and promised that he would find employment for these people as soon as positions became available. Through these appointments, Duanfang strengthened his connections to supervisors in the court (officials in the Grand Council, Ministry of War, and Civil Appointments) as well as with men in other provinces (Zhili, Jiangsu, Zhejiang, Guangdong, Shandong, and Xinjiang).

However, the exchange of favors centered around positions was also a double-edged sword. On the one hand, having close connections with a number of supervisors and colleagues not only helped a governor or viceroy to secure his place and move up the court ladder but also saved him a considerable amount of internal conflict and smoothened the implementation of his various projects— including reform. On the other hand, the burgeoning number of positions created enormous financial pressures. Take the provincial-supported Lianghu Academy in Hubei province, for example, where the annual salary of the lowest-level staff was 250 taels of silver—equal to the price of 5,000 pounds of rice. Administrators and professors received more than 1,200 taels a year.[40] Foreign engineers and military tutors were paid even more—3,600 to 4,000 taels each per year.[41] The total expenses add up to more than 60,000 taels annually for a single academy. Other examples such as these follows: The Telegram Bureau of Liangguang posted an annual deficit of 56,000 taels of silver, with expenses of 67,000 taels and an income of only 11,000.[42] In Henan in 1908, the operation of an elementary military school alone cost 37,259 taels.[43] In Sichuan in 1909, provincial administrative expenses reached 2,500,000 taels—14.4 percent of the total provincial revenue.[44]

To visualize the inverse relationship between the financial resources at a governor's or viceroy's disposal and the broadness of his network, I have drawn Chart 2. In this chart, Point A signifies the start of a governor's or viceroy's term when the resources at his disposal were sufficient and his connections limited. From Point A to Point B, he used positions and money as favors to bond with supervisors and colleagues. As he spent his resources, his network developed and the efficiency of his political operations increased but the investment in networking, with its long-term nature, would not pay returns that soon. Eventually every networker would reach the worst point, Point B, when he perhaps discovered that he was running out of resources, the exploited masses were planning a rebellion, floods were imminent, and dams were inadequate. Furthermore, he was on the verge of dismissal. If he managed to survive this risky period, he could move from Point B to Point C and start to make his way to a positive feedback loop between resources and his networks. The reform-related projects he established, such as building factories, would begin to bring in revenues and give him more positions from newly created reform institutions or money to trade for connections. Meanwhile, with well-established relationships in both the central and provincial bureaus, his position would be secure, and his further proposals would have a better chance of obtaining the court's approval and cooperation. The link between resources and network would thus evolve into a mutually prosperous relationship. However, if he failed to survive the low period, Point B would be the end of his career. As we saw in the first part of this chapter, the official would not be demoted but simply fired outright and would lose almost all of the political credentials he had been building over several decades.

If reform-oriented networking inevitably cost resources, when might one reach point B? Among the famous networkers of the 1900s, Zhang Zhidong remained a top official until his death in 1909, Yuan Shikai got demoted in 1908 but reemerged as a national leader after 1911, and Duanfang was dismissed in 1909 and died tragically during the mutinies of 1911. For a governor or viceroy, is the track from point A to B point calculable, and if so, what major elements constituted this track, and how can we discover and evaluate them? Duanfang and

Chart 2. Investing in Networking

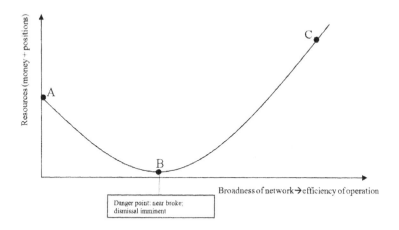

his colleagues have provided us with clues on how to proceed in future research and how to understand the ways in which an individual reform-minded governor's personal networking helped shape the course of the reform and therefore the fate of the dynasty.

In this chapter I reconsidered the centrality and marginality of several issues in the political life of the last Qing decade and suggest two interpretations: reform as a marginal qualification of high officials and the organization of personal relationships as the central factor behind institutional changes. The questions raised here suggest how we might seek a network approach to frame the complex process of the fall of the Qing dynasty and the transition to the Republic of China. If reform was a bonus and required large investments in networking, then those networks should be located at the center of our analysis, not on the margins of institutional changes.

Appendix

The Dismissed Governors, Viceroys, and Grand Councilors from 1881 to 1910

NAME	POSITION	START	END	OFFICIAL REASON	ACTUAL REASON	LABEL
Chen Baozeng 陳寶箴	Governor of Hunan	1895.9.12	1898.10.6	緣事革職	Dismissed for participating in the Hundred Days Reform.	1898
Hu Pingzhi 胡聘之	Governor of Shanxi	1895.10.7	1899.9.12	解職	Dismissed for participating in the Hundred Days Reform.	1898
Liao Choufeng 廖壽豐	Governor of Zhejiang	1894.1.8	1898.11.18	因病解職	Dismissed for participating in the Hundred Days Reform.	1898
Tan Jixun 譚繼洵	Governor of Hubei	1889.12.22	1898.8.30	裁缺	Fired for being the father of Hundred Days reformer Tan Sitong.	1898
Weng Tonghe 翁同龢	Grand Councilor	1897.9.11	1898.6.15	緣事開缺	Dismissed for participating in the Hundred Days Reform.	1898
Gangyi 剛毅	Grand Councilor	1898.6.10	1900.9.25	緣事父部察院史文部議處	Dismissed for participating in the Boxers debacle.	Boxers
Liu Shutang 劉樹棠	Governor of Zhejiang	1898.11.18	1900.11.25	開缺候簡	Dismissed for participating in the Boxers debacle.	Boxers
Songchun 松椿	Viceroy of Caoyun		1900.11.25	緣事革職	Dismissed for participating in the Boxers debacle.	Boxers
Wang Yuzao 王毓藻	Governor of Guizhou	1897.3.7	1900.3.13	因病開缺	Dismissed for participating in the Boxers debacle.	Boxers
Xu Tong 徐桐	Grand Councilor	1896.12.9	1901.1.5	自盡	Forced to commit suicide as a result of the Boxer debacle.	Boxers
Yu Lu 裕祿	Viceroy of Zhili	1898.9.28	1900.7.8	免	Dismissed for participating in the Boxers debacle.	Boxers

NAME	POSITION	START	END	OFFICIAL REASON	ACTUAL REASON	LABEL
Li Bingheng 李秉衡	Viceroy of Sichuan	1897.9.27	1897.12.11	緣事解職	Dismissed at the request of German Ambassador; two German missionaries were murdered when Li was the governor of Shandong.	Death of missionaries
Liu Binzhang 劉秉璋	Viceroy of Sichuan	1886.6.6	1894.11.19	到京另候簡用	Dismissed at the request of British ambassador for the murder of a missionary under his jurisdiction.	Death of missionaries
Ding Zhenduo 丁振鐸	Viceroy of Minzhe	1906.9.11	1907.3.4	開缺	Transferred out of his position so that Cen Chunxuan, viceroy of Liangguang, could take his spot.	Expendable
Tan Zhonglin 譚鍾麟	Viceroy of Liangguang	1895.4.16	1899.12.19	到京陛見	Transferred out of his position to open it for Li Hongzhang.	Expendable
Lin Zhaoyuan 林肇元	Governor of Guizhou	1881.10.5	1883.12.21	緣事革職	Dismissed because of a shortfall in the provincial treasury.	Fiscal shortfall
Pan Xiaosu 潘效蘇	Governor of Gansu-Xinjiang	1902.10.6	1905.9.16	緣事革職	Dismissed for a shortfall in the provincial treasury.	Fiscal shortfall
Zeng He 曾鉌	Governor of Hubei	1898.11.1	1899.1.17	緣事革職	Dismissed for forging memorials in the name of the viceroy of Shaan-Gan to propose his own reform ideas.	Forging documents
Xu Yingkui 許應騤	Viceroy of Minzhe	1898.10.25	1903.4.5	緣事解職	Dismissed for bungling court cases.	Judiciary complaints
Chen Shijie 陳士杰	Governor of Shandong	1883.1.17	1886.6.2	到京候簡	Transferred out of his position for inadequate flood control measures that became apparent after a disaster.	Natural disaster
Li Henian 李鶴年	Governor of Henan	1881.10.5	1883.4.6	緣事革職	Dismissed for inadequate flood control measures that became apparent after a disaster.	Natural disaster

NAME	POSITION	START	END	OFFICIAL REASON	ACTUAL REASON	LABEL
Mei Qizhao 梅啟照	Director-General of Conservation of Yellow River and Grand Canal	1881.10.20	1883.4.6	緣事革職	Dismissed for inadequate flood control measures that became apparent after a disaster.	Natural disaster
Ni Wenwei 倪文蔚	Governor of Guangdong	1883.10.9	1886.6.2	因病解職	Dismissed for inadequate flood control measures that became apparent after a disaster.	Natural disaster
Bian Baodi 卞寶第	Viceroy of Minzhe		1892.6.22	因病解職	Forced to resign because Bian opposed Cixi's allocation of navy funds to build the Summer Palace.	Offended Cixi
Yan Jingming 閻敬銘	Grand Councilor	1886.1.18	1888.8.23	因病開缺	Dismissed for opposing Cixi's allocation of navy funds to build the Summer Palace.	Offended Cixi
Baojun 寶鋆	Grand Councilor	1877.4.2	1884.4.8	緣事休致	Baojun was close to Prince Gong; dismissed together with Prince Gong.	Power struggle
Cen Chunxuan 岑春煊	Viceroy of Liangguang	1907.5.28	1907.8.12	因病開缺	Lost position in power struggle with Prince Qing and Yuan Shikai.	Power struggle
Cheng Fu 成孚	Director-General of Conservation of Yellow River and Grand Canal	1884.1.19	1887.11.14	開缺	Dismissed for inadequate flood control measures that became apparent after a disaster.	Power struggle
Duanfang 端方	Viceroy of Zhili	1909.6.28	1909.11.20	革	Dismissed for offending Regent Zaifeng.	Power struggle
Ding Baoquan 丁寶銓	Governor of Shanxi	1909.11.23	1911.6.18	因病乞休	Forced to resign for ordering troops to fire on peasants resisting the opium ban.	Riot/uprising/Bandits
Kuijun 奎俊	Viceroy of Sichuan	1898.7.12	1902.8.5	命开缺	Dismissed for inability to put down the Sichuan Boxer uprising in 1902.	Riot/uprising/Bandits
Ruicheng 瑞澂	Viceroy of Huguang	1910.6.12	1911.10.12	緣事革職	Dismissed for inability to put down Wuchang uprising;	Riot/uprising/Bandits

NAME	POSITION	START	END	OFFICIAL REASON	ACTUAL REASON	LABEL
Shi Nianzu 史念祖	Governor of Guangxi	1895.7.23	1897.10.14	緣事革職	Dismissed for inability to put down bandits in Guangxi.	Riot/uprising / Bandits
Wang Zhichun 王之春	Governor of Guangxi	1902.7.3	1903.7.7	緣事革職	Dismissed for inability to put down bandits.	Riot/uprising/ Bandits
Yang Changrui 杨昌濬	Viceroy of Shanggang	1888.4.6	1895.11.20	开缺回籍	Dismissed for inability to put down Muslim uprising.	Riot/uprising/ Bandits
Zeng Guoquan 曾国荃	Viceroy of Shanggang	1881.2.28	1881.10.16	因病开缺	Dismissed for inability to put down Nian uprising in Northwest.	Riot/uprising/ Bandits
Liu Changyou 劉長佑	Viceroy of Yungui		1883.5.30	因病乞休	Forced to resign; the Sino-French war was lost, so heads needed to roll.	Sino-French war
Pan Dingxin 潘鼎新	Governor of Guangxi	1884.3.26	1885.3.24	緣事革職	Dismissed; the Sino-French war was lost, so heads needed to roll.	Sino-French war
Xu Yanxu 徐延旭	Governor of Guangxi	1883.10.9	1884.3.26	緣事革職	Dismissed; the Sino-French war lost, so heads needed to roll.	Sino-French war
Tang Jiong 唐炯	Viceroy of Yunnan	1883.7.25	1884.3.26	緣事革職	Dismissed; the Sino-French war was lost.	Sino-French war
Zhang Shusheng 張樹聲	Viceroy of Liangguang	1883.7.13	1884.5.22	因病開缺	Dismissed; the Sino-French war lost, so head needed to roll.	Sino-French war
Zhang Zhaodong 張兆棟	Viceroy of Fujian	1883.5.30	1884.9.19	緣事革職	Dismissed; the Sino-French war lost, so head needed to roll.	Sino-French war
Tang Jingsong 唐景崧	Viceroy of Taiwan	1894.10.13	1895.5.20	解職到京	Dismissed; the Sino-Japanese war was lost, so heads needed to roll.	Sino-Japanese war
Wu Dacheng 吳大澂	Governor of Hunan	1895.3.26	1895.7.5	到京另候簡用	Wu volunteered to lead Hunan army into the Sino-Japanese war; dismissed when the war was lost.	Sino-Japanese war
Li Hanzhang 李翰章	Viceroy of Liangguang	1889.8.8	1895.4.14	因病開缺	Li Hongzhang's elder brother; forced to resign because of the unpopularity of his tax measure to support Sino-Japanese war.	Tax complaints

NAME	POSITION	START	END	OFFICIAL REASON	ACTUAL REASON	LABEL
Dexin 德馨	Governor of Jiangxi	1884.11.4	1895.9.11	緣事卑職	Unable to identify.	Unspecified
Lian Kui 聯魁	Governor of Gansu-Xinjiang	1905.9.16	1910.8.25	到京另候簡用	Unable to identify.	Unspecified
Niu Jigui 聶緝槼	Governor of Zhejiang	1902.10.6	1905.10.10	緣事開缺	Unable to identify.	Unspecified
Pan Hongshu 龐鴻書	Governor of Guizhou	1906.9.4	1911.5.21	解職	Unable to identify.	Unspecified
Ren Daorong 任道鎔	Governor of Zhejiang	1901.5.23	1902.10.6	因病解職	Unable to identify.	Unspecified
Songkun 嵩崑	Governor of Guizhou	1895.7.7	1897.2.24	緣事卑職	Unable to identify.	Unspecified
Wu Chongxi 吳重憙	Governor of Henan	1908.8.29	1910.4.26	到京另候簡用	Unable to identify.	Unspecified
Zhang Liangui 張聯桂	Governor of Guangxi	1892.2.27	1895.7.21	因病開缺	Unable to identify.	Unspecified

Source: Zhao Erxun et al., *Qing shigao* [Draft of Qing history] (Beijing: Zhonghua shuju, 2006).

NOTES

1. Examples include: Benjamin Isadore Schwartz, *In Search of Wealth and Power: Yen Fu and the West* (Cambridge: Harvard University Press, 1961); Mary C. Wright, *The Last Stand of Chinese Conservatism: The T'ung-Chih Restoration, 1862–1874* (Stanford: Stanford University Press, 1962); Samuel C. Chu, *Reformer in Modern China: Chang Chien, 1853–1926* (New York and London: Columbia University Press, 1965); and Roger V. Des Forges, *Hsi-liang and the Chinese National Revolution* (New Haven and London: Yale University Press, 1973).

2. R. Kent Guy, "Rule of Man and the Rule of Law in China," in Karen G. Turner, James V. Feinerman, and R. Kent Guy, eds., *The Limits of the Rule of Law in China* (Seattle: University of Washington Press, 2000), 89. Guy's research focuses on the channels through which the political officials were accused and divides them into three sorts: imperial accusations, accusations by secret memorial, and accusations by routine memorial. My writing here focuses on the misdeeds that could cause the dismissal of officials.

3. Shen Xuefeng, *Wanqing caizheng zhichu zhengce yanjiu* [Research on the financial expenses of the late Qing government] (Beijing: Zhongguo renmin daxue chubanshe, 2006), 159.

4. Ibid., 159.

5. Ibid., 160.

6. Li Renkai, *Zhang Zhidong mufu* [Zhang Zhidong's private administration] (Beijing: Zhongguo guangbo dianshi chubanshe, 2005), 300.

7. Liu Zenghe, "Yapian shuishou yu qingmo xingxue xinzheng" [Opium revenues and late Qing educational reform], *Shehui kexue yanjiu*, 1 (2004): 120.

8. Li Shisun, "Zhang Zhidong shiji shuwen" [Things about Zhang Zhidong], in Zhongguo renmin zhengzhi xieshang huiyi quanguo wenshi ziliao weiyuanhui, ed., *Wenshi ziliao xuan* [Selected collection of historical materials] (Beijing: Zhongguo wenshi chubanshe, 1980), v. 34, 73–74.

9. Li Qiao, *Qingmo guanchang tuji* [Illustrated compendium of officialdom during the late Qing] (Beijing: Zhonghua shuju, 2005), 90.

10. Xu Yishi, *Yishi leigao* [Collected writings of (Xu) Yishi] (Beijing: Shumu wenxian chubanshe, 1983), 191.

11. Zhang Shouzhong, ed., *Zhang Renjun jiashu riji* [Letters and diaries of Zhang Renjun] (Beijing: Zhongguo wenshi chubanshe, 1993), 3–5.

12. Ray Huang, *1587: A Year of No Significance* (New Haven: Yale University Press, 1981), 105.

13. Mary Backus Rankin, *Early Chinese Revolutionaries: Radical Intellectuals in Shanghai and Zhejiang, 1902–1911* (Cambridge: Harvard University Press, 1971), 79.

14. Ibid, 80, 77–95 for further discussions about the *Subao* articles; see also J. Lust, "The 'Su-pao' Case: An Episode in the Early Chinese Nationalist Movement," *Bulletin of the School of Oriental and African Studies* 27.2 (1964): 408–29.

15. Zhongguo shi xuehui, ed., *Xinhai geming* [The 1911 Revolution] (Beijing: Zhonghua shuju, 1986), v. 1, 408–80.

16. *Subao* (May 20, 1903). See also "Jingshi daxuetang xuesheng zhi E ge xuetang shu" [Open letter to Hubei students from students in Capital University], in Yang Tianshi

and Wang Xuezhuang, eds., *Ju E yundong* [The anti-Russian movement] (Beijing: Shumu wenxian chubanshe, 1981), 154.

17. Ibid., 156.

18. *Subao* (May 18, 1903).

19. Jin Ding, "Jin Ding zhi Liang Dingfen shu" [Jin Ding's letter to Liang Dingfen], in Zhou Kangxie, ed., *Xinhai geming ziliao huiji* [Collected documents on the 1911 Revolution] (Xianggang: Dadong tushu gongsi, 1980), v. 1, 25.

20. Lo Hui-min, *The Correspondence of G. E. Morrison* (Cambridge: Cambridge University Press, 1976), v. 2, 692.

21. Thomas Lawton, *A Time of Transition: Two Collectors of Chinese Art* (Lawrence: University of Kansas, 1991), 19.

22. Jin, "Jin Ding zhi Liang Dingfen shu," 25.

23. For a detailed study of the avoidance system during the Qing dynasty, see Wei Xiumei, *Qingdai zhi huibi zhidu* [The avoidance system during the Qing dynasty] (Taibei: Zhongyang yanjiuyuan jindai shi yanjiusuo, 1992).

24. See "Jianfang daofu chengli" [The appointment of *dao* and *fu*], in Hu Sijing, ed., *Guowen beicheng* [Collection of political anecdotes from the late Qing period] (Shanghai: Shanghai shudian, 1997), 127.

25. Liu Fengyun, "Qingdai dufu yu difangguan de xuanyong" [Viceroys and governors and the appointment of local officials], *Qingshi yanjiu* 3 (1996): 22.

26. For Hu Sijing, see note 24. For other scholars, see Du Jiaji, "Qingdai guanyuan xuanren zhidu shulun" [An approach to the mandarin selection and appointment system during the Qing dynasty], *Qingshi yanjiu* 2 (1995): 18.

27. Xu Daling, *Qingdai juanna zhidu* [The *juanna* system of the Qing dynasty] (Taibei: Wenhai chubanshe, 1987), 111–12.

28. Du Jiaji, "Qingdai guanyuan xuanren zhidu shulun," 11.

29. Xie Junmei, "Juanna zhidu yu wanqing lizhi de fubai" [The *juanna* system and the corruption of late Qing officialdom], *Tansuo yu zhengming* 4 (2000): 45.

30. Lu Zijian, *Juanna: Qingdai de maiguan yujue zhidu* [*Juanna*: The "selling-office" system in the Qing dynasty], *Wenshi zazhi* 6 (1999): 76.

31. Xie, "Juanna zhidu yu wanqing lizhi de fubai," 43.

32. Ibid., 76.

33. Ibid.

34. Zhang was promoted directly by Empress Dowager Cixi. See "Jianfang daofu chengli" in Hu Sijing, ed., 127.

35. Liu Fengyun, "Qingdai dufu yu difangguan de xuanyong," 27–28.

36. See Ch'ü T'ung-tsu, *Local Government in China under the Ch'ing* (Cambridge: Harvard University Press, 1962) and Bradley W. Reed, *Talons and Teeth* (Stanford: Stanford University Press, 2000).

37. For studies of *mufu* during the late Qing, see Kenneth E. Folsom, *Friends, Guests, and Colleagues: The Mu-Fu System in the Late Ch'ing period* (Berkeley: University of California Press, 1968) and Jonathan Porter, *Tseng Kuo-fan's Private Bureaucracy* (Berkeley: University of California, 1972).

38. Li Renkai, *Zhang Zhidong mufu*, 121–66.

39. See Li Qiao, *Qingdai guanchang tuji*, 25–29.

40. Li Renkai, *Zhang Zhidong mufu*, 53.

41. Ibid., 83.

42. Shen, *Wanqing caizheng zhichu zhengce yanjiu*, 161.

43. Ibid., 139.

44. Liu Wei, *Wanqing dufu zhengzhi* [Viceroys and governors during the late Qing] (Wuchang: Hubei jiaoyu chubanshe, 2003), 254.

9

DEMOCRACY IS IN ITS DETAILS

The 1909 Provincial Assembly Elections and the Print Media

David Cheng Chang

"Today is the first day for China to break away from despotism; today is the first day for the Chinese people to participate in government," proclaimed *Shenbao* editors on October 14, 1909, when elected Provincial Assemblies (*Ziyiju*) convened for the first time across China. On this day when "provincial assemblymen are born, and a constitutional government is born," citizens could now look forward to "rescuing China from the catastrophe of sinking, and engendering [a nation equivalent to] America and Europe and bringing glory to our ancestors."[1] *Shenbao* and *Shibao*, the two most influential newspapers in Shanghai, printed newsmen's congratulations and good wishes in auspicious red ink on cover pages that were normally reserved for advertising. The Tianjin-based *Dagongbao* proclaimed, "Out of the abyss of misfortune comes bliss," declaring this event a potential turning point in Chinese history.[2]

Just three months earlier, in stark contrast to this exultant portrayal of China's first experiments in elections and democracy, another report had painted a grim picture of the far-flung margins of this vast country. "Brutal Murder of an Election Worker" was the spectacular headline on June 9, 1909, in *Zhengzong aiguobao* (Authentic patriotic news), a vernacular newspaper based in Beijing. The election worker reportedly had gone into villages in Jingbian county, Shaanxi, giving speeches to promote elections and self-government. Villagers presumed that this man must be a spy for the "foreign devils." "The crowd first ripped out his two eyes. Then they tied his arms and legs with heavy ropes." Evoking images of the ancient punishment of drawing and quartering by horses, the paper continued, "The mob pulled ropes in four different directions, and he was quartered."[3] These "ignorant yokels" stormed into the county seat and demanded annulment of all reforms, including elections and new schools. "This kind of mindset of the ignorant is not unique to Shaanxi," lamented the editor of *Zhengzong aiguobao*. If reforms required extra taxes from the people, violent resistance, if not uprisings, would recur. The paper ominously declared, "The prospect is horrifying."[4]

These two conflicting images of the elections highlight the enormous regional differences in Chinese politics and society in 1909, particularly the contrast between the eastern seaboard and the western hinterland. These two contradictory assessments of political reforms accentuate the hopes and fears of the time. The final years of the Qing were an era of reform, when China's first democratic experiments took place—the 1909 Provincial Assembly elections. At this historic juncture, in a country ruled by emperors for more than two thousand years, unprecedented numbers of people were mobilized to participate in elections to establish representative assemblies. About 1.7 million men, or 0.42 percent of a population of 410 million, were registered as eligible voters.[5] At the time this was an extraordinary feat of political mobilization.

The significance of the 1909 elections has been overshadowed by wars and revolutions. Both the Nationalist and Communist historians derided the 1909 elections as a last-ditch attempt by the Qing court to salvage the moribund dynasty by introducing "sham" elections and self-government. Not surprisingly, the role of constitutionalists was marginalized in histories written by both Leninist parties. P'eng-yüan Chang observed, "Because the Revolution of 1911 resulted in the overthrow of the Qing dynasty and the establishment of a republic, the revolutionaries have been regarded by some as champions of China's salvation, and the constitutionalists as conservatives and stubborn reactionaries who placed obstacles in the way of the revolutionary movement."[6] In 1968, along with Mary C. Wright and John Fincher, Chang made a pioneering breakthrough, challenging this dismissive view of the late Qing political reforms.[7] Similarly, Joseph Esherick highlighted the significance of this process; "There was no more important political development in the final years of the Qing dynasty than the constitutional movement and the establishment of the provincial assemblies."[8]

In some ways reforms precipitated revolution, but constitutional reformers and revolutionary radicals presented two fundamentally different visions of social change. In sharp contrast to the revolutionary belief that "the ends justify the means," the constitutionalists emphasized the importance of process. Eschewing the immediately gratifying appeal of populist justice, they focused on procedural justice. Instead of shouting lofty slogans of revolutionary change, they practiced the mundane details of reforms to bring about incremental improvement. In Jeremy Murray's chapter in this volume, Zhang Yaozeng, one of republican China's foremost legal reformers, is described as a constitutionalist who lived his life practicing these values.

The most important legacy of the constitutional movement and the 1909 Provincial Assembly elections lies in the fact that after this early democratic experiment, complete with a vibrant print media, China went through a "democratic enlightenment." Concepts such as "people's rights (vis-à-vis the state)," "government's responsibilities" (to its people), "checks and balances," and "no taxation without representation" entered into the popular vocabulary. "Chinese sources confirm the impression of a new era, indeed of a new world." Wright made a hopeful assessment when she discussed the print media: "The headlines, the cartoons, the featured stories, the letters to the editor belong to our own era. They are not reminiscent of the end of any earlier dynasty ... "[9] However, the interaction between election processes and the media is not explored in depth in Chang and Fincher's chapters in *China in Revolution* and in their later monographs. In *Print and Politics*, Joan Judge does not examine the pivotal role played by the media in facilitating elections, despite her discussion of the role of *Shibao* writers as assemblymen.[10] In this chapter, I seek to investigate how elections and the print media interacted and reinforced each other to bring about a large-scale democratic experiment.

Today, as we observe the centennial of the 1909 elections, students of democracy and history are rediscovering this era of reform, a process of nonviolent evolution. In this chapter, the focus is not on men powerful or famous, but on the little known and the down-to-earth; the attention is not on ideas lofty and abstract, but on actions concrete and mundane, even tedious. It is a narrative about the nitty-gritty, the nuts and bolts of the 1909 elections. This is also a story about how the print media, emerging from the margins, courageously and intelligently challenged the state in the center. This is an account of a new generation of journalists speaking out for fellow citizens' rights, for a new vision for the nation. In the great Confucian tradition of *weiyan dayi*, I will recount "subtle actions that embody profound meanings" in the following sections. Before us unfolds the history of the 1909 elections against the backdrop of wars and revolutions in twentieth century China.

A Zeitgeist of Constitutional Reforms: Self-government and Elections

Stumbling into the twentieth century, China under the Qing was in a state of deep crisis. It had suffered humiliating defeats in the first Sino-Japanese War in 1894–1895 and the Boxer War in 1900, and experienced an abortive "Hundred Days Reform" in 1898. Only after witnessing the trouncing of the autocratic Russian empire by the constitutional monarchy of Japan in the Russo-Japanese War (1904–1905) did Empress Dowager Cixi begin to consider political reforms in earnest. In 1905 the two most influential officials, Zhang Zhidong and Yuan Shikai, jointly memorialized the throne, suggesting a twelve-year transition to constitutional monarchy.[11] Duanfang, one of the five officials sent by Cixi to tour the West and Japan to study political systems, indicted the earlier self-strengthening movement and other reform policies as "only capable of affecting the superficial (*mo*) but not the fundamental (*ben*)." China had to emulate the West in abandoning despotism and adopting a constitutional government.[12] These forceful arguments prompted Cixi's decision to initiate constitutional reforms.

Parallel to this shift in political outlook among the ruling elite in the political center, China witnessed a groundswell of support for constitutional reform in society, a process instigated by political forces at the margins, sometimes outside its border. This constitutionalist movement was initially led by the surviving leaders of the "Hundred Days Reform," Kang Youwei and Liang Qichao, operating in exile in Japan. In 1902, Kang proposed the establishment of self-government councils at local levels before the opening of a national parliament.[13] In 1904, Kang's disciple Di Baoxian founded *Shibao* in Shanghai, with the express purpose of educating the people for future political reforms. Leveraging on top officials Yuan and Zhang's proposal for a twelve-year transition to constitutional monarchy, *Shibao* called for a ten-year time frame.[14] The new media emerging from the margins of traditional power structure began to make its influence felt at the center.

During 1906–1908 the Qing court finally came to terms with what the constitutionalists had been advocating all along. In 1907 the Constitutional Commission (*Xianzheng bianchaguan*) was established directly under the Grand Council (*Junjichu*). The court chose to start with local assemblies, as a way to deflect pressure from the central government. In July 1908, the court promulgated the 62-clause "Regulations for Provincial Assemblies" and the 115-clause "Regulations for Provincial Assembly Elections," which included property and education requirements for candidates.[15] Provincial governments were required to set up preparatory bureaus jointly run by officials and local elites. Under an indirect voting system, in the first-round elections eligible voters chose electors, akin to an electoral college, who would in turn elect the actual provincial assemblymen in the second-round elections. When provincial assemblies convened on October 14, 1909, assemblymen would elect their representatives to the National Assembly (*Zizhengyuan*), which would serve as a proto-parliament until the establishment of a full-fledged National Parliament (*Guohui*) in 1917.

On August 27, 1908, the court announced the "Principles of the Constitution," promising a nine-year transition to constitutional monarchy. In view of the nine-year transition period, some reformers questioned the court's sincerity in reforms. However, it is hazardous if not futile to speculate about the intentions of historical figures. There are few sources that confirm or disprove the sincerity of Cixi and her successor, Prince Regent Zaifeng, who effectively reigned in place of his son, the infant emperor Xuantong. What we do know is that soon after Cixi died in November 1908, Zaifeng reaffirmed the 1917 deadline for the completion of the transition to a constitutional monarchy: "There is no reason whatsoever to reverse course, and the plan must be carried out."[16] Throughout 1909 his repeated edicts demanding timely implementations of elections suggest a significant level of commitment.

Ultimately, the motives of rulers are not crucial to our analysis. While the court certainly had its own calculations regarding constitutional reforms, to a large degree it was responding to a sea change in political outlook in officialdom and society. The central state was an important element in the equation of reforms, but the outcome was largely determined by a resourceful society aided by the print media. As *Shibao* commentator Bao Tianxiao (known by the pseudonym Xiao, or laughter) judiciously pointed out, despite the long transition period stipulated by law, once the local self-government regulations were promulgated, local people could start to prepare immediately. Local self-government could be set up within half a year, or three months. After all, "It will be determined by the capacities of our *guomin* (citizens)."[17]

Although the self-government movement was initiated by the center, it would be appropriated by society, including new social forces operating at the margins. The movement would assume a life of its own. Just as Zaifeng had recognized, constitutional reform was at a point of no return. By focusing on citizens and the media in action, we can see that regardless of the intent or sincerity of the court, citizens and the media had the potential to make elections real and make democracy work.

Institutional Preparations

In a country without any prior experience in elections or self-government, the preparatory stage proved to be a critical element in the 1909 elections. Following the creation of the Constitutional Commission in Beijing, each province established its own Provincial Assembly Preparatory Bureau. At the local level, self-government research institutes and election affairs offices emerged. There were some regional variations in terms of the structure and pace of reforms. In some localities, the preparatory agencies for local self-government and elections were essentially one organization. In many places Election Affairs Offices or Election Research Bureaus were affiliated with Local Self-Government Research Institutes, sharing human resources and expertise. However, in Hunan the Election Survey and Research Institute was founded under the provincial Education Association, highlighting the influence of the educated elites.[18]

The preparatory stage was in its own right a microcosm of the larger election process. And the difficulties in setting up local self-government organizations underscored the dilemma faced by local elites: how should one practice democracy before democratic institutions are in place? In concrete terms, how should one conduct small elections in order to create preparatory institutions for larger elections? In many cases, methods of selection and election were combined to resolve this dilemma. For instance, in Zhejiang's Renhe and Qiantang counties, in order to elect 20 election workers, the business and education sectors were each expected to select 25 men to make a total candidate pool of 50. While the education group went through an election to choose 25 out of 46 nominees, the business group came up with a list of only 22 candidates, still short by 3.[19]

In theory, these self-government preparatory agencies were to be jointly run by local officials and elites, more precisely representatives from gentry (*shen*), commercial (*shangjie*), and education sectors (*xuejie*). However, these terms were often undefined and fraught with internal contradictions. It would be facile to assume that local elites were a coherent entity in relation to the state. Under the heartening title "Harbinger of constitutional government," *Zhengzong aiguobao* reported the founding of Tongzhou district's Self-Government Research Institute and the plan to elect its chairman and first batch of trainees. "If proper people are elected, and they can work together, it will be a true blessing for the people of Tongzhou."[20] However, this early enthusiasm soon soured when allegations of improper networking to win votes were leveled at the chairman-elect. Rumor had it that even "waiters and coolies from a certain restaurant cast many votes!" As a result, among the local gentry there was widespread opposition to the chair. The paper protested: "Alas, how rotten!"[21]

Inertia or foot-dragging from officials was to be expected, since the rise of self-governing bodies would certainly erode their power. In many cases, society demonstrated a high level of initiative and determination to take officials to task for failing to set up research institutes and carry out election preparations promptly. In some cases, the state appeared to respond to society's pressures with concrete actions. Magistrate Xu Baoqing of Haiyan county, Zhejiang, for example, discovered to his dismay that his failure to collaborate with local gentry to prepare for elections had cost him his job.[22]

One early product of the collaboration between government and society was the creation of election training centers. With support from the Provincial Assembly Preparatory Office, Hunan's Election Survey and Research Institute offered a three-week training course. It was open to any man interested in politics who could obtain the endorsement of one prominent member of the gentry, scholar, or businessman in his native county.[23] In Shanxi province, the research institute required each county government to select two or three candidates to undergo free training in the provincial capital.[24]

To reach out, various institutes or bureaus sent election workers to give speeches in local areas explaining the process and encouraging participation. In Zhejiang, one of the leading provinces in the preparations processes, the Provincial Preparatory Bureau, mailed local bureaus 24,000 copies of posters and an "Open Letter to Gentry, Businessmen and Educated Elites" written in vernacular Chinese, 2,700 copies of the "Regulations on the Provincial Assembly and Elections," and 350 copies of the "Charter for Preparatory Bureaus."[25] In Hangzhou, the Renqian District Election Office printed large quantities of posters and fliers with such titles as "The right to vote is a right that must not be forsaken" and "Local gentry's responsibilities in promoting elections."[26]

Enthusiasm and determination on the part of society in some localities did not necessarily mean expertise in election affairs across China. Few of the local gentry had studied modern politics or law. As a result, students of politics and law, especially those trained in Japan, became highly sought after as many local self-government agencies tried to recruit them. Frequently, the educated elite, both old and new, became the leading force in these bodies. For instance, in Henan's provincial Election Research Institute five scholars, three with traditional educations, two with training in law and politics in Japan, assumed teaching positions *pro bono* in order to "complete this magnificent endeavor."[27] However, in some cases the role played by the educated elites often became so dominant that the gentry and businessmen felt marginalized. In *Shibao*'s "criticism" column, one writer bitterly complained, "Today provincial assembly affairs are commonly understood as the prerogatives of the educated elites, as if rights to participate in politics are privileges reserved for them." He exhorted the business elites of Shanghai to participate in elections, thus "washing away this humiliation once and for all!"[28] This exhortation can be seen in the context of the spirit of fair competition among different social groups in the dual pursuits of their own interests and larger social ideals.

Thanks to an emerging press, knowledge of and experience with elections were readily shared across regions; laws were interpreted, questions debated, good examples praised, and bad practices lambasted. In Zhili, *Dagongbao* provided painstaking details on self-government activities in Tianjin, a pacesetter of the time. Shanghai's *Shenbao* and *Shibao* reported exhaustively on election affairs across the country on a daily basis from late 1908 through 1909. Starting in mid-1908 *Shenbao* devoted an entire section on page three to "Preparations for Provincial Assemblies in Various Provinces." The purpose of such thorough reporting was to "facilitate research and learning, and generate competition among provinces."[29] Similarly, *Dongfang zazhi* allocated its first dozen pages or so to "Constitutionalism." It also regularly featured a series of charts comparing each province's progress in the preparations "race." As early as November 1908, Zhili province and two counties in Jiangsu were leading the way, while Guangdong, Fujian, and some parts of Jiangsu and Zhejiang languished.[30] *Shenbao* bluntly characterized Guangdong's poor progress, which placed it behind Xinjiang, Yunnan, and Guizhou, as "a shame on Guangdong officials and gentry."[31] This type of public pressure pushed laggards to shape up. By early 1909, Jiangsu and Zhejiang had become leaders. The press made its impact felt by transforming public opinion from traditional local criticism to nationally transmitted public pressure. Thus voices from the margins had the opportunity to become the mainstream.

In the preparatory phase of the 1909 elections, three identifiable and overlapping driving forces emerged: an assertive gentry, a new generation of educated elites, and a vibrant press. If the court's decision to establish provincial assemblies had drawn a general outline for a future course, the three social forces worked in tandem to define the texture and details of the electoral process. Our examination of details starts with suffrage and voter registration.

Suffrage

While suffrage determines enfranchisement, voter registration is effectively the verification and mobilization of eligible voters. Together, the level of enfranchisement and the quality of voter registration largely decide the democratic content of an election. The 1909 elections allowed a very limited suffrage, which was in line with the early electoral experiences of most countries. Women were excluded, just as women in the United States were until full suffrage was achieved in 1920, in Britain in 1928, in France and Japan in 1945, and in Switzerland in 1971.[32] It would be absurd to judge elections held a century ago by the standards of today. For China the 1909 elections were a starting point. Therefore, our focus should not be fixed upon what these elections were not. Instead we need to explore how eligible voters experienced elections.

The 1908 "Regulations on Provincial Assemblies" restricted the right to vote to males over the age of 25 *sui*, natives of the province who had either (1) made important contributions to local education and public interest projects, or (2) had the equivalent of a Chinese or foreign middle-school education, or (3) had a traditional *gongsheng* degree, (4) had served as a seventh-rank civil official or fifth-rank military officer, or (5) possessed capital or properties worth at least 5,000 *yuan*. And nonnatives could qualify if they had been resident for ten years and owned property worth at least 10,000 *yuan*. The right to be elected required a minimum age of 30 *sui*, as the same in Japanese parliamentary elections.

Various types of individuals were deprived of voting rights: those who were deemed to possess "unsavory, selfish character, or presumptuous personality;" those who had been convicted and jailed, those who engaged in improper businesses (a code word for prostitution, opium trade, etc.), those charged with and not cleared of financial wrongdoing, those of disreputable family background, opium smokers, the mentally ill, and illiterates. In addition, the rights of several types of people were suspended as long as they remained officials or private secretaries to officials, active soldiers and reservists, police officers, Buddhist, Daoist and other priests, and current students. Following the Japanese rule, elementary school teachers could not be elected, as serving in the assembly was thought to conflict with their teaching duties.[33] Some of the rules were rather progressive, most notably those that banned officials, their private staffs, and military men from running or serving, consistent with the concept of separation of powers.[34]

However, many of these qualifications involved ill-defined or arbitrary standards. Nearly every clause of the "Regulations on Provincial Assemblies" and the election rules sparked challenges and controversies. A torrent of differing interpretations springing from the Constitutional Commission in Beijing, local governments, and society were reported verbatim in the press. Local magistrates asked provincial governors for interpretations, and governors in turn asked the Constitutional Commission. Provincial Assembly Preparatory Bureaus also provided their own interpretations, and newspapers weighed in to offer their opinions through editorials or letters to the editors. This was indeed a remarkable phenomenon for a country termed by *Shibao* as a "secretive society," where "secrecy was the guiding principle for all government."[35]

One of the most controversial issues involved the denial of voting rights to "those who engaged in improper businesses" and "those of disreputable family background."[36] These poorly defined terms left considerable room for interpretation. In its reply to an inquiry from Zhenghai county, the Zhejiang Provincial Assembly Preparatory Bureau limited the prohibition to prostitutes, actors, actresses, and yamen runners (*chang you li zu*), while it affirmed the right of butchers to vote. However, at the same time, this interpretation ruled that petty functionaries and clerks (*xuli*) did not qualify as "officials." Therefore, while "officials" and their private staff could not vote, these functionaries were not banned from voting.[37] Three weeks later, the Constitutional Commission in Beijing issued a contrary ruling: "Since petty functionaries serve in a government capacity, the right to vote of all those who are on active duty is suspended to prevent collusion and interference."[38] *Shibao* columnist Xiao applauded this ruling and gloated, "Today's scribes have so much power, enough to double-cross their superiors. They manipulate writings and fiddle with words." To Xiao, the denial of suffrage to petty functionaries was even more urgent than the ban imposed on the private secretaries of officials.[39]

Press support for one particular ruling by Beijing does not necessarily suggest a general agreement between the central state and the media. On the contrary, the press had consistently criticized the "Regulations" and subsequent interpretations made by the Constitutional Commission. *Shibao* criticized provincial preparatory bureaus for turning to the Commission on all matters, while pointing out that the original "Regulations" and interpretations were fraught with contradictions and "careless omissions."[40] *Shibao* printed a series of editorials entitled "Doubts and questions regarding the Constitutional Commission," bluntly challenging the authority of this "highest legislative institution of the day." It pointed out that in the "Regulations," language was "vague," and there were "numerous points that were hard to make sense of."[41] To make matters worse, the Commission's interpretations often contradicted the original Regulations. *Shibao* raised an audacious question, carefully couched in a language that exalted the throne as a way to criticize the Commission: "Should local officials and citizens follow the opinions of one government agency and thus bend the Regulations sanctioned by the throne, or should they faithfully stick to the Regulations and reject the opinions of one agency?" Then *Shibao* "humbly" proposed that "we should settle issues together with all officials and citizens under heaven; moreover, we are also willing to settle issues with the officials at the Commission."[42] *Shibao* exhorted the Commission to heed public opinion, and to make an effort to correct its mistaken interpretations. After all, making mistakes is as natural as the "eclipses of the sun and moon," and people's respect would only grow after these corrective measures were taken.[43]

Shibao made a forceful claim when it declared, "The Commission should know that the law is a public instrument."[44] Here, the newspaper was openly questioning the authority of an unelected government body that paradoxically was in charge of creating elected bodies. It made abundantly clear the idea that no government bodies or individual officials had a monopoly on interpretation of the law. Society had a say as well. Here we see how the margins could challenge the center. Early on in the election process the print media confidently assumed the roles of promoter of participation and watchdog on the government. They set the tone for future interaction between government, citizens, and the press.

Voter Registration

The challenges in voter registration were daunting, largely because the Qing government had never conducted a comprehensive national census, and a new one "would take months to complete."[45] As a makeshift measure, the Constitutional Commission used traditional examination and tax quotas to fix the size of each provincial assembly. However, a nationwide survey was still required to verify voter eligibility. As the government was totally unequipped to carry out such a vast endeavor, local gentry were mobilized to conduct surveys. This was part of the logic behind the court's promotion of local self-government bodies, which actually carried out the bulk of the survey work. Local preparatory bureaus and research institutes established survey offices for this specific task. Election surveyors were trained and then sent out to towns and villages to register voters. Moreover, surveyors also worked as election lecturers (*xuanjiangyuan*), giving speeches and explaining laws to voters and nonvoters alike.

Although details across China are scattered, we can get a sense of the organizational difficulties faced by the surveyors from a number of news reports. The research institutes in Renhe and Qiantang counties, Zhejiang, had selected their election surveyors more or less democratically. Before long some of the surveyors decided to quit because of low pay and hard work.[46] Nevertheless, immediately after the Chinese New Year, twenty-five surveyors were dispatched to towns and villages, and local guides were appointed to accompany them to visit each potentially eligible voter and verify his education and wealth status.[47] In these relatively developed areas election surveys were already quite difficult to compile. In rural, mountainous, or sparsely populated places, surveys could present almost insurmountable logistical challenges.

The most extreme case was the murder of an election worker in Shaanxi reported by *Zhengzong aiguobao* and mentioned at the start of this chapter. A similar tragedy nearly befell another surveyor named Guo Haonan in Nanchang county, Jiangxi. When he went down to the villages, the peasants "did not understand the purpose and became agitated." Villagers convened in their lineage hall and declared their intention to "tie up Guo and sacrifice him to their ancestors" if he dared to come close. Guo fled at once and promptly quit his job.[48] Reading these harrowing reports, one is tempted to conclude that the survey process was often violent. However, to date I have found only these two specific reports of violence against election workers. Furthermore, the first report by *Zhengzong ai-guobao* was uncorroborated by other newspapers, while the latter case constituted a threat. Available sources suggest that the survey process was peaceful overall.

While violent reactions were rare exceptions, skepticism and enthusiasm were the two most common attitudes. On the one hand, people were suspicious of the true intention of the surveys, fearing new tax burdens. As in numerous other places, many people in Sichuan did not understand the concept of elections. When election workers came to town to give speeches, "they were stared at as if they were foreigners, and their messages were entirely ignored."[49] Not only in the underdeveloped hinterland, but also in the Yangzi River delta, survey workers experienced frustrations. In Wuyang county near Shanghai, surveyors put up posters and announced an extra voter registration session in case any eligible voters were missed during the house-by-house registration drive. To their great surprise and dismay, no one showed up to register. Instead, a few businessmen came to ask for the removal of their names from the voter roll, because rumors of new taxes ran rampant.[50] In metropolitan Shanghai, the showing was not any more presentable. In a sarcastic tone, *Shibao* admonished Shanghai residents for their pathetic response to the survey: "How could populous Shanghai be worthy of its reputation as the first city opened to the world" when it lagged behind its small neighboring counties?[51] To a degree, this type of voter apathy contributed to the low national voter base of 0.42 percent, with provincial variations ranging from 0.19 percent in Gansu to 0.62 percent in Zhili.[52]

On the other hand, many citizens eagerly embraced elections, regarding it either as a path to officialdom after the abolition of the civil service examination system in 1905 or popular recognition of their status in the community. Voting rights were pursued vigorously by the educated and propertied. Although the Regulations clearly stated that people with the equivalent of a Chinese or foreign middle-school education were eligible to vote, the graduates of two American schools in Fuzhou were denied voting rights on the pretext that the schools were not properly registered with the local government and that their students did not receive any government award, two claims with no legal ground. The American consul in Fujian cabled the U.S. ambassador to lodge a protest with the Chinese Foreign Ministry, claiming that the loss of voting rights would "damage the reputations of these schools." However, the students did not appreciate American involvement. "They felt ashamed of the interference of foreign powers in Chinese domestic affairs, and they would rather win back their voting rights on their own."[53] *Shibao* columnist Xiao unequivocally defended their rights, and pointed out that graduates from foreign schools were "still Chinese nationals, not foreigners."[54] He also rejected foreign interference in China's self-government movement.[55] Apparently, these students and Xiao had found faith in the new concept of citizen's rights.

For those lacking status or wealth, the "Regulations" made a special provision to include "good citizens" who had made important contributions to either local education or other public interest projects for more than three years.[56] When election surveyors in Minhou county, Fujian, transcribed the names of staff members of several public interest associations, these members were delighted. But when the actual voter roll was posted, they could not find their names, and were duly outraged. Twelve representatives were chosen to press their complaints at the county Election Affairs Bureau, and threatened lawsuits.[57] A few days later, the Bureau yielded to one of the most prominent associations, the Anti-Opium Society, and reinstated the voting rights of its employees.[58] Successfully these proto-NGO (Nongovernmental Organization) activists made a rigorous defense of their citizens' rights.

Probably the most problematic regulation was the prohibition of opium addicts from voting, and few of the drafters of the "Regulations" could have anticipated the logistical nightmare that moralistic qualifications would bring. To enforce this requirement, Magistrate Sheng of Yongjia county, Zhejiang, set up an opium test center in the local Education Bureau and designed elaborate procedures for its operation. Any person with an opium-smoking history who now claimed he was clean "must come forward to take the test and receive a certificate." Two examiners presided over the center, with one doctor verifying the absence of opium craving and one official conducting the body search. "The examinees are not allowed to smuggle in any opium substitutes or pills into the test center; they are not allowed to meet any family members or friends." And "meals are exclusively provided by the center at the price of three *jiao* per day." Despite measures that were so stringent they seemed designed to "treat arrested thieves," resourceful voters were still able to frustrate the government in some cases. Since most of the gentry examinees enjoyed a degree of social status, the examiners dared not "remove their shirts and strip off their pants to perform a thorough body search." Thus, several small pills still could still get smuggled in, and "these pills are enough to last three days or more."[59] One satire in *Shenbao* described a potential voter who even contemplated concealing opium pills in his rectum to pass the test.[60] Commentator Xiao was baffled to the point of asking, "Is there any solution? Is there any solution?"[61] However, beneath the farcical appearance of these reports, the numerous legal disputes over opium addiction highlight the contested nature of voting rights.

Election *Yundong* (Campaign)

Once local governments completed the voter rolls with information on eligible voters' names, addresses, family origins, official rank, property, and special contributions made to the community, the lists were submitted to upper level government. Upon approval, local bureaus were required by the "Regulations" to publicize the voter rolls three months before the voting date, and the public notice was to remain available for twenty days. If voters found mistakes in the rolls, they were entitled to raise objections with election inspectors within the twenty-day public notice period. Local magistrates, who were required to serve as inspectors, had to make a judgment within twenty days of receiving complaints.[62] Lists of eligible voters appeared in market towns, cities, and on bulletin boards outside local bureaus. Some localities took a further step and utilized newspapers to spread the word. Shanghai county, for example, placed an advertisement on the front page of *Shenbao*, announcing the public notice period and deadlines for complaints as well as eligibility judgments.[63] However, in reality local practices were sometimes inconsistent with the law. Fujian's Minhou county government shortened the notice period without any explanation, first to fifteen days, then to ten days. After some additional delays in the delivery of voter rolls back to the towns and villages, only five days were left.[64] A shortened public notice period most likely had left some voters uninformed.

However, for some enthusiastic candidates, well before the voter list was announced election campaigns had been underway for some time, though often in an underhanded fashion, or so it was claimed in the newspapers. The usual suspects were none other than the surveyors themselves. In Hunan province, some surveyors went to the countryside and taught people "how to vote." "Write down my name on the ballot and drop it in the box," they explained. As it turned out in this case, surveyors did indeed receive the highest number of votes in the primary.[65] In the Shanghai area, an election lecturer dispatched a team of six or seven, including his sons and students. "Starting from the Temple of Confucius," it was alleged, "they toured towns and villages and gave speeches, telling people which gentry men they should not vote for, and why they should not vote for them." Moreover, the lecturer personally went around telling people to "remember this name [his own name]" and the names of his disciples. "If you cannot remember, go home and practice these names. Besides us, no one is worth voting for."[66] This is probably the earliest report of negative campaigns in the history of Chinese elections. While the second case was an example of conflict of interest, the first constituted outright deception. They were among the more egregious examples of *yundong*.

While *yundong* in later history generally refers to a political movement or campaign, in 1909 its meaning was ambiguous, often with a negative connotation suggesting improper networking or corrupt dependence on *guanxi*. Xiao defined *yundong* as "using pull to get what one wants, soliciting support, or currying favor with others." In the meantime, other commentators acknowledged the fact that campaigning was a legitimate part of electoral politics in the West.[67] "Whenever there is an election, there will be various forms of *yundong*," another *Shibao* commentator admitted. However, he continued, "*Yundong* is like aping other countries without learning the essence."[68] Reflecting a deep-seated Confucian prejudice against partisan politics (*pengdang*) and self-promotion, opinion leaders were adamant in their opposition to improper *yundong*, as they believed in choosing candidates based purely on their virtue and ability. The ideal candidates should "have some basic education, possess some wealth, have some knowledge. Through rich life experience they should be capable. By taking care of their own reputation they should be of good character."[69] Clearly, these constitutionalists in China had very high expectations for candidates, and demanded a lot from voters.

Using cartoons, *Shibao* vividly portrayed various methods of *yundong*. Based on a news report, one cartoon humorously sketched a scene in a restaurant, in which a candidate treats a voter to a local delicacy of supersized quick-fried fish noodles (Figure 1).[70] In addition to criticism and ridicule, nuanced messages were conveyed as well. In Figure 2 we see a gentry-looking young man humbly bowing to a peasant woman who has a pole in her hand and two water buckets behind her.[71] Since the electorate was restricted to male propertied or educated elites, a peasant woman was unlikely to have any influence in the outcome of the elections. In a local context, the gentry are at or near the center of power, and a peasant woman at the remotest margins. However, the deferential gesture made across class and gender lines raises an intriguing question. Does it suggest a shift in political culture in the direction of populism despite the limited suffrage? Perhaps this was emblematic of the humbling effect of democratic elections on the elite.

As we witness the massive voter registration drive and the comings and goings of *yundong*, we should not assume that the elections were speeding ahead unopposed. In Wuyang county, Jiangsu, a member of the local gentry named Ma went out in the street to exhort people not to vote. Citing the Confucian classics, he cried, "When commoners are participating in politics, that is the end of the Dao." To add drama, he predicted ominous deaths for those who dared to vote.[72] However, this odd act seemed to belong to a bygone era; "Go to the ballot box" was the order of the day.

Go to the Ballot Box!

With the voting day approaching, both the government and society mobilized to draw more voters to the ballot boxes. Some local government and self-govern-

Figure 1. Election *yundong* in a restaurant (*Shibao,* March 31, 1909).

Figure 2. Election *yundong* in the countryside (*Shibao,* March 30, 1909).

ment institutes arranged additional rounds of speeches and meetings to explain the importance and mechanics of the elections. In Yongjia county, Zhejiang, for example, speakers covered a range of issues: the relations between the nation and the people, between provincial assemblymen and the local people, and the methods of allocating seats.[73]

In an extraordinary move, both *Shenbao* and *Shibao* published the same editorial on March 18, the day of first-round elections in Jiangsu. It made an emotional appeal to Jiangsu citizens: "Foreigners have long derided us Chinese as a people lacking the spirit of cooperation. For Jiangsu people, this is a grave slander." The article pleaded with each eligible voter to make the effort to vote. "Please make sure we wash away this reputation!"[74] To convince voters to go to the polls, seven reasons were given. In addition to six moral and instrumental arguments, the seventh bordered on coaxing: "Since numerous district poll stations are set up in town and country, voters can walk to one within 10 *li*. Therefore, it is not tiring on the body." Moreover, "Writing down a candidate's name in a few characters is simple. Therefore, it is not taxing on the brain." Furthermore, "The voting station is open from 8 A.M. to 6 P.M. Therefore, it is convenient." Still not convinced? "After all this, don't worry about the theory of the right to vote. Even if you think of it as a game, it is extremely interesting."[75]

Appealing to the noble side of human emotions, the idea of making history through voting was emphatically repeated by the media. *Shibao* implored Jiangsu voters to cherish the first ballot day, "the most important, most precious first day ... Oh! Don't forget this first day!"[76] On May 4, the day of the second-round of voting in Jiangsu, when electors who emerged from the first-round were to vote for the actual provincial assemblymen, *Shibao* asked, "What day is today?" The answer was delivered in large font: "This is the first day in Chinese history that people can elect their representatives. This is the first day in the land of China that people can elect their representatives. Electors should cast their vote with a pure heart and mind." On the same page a cartoon sketched a human pyramid made of voters holding up a globe. The message jumped off the page, "Together, the future of China is in our hands."[77]

Despite the fact that "it rained like a torrent," on March 22, Jiangsu citizens made history when they streamed into polling stations across the province."[78] In an illustration in *Shibao* entitled "*yundong* in the rain," we can see four candidates lining up outside the station, making a last-minute effort to woo voters (Figure 3). These young local elites were standing in a downpour, visibly smiling but probably shivering, since their umbrellas provided little protection.[79] Understandably, the inclement weather had an adverse effect on voter turnout. Voting statistics were published in newspapers in detail for each county and many districts in the days after the votes were counted. More comprehensive data suggest an overall turnout of 54.8 percent.[80] Given the terrible weather, it was a respectable turnout for a local election, especially when compared to rates in modern democracies. On June 2, Zhejiang had its first-round elections. Based on a sixteen-county tally, the turnout was a whopping 69.4 percent.[81] Rates at these levels certainly indicate strong participation in these two leading provinces.

Critics may have found election day *yundong*, along with other irregularities, to be objectionable. Despite some reports of vote buying, there is little evidence to suggest it was a widespread phenomenon. Though there was one case of a violent clash between the lineage groups of two voters in Ansu county, Zhili, it was a new flare-up of a very old rivalry, triggered by the encounter of two foes at the polling station.[82] I have yet to find reports of officials using state violence to influence voter decisions.

Figure 3. Election *yundong* in the rain (*Shibao*, March 23, 1909).

Among all the scandals, one report stood out, though it turned out to be entirely untrue. After the first-round election in Changsha county, Hunan, it was said that one vote went to the famous local courtesan Yang Cuixi. The media had a picnic, and commentators deplored the sad state of voter quality in Hunan, and in China in general.[83] A full investigation was duly launched. "All ballots, including valid and invalid ones, were checked one by one, and there were no missing ballots." The suspect ballot could not be found. The Changsha election bureau cabled Beijing, requesting all major newspapers to make a correction.[84] The author of a *Shenbao* editorial expressed a deep sense of relief. "Upon hearing the strange rumor, initially I was skeptical, nevertheless disturbed ... Now it has become clear that the scandal was a rumor spread by the opponents of elections to discredit the process."[85] This episode cautioned readers that skepticism must be exercised in dealing with the many outlandish allegations.

The biggest challenge in the 1909 elections was not created by the detractors of elections or voter irregularities, but rather by the Election Regulations themselves. Encapsulating the tension between open and competitive elections and the Confucian prejudice against partisan politics and self-promotion, Clause 45 stipulated, "Each voter should cast a secret ballot to select one candidate, but not oneself."[86] Certainly, to enforce the prohibition on self-voting would violate the very idea of the secret ballot, leaving the door open for election inspectors to check ballots. As they had so in expressing their opposition to *yundong*, some reformers tried to uphold Confucian beliefs by attempting to reconcile the two conflicting principles. Much discussion about this effort took place in the media, but to no avail. Three days before the first voting in Jiangsu, *Shenbao* tentatively suggested, "It is not necessary to insist on inspecting each ballot for self-endorsement."[87] In the end, it would become abundantly clear that no reconciliation could achieve both goals without compromising one of the principles.

Indeed, Clause 45 created a lot of chaos. Secret ballots were never a priority, as evidenced by the absence of provisions requiring partitioned booths for ballot writing (*xiepiaochu*). On the floor map of the polling station in Changzhou, Jiangsu, the area for filling out ballots was alongside the wall but adjacent to the election inspectors' desk.[88] In Wanping county, Beijing, a separate room was allocated for ballot writing, but was not partitioned for each voter.[89] Even if there had been partitioned areas for voters, they would not have shielded voters from the prying eyes of election inspectors and their attendants. The most infamous disaster area was Hualou county near Shanghai, where one allegation bordered on electoral violence. When voter Du was writing his ballot, a certain Zhu who was a "helper" at the polling station "suddenly grabbed his hand" and told him to vote for Qian, "or else." Citing the Regulation on electoral violence, *Shenbao* decried this incident as "a brutality that threatened and violated voting rights," and lambasted local government officials and election staff for dereliction of duty and outright illegal actions.[90] It was no surprise that Hualou had the largest number of signed and anonymous complaints lodged to newspapers.[91]

The poster boy of election irregularities was none other than Cao Zuanming, the same gentry man who had dispatched his sons and students to *yundong* and dished out fifty bowls of fish noodles to garner support. From letters to the editor and other reports, we can see a profile of his alleged outrages during the time he served as the chief inspector for the local polling station. Before the election, he summoned voters and instructed them to vote for him. On election day, his polling station staff brought opium pipes to the premises. Cao smoked all day while lying on a bed, and his staff members took turns puffing. When voters trickled in, Cao's attendants gathered around them, "leering at their ballots," purportedly to "prevent mistakes." They filled out the ballot for one illiterate peasant, and "patiently taught" another less educated voter how to write the name of one staffer. At the end of day, Cao and his men filled in all the unclaimed ballots.[92] Not surprisingly, Cao was elected in the first-round of voting.

In view of the irregularities during the first round of election, a letter to the editor published by *Shibao* confronted the state by declaring "the illegality of inspectors monitoring ballot writing."[93] In discussing "problems with today's elections," *Shenbao* editor Ouyang put much of the blame on a government that "never had much credibility." People had little knowledge of the law and politics, so the sudden advent of elections made the selection of good candidates "as difficult as finding needles in the sea." People would either vote "without much thought or with selfish motives." However, it was an important first step in "the participation of citizen in government," and an opportunity for Chinese citizens to "emerge out of darkness to see the light." Readers were reminded not only of "the unavoidable difficulties a constitutional country has to experience," but also of the "signs of an emerging new society." At this stage, China's experiment in democracy and self-government was like "a ferry boat yawing in stormy waters," or "an early sprout without a strong stem or deep roots." Through "continuous practice and incremental improvement," the author asserted, it can reach the "state of perfection."[94]

Elections, Media, and Democracy

Although in 1909 the word *minzhu* (democracy) was not a regular ingredient of Chinese vocabulary, the experience of the 1909 elections and self-government movement sheds much light on the discourse of democracy in early twentieth-century China and in our own time. It was a classic textbook case, underscoring two fundamental components of democracy: elections and freedom. Nobel Prize laureate, Indian-born economist Amartya Sen observes, "Democracy has complex demands, which certainly include voting and respect for election results, but it also requires the protection of liberties and freedoms, respect for legal entitlements, and the guaranteeing of free discussion and uncensored distribution of news and fair comment."[95] Sen emphasizes, "We must not identify democracy with majority rule."[96] The protection of liberties and freedoms is the main distinction between the modern concept of liberal democracy and the Platonic notion of democracy as majoritarian mob-rule.

The vibrancy of the print media in 1909 points to the democratic spirit of China in those days. Emerging from the margins of existing political structure, the press eagerly took on the tasks of educating citizens, debating the issues, scrutinizing the process, and monitoring the government. These journalist pioneers bravely challenged the state and stood for the rights of common citizens. The media took many officials to task, and even brought down the antireform governor-general of Shaanxi-Gansu.[97] Empowered by the legitimacy conferred by elections, and pressed by the media to take action, elected citizens weighed in on local and national politics. After the first-round elections, electors in Hunan who had no official status collectively declared their opposition to railroad loans from the West.[98] This action presaged the widely popular Railroad Protection Movement that later proved to be the last straw for the Qing dynasty.

In editorials, government hypocrisies were exposed and official incompetence were criticized. A *Shenbao* editorial attacked "fallacies in the Jiangsu governor's political views." The author made a searing indictment of the authoritarian government: "The greatest evil of despotic government lies in the fact that officials have the ultimate authority, while the people have little right to participate in governance. Officials control all local affairs, manipulate and confuse white and black … That's why the country has fallen into such a precarious state, with almost no hope of salvation."[99] *Dagongbao* advocated an end to the ban on political parties, because meaningful elections required parties.[100] It also made an unequivocal call to end the millennia-old practice of local magistrates serving concurrently as judges, thus effectively demanding an independent judiciary.[101]

Even though they were enthusiastic promoters of democratic elections, reformers did not blindly subscribe to the magic of elections. "The power of the government is checked by assemblymen, but who is to check the power of the assemblymen?" *Dagongbao* concluded, "Citizen's representatives should be checked by the newspapers."[102] *Zhengzong aiguobao,* a lowbrow paper that catered to the working class, captured the essence of democracy in down-to-earth Beijing colloquialisms: "What is constitutionalism? It is nothing more than setting up rules. From now on the emperor and people must all abide by them. No matter whether one is educated or ignorant, noble or mean, nobody can break these rules."[103] Essentially it argued that all individuals, no matter at the center or at the margins, should be treated equally before the law. Evidently, a culture of democracy was in the making.

The early constitutionalists were not only ahead of their time, their messages still resonate with the best minds of our time. In her "In Defense of Democracy in Taiwan," Lung Yingtai, one of the most influential contemporary Chinese-language writers, made a rigorous yet moving case for democracy in the aftermath of Taiwan's controversial presidential election of 2004. "Democracy is not just about elections and voting. It is a way of life, a way of thinking. It is like the air you breathe everyday, the way one carries oneself, and the space individuals possess."

She suggests that the true meaning of democracy "permeates the details of people's lives" without people actually noticing it.[104] In 1909, Liang Hong made a similar argument in a *Shenbao* editorial, when he compared self-government to the natural desire of human beings for food and drink in both the East and West. "Self-government is what people's livelihoods depend on, where life's vitality resides." In order to save the nation and protect individuals, he urged the Chinese people to pursue self-government in earnest, because "if not self-government, what else can be used [to achieve these goals]? What else can?"[105] Across time and space, both Liang and Lung would have found comfort in the words of a grassroots democracy reformer in Yunnan in 2004, "Democracy is a natural desire of the people."[106]

The reasoning of these writers and the experiences of the 1909 elections refute the reactionary elitist claim that the Chinese people are not ready or fit for democracy. The question of whether a country is "fit for democracy" is fundamentally misguided. Sen argues that in the twentieth century, a new belief has gained ascendancy: "A country does not have to be deemed fit for democracy; rather, it has to become fit through democracy."[107] While apologists for authoritarianism in the East and West still raise this question today, the reformers of 1909 did not ask whether China was fit for democracy. Instead, they saw the intrinsic and instrumental value of democracy, and they believed in the human potentiality for good. Most importantly, progressive reformers like the writers of *Zhengzong aiguobao* treasured the fundamental premise of democracy—the belief in equality, regardless of one's status, wealth, or education.

In many ways, the 1909 elections laid the foundation for a much-expanded national parliamentary election in the new republic in 1913. The voter base was expanded more than twenty fold to approximately forty million men, around 10 percent of the total population.[108] Had China not fallen victim to monarchical restoration attempts and internecine wars, had the new democracy survived and been consolidated, this election would have made China the largest democracy in Asia, if not the world.[109]

China's own home-grown experiments in elections and free media a century ago reveal its democratic potential. This long-marginalized historical process reminds us that it is misleading to think that the culture of democracy is entirely foreign to China. Our understanding of the past can have some impact on the future of China, because the democratic experiments of 1909 demonstrate the capacity of common citizens to collaborate and compete in fair and open elections, in pursuit of both their personal aspirations and social ideals. Given a reform-minded government initiative and a more liberal media, China has the potential to restart its history of democracy, especially from the grassroots and from the margins of the existing political structure.[110]

NOTES

1. *Shenbao* (October 14, 1909), 1.3.

2. "Lun ziyiju zhi qiantu" [On the future of provincial assemblies], *Dagongbao* (October 14, 1909), 4.

3. *Zhengzong aiguobao* (June 8, 1909), 5.

4. *Zhengzong aiguobao* (June 9, 1909), 1.

5. P'eng-yüan Chang, "The Constitutionalists," in Mary C. Wright, ed., *China in Revolution: The First Phase 1900–1913* (New Haven: Yale University Press, 1968), 150.

6. Ibid., 143.

7. Mary C. Wright, P'eng-yüan Chang, and John Fincher in *China in Revolution*.

8. Joseph W. Esherick, *Reform and Revolution in China: The 1911 Revolution in Hunan and Hubei* (Berkeley: University of California Press, 1976), 91.

9. Mary C. Wright, "Introduction," in *China in Revolution*, 3.

10. Joan Judge, *Print and Politics: 'Shibao' and the Culture of Reform in Late Qing China* (Stanford: Stanford University Press, 1996), 181.

11. *Shibao* (July 2, 1905).

12. Quoted in Bian Xiuquan, *Lixian sichao yu qingmo fazhi gaige* [The trend of constitutional thought and legal reforms at the end of the Qing] (Beijing: Zhongguo shehui kexue chubanshe, 2003), 29.

13. Kang Youwei, "Gongmin zizhi pian" [Treatise on citizen's self-government], in Zhang Zhan and Wang Renzhi, eds., *Xinhai geming qian shinianjian shilun xuanji* [Commentaries on current affairs in the ten years before the 1911 Revolution] (Beijing: Sanlian shudian, 1960), v. 1.1, 174.

14. "Lun jin renmin dui lixian zhi zeren" [The people's responsibility toward constitutionalism today], *Shibao* (September 8, 1905).

15. Xianzheng bianchaguan, *Qingmo minchu xianzheng shiliao jikan* [Collection of historical records on constitutionalism at the end of the Qing and in the early Republican period] (Beijing: Beijing tushuguan chubanshe, 2006), v. 1, 1–83.

16. Gugong bowuyuan mingqing dang'anbu, ed., *Qingmo choubei lixian dang'an shiliao* [Historical records on constitutional preparation at the end of the Qing] (Beijing: Zhonghua shuju), v. 1, 69.

17. Xiao (Bao Tianxiao), "Shuo chengxiang difang zizhi" [On urban and rural local self-government], *Shibao* (February 9, 1909), 3.

18. *Shibao* (January 11, 1909), 3.

19. *Shibao* (December 12, 1908), 3.

20. *Zhengzong aiguobao* (April 13, 1909), 5.

21. *Zhengzong aiguobao* (April 29, 1909),5.

22. "Xianling yi xuanju shi cheren" [Magistrate sacked due to election-related affairs], *Shibao* (February 27, 1909), 3.

23. *Shibao* (January 12, 1909), 3.

24. *Shenbao* (March 1, 1909), 3.2.

25. *Shibao* (December 12, 1908), 3.

26. Ibid.

27. *Shibao* (January 5, 1909), 3.

28. *Shibao* (December 14, 1908), 4.

29. *Shenbao* (October 14, 1909), 3.2.

Democracy Is in Its Details 217

30. *Dongfang zazhi* (November 18, 1908), 108–09.

31. *Shenbao* (January 5, 1909), 3.2. Although some initial preparations were carried out in Xinjiang, the elections and the establishment of the provincial assembly were postponed. Thus Xinjiang became the only province that did not have a provincial assembly on October 14, 1909, while all other twenty-one provinces did.

32. Inter-Parliamentary Union, http://www.ipu.org/wmn-e/suffrage.htm#Notel, accessed on April 28, 2007.

33. *Qingmo minchu xianzheng shiliao jikan*, v. 1, 14–23.

34. In view of today's People's Congress in the People's Republic, where 50 to 70 percent of the People's Representatives are officials and military officers, China's first elections in 1909 remain a hard act to follow. Estimates vary. Wang Guixiu, a Chinese Communist Party Central Party School professor gave his estimate of 70 percent in *Huaxia shibao* (February 23, 2006).

35. "Mimi zhi Zhongguo" [China the secretive], *Shibao* (August 10, 1909), 3.

36. Although the Yongzheng emperor eliminated a number of hereditary debased-status categories in 1723, the stigma was still manifest in the Regulations.

37. "Zhejiang sheng Ziyiju choubanchu jinshi huizhi" [Recent development of Zhejiang Provincial Assembly Preparatory Bureau], *Shibao* (December 13, 1908), 3. This interpretation distinguished between yamen runners and petty functionaries, though in practice the line between them could be quite blurred. The decision not to count petty officials as proper "officials" probably had to do with the fact that they were not on regular government payroll (*shique*).

38. Ibid.

39. "Shuli bude you xuanjuquan" [Scribes should not have the right to vote], *Shibao* (January 5, 1909), 3.

40. "Xianzhengguan zhi jieshi" [The Constitutional Commission's interpretation], *Shibao* (December 13, 1908), 3.

41. "Duiyu xianzhengguan zhi yiwen qi san" [Questioning The Constitutional Commission, part III continued], *Shibao* (December 16, 1908), 1.

42. "Duiyu xianzhengguan zhi yiwen qi san" [Questioning The Constitutional Commission, part III], *Shibao* (December 15, 1908), 1.

43. "Duiyu xianzhengguan zhi yiwen qi san" [Questioning The Constitutional Commission, part III continued], *Shibao* (December 16, 1908), 1.

44. Ibid.

45. *Qingmo minchu xianzheng shiliao jikan*, v. 1, 15.

46. *Shibao* (December 12, 1908), 3.

47. *Shibao* (January 30, 1909), 3.

48. *Shenbao* (August 6, 1909), 2.4.

49. "Sichuan zhengjie pianpianlu" [Political news from Sichuan], *Shibao* (March 23, 1909), 3.

50. "Wuyang xuanju diaocha shiwusuo jinshi" [New report from Wuyang election survey office], *Shibao* (December 18, 1908), 3.

51. *Shibao* (December 12, 1908), 4.

52. Zhang Pengyuan, *Lixianpai yu xinhai geming* [The Constitutionalists and the 1911 Revolution] (Taibei: Zhongyang yanjiuyuan jindai shi yanjiusuo, 1969), 15–16.

53. "Fujian Ziyiju choubanchu jishi" [Report on Fujian Provincial Assembly Preparatory Office], *Shibao* (March 6, 1909), 3.

54. "Waiguoren suokai xuetang xuesheng zhi xuanju quan" [Voting rights of students in foreign-run schools], *Shibao* (March 5, 1909), 3.

55. "Jiaohui xuetang biyesheng zhi xuanju quan" [Voting rights of graduates of church schools], *Shibao* (March 9, 1909), 3.

56. *Qingmo minchu xianzheng shiliao jikan*, v.1, 17.

57. *Shibao* (February 17, 1909), 3.

58. *Shibao* (February 20, 1909), 3.

59. *Shenbao* (March 20, 1909), 3.2.

60. *Shenbao* (February 19, 1909), 2.4.

61. *Shibao* (February 21, 1909), 3.

62. *Qingmo minchu xianzheng shiliao jikan*, v.1, 60.

63. "Shanghai xian xuanshi xuanjuren mince" [Shanghai county announces voter roll], *Shenbao* (February 7, 1909), 1.2.

64. "Fujian Ziyiju choubanchu jishi" [Report on Fujian Provincial Assembly Preparatory Office], *Shibao*, March 6, 1909), 3.

65. *Shenbao* (July 5, 1909), 3.2. Also reported in *Dagongbao* (June 24, 1909), 3.

66. *Shenbao* (March 13, 1909), 2.4.

67. *Shenbao* (March 30, 1909), 1.3.

68. "Shiping" [Editorial on current affairs], *Shibao* (April 1, 1909), 4.

69. *Shenbao* (March 30, 1909), 1.3.

70. *Shibao* (March 31, 1909), 2.

71. *Shibao* (March 30, 1909), 2.

72. *Shenbao* (March 18, 1909), 3.2.

73. *Shenbao* (May 30, 1909), 3.2.

74. Qin Ruijie, "Runeryue chuyi zhi Jiangsuren" [Jiangsu people on the election day], *Shenbao* (March 18, 1909), 1.2, and *Shibao* (March 18, 1909), 1. *Shenbao* placed it as an editorial on its front page, and *Shibao* ran it as a letter to the editor on page one. They printed different surnames for the author: Qin Ruijie in *Shibao*, Chen Ruijie in *Shenbao* (a mistake acknowledged by *Shenbao* on March 19).

75. Ibid.

76. "Runeryue chuyiri" (March 22), *Shibao* (March 16, 1909), 3.

77. "Jinri" [Today], *Shibao* (May 4, 1909), 2.

78. *Shibao* (March 24, 1909), 3.

79. *Shibao* (March 23, 1909), 2. This is probably a classic rendition of the humbling effect of elections and democracy.

80. Fu Huaifeng, "Shixi qingmo minchu minzhong de zhengzhi canyu: jiyu qingmo jiangzhe Ziyiju xuanju de gean yanjiu" [An analysis on people's political participation at the end of the Qing and early Republican period], *Ershiyi shiji* 23 (February 28, 2004), accessed at www.cuhk.edu.hk/ics/21c/supplem/essay/0211034.htm.

81. Shen Xiaomin, *Chuchang yu qiubian: Qingmo michu de Zhejiang Ziyiju he shengyihui* [Maintaining status quo and seeking change: Zhejiang Ziyiju and provincial assembly at the end of the Qing and the early Republican period] (Beijing: Sanlian shudian, 2005), 26.

82. "Zhili Ansu xian xuanju fengchao" [Election disturbance in Ansu, Zhili], *Shenbao* (June 30, 1909), 3.2.

83. "Changsha chuxuan" [First-round election in Changsha], *Shenbao* (June 10, 1909), 3.2.

84. "Hunan," *Shenbao* (July 27, 1909), 3.2.

85. "Duiyu Hunan Ziyiju zhi ganyan" [Comments on Hunan Provincial Assembly], *Shenbao* (August 2, 1909), 1.2.

86. *Qingmo minchu xianzheng shiliao jikan*, v. 1, 66.

87. Shanyue, "Jinggao Ziyiju zhi toupiao guanliyuan jianduyuan" [To election inspectors and staff members], *Shenbao* (March 19, 1909), 1.3.

88. "Changzhou chuxuan toupiaosuo guanliyuan jianchayuan xuzhi" [Inspector and staff instructions for first-round election in Changzhou], *Shenbao* (March 11, 1909), 3.2.

89. "Jingshi chuxuan qingxing" [First-round election in Beijing], *Shibao* (June 27, 1909), 2.

90. "Lun Hualou zhi weifa xuanju" [On election illegalities in Hualou], *Shenbao* (April 2, 1909), 1.3.

91. *Shenbao* (April 19, 1909), 2.4.

92. "Laihan" [Letter to the editor], *Shenbao* (March 29, 1909), 3.3.

93. "Lun jianchayuan jianshi xiepiao zhi bufa" [The illegality of inspectors monitoring ballot writing], *Shibao* (April 20, 1909), 1.

94. "Lun jinri xuanju zhi bi" [On the problems of today's elections], *Shenbao* (March 30, 1909), 1.3.

95. Amartya Sen, "Democracy as a Universal Value," *Journal of Democracy*, 10.3 (1999): 9–10.

96. Ibid., 9.

97. *Shibao* (June 25, 1909), 1.

98. "Chuxuan dangxuanren dian zheng jiekuan" [Protesting railroad loans by those elected in the first round], *Shenbao* (July 13, 1909), 1.5.

99. "Lun xufu zhengjian zhi miu" [Fallacies in the Jiangsu governor's political views], *Shenbao* (April 22, 1909), 1.5.

100. "Zhengdang yu xuanju" [Parties and election], *Dagongbao* (April 19, 1909), 2.

101. "Zhouxian guan buyi zai jian caipan" [Magistrates should no longer serve as judges], *Dagongbao* (May, 15, 1909), 3.

102. "Guomin daibiao ying shou baozhi jiandu" [Citizen's representatives should be checked by newspapers], *Dagongbao* (July 17, 1909), 3.

103. "Min zhiyi" [The people's will], *Zhengzong aiguobao* (June 27, 1909), 2.

104. Long Yingtai, "Wei Taiwan minzhu bianhu—yu huaren shijie duihua" [In defense of Taiwan democracy—a dialogue with the Chinese world], *Zhongguo shibao, Lianhe zaobao, Mingbao* (April 15, 2004).

105. *Shenbao* (September 20, 1909), 1.3.

106. Reported by Li Fan, a grassroots election expert and the director of The World and China Institute (a grassroots democracy research NGO based in Beijing), after his field research in Honghe prefecture, Yunnan, in 2004.

107. Sen, 4.

108. John Fincher, "Political Provincialism and the National Revolution," in Wright, ed., *China in Revolution*, 209–10.

109. The concept of election became so entrenched that even its foes felt obliged to go through elections to demolish the new republic. In 1915 President Yuan Shikai set up a rubberstamp National Congress of People's Representatives, and the resolution to restore "constitutional monarchy" garnered 1,993 votes out of 1,993 ballots. In January 1916 Yuan became the new emperor, but 83 days later he was forced to abandon his emperorship. Concomitant with the demise of elections and democracy, press freedom had been under attack, as Yuan suppressed the once-vibrant media to clear the way for his restoration propaganda. Ding Baochen, the founder of *Zhengzong aiguobao* was arrested and executed in

1913. He became the first among a number of independent newsmen killed by Yuan and other warlords. When these advocates of political participation and citizen's rights were muzzled, Yuan's henchmen brazenly labeled republicanism as "unfit for China's national condition" (*guoqing*). See *Junxian jisheng* [Celebrating constitutional monarchism], photocopy of a collection of restoration documents compiled by Toyo Bunko, Tokyo, stored at Stanford University East Asian Library. Acquisition is dated 1976.

110. The notion of "restarting Chinese history" is borrowed from Merle Goldman. See "Restarting Chinese History," *The American Historical Review* 105.1 (February 2000), 153–64.

10

A BULWARK NEVER FAILING

The Evolution of Overseas Chinese Education in French Indochina, 1900–1954

Tracy C. Barrett

In Indochina, the creation of Chinese schools relied heavily upon the long tradition of overseas Chinese education established before the arrival of French colonialists and their regulatory influences. In the late nineteenth and early twentieth centuries, following a pattern common to the Southeast Asian Chinese diaspora, this educational tradition started with the native place associations, or *huiguan*, that operated Chinese language schools wherever suitable populations of young Chinese were present. As the Chinese population grew, the number of schools increased as well, until they became a ubiquitous fixture in cities and small towns across present-day Vietnam and Cambodia. French efforts to use education as a means of courting southern Chinese officials—thus facilitating France's access to the markets of southern China—also contributed significantly to the development of Chinese education in the colonies. But despite French plans, real educational success rested in the hands of Indochina's overseas Chinese, the wealthy and powerful merchant and business families from various native places who invested their own money and energy in the schools as insurance on the future.

This chapter examines the efforts of overseas Chinese living outside the Qing empire to mobilize their communities in relation not just to the Chinese state, but also to the French colonial state in Indochina. In the rapidly changing environment of colonial Indochina, what roles did Chinese schools play? Did the intent of education in small, perhaps even rural, Chinese schools differ from its purpose in larger, more pan-Chinese schools in large urban areas such as Hanoi and Saigon? If so, how and why? What new forms of education awaited overseas Chinese on the twentieth century horizon? These are just a few of the questions that this chapter hopes to address, but before turning more specifically to these issues, a clearer picture of the nature of overseas Chinese society in French Indochina at the turn of the last century will facilitate a better understanding of the educational requirements and priorities of Indochina's overseas Chinese communities. Thus, we shall shift our focus briefly to Indochina's colonial milieu.

Native Place and the Congregations

No discussion of Indochina's overseas Chinese can occur without first mentioning the Chinese congregations. As the fundamental organizational component of Indochina's Chinese community, congregations are unique to Indochina, although similar groups of Chinese existed wherever large native place communities settled outside of China. Local members referred to these organizations as *huiguan*, meaning temple or meeting place, but the French version of these associations differs significantly from *huiguan* found elsewhere in the Chinese diaspora. In their colonial incarnation, congregations emerged on October 5, 1871, three years before the French officially consolidated their hold on Cochinchina.[1] The institutions that were to govern the overseas Chinese in Indochina for the next eighty years attained their first colonially sanctioned form with the passage of a law that encompassed the two fundamental components of the congregation system. First, it officially recognized seven Chinese congregations, the congregations of Canton, Fujian, Hakka, Hainan, Chaozhou, Fuzhou, and Quanzhou.[2] Second, it established that all Chinese nationals residing in Cochinchina were required by law to belong to one of the seven congregations if they desired to remain in the country. Chinese subjects employed by European firms were the only exception to this law.[3] Although a number of other laws in later years developed and refined the French system of monitoring and controlling the overseas Chinese,[4] the 1871 law created the very first pitch upon which the game of Franco-Chinese relations within Indochina would be played throughout the colonial period until the French departure from Vietnam in 1954.[5]

Across Indochina, Chinese congregations created a niche in which overseas Chinese could interact with others from the same general region of China who, in many cases, shared the same dialect and worshipped the same deities. However, to view the congregations simply as institutions providing open access to a homogenized population would be to ignore the complexity and depth of the congregations as organizations. As the legal scholar Nguyễn Quốc Đinh wrote at the time, within each congregation, "all the members of each trade, of each insurance group, assistance group, and cult join together to form many distinct groups, and the congregation is the sum of all these."[6]

The first and foremost obligation of any congregation was to provide a meeting place for its congregants. Thus, Chinese congregations were responsible for constructing and maintaining temples and other cultural sites for their dialect community. In keeping with this particular obligation, congregations were also charged with celebrating native-place holidays and ensuring the observance of local religious festivals. Over time, locally oriented cultural responsibilities began to assume a more nationalistic flavor as congregations took on the task of collecting remittances, first for Qing-sponsored causes and anti-Qing activities, and later for the new Republic. In Indochina, as was the case in many of Southeast Asia's colonies, functions of economy and mutual aid overshadowed the more spiritual roles of the *huiguan* in the public eye, and this phenomenon became more marked as time passed. A colonial environment required institutions capable of performing intermediary roles, whether politically, economically, or personally. In Indochina, the vital necessity of mediation took precedence over daily piety, at least in the big picture.[7]

The very nature of *huiguan* observances also changed dramatically as the twentieth century progressed. The crucial, and even cataclysmic, events of the early twentieth century shifted the *huiguan*'s focus from the mundane to the monumental. Parades for the goddess Mazu lost ground to massive pan-Chinese nationalist movements and the idea of a "Chinese" spirit overtook many of the intricacies of subethnicity in the process. This is not meant to imply that each subethnic community lost the specificities which made it unique—e.g., Mazu retained her cultural and religious significance—however, new global political influences required the attention of the Chinese community as a whole and the community responded to that need with enthusiasm.

Congregations possessed great significance in several respects. As the cornerstone of Chinese social, cultural, religious, political, and economic life in Indochina, congregational membership allowed overseas Chinese to tap into a vast network of personal connections that could assist them in any aspect of their legal, personal, or professional lives. Intra-congregational contacts assisted Chinese with such things as religious or commemorative ceremonies specific to a native place; hospitalization, burial, or repatriation of bones back to the native place; and even mutual aid insurance to support the elderly or infirm during times of great difficulty. But while congregations performed mutual aid functions that sustained overseas Chinese in the most critical periods of their lives, the services they provided far exceeded social welfare. Congregations assumed responsibility for nurturing the very souls of their communities by taking on the tasks of engineering religious and secular festivals, organizing political commemorations, and attending to the education of young Chinese students in Indochina.

In his chapter, Soon Keong Ong confronts the common assumption that overseas Chinese pursued activities in China out of loyalty to their native place, a stereotype he refers to as the "love of homeland" thesis. His critique reminds us of the dangers of oversimplification, and in particular, that each overseas Chinese citizen, irrespective of native place, was an individual with motivations unique to his own life and experiences. But even though the heterogeneity of Indochina's overseas Chinese community cannot be overemphasized, members of the diaspora still frequently identified themselves in categories drawn by dialect and subethnic place. In Chapter 12 Paola Iovene's discussion of the Shanghai barbers' revolt reminds us that in the Shanghai of the 1940s, native place took precedence over professional associations, a fact clearly evident in her descriptions of the resentment expressed by the Yangzhou barbers for being lumped in with their callow Subei countrymen. These two ideas are certainly not contradictory and both are useful to keep in mind during any discussion of the Chinese diaspora. Each overseas Chinese had unique motivations and aspirations, but in Indochina, each also belonged to a larger community, a congregation, with institutional goals and priorities of its own.

In Indochina, by both choice and colonial design, Chinese congregations were inextricably involved in overseas Chinese education. The significance of this involvement can be found in the vast cultural differences between Chinese in each of the Indochinese congregations. Overseas Chinese might have shared a nationality, but for the most part, they did not share a spoken language. The values and concerns of each dialect group differed, as did the gods they worshipped and the professions they tended to pursue. In fact, members of different dialect groups frequently engaged in open, sometimes bloody, conflict with one another, especially in periods preceding the consolidation of French colonial control. Living in Indochina at a time of great susceptibility in their lives, adolescent overseas Chinese, constantly bombarded by non-Chinese influences and values, found themselves buffeted by a variety of cultural stimuli. Thus, the establishment of schools unique to each native place or dialect not only represents a concerted effort to indoctrinate young Chinese students in the ways of their native place, but also casts the congregations in the role of cultural defenders, bulwarks against the many alien influences, Chinese and other, that sought to dilute the values and traditions of each native place.

Education: The Funding, Establishment, and Operation of Schools

Perhaps the most interesting aspect of overseas Chinese organizations in general is the concerted effort they directed towards maintaining the social and cultural integrity of their settlements abroad. The significance of these schools to the overseas Chinese community is borne out in the numbers. By 1929, somewhere in the vicinity of one hundred and thirty private Chinese schools existed in the southern colony of Cochinchina alone, and requests to open them came in at such a pace that French authorities found themselves buried beneath applications they had increasingly less time to process.[8] Existing schools proved to be the least of the French worries. As early as 1925, the Residents Superior in Tonkin and in Cambodia expressed concerns about the proliferation of and ideological leanings of Chinese education, resulting in the inauguration of a French campaign against unauthorized Chinese schools. Hanoi's Governor General demanded detailed intelligence estimates of the scale and number of these institutions, concerned by the risk they posed to public order, particularly if they became politically adversarial.[9] French apprehension stemmed largely from incidents happening elsewhere in Southeast Asia, in particular among the Chinese of Thailand, rather than deriving from unrest among Indochinese-based Chinese. Despite the relative absence of havoc, French authorities were unwilling to take any chances with the spread of civil disorder.

In Indochina, congregations and schools enjoyed a unique relationship that nurtured the youngsters from each native place and ensured the perpetuation of Chinese language and culture among children whose actual experience in their homeland was often quite limited. In addition, by encouraging multidirectional ties between the colonies and the native place, congregations and schools strengthened the relationship between each native place and the congregation that called it home. This strengthening of ties occurred in a number ways. Most commonly, instructors from the native place were brought to Indochina to direct local schools or to teach, especially at the elementary level; however, congregations also worked to strengthen education back in the native place, offering more than teaching jobs to their fellow countrymen when the situation allowed. In both situations, the symbiotic relationship between congregation and native place offered benefits to the homeland as well as to the expatriate community.

In 1902, the Fujian congregation in Cholon, which bordered Saigon, sought permission to open a collection among its members in order to raise money for the establishment of a school in Xiamen where young Chinese students would learn to speak French.[10] This institution became one of the earliest examples of a Cochinchinese diaspora-sponsored school in China. At the time, the sole non-Chinese school in Xiamen was an American-sponsored school with English as the primary language of instruction. Cholon's Fujianese community thought that the establishment of its school would serve to enhance the trade in Indochina and improve commerce by strengthening ties with the French.[11] From the French perspective, closer ties with Chinese resident in Indochina and an improved image among the Fujianese had much to offer; however, Cochinchina's lieutenant governor remained quite skeptical of the undertaking, concerned that curriculum at the school would be completely outside of French control, and therefore potentially subversive.[12] Surprisingly, the lieutenant governor did not seem tempted by the opportunity to counterbalance the English-speaking influence in Xiamen.

Cholon's Fujianese community had already successfully established a school for Fujianese children in the city of Cholon; however, a French-oriented Fujianese school in Xiamen offered certain benefits as well. While from the Fujianese perspective, the advantages of such a school and the accessibility it provided to French language instruction seem clear, the benefits for the Fujian congregation in Cholon were not insignificant either. By creating a school to which the congregation's name would certainly be affixed, the congregation ensured good publicity in the native place. After all, the quantity, frequency, and significance of remittances from Cholon to Xiamen played a major role in determining local prestige. More practically, the ability to speak a colonial language did wonders for an individual's success in the colonial environment. Easy access to French instruction in Xiamen virtually guaranteed a steady influx of young laborers and fortune seekers capable of dealing with the vicissitudes of the French administration in Indochina, thereby preparing them to achieve personal success in their new diasporic lives.

Requests for permission to establish, direct, or teach at a Chinese school reached colonial desks most frequently, and although these requests have the appearance of mere formalities, certain impressions gleaned from them cast light upon the complex, and even transnational, connections involved in primary and secondary Chinese education in Indochina. French records enumerating annual requests to establish Chinese schools suggest that the Chinese education movement reached its apex between 1926 and 1929. Although it is difficult to say for certain why Chinese schools were most prolific during these particular years, transnational politics certainly played a major role in this phenomenon. In Guangzhou and Nanjing, the Nationalist Party's calls for Chinese solidarity and for the material and ideological support of the overseas Chinese community at large must have influenced the increasing numbers of Chinese schools. Furthermore, the gradual politicization, not only of China, but of Southeast Asia's overseas Chinese communities as well, was underway, and wars waged on Chinese soil had not yet refocused Indochina's overseas Chinese community on national relief, supporting the war efforts, and opposing the Japanese invasion.

Internal Chinese politics had a history of disrupting study abroad for Chinese students. In one particular case, that of the Chinese student Tchêng Tchong Hoa, the massive upheavals that occurred in China during the 1911 revolution forced him to abandon his education at the College of the Protectorate in Tonkin in order to return to China to help his family, who had been ruined by the events of the revolution.[13] The situation did not improve as the century progressed. The abrupt and bloody split in 1927 between the Communists and the Nationalists in China meant that young Chinese students were likely safer in Indochina than in major Chinese cities, particularly Guangzhou, the city through which many of Indochina's Chinese reached the colonies.[14] In fact, this event was likely responsible for much of the increased demand for Chinese education in Indochina. Chinese schools also became one of the focal points of the movement for speaking Mandarin (*guoyu*) in Indochina. Unifying the national spoken Chinese language meant that greater national unity and pan-Chinese solidarity became more likely. Chinese schools and associations seemed the most logical places to pursue the task of linguistic standardization.[15]

The Ecole Pavie

French authorities also tried their hand at establishing schools for Chinese students. In 1904, the founding of Hanoi's Ecole Pavie heralded a new age for Chinese education in Indochina. Established by the French to instruct the sons of southern Chinese scholar officials, the school formed the heart of an educational web extending throughout Indochina and into southern China. It maintained close ties with the Chinese imperial government, as well as regularly interacting with the students' congregations. Although a colonial institution, this school ironically played a major role in fostering rebellion among its young Chinese students. Students there learned the arts of politics and war, knowledge they took back with them to China where they used it to foment unrest and rebellion, to the dismay of imperial officials and French colonial authorities alike.

This sort of irony is certainly not unique to Indochina. Historian Michael Hunt suggests that the increasing acceptance in China of republican and democratic ideals paradoxically served to strengthen anti-Western resistance among young Chinese students and revolutionaries.[16] He also points to the growing resentment among Chinese subjects who felt that western imperial powers, in particular the United States, used a vocabulary of national friendship and "cultural investment" to justify their economic exploitation of China.[17] But despite the paradox that Chinese students receiving French education became increasingly anti-French, the ideological difficulties emerging from the Ecole Pavie paled into insignificance beside the impact of the institution upon overseas Chinese education in Indochina.

The Ecole Pavie, located in Hanoi, was the first school created in Indochina for the Chinese in general, and for the sons of official elites in particular. Although far from representative of Chinese education in Indochina, the Ecole Pavie as an institution holds a place of paramount importance. Scholar officials from the Chinese provinces bordering Tonkin, primarily Yunnan and Guangxi, sent their sons to Hanoi to study at this school. In Hong Kong, the British were concurrently in the process of establishing an Anglo-Chinese University. The French inability to compete with the English in attracting young sons of Chinese elites to their schools caused Indochina's colonial administration quite a bit of anxiety. The Ecole Pavie, founded in 1904, was one of the first French efforts to rectify that perceived imbalance, and it was at once a great success and a terrible failure.

In June 1904, Li Caotian, the *taotai* and minister for foreign affairs in Yunnan, sent a letter to the governor general inquiring about French options for educating his two sons, who were 22 and 16 years of age. In particular, he wanted to know if there was a school for French students that his sons could attend in order to learn French and to become more acquainted with Yunnan's neighboring colonialists.[18] No such school existed, but after the governor general's inquiry, Tonkin's resident superior suggested opening a boarding school for sons of Chinese officials, where, for example, Yunnan's *taotai*'s sons could mingle with the sons of the Longzhou's *taotai*, who were already based in Hanoi.[19] To French and Qing officials, closer cooperation and friendship between Indochina's colonial administration and the Chinese government in provinces bordering Tonkin promised to be mutually beneficial. Plans were immediately underway to establish the school. On September 17, 1904, the governor general told his chief of cabinet that he was "of the opinion that the school for the sons of the Chinese mandarins should be formed at once." Also in this response, he approved the school's rather steep annual fee of 1,200 francs per student and said that he would inform the French consul at Yunnan of the plans to create the school.[20] In just a few weeks, the response of Yunnan's minister arrived.

> I would suggest sending, every year, to Hanoi, a certain number of pupils, some of whom would go on, after [finishing in Hanoi], to complete their studies in France. Given the movement that exists in all the parts of the Empire to entrust the care of educating young Chinese men to the Japanese, there would perhaps be enough interest to create a university in Hanoi where one could fight against this anti-foreign influence.[21]

After receiving such a positive response from China, matters unfolded with surprising speed. By December, twenty-two Chinese students from Yunnan, ten of whom had already been admitted to the new school by examination, departed for Hanoi, escorted by Léang Siang, a provincial official.[22] The French were pleased with the initial enrollment of ten students but realistic about the importance of it. As an early report from the school's administration commented, the Chinese "wanted to try an experiment, and, to prove it, sent forty students to Japan and ten to Tonkin. If they are satisfied, next year the proportion can be reversed."[23]

As the end of the first year approached, prospects for the young school looked bright; the students had progressed nicely, no issues of discipline had arisen, and both the Chinese and the French seemed optimistic.[24] Even the minister of Asian affairs in Paris applauded the colonial efforts, encouraging them to increase enrollment at the school and to look into founding an Indochinese university, all for purposes of garnering international political equity and increasing the spread of French influence. For the minister, the use of French as the educational medium in Hanoi's schools for young Chinese was of paramount political importance. "The increasing importance for us of counterbalancing Japanese influence in China will seem to you, certainly, to justify all of the measures intended to propagate the use of our language."[25]

In 1906, the timbre of the school began to change when several students submitted a petition requesting permission to be allowed to practice military tactics half a day every day.[26] At first, the request was denied. The governor general had consulted with the minister of foreign affairs in Yunnan, who had demurred, commenting, "These young people are destined for civil service careers."[27] Despite this official reluctance, the request was granted a short time later, and the ecole's students began to study the art of war under French soldiers in Hanoi.[28]

The first indication that the French might regret that decision came quickly when an excerpt from a letter sent by an Ecole Pavie student appeared in the Chinese press:

> Yunnannese students in Hanoi sent a letter to Peking addressed to the ministry in charge of the reorganization of the armies saying that during their holidays, they traveled along the border of Indochina and Yunnan. They noticed that the French had established many fortresses and that in the territory of Yunnan, all are along the railroad line ... The province of Yunnan is therefore endangered because everyone knows the ambitions of the French. It is necessary to organize a very strong army for the defense of the border.[29]

The French investigated the incident, spoke to the students en masse, and, while unable to identify the offending party, did manage to determine that the students had received the information second-hand from reading Chinese publications. The director of the Ecole Pavie attempted to convince the students that France represented no danger to Yunnan, but to no avail: "Chinese, with the mentality that is theirs, will never believe that a Frenchman can, on this point, tell them the truth."[30]

Political activism among students at the school did not stop there. A sixteen-page pamphlet called "Yunnan Warning" (*Yunnan jinggao*) circulated through the province in 1906, and French sources were able to trace the anti-French tract back to Ecole Pavie students. The document spoke of the danger posed by the French to Yunnan's sovereignty, comparing the French in China to the Russians in Manchuria, and citing the French in Algeria as proof of French duplicity and savagery.[31] Another bulletin, entitled "Advice for Yunnan's Population," condemned the way the French grew wealthy as the people of Indochina starved. "Annam's realm has been conquered for twenty years. A part of the population has disappeared. At the beginning of the French occupation, the population was not too miserable because the country was not dominated. France was afraid of an uprising and it was important to achieve pacification; peace was advised. Later the population returned to misfortune. Now, all of the dangerous rebels are dead."[32] The authors of this piece of propaganda claimed to be students in Hanoi; once more, the Ecole Pavie was implicated in anti-French agitation.

The French government quickly realized that the difficulties that they were having with Ecole Pavie students paled in comparison to the problems facing Yunnanese authorities. In 1908, with no explanation, Yunnanese officials informed the governor general that it would no longer be possible to send a new class from the province to the Ecole Pavie. After a bit of confusion, the French vice-consul in Yunnan met privately with the provincial treasurer[33] who explained why Si-Léang, Yunnan's provincial governor, had ordered that no more students be sent to the school.

> These pupils, after ending their studies at the Ecole Pavie, were, upon their return, the cause of real difficulties for the authorities in the schools that they entered or the places in which they live. They have not stopped provoking unfortunate unrest, either by means of public or private speeches, or by wanting to get involved in local affairs and in international issues by [writing and distributing] pamphlets or by making charges [against those] high authorities. This revolutionary spirit, said the treasurer, is no less dangerous because it hampers local administrations and it risks compromising international relations.[34]

At first, the sudden decision of the Yunnan government to stop patronizing the school seemed to have taken the French government aback, but it is also clear that the French were aware of the many problems being caused in China by Ecole Pavie students. As previously discussed, at least three different sets of lengthy and detailed pamphlets full of anti-French propaganda and written by Ecole Pavie students circulated throughout Yunnan in late 1905 and early 1906 alone. Additionally, the head of Indochina's political bureau was aware of the involvement of Ecole Pavie students in revolutionary activities propagated by one of the most dangerous opponents of the Qing dynasty. "Antidynastic and revolutionary sentiments professed by these students are not in doubt; during the Nam-Quan fort escapade, three of them were convinced to travel to Lang Son, at least, with Sun Yat-sen and his companions."[35] When Ecole Pavie graduates became implicated in revolutionary forays involving the future father of the Chinese Republic, Yunnan's provincial officials could not ignore the threat they posed. In the end, the scandal over political unrest fomented by former students signaled the death knell for the unique, if short-lived, school.[36]

The Ecole Pavie was officially disbanded by an order of the governor-general dated July 11, 1908.[37] The reasons behind the institute's abrupt closure are complex, but fundamentally, even though the French had previously bandied around the idea of closing the school, the ultimate decision came from China, and its meaning was unmistakable. Yunnan authorities would no longer send students from their province to the Ecole Pavie. Only two solutions remained: send all of the students back to Yunnan immediately, or let them enroll for the rest of the school year in a normal school in Hanoi that accepted Asian students who were not Vietnamese.[38] The viceroy of Yunnan agreed to let the students return immediately on two conditions. First, that the fall tuition already paid to the French be returned to Yunnan's government, and second, that if the students could not afford the return fare of fifty taels per person, that the governor-general of Indochina advance them the money, which would later be reimbursed.[39] Thus, with a brief bureaucratic squabble over finances, the school was closed.

In a confidential letter sent to the governor-general, the head of Indochina's political bureau condemned the entire Ecole Pavie venture as a disastrous failure.

> As a matter of fact, the Ecole Pavie did not produce any of the hoped-for results. Intended especially to develop French influence in Yunnan, most of the pupils that it educated gave evidence, afterwards, of their hostility towards France. Intended to contribute to the development of friendly relations between France and China, it threatens to become, on the contrary, a source of difficulties because of the revolutionary spirit that moves the students.[40]

Despite the early success of the Ecole Pavie in attracting the attention of southern China's ranking officials in another major respect, the school was a failure. It never managed, despite several attempts, to recruit students successfully from wealthy Chinese merchant families with ties to Indochina. This failure can be attributed to two factors. First, the school's focus upon attracting sons of Qing officials gave it an initially elitist flavor, both in China and in the northern colony of Tonkin. Second, before the school had a real chance to become well established, it had already been implicated in political radicalism and anti-establishment ideology. Either of these two indictments could easily prove fatal for an individual's livelihood or residence in French Indochina. With Indochina's wealthy Chinese merchants having so much at stake in the colony, it is hardly a surprise that no overseas Chinese families stood clamoring at the door of the Ecole. Had the school effectively shifted gears to allow admittance to those types of students, it might possibly have managed to maintain a less politically charged environment. With a dramatically larger pool of prospective students, it also would have had less trouble attracting a complete enrollment from year to year.

The Lycée Franco-Chinois

In spite of these failings, efforts to educate Chinese in French-style schools continued unabated. In fact, I would like to suggest that the failure of the Ecole Pavie, combined with the support and cooperation of Cochinchina's Chinese merchant elites eventually allowed the emergence of a school that did not fail but stalwartly endured right up until the collapse of the French regime in 1954. This school was known as the Lycée Franco-Chinois. Colonial attention turned to the fledgling Lycée Franco-Chinois as the bearer of French hopes for shifting the minds of young Chinese students toward the French and away from both the English and the Japanese, who were so much better positioned geographically for admitting Chinese to their educational institutions. This idea gains further credence when one considers that the school's native-place ties with Fujian were quite strong and that the school's board of directors, along with the general government, recruited quite heavily from places like Xiamen and Fuzhou—a region where English influence was less evident than in Guangzhou and hopes for French success could be higher.

While the Indochinese University did not come to be, the English plan to open universities in China gradually morphed into a plan to open the University of Hong Kong. French colonial authorities were already distressed by the fact that wealthy Chinese merchants in Cochinchina educated their sons in English secondary schools, and they tried to figure out a way to consolidate French influence in Asia, particularly in Indochina and among the merchant Chinese. This was the primary colonial justification for establishing the Franco-Chinese Secondary School in Cholon, known as the Lycée Franco-Chinois, but the Lycée Franco-Chinois was also significant within the Chinese community. For Cholon's Chinese, and arguably for the Chinese throughout Cochinchina, the Lycée Franco-Chinois was one of the crown jewels, not only of Sino-French cooperation, but of inter-congregational cooperation as well.

That the French were integrally involved in the planning and implementation of the Franco-Chinese Secondary School cannot be denied; however, the early efforts for the establishment of a modern, Western school for Chinese students came from other sources in addition to the French. In fact, as early as December of 1907, a group of Chinese merchants living in Cholon established an association whose sole purpose was to create a school that would "give Chinese children a modern education."[41] These same Chinese merchants even commissioned a French notary, Mr. Gigon-Papin, to investigate the feasibility of such an institution.[42] With such active support from the Chinese community in Cholon, the colonial government quickly agreed to facilitate the creation of the Franco-Chinese Secondary School.

The desire for a French school expressed by Cholon's wealthy Chinese proved to be a valued lifeline for the colonial administration. On January 27, 1908, colonial authorities met in a general assembly at which they appointed a board of directors for the as-yet-unformed school. Six members of this board, including the first president of the board, Mr. Schneegans, were European; the other twelve members, including the first vice-president of the board, Mr. Ta-Mah-Yan, were Chinese businessmen and heads of the four major Chinese congregations.[43] On February 10, 1908, about two weeks after the creation of the school's board of directors, the new company received its official seal of approval when the lieutenant governor of Cochinchina, Mr. Bonhoure, endorsed the establishment of both the association and the school it sought to create.[44] Three years later, the joint committee of Chinese and Frenchmen got their project underway.

When petitioning the French government for a subsidy to meet the school's budget shortfall, the president of the committee commented on the early days of the association, writing that its purpose

> ... was to create, in the most important Chinese center of the colony, an establishment similar to those which had already existed for several years in Hong Kong, Shanghai, and Singapore, where well-to-do Chinese based in Indochina had not hesitated, despite the relatively high expense, to send their children. These [children], their studies completed, returned to us educated like the English and speaking English exclusively. It seemed that it would be possible to keep [those students] in Indochina by offering the same education but in French.[45]

By highlighting the ever-present competition with Great Britain, the Association of the Franco-Chinese Secondary School managed to maintain the interest and support of the colonial administration throughout the early years of its existence, not a mean feat considering that the school ran with a perpetual budget shortfall and required significant yearly subsidies in order to continue its operations.

When considering the local value of an institution like the Lycée Franco-Chinois, it is important to remember the depth of penetration of congregational schools into rural areas. All regions of Indochina maintained Chinese-run, congregationally supported elementary schools for local Chinese children. Only the best and the brightest of Chinese pupils, those destined for higher education, were affected by the flight to foreign schools and universities. By establishing a Chinese secondary school in Cholon, the French, with the help and cooperation of the Chinese congregations, had gone a long way toward obviating the need for travel to Hong Kong or Guangzhou for further education.[46]

Despite its stalwart support of the endeavor, it would be incorrect to assume that the colonial government bore the primary pecuniary responsibility for building and operating the school. After Lieutenant-Governor Bonhoure approved the establishment of the Association of the Franco-Chinese Secondary School,[47] the association called upon the European and Chinese communities in Saigon and Cholon to pledge financial support to the school. The resulting signatures promised a sum of $159,160 piastres, only $15,160 piastres of which were paid by European donors. The remaining $144,000 piastres of the initial sum collected came directly from members of Cholon's Chinese community. Prompted by the generosity of the network of Chinese businessmen based in Cholon and no doubt relieved that wealthy Chinese youth would no longer be required to seek education from the English, the French General Government added its own donation of $20,000 piastres to the amount collected by the board of directors.[48]

Although technically in the town of Cholon, the proposed site for the school actually sat on the border between Cholon and Saigon, offering easy access to Chinese pupils from both cities. The colonial government, led by Governor General Beau, donated a substantial tract of land to the association for the construction of the school's facilities, and the governor general himself laid the cornerstone of the new school on February 26, 1908. At the ceremony marking the commencement of construction, five of the Chinese founders of the secondary school were awarded the distinguished Decoration of State Education[49] for their efforts on behalf of the new institution of learning.[50] During the period of construction, the board of directors desired that the school commence operations despite the lack of suitable facilities. To that end, the board sought temporary space in which to house and teach the students and their professors. The Chinese community came up with a solution to the dilemma of space when the Fujian congregation volunteered the use of its pagoda in Cholon to the students and faculty of the school until the school's actual building was completed. The association quickly accepted this generous offer and the Franco-Chinese Secondary School sprang to life.[51]

On April 7, 1909, Governor General Klobukowski addressed the assembled students and an audience of French and Chinese dignitaries during an ornate ceremony at the Fujian pagoda, the temporary site for the newly inaugurated school. In his speech, he spoke little of education and his hopes for the school's success; rather, he delivered a stern address with heavy political overtones. Discussing the long relationship between China and Indochina, Klobukowski warned the Chinese to remain obedient to local laws, saying

> Indochina has always welcomed [the Chinese] warmly and has given them the greatest opportunities to work. [Here] they are entitled to appeal either to indigenous statutes or to French law. Therefore, the colonial government counts it as absolutely required that [the Chinese] always remain respectful of the regulations and of the laws which ensure a privileged position for them in Indochina. That is why their absolute and complete loyalty can be claimed.[52]

In his speech, Klobukowski went on to acknowledge the fundamental condition of the Chinese community in Indochina. They consistently participated in the commerce, labor, and communities of Saigon and Cholon, he acknowledged, but he doubted their loyalty and commitment to the governing bodies of Vietnam, fearing instead that the numerous Chinese nationals in Indochina remained loyal only to China and to their political and economic interests there. The political climate in Indochina at the time goes a long way toward contextualizing this speech. The Vietnamese peasant uprising of 1908, the closing of the University of Hanoi, and a number of similar incidents had served to darken considerably the colonial mood, a mistrust clearly conveyed in the severe and stern nature of Klobukowski's address.

Despite his 1909 severity, Klobukowski himself generally supported Chinese organizations in Indochina[53] and the Franco-Chinese Secondary School proved to be no exception to this unwritten policy. Still, he expected something more than good stewardship in return for the financial support of the colonial authority, as the above passage from his speech indicates. In fact, what was perceived as his permissive attitude toward the Chinese population of Indochina led to quite a bit of friction within the administration, and on occasion, scathing letters of protest were sent to the minister of colonies in Paris, who then required explanations of and even defenses for Klobukowski's decisions. The subsidy granted to the Franco-Chinese Secondary School by Klobukowski's administration was just one of a number of issues for which the minister of colonies demanded justification.[54] The financial pressure that the administration faced from Paris also shines through in the speech Klobukowski gave at the opening of the school, in which he urged the school's board of directors to adhere to the "the strictest economy in the construction of this establishment. Needless use of luxury is not preferable to reserving the collected capital sums necessary for the normal functioning of the school for one or two years."[55]

The school's builders paid heed to Klobukowski's plea for economy. Construction of the school building only cost $109,800 piastres, considerably short of the $179,160 piastres that had been raised by the Board in its initial collection; however, the remaining funds quickly dwindled with the purchasing of furniture, educational supplies and books that had to be ordered from France, equipment for the dining halls, and so on. The financial shortfall was exacerbated because the pupils cost more money to keep, feed, and educate than they paid for tuition and board. By 1912, when the board of directors decided to install electricity in the new building (at the cost of $10,000 piastres for the entire project) the school's financial struggles had become abundantly clear.[56]

In fact, the most serious issue challenging the success of the school concerned its irregular funding, a problem so severe that it once actually halted the operation of the institution for several months in 1917. Financial woes beset the school as early as 1911, when, before the institution was even operational, $10,000 piastres were lost due to the unexpected bankruptcy of one of the Chinese businesses that had pledged to support it. The money donated for the founding of the school had been exhausted by 1914. The closure of 1917 represented a real low point for the institution, but in 1918, the French stepped in to subsidize the running of the place. These subsidies took many varied forms, including large donations of funds levied by the congregations from the Chinese community[57] and various supplements donated by the government of Cochinchina.[58] In fact, the most consistent source of funding enjoyed by the school in the 1920s was money funneled to the school out of the amounts paid to France by the Chinese government as part of the reparations remaining from the Boxer Rebellion.[59]

These funding problems were not alleviated until the President of Cholon's Municipal Council had the inspired idea to add five cents to the taxes paid by each of Cholon's Chinese merchants and businessmen, money that was to go directly into the Lycée's budget. Cholon's Chinese Chamber of Commerce welcomed a solution that was at once simple and effective but not too onerous for smaller businessmen to bear.[60] The Chinese Chamber of Commerce and the leaders of Cholon's congregations felt that an increased tax would present fewer problems for them than had the old method of laboriously collecting pledges from the entire Chinese community.[61] The only major complaint was that Cholon merchants bore the brunt of a tax that was used to support a school that was attended by Chinese from all across Cochinchina and Cambodia. Even more off-putting to Cholon's Chinese, Saigon's Chinese community members were also not initially subject to taxation.[62] After a complaint by the president of Cholon's municipal council, the government reexamined the taxation notion. With the endorsement of the Chinese Chamber of Commerce and of the Chinese congregations of Saigon and Cholon, the Cochin-chinese government extended the tax to include all Chinese residents of Cochinchina.[63] With the combined money from taxes and the Boxer reparations, the school could finally keep its financial head above the water.

This solution offers insight into one of the most fundamental realities of the congregation system. In Indochina's hierarchy of Chinese congregations, the congregations in Cholon sat unchallenged at the top; Saigon's congregations were just a small step below. Thus, when the Chinese community in Cholon felt that something was unfair, the French government, as in this case, paid attention. This is not meant to imply, by any means, that the French always capitulated to Cholon's Chinese. Instead, a strong opinion voiced by that Chinese community guaranteed at least a hearing from the French. The second point worthy of note is that when the united congregations of Cholon and Saigon agreed to measures such as a Cochinchina–wide tax increase to support the Lycée Franco-Chinois, the opinions of smaller congregations outside of the city were irrelevant. In this case, the congregations' decision was certainly not capricious. The institution of the new tax guaranteed the school a source of funding that would remain as long as Chinese remained in Indochina to attend the institution.

The connections between the Lycée Franco-Chinois and the Chinese congregations also warrant closer attention. Statutes published in 1908 by the Lycée Franco-Chinois are essentially a list of all of the very prominent Chinese business-men. Phong Nhut, Cantonese congregation president and future president of Cholon's Chinese Chamber of Commerce, appears on the list, as does the Cantonese merchant Ly Dang, a businessman who enjoyed a brief period of unusual success in the first decade of the twentieth century. For the French, the high degree of Chinese involvement in the affairs of the Lycée spoke favorably about the institution. From one perspective, the Lycée largely avoided the anti-French sentiments and revolutionary inclinations that had doomed the Ecole Pavie. By enrolling students who were personally invested in Indochina by virtue of family ties, the risk of radical reformism and general xenophobia was greatly reduced.[64] As the head of the school's council wrote,

> You will doubtless consider with us that the question of the educa-
> tion to be given to the Chinese upper class is not only educational,
> but above all, political. Our neighbors in Hong-Kong have consented
> to large sacrifices to drain the intellectual Chinese elite, and it would
> be certainly annoying if the Chinese businessmen of the Colony were
> forced to send their children to British territory to receive an education
> for which no need was foreseen in Indochina, except for our establish-
> ment.[65]

From the Chinese perspective, this school also seems to have been a success. Books and pamphlets commemorating various classes and reunions at the school were still being published well into the 1950s, a clear indication of the institution's longevity.

Conclusion

In Indochina, the Ecole Pavie represented an independent foray by the French into Chinese education, a venture that entirely circumvented the colony's resident overseas Chinese. Prior to its 1904 inception, individual Chinese schools and congregations all across Indochina typically worked independently—even discretely—to address issues of Chinese education in the colony. These *huaqiao* communities on the Chinese margin had traditionally looked away from the colonial "center" surrounding them and toward their original loci in China itself. Dozens of tiny Chinese schools across the five regions of Indochina emphasized culture, language, and the heritage of a pupil's subethnic place; in other words, they acted as instruments intended to bolster the existence of native place identity and recenter the members of their communities upon the native place values by which each community was defined. The Ecole Pavie, though catalyzed by the French, represented the other side of the coin, an educational endeavor managed by the French with the goal of providing students with an international education, irrespective of the native places from which the students hailed. Thus, the institution of the Ecole Pavie represented the re-envisioning of the French center, the construction of a competing sphere, which, through skillful exploitation and remolding of young Chinese minds, was intended to replace China's influence upon youthful Chinese expatriates with an affection for the French colonial regime. But despite its French orientation, the history of the school proves that it could not survive without support from China.

The Lycée Franco-Chinois, unlike the Ecole Pavie, was a cooperative effort. While the idea was French, the overseas Chinese themselves were far more successful at developing the pan-Chinese school than the colonialists had been. The Lycée Franco-Chinois could not have existed without the stalwart support offered by Saigon-Cholon's overseas Chinese merchant community, backing that never faltered from the moment in 1907 that the French first mentioned the plan, through the economic woes of the 1910s, right up until the abrupt departure of the French in 1954. In fact, in some respects, the Lycée Franco-Chinois owes it success to a redefinition of Chinese identity. In an era of spreading pan-Chinese sentiment, a Chinese school open to all overseas Chinese, while still respecting the values of native place, offered unique possibilities for reorienting overseas Chinese loyalties to a larger Chinese "center." In fairness, the support of overseas Chinese was not the only deciding factor in the Lycée's success. Political realities also served to bolster the effectiveness of the vital patronage provided to the school by the overseas Chinese.

By the mid-1920s, frequent French refusals to allow political activism in the form of commemorations and demonstrations led to open Chinese resistance to colonial prohibitions. While politicized cultural activities occasioned friction, French and Chinese leaders found common ground over the issue of education. French officials were concerned about the flight of Indochina's best and brightest overseas Chinese pupils to British, Japanese, and American schools and universities. By establishing a Chinese secondary school in Cholon, the French, with the help and cooperation of the Chinese congregations, went a long way toward obviating the need for overseas Chinese students to travel to Hong Kong or Guangzhou for further education. Presumably, education in Indochina benefited both the French and the Chinese by creating a class of overseas Chinese pupils that was fluent in French, likely friendly to French interests, and able to interact successfully with colonial authorities. In this sense, the French colonial "center" that governed Indochina had much to gain from the creation of the Lycée Franco-Chinois. But when it came to issues of educational funding, colonial imperatives once again carried the day. Despite stalwart French colonial support of the endeavor, the overseas Chinese community itself still bore the primary pecuniary responsibility for building and operating the school.

The significance of Chinese youth and the importance of education were also acknowledged by the French, as evinced by their own intense concern for Chinese instruction. The two French schools intended solely for Chinese students, the Ecole Pavie in Hanoi and the Lycée Franco-Chinois in Saigon, demonstrate the significance of education as a nexus of interaction between the Chinese in Indochina and the French colonial authorities. Despite the fact that the shadow of French authority touched upon nearly every aspect of overseas Chinese life in the colonies, the strength and autonomy of Indochina's overseas Chinese community is clear. Without French involvement—and occasionally in the face of French resistance—congregations successfully operated their own Chinese schools throughout Indochina. When French authorities attempted to operate a Chinese school of their own, the endeavor failed disastrously, due in part to the withdrawal of Chinese imperial officials from the agreement but also as a result of the unwillingness of the French to involve Indochina's overseas Chinese, with their powerful networks, close connections to their native places, and vested interest in the life of the colony. When the opportunity arose to establish a Chinese school in Saigon, the French welcomed overseas Chinese involvement and the school thrived, thanks more to the tenacity and devotion of Saigon-Cholon's congregations than to the commitment of French authorities to the institution.

As for the significance of accessible, local Chinese education sponsored by the congregations, the answer lies rooted in the realities of a sojourning life. Overseas Chinese connections to native place gave overseas Chinese a base of support for business ventures and a place of retreat in the event of disaster, but there was a price to be paid. In return for this nurturing, these ties implicitly required that overseas Chinese communities retain as many as possible of the linguistic, cultural, and social practices of the native place. One of the most efficient ways to achieve this cultural continuity was through the establishment of Chinese schools. Not only did schools provide the fundamental language training required to keep young *huaqiao* functionally literate in Chinese and fluent in their native tongues, but, as schools were typically affiliated with specific congregations, they ensured that many of the cultural and religious practices of the native place were transmitted as well. In this way, for Indochina's overseas Chinese community, Chinese schools acted as a bulwark, a primary line of defense for the preservation of native place identity and culture in a strange, if not so distant, land.

NOTES

Abbreviations used in the notes:

CAOM	Centre des Archives d'Outre Mer [Overseas archive center] (Aix en Provence, France).
INDO GGI	Files of the General Government of Indochina (Aix en Provence, France).
GOUCOCH	Files of the Governor/Lieutenant Governor of Cochinchina (Ho Chi Minh City, Vietnam).
GOUV GAL	Files of the General Government of Indochina (Hanoi, Vietnam).
RST	Files of the Resident Superior of Tonkin (Hanoi, Vietnam).
TTLTQG1	Trung Tam Luu Tru Quoc Gia 1 [Central National Vietnamese archive 1] (Hanoi, Vietnam).
TTLTQG2	Trung Tam Luu Tru Quoc Gia 2 [Central National Vietnamese archive 2] (Ho Chi Minh City, Vietnam).

1. In 1874, Nguyễn Emperor Tự Đức signed the treaty that formally ceded the six provinces of Cochinchina to the French imperialists.

2. The seven official congregations were later reduced to five, when the Fuzhou (Phuoc-chau) and Quanzhou (Quinh-chau) groups were removed from the list.

3. Nguyen Quoc Dinh, *Les Congregations chinoises en Indochine française*, Claude Reed, trans. (Paris: Libr. du Recueil Sirey, 1941), 46.

4. A second law governing Chinese congregations in Indochina, also quite notable, was the declaration made on January 23, 1885, by the Governor of Cochinchina within which no less than seven articles exclusively addressed the regulation of Chinese congregations. Nguyen Quoc Dinh, *Les Congregations chinoises en Indochine française*, 46.

5. In its emphasis on mutual responsibility and community accountability, the congregation system, which was borrowed at least in part from the system existing under the Nguyễn dynasty, bore considerable resemblance to the traditional Chinese *baojia* system.

6. Nguyen Quoc Dinh, *Les Congregations chinoises en Indochine française*, 73.

7. Whether in Hanoi, Haiphong, Saigon, Cholon, or the remoteness of the Mekong Delta, many of these temples are still in active use today. This is particularly interesting in the case of Cholon's temples, which have often effectively been abandoned by the Chinese who established them. The pious functions of these pagodas endure long after the majority of the community has departed.

8. Letter from the Governor of Cochinchina, January 11, 1929, CAOM, INDO GGI 51557.

9. Private Chinese Schools in Indochina, 1925, CAOM, INDO GGI 51556.

10. Letter from the President of Cholon's Fujian congregation, October 17, 1902, CAOM, INDO GGI 18331.

11. Letter from the French Consul in Amoy, January 15, 1903, CAOM, INDO GGI 18331.

12. Letter from the Lieutenant Governor, October 21, 1902, CAOM, INDO GGI 18331.

13. Letter from Tonkin's Head of Public Education, January 2, 1912, TTLTQG1, RST 8279.

14. David Marr also mentions the violence of the CCP-GMD split as another reason for the increase in Vietnamese students staying home for their education. David Marr, *Vietnamese Tradition on Trial, 1920-1945* (Berkeley: University of California Press, 1981), 40.

15. Summary of Anniversary of Sino-Japanese Hostilities in Shanghai, August 13, 1938, TTLTQG2, GOUCOCH IIA.45/254(4).

16. For a more detailed account of Hunt's argument, see Michael Hunt, *The Making of a Special Relationship: The United States and China to 1914.* (New York: Columbia University Press, 1983).

17. Michael Hunt, "The American Remission of the Boxer Indemnity: A Reappraisal" *Journal of Asian Studies* 31.3 (May 1972): 558.

18. Letter from the Consul for Foreign Affairs in Yunnan, June 19, 1904, TTLTQG1, Gouv Gal 4820.

19. Letter from the Resident Superior, August 8, 1904, TTLTQG1, Gouv Gal 4820.

20. Telegram from the Governor General to the Head of Cabinet, October 8, 1904, TTLTQG1, Gouv Gal 4820.

21. Letter from the Consul for Foreign Affairs in Yunnan, October 8, 1904, TTLTQG1, Gouv Gal 4820.

22. Letter from the Consul for Foreign Affairs in Yunnan, December 18, 1904, TTLTQG1, Gouv Gal 4820. Subsequent documents give this official's name as Léang Yu.

23. Ecole Pavie: Monthly Report from January 1905, January 31, 1905, TTLTQG1, Gouv Gal 4821.

24. Letter from the Resident Superior, November 11, 1905, TTLTQG1, Gouv Gal 4821.

25. Letter from the Minister for Asian Affairs, January 24, 1905, TTLTQG1, Gouv Gal 4817.

26. Petition from students at the Ecole Pavie, March 1906, TTLTQG1, Gouv Gal 4817.

27. Letter from the Governor General, September 14, 1905, TTLTQG1, RST 38099. This exchange clearly shows that from the perspective of Yunnan officials, the future prospects of these "sons of mandarins" included service in government or as officials.

28. Order of the Governor General, May 16, 1906, TTLTQG1, Gouv Gal 4817.

29. Press excerpt, September 19–20, 1906, TTLTQG1, Gouv Gal 4817.

30. Letter from the Director of the Ecole Pavie, October 25, 1906, TTLTQG1, Gouv Gal 4817.

31. *Yunnan Jinggao* [Yunnan warning], n.d., TTLTQG1, Gouv Gal 4817.

32. Advice for Yunnan's Population, n.d., TTLTQG1, Gouv Gal 4817.

33. A man with the surname Chen.

34. Letter from the French Vice-Consul assigned to the Ministry of Foreign Affairs in Yunnan, March 21, 1908, TTLTQG1, Gouv Gal 4815.

35. Letter from the Head of the Political Bureau, April 28, 1908, TTLTQG1, Gouv Gal 4815. This quote refers to the rather mysterious events that transpired at the French post in Nam Quan, when a band of revolutionaries, allegedly accompanied by Sun Yat-sen, were involved in some unrest along the Sino-Tonkin border. Details of the actual "escapade" are unclear, but the important part of this anecdote concerns the connection between graduates of the Ecole Pavie and Sun Yat-sen, a relationship that clearly implies the close ties of some Ecole Pavie students with China's most radical figures. The fact that this whole episode predates the 1911 revolution meant that Sino-French relations could have easily been jeopardized had the crippled imperial Chinese regime determined that a French colony bore responsibility for offering sanctuary to one of the empire's most eloquent critics.

36. Hanoi's Ecole Pavie has parallels, if a bit later, in Republican China. Wen-hsin Yeh describes a similar dissatisfaction with Western educational methods and motives in Shanghai in 1925. There, frustration with the "cultural imperialism" of the Western administrators and teachers at St. John's University led to the mass withdrawal of more than half of the university's student body. The acrimony and resentment surrounding the schism at St. John's resulted ultimately in the establishment of Guanghua University, an institution immediately favored by Chinese nationalists and significantly empowered by its apparent resistance to western imperialism. Wen-hsin Yeh, *The Alienated Academy: Culture and Politics in Republican China, 1919–1937* (Cambridge: Harvard University Asia Center, 2000), 84–85.

37. Order of the Governor General, July 11, 1908, TTLTQG1, Gouv Gal 4815.

38. Telegram from the Governor General to Yunnan and Mongtseu, 1908, TTLTQG1, Gouv Gal 4815.

39. Telegram from Yunnan's Minister of Foreign Affairs to the Governor General, August 3, 1908, TTLTQG1, Gouv Gal 4815.

40. Letter from the Head of the Political Bureau, April 28, 1908, TTLTQG1, Gouv Gal 4815.

41. Note No°1317 G, January 16, 1912, CAOM, INDO GGI 44042.

42. Ibid.

43. Ibid. The four congregations represented on the Board of Directors of the Franco-Chinese Secondary School were Guangzhou (Canton), Fujian (Fou-kien or Phuc-kien), Chaozhou (Trieu Chau), and Hainan (Hainam).

44. Note No°1317 G, January 16, 1912, CAOM, INDO GGI 44042.

45. Letter to the Governor General from the President of the Association du Lycée Franco-Chinois, May 8, 1912, CAOM, INDO GGI 44042.

46. Letter from the President of Cholon's Municipal Council, June 29, 1922, TTLTQG2, GOUCOCH IA.8/056(8).

47. The Association du Lycée Franco-Chinois still exists today with a membership composed primarily of students who graduated from the institution in the 1950s and 1960s.

48. Note N°1317 G, January 16, 1912, CAOM, INDO GGI 44042.

49. They were awarded "les palmes de l'Instruction Publique" by the French authorities.

50. Note N°1317 G, January 16, 1912, CAOM, INDO GGI 44042.

51. N°394ster, letter from Governor General Klobukowski to the Minister of Colonies in Paris, April 12, 1909, CAOM, INDO GGI 44042.

52. N°394ster, letter to the Minister of Colonies, April 12, 1909, CAOM, INDO GGI 20046.

53. Klobukowski's administration presided over the creation of a number of Chinese institutions, including the Franco-Chinese Secondary School and the Chinese Chamber of Commerce of Cholon. Although Klobukowski himself might have resisted the creation of some of these institutions, the very fact that a number of them emerged during his tenure as Governor General indicates that he was considerably more receptive to such non-native organizations than some of the Governors General who came before and after him.

54. No 848bp, Rapport from the Governor General p.i. to the Minister of Colonies in Paris, June 8, 1911, CAOM, INDO GGI 50950.

55. No 394ster, Letter to the Minister of Colonies, April 12, 1909, CAOM, INDO GGI 22046.

56. Note No 1317 G, January 16, 1912, CAOM, INDO GGI 44042.

57. In 1922, the Chinese community offered 80,000 piastres toward maintaining the institution.

58. Letter from the President of Cholon's Municipal Council, June 29, 1922, TTLTQG2, GOUCOCH IA.8/056(8).

59. Letter from the Governor General, May 2, 1923, TTLTQG2, GOUCOCH IA.8/284(12).

60. Circular from the Governor of Cochinchina, June 13, 1923, TTLTQG2, GOUCOCH IA.8/056(8).

61. Letter from Yip Pak Ky, the President of Cholon's Chinese Chamber of Commerce, June 19, 1922, TTLTQG2, GOUCOCH IA.8/056(8).

62. Letter from the President of Cholon's Municipal Council, October 27, 1922, TTLTQG2, GOUCOCH IA.8/056(8).

63. Circular from the Governor of Cochinchina, June 13, 1923, TTLTQG2, GOUCOCH IA.8/056(8).

64. The records of the Ecole Pavie and the Lycée Franco-Chinois seem to suggest that officials' sons were troublemakers while merchant's sons were obedient and docile. While it is tempting to claim that scholar-officials' sons were more politicized and merchants' sons were more practical, it seems more likely that in the case of the Lycée Franco-Chinois, merchant parents were involved quite deeply in the functions of the school, whether by monitoring their children, paying tuition, or even administering some part of the institution's operations. In a colonial environment, the cost of bad behavior could be family ruin, therefore merchant parents watched their children closely and worked to curb their adolescent excesses.

65. Letter from the President of the Lycée Franco-Chinois Council, May 8, 1912, TTLTQG2, GOUCOCH IA.9/142(2).

11

"TO SAVE *MINNAN*, TO SAVE OURSELVES"

The Southeast Asia Overseas Fujianese Home Village Salvation Movement of the 1920s and 1930s

Soon Keong Ong

On June 22, 1924, a group of overseas Chinese, all originally from the southern parts of Fujian province in China, gathered at the Asia Theatre in Manila in the Philippines to found the Southeast Asia Overseas Fujianese Home Village Salvation Association (*Nanyang minqiao jiuxiang hui,* hereafter the association). Stirred by economic and political woes in China's Southern Fujian province (Minnan), the association called upon overseas Fujianese in every port of Southeast Asia to join hands in restoring social order and improving people's livelihood in their home region. Lasting almost a decade (1924–1933), the transnational efforts of the association inaugurated a zealous movement among overseas Chinese to save their home villages and make a real impact on the lives of the people in Minnan through their activism in local politics, philanthropy, and efforts in bandit suppressions.[1] By studying the activities of the association, its leadership, and its accomplishments and failures, this chapter will analyze the motivations behind overseas Chinese's continual involvement in affairs in China, and interrogate conventionally held assumptions regarding overseas Chinese and their homeland.

The "Love-of-Homeland" Thesis

From the view of China, the geopolitical and cultural center, overseas Chinese are necessarily marginal figures. This is because in a culture that extols the virtues of filial piety and agricultural labor, any movement away from home, thus leaving one's parent unattended and the fields untilled, poses a threat to social order.[2] By leaving China, the Chinese migrants have become potential deserters and outlaws, and for the most part of the Qing dynasty, the threat of capital punishment by beheading was imposed in an effort to stop overseas travel.[3]

Because Chinese migrants faced legal sanction and also moral reprimand, they are often portrayed as reluctant travelers who yearned to return home eventually, if they could, and Chinese migration is thus seldom considered as a mono-directional relocation, but rather a circular process undertaken by the Chinese to make the most of economic opportunities abroad so as to finally return to benefit those they left behind.[4] It is not surprising that the study of Chinese migration is predominantly China-centered, with China presupposed as the appropriate center from which overseas Chinese experiences in the margins are to be described and understood.

One revealing example of how the historical trajectory of the overseas Chinese is seen as dependent on China is in the study and treatment of overseas Chinese nationalism. According to Wang Gungwu, a pioneer scholar on the overseas Chinese, overseas Chinese nationalism is "a periphery and dependent nationalism which did not have the capacity to generate itself."[5] Instead, overseas Chinese nationalists depended on China to continue to take an interest in them and on expatriate Chinese to help jump-start nationalism for them.[6] Yen Ching-hwang, another prominent scholar in the field, further reasons that not only was overseas Chinese nationalism "an extension of modern Chinese nationalism" overseas, it was also the demonstration of "common feelings" among the Chinese immigrants for China:

> From the time when overseas Chinese donated tens of thousands of dollars to relief funds for China at the end of the nineteenth century, through the time of their active participation in the 1911 revolutionary moment, and on to the strong support given to the anti-Japanese resistance movement in the 1930s and 1940s, they have demonstrated deep emotional attachment to China's destiny. *This keen concern for China's fate is the main characteristic of the overseas Chinese nationalism.*[7] [Emphasis added]

In Yen's view, it is "natural" for overseas Chinese to have a deep emotional attachment to their homeland, which turns their attention to China and leads them to be keenly concern with China's fate.

Yen Ching-hwang was not alone in celebrating overseas Chinese's undying love for and connection with their place of origin. Scholars of overseas Chinese have conducted detailed research in the areas of overseas Chinese nationalism,[8] their involvement and participation in Chinese revolutionary movement[9] and resistance to Japanese encroachment,[10] their economic activities in China,[11] their social and religious organizations,[12] remittances,[13] and fundraising activities and donations for disaster relief or philanthropic purposes in China.[14] Notwithstanding the disparity in subject matter, these works are all undergirded by a shared premise of a primordial tie between overseas Chinese and China, often expressed as overseas Chinese's deep emotional attachment to, or even obsession with, China. It was this single enduring bond, several scholars argue, that motivated overseas Chinese to be involved in various activities in China. In the preface to their important work on pre-1949 overseas Chinese investments in Fujian province, Lin Jinzhi and Zhuang Weiji proclaim:

> In the course of survey and preparation for the present volume, we have come to recognize and deeply appreciate an honorable tradition among our overseas Chinese, i.e., their enduring love for the motherland and the hometown. Before Liberation [in 1949], they supported and participated in the motherland's revolutionary struggles, leaving an indelible contribution in the history of Chinese political development. In the economy, overseas Chinese have also longed to see prosperity and strength in their motherland, hence they poured in their money and partook in our country's economic construction. ... Factories and enterprises built or expanded with overseas capital have done much to improve the livelihood of the people in their home villages (*qiaoxiang*), and provided much impetus to industrial and agricultural development.[15]

There is certainly some truth to the idea that overseas Chinese have been attached to and have even loved China, as a perusal of early twentieth century overseas Chinese newspapers will testify. However, using these sentiments as a historical explanation is both limited and limiting. In the first place, to regard overseas Chinese's love for the homeland as something intrinsic and instinctive immediately endows it with the authority of the commonsensical, such that once cited as the underlying cause to a historical phenomenon, it effectively terminates further investigation. Second, to reduce overseas Chinese's intricate relations with China to a singular psychological motivation not only homogenizes and depersonalizes the vast number of overseas Chinese, it also makes China the central focus and ultimate point of reference. Overseas Chinese's experiences abroad are consequently underestimated and factors not China related are also disregarded. In more extreme cases, overseas Chinese who are presumably not loyal or do not love the homeland are excluded from Chinese history altogether.

The purpose of this chapter is to complicate the idealized image of overseas Chinese's single-minded devotion to the homeland. By looking at the overseas Chinese's village salvation movement—a movement widely regarded as a quintessential example of patriotism—it will attempt to avoid historical reductionism, and to de-center China by restoring overseas Chinese as real people whose actions are guided by personal needs and concerns.[16] Through an analysis of the historical backgrounds, leadership, motivations, and goals of the village salvation movement, this chapter will reveal that human will and exigencies, together with historical contingencies at home and abroad, are just as important, if not more so, as any sentimental attachment in the Chinese migrants' relationship with the homeland.

The Order of Things in Fujian, Early Twentieth Century

As a source for Chinese emigrants in the modern era, Fujian province is second only to Guangdong province. Between 1841 and 1949, it has been estimated that almost 5.8 million Fujianese made a trip overseas.[17] Discounting those who eventually returned, by 1955, Fujianese constituted 3.7 million or a little over 30 percent of the 12 million overseas Chinese worldwide.[18] Among the overseas Fujianese themselves, more than three-quarters would trace their origin back to southern Fujian (including the cities of Xiamen, Zhangzhou, Quanzhou, and their environs).[19] There are of course many reasons behind the exodus of Fujianese once the floodgates to emigration opened in the mid-nineteenth century. Chief among them were the miserable living conditions in Minnan.

Lapped by the sea on one side and girded by highlands on the other, the topography of Fujian made life hard for those who worked the land. With over 90 percent of the province mountainous, there was little room left for river plains, thus limiting the total acreage available for growing grain. Competition for arable land became a persistent source for violence in the province. As one seventeenth-century observer noted, the hunger for land has led Fujianese tillers "to quarrel like dogs barking with bared teeth, and even to fight with and kill one another."[20]

Those fortunate or powerful enough to acquire a piece of land, often found Fujian's soil acidic and leached, requiring much effort and heavy fertilization to re-establish productivity—a luxury not all farmers could afford. Little wonder rice was chronically in short supply in Fujian, and the lament of "barren land and impoverished people"(*di chi min pin*) became a stock comment in memorials to the imperial courts throughout the Qing dynasty.[21] The rapid increase in population since the late Ming dynasty—7.6 million in 1749, 11 million in 1776, 15.9 million in 1819, and 20 million in 1851[22]—put still more pressure on the land, such that even with the introduction of New World crops like taro and sweet potato, famine remained a recurrent phenomenon through the Qing dynasty and into the Republican era.[23]

Adding to the woes of the Fujianese was the constant threat of natural disasters. The distress these brought about is easily imaginable from the following data: in the 38 years of the Chinese Republic, floods occurred in 33 years of them, droughts in 24, typhoons in 22, earthquakes in 20, and epidemics in 10.[24] With the exception of 1930 when only one earthquake struck Fujian, two or more forms of calamity normally frequented the province yearly. On average, 30 percent of the province was affected by natural calamities annually; and in the single year 1933, as many as four hundred thousand Fujianese were displaced from their homes.[25]

As the Chinese saying goes, *tianzai renhuo*, natural disasters and man-made calamities often come together. This was especially true in the Republican era. The end of imperial rule in 1912 did not bring about peace and the rejuvenation of Fujian. Instead, Fujian soon became the arena for power struggles among strongmen of different factions. Amid the unrestrained striving for personal and provincial goals, these warmongers brought terrible suffering to the people of Fujian through unremitting hostilities, rapacious exploitation, and banditry.

From 1913 to 1922, the most powerful political and military figure in Fujian was Li Houji. Initially sent to Fujian on orders of Yuan Shikai, the president of the republic at the time, Li was promoted to governor of the province by Duan Qirui after he associated himself with Duan's Anhui clique upon Yuan's death in 1916.[26] In 1917, Li initiated an offensive to capture Guangdong province for Duan Qirui as part of the latter's master plan to unite China militarily. In response, Cantonese warlords banded together with nationalist government forces to launch their own assault against Fujian. This Fujian-Guangdong War set in motion incessant warfare between northern and southern warlords in Fujian for the next decade. The devastation caused by troops fighting over southern Fujian was plain for all to see. In September of 1918, the defeated Zhangzhou division of Li's army retreated to the town of Anhai in Jinjiang and pillaged for three days. In addition to Jinjiang losing 620,000 yuan in damages, it also lost thirteen townsmen who were killed. Again in Anhai in 1920, the invading Cantonese army robbed over two thousand homes, riding off with 1.5 million yuan after taking several lives.[27]

The behavior of government troops on both sides of the war led one contemporary to comment that "the government and the bandits were the same; the government was just like the bandits and the bandits were just like the government."[28] Into this virtual anarchy, local powers in Fujian introduced the so-called people's army (*minjun*) in the name of self-defense. Unfortunately, these people's army units were equally apt to pillage, kidnap, extort, and kill. They behaved more like bandits than protectors of the people, and their presence added much volatility to an already violent environment.

The unceasing loss of lives, property, and means of subsistence among the Fujianese created a strong sense of insecurity that forced many to move abroad. For example, Wu Shuige (Goh Tjoei Kok) of Anxi left for Singapore at the tender age of sixteen because his family's business was ruined in the chaotic environment; Huang Chaoyuan (Ng Teow Yhee) was forced to flee from his home in Nanmen, Jinjiang, at age fifteen to avoid conscription. He first headed for the relative security of Xiamen before venturing to Hong Kong and Singapore.[29] In 1923, the village of Chaodai in southern Jinjiang was emptied when 80 percent of its inhabitants left for Southeast Asia to escape from bandit harassment.[30] As a matter of fact, one survey in 1935 revealed that banditry was cited by 33 percent of Fujianese abroad, more than any other single factor, as the main reason behind their initial decision to leave home.[31]

Chinese in the Philippines, Early Twentieth Century

Although the majority of Chinese relocated overseas to extricate themselves from the predicament at home, they did not always find conditions in their place of settlement congenial. This is certainly true of the Philippines in the 1920s, where more than 80 percent of its Chinese were southern Fujianese.

While it is true that the Americans, who replaced the Spaniards as colonial overlords of the Philippines in 1898, were less prone to use violence to solve the "Chinese problem," they too discriminated against the Chinese. The infamous Chinese exclusion act was extended to the Philippines in 1902,[32] and on February 21, 1921, in one of his last acts as governor general of the Philippines, Francis B. Harrison passed a law that made it illegal for any person or company "to keep their books of account in a language other than English, Spanish, or any native dialect."[33] Known as the Bookkeeping Law, it was scheduled to come into force on November 1, 1921. The government's rationale for passing it was to facilitate the work of revenue collectors and prevent fraudulent tax returns. It was alleged by the government that because an estimated fifteen thousand Chinese stores in the Philippines kept their records in Chinese, which naturally posed a major handicap to inspectors of the Internal Revenue Bureau, the government lost one and a half to two million pesos in tax revenue annually.[34]

Despite the government's claim that the enactment of the Bookkeeping Law was simply a fiscal measure, the Chinese insisted that the law was a racist act targeting the Chinese on the islands and that it was designed to prevent them from advancing in the country's economy.[35] Under the leadership of the Philippine Chinese General Chamber of Commerce headed by Li Qingquan (Dee C. Chuan), a lumber magnate and dominant force of the Chinese community in the 1920s, the Chinese in the Philippines petitioned Governor General Harrison, clearly stating their objections:

> [T]he Chinese people are the only considerable population in the Philippines engaged in commercial pursuits that do not speak as their native tongue one of the languages or dialects aforesaid;
> [T]his proposed law therefore protects all English-speaking, Spanish, and native merchants and places onerous burdens upon the Chinese people which it is sincerely believed it will be impracticable, if not impossible for them to bear, regardless of their entire willingness and desire to do so;
> [F]rom every point of view, the proposed legislation must be regarded as highly prejudicial and unfriendly to the Chinese people of the Philippines Islands and, in effect, destructive of their commercial and property interests, vested and otherwise, and is of extremely doubtful validity.[36]

Besides resenting the racist overtones, the Chinese also found it hard to comply with the new law because *sari-sari* (miscellaneous goods) store owners, which comprised the majority of Chinese businessmen in the Philippines, were not able to spare the extra 50 to 100 pesos a month to hire a bookkeeper.[37] Moreover, showing one's account book was as good as revealing one's trade secrets, which Chinese businessmen adamantly refused to do.[38]

Seeing that the law was passed despite vehement local protests, the chamber marshaled resources to expand its fight. It organized the first nationwide convention of Chinese merchants in May 1921, when it was agreed that they would fight against the enforcement of the law with all lawful means available.[39] Li later dispatched Xue Minlao (Albino Sycip)—a lawyer with a University of Michigan degree—and Wu Kecheng (Rafael Gotauco) as special envoys to Washington, D.C., to lay their plight before the President and the Congress.[40] On their way to the United States, Xue and Wu detoured to Hong Kong, Shanghai, Tianjin, and Beijing, where they held conferences with Chinese authorities, local Chinese chambers of commerce, and the American minister. Concurrently, circulars condemning the law were also printed by residents in Manila and distributed to Chinese and non-Chinese business houses in China and other foreign countries.[41]

Because of the chamber's effort in publicizing the impracticality and unjustness of the new law, it won the support of not only their compatriots in China, the United States, and other parts of Southeast Asia, but also important foreign firms—including American ones—in Manila.[42] The stir created by protests and petitions from Chinese and non-Chinese within and outside the Philippines alerted the new Governor General, Leonard Wood, to the difficulties involved in enacting the law. He then advised the legislature to postpone the Bookkeeping Law until January 1, 1923. As a compromise, the Philippines Legislature agreed to the postponement but refused to modify it in any manner.[43]

In March of 1923, criminal charges were brought against Yang Kongyin (Yu Cong Eng), who still kept his account books in Chinese deliberately, for violating the Bookkeeping Law. The accused, in response, filed a lawsuit in the Supreme Court against the collector from the Internal Revenue Bureau, the City Fiscal, and Judge Pedro Concepcion. Yu made it very clear that the suit was filed on behalf of all Chinese merchants in the Philippines and hoped that the Supreme Court would rule the Bookkeeping Law unconstitutional and void.[44] Unfortunately for the Chinese merchants, on February 6, 1925, the Supreme Court of the Philippines upheld the Bookkeeping Law as valid and constitutional.

Failing to find legal redress in the Philippines, the Chinese again took their fight to the United States. As representatives of the Chinese in the Philippines, Xue Minlao and Wu Kecheng filed a suit in the United States Supreme Court challenging the legality of the Bookkeeping Law. This time they had better luck. On June 7, 1926, the United States Supreme Court officially declared the Bookkeeping Law unconstitutional, thus vindicating the Philippine Chinese in their fight to assert their rights to trade under conditions of justice. This legal battle took five years and five months and cost the Chinese Chamber of Commerce in excess of 167,000 pesos.[45]

An unexpected consequence of the rancor over the Bookkeeping Law was that it further united the Chinese community in the Philippines. As already mentioned, the Chamber held its first nationwide convention in the wake of the passing of the Bookkeeping law in 1921. Besides passing a resolution to defeat the law, the convention also decided to carry out a comprehensive program. The Chinese formed a solid union in the Philippines, extended Chinese trade and commerce in the islands, established closer relations and understanding between Chinese dealers and the consumers, aroused greater interest in internal and foreign questions that affected the Chinese community, founded a federation of all Chinese education agencies, generated greater interest in Chinese relief work, extended branches of the Chinese Chamber of Commerce to the provinces, and united the Chinese stores association, hardware association, dry goods association, and other Chinese commercial organizations.[46]

But as scholar Antonio Tan pointed out, the Chinese demonstrations and protests, the cohesiveness they showed in mobilizing their community, and their ability to marshal public opinion in their favor caused considerable apprehension in various Philippine quarters.[47] The Philippine government considered their move to bypass its legislature and bring their petitions to the United States Supreme Court a sign of disrespect, while the natives of the islands saw the same gesture as using the Americans to oppress their government. Relationships between the Chinese and the Filipinos became very strained.

The precariousness of the positions of the Chinese in the Philippines was fully exposed when a minor altercation between a Chinese shopkeeper and a Filipino salesman in Manila grew into an all-out anti-Chinese riot that spread across the country. On the night of October 18, 1924, a dispute arose between a Chinese shopkeeper and his Filipino supplier. A Filipino policeman nearby arrived at the scene just as verbal insults were escalating to the exchange of blows. According to the Governor General's report, the policeman was "greeted with a bottleful of lemonade on the head, bottle and all."[48] Incensed by the disrespect, the policeman opened fire into the crowd, leaving a Chinese merchant surnamed Zhuang dead.

A rumor began to spread that two or more Filipino policemen had been killed by the Chinese.[49] The next day, a Sunday, saw small bands of Filipinos gathering here and there throughout the city. A few Chinese stalls were stoned at first, and later, older students and workers intercepted and beat up Chinese passersby.[50] The Chinese practice of flying the flag of the Chinese Republic on Sundays also came to be interpreted as a declaration of war against the Filipinos. Fueled by increased agitation and emboldened by growing mobs, the rioters began breaking into, looting, and destroying Chinese shops.[51]

The riot in Manila quickly spread to other provinces, especially Cabanatuan, Nueva, and Ecjia, where Chinese injuries and property damages were widely reported.[52] The culprit behind the dissemination of violence was a special afternoon edition of a vernacular paper, *Ang Watawat*, which hit the streets of Manila before 2 P.M. on October 20. It fabricated the news that Chinese had murdered eighty Filipinos in Shanghai, and that Chinese in the Philippines were preparing to poison the Filipinos.[53] Fortunately for the Chinese, the mayor of Manila, Mayor Romualdez, urged restraint and ordered the protection of Chinese before the riot got out of hand. The city police efficiently handled the situation, arresting one American, 47 Chinese and 252 Filipinos.

Compared to earlier Chinese massacres,[54] the Philippine Chinese were exceedingly lucky to survive the 1924 riot with only one death—the Chinese merchant who started it all.[55] However, events in the 1920s made plain to them their general helplessness in the face of colonial discipline and native harassment. Hence while it is true that the prospects of financial betterment originally enticed many Chinese to the Philippines, the anti-Chinese conditions of the 1920s in the Philippines predisposed the Philippine Chinese to long for a safe haven in their home villages where they could return when circumstances in the Philippines really became unbearable. Moreover, compared with their subordinated positions in the Philippines, their home villages, despite—or perhaps, because of—the chaos and dilapidation, afforded them an opportunity to impose their will and achieve rehabilitation. One can imagine the immense satisfaction and sense of self-worth overseas Chinese would feel when they knew their money was making a difference at home.

Saving the Home Villages

Roused into action by news of the grievous damages and great affliction inflicted on their home villages and fellow townsmen in southern Fujian, overseas Chinese of means began to come together to find ways to relieve the misery caused by natural disaster and to halt the exploitation by rapacious warlords. On October 17, 1920, Wu Kecheng (Rafael Gotauco), Zheng Huancai, and Li Wenxiu, all southern Fujianese who found their own pots of gold in the Philippines, called an informal symposium on the island of Gulangyu off Xiamen to discuss hometown affairs. The forty-four present, many of them distinguished overseas Chinese, came to the consensus that in view of the chaos created by political disunity, the only way Fujian could have a future was for Fujianese to work toward self-government.[56] After the symposium, Wu returned to Manila to garner support for the self-government cause among Fujianese communities throughout the Philippines. In November that year, a preparatory committee for the Fujian Self-Government Association (*Fujian zizhi hui*) was organized with Li Qingquan as chairman and Wu himself as vice chairman. This association took the lead in promoting the home village salvation movement among overseas Fujianese.[57]

In 1922, as a new wave of hostilities swept across Fujian, over seventy overseas Chinese leaders in the Philippines convened in an ad hoc "overseas Chinese public security meeting" to discuss immediate measures to defuse the crises. It was agreed that an Association for the Eager Pursuit of Fujian Self-Government by Overseas Chinese in the Philippines (*Lufei huaqiao zizhi jijin hui*) be formed, and in its name, Li Qingquan and Wu Kecheng, as chairman and vice-chairman, would send telegrams to key Fujianese organizations like the Singapore Chinese Chamber of Commerce, the Fujian Province Congress, the Xiamen Chamber of Commerce, the Xiamen Education Association, and the various Fujianese associations in Shanghai and Beijing, to state the association's position:

> In view of the devastations caused by marauding troops and roving bandits, your overseas compatriots know that if moves are not taken to save our ancestral villages, there can be no peace at home. Hence we propose to follow the new trend of promoting self-government and to establish a foundation for construction by drafting our provincial constitutions ... we also propose to pull together resources to vitalize the education, build better transport, and develop industries and commerce. By so doing, we may turn our beloved native place into a land of happiness. *Not only can our fellow townsmen at home enjoy peace and security, but our brethren overseas, when aggrieved by government policies in their place of settlement abroad, can look to their hometown as their final resting place.* ... We specially organized this new association to emphasize our goal for true self-government and our determination to achieve it speedily. For a new Fujian after the eleventh year of the Chinese Republic, we must depend on our overseas Fujianese, we must depend on our 20 million Fujianese![58] [Emphasis added]

On June 22, 1924, the Association for the Eager Pursuit of Self-Government by Overseas Chinese in the Philippines was renamed the Southeast Asia Overseas Fujianese Home Village Salvation Association (*Nanyang minqiao jiuxiang hui*) so as to open it to Fujianese beyond the shores of the Philippines. Representatives from the association were sent to key Chinese communities in British Malaya and the Dutch East Indies to convince "southern Fujianese of every port in Southeast Asia" to unite and work toward the goal of an independent Fujian.[59] For it was only when Fujianese ruled Fujian, they believed, that peace would return to its sixty-three counties and happiness would be possible for its thirty million inhabitants.[60] According to the association's report, the result of its propaganda campaign was "outstanding." Besides setting up over twenty branches across the Philippines, an additional eighteen adjunct divisions were also organized by Fujianese in various parts of Southeast Asia.[61]

Between May 17 and 29, 1925, the association held its first official congress in Manila. Li Qingquan was again elected as president of the association, and Xue Minlao (Albino SyCip), Li's comrade-in-arms in the Bookkeeping Law litigation,

served as his deputy.[62] The congress agreed that the following five goals would
serve as the Association's purpose:

(1) Restore social order with proper means;
(2) Ensure long-lasting peace through fundamental construction;
(3) Improve people's livelihood by developing industries;
(4) Strive for local prosperity through coordination with other
    legitimate organizations;
(5) Encourage the spirit of self-sacrifice in the cultivation of
    high moral character.

It was also agreed that besides expanding the association and soliciting funds, the
association would set as its top priorities the promotion of education, the construction of province-wide road networks, the organization of local militias, and
the preparations for local self-government.[63]

By the end of the year, the association had already made significant strides
toward its goals. According to its report published in Singapore's *Nanyang Siang
Pau (Nanyang shangbao)*, the association played a crucial role in settling two cases
of armed feuds (*xiedou*) between different southern Fujianese clans; ended the
misunderstanding between the local militia and the government army; presented
the association's purposes and goals to the governor of Fujian; propagandized the
principle of "self-government and self-protection" to villages and schools through
public speeches and textbooks; lodged appeals against the conscription of laborers
in Quanzhou; and planned to start the publication of a Chinese newspaper, the
Fookien Times (Xinmin ribao).[64]

The association gained such momentum that it moved its headquarters
from Manila to the international settlements of Gulangyu in Xiamen, which
provided relative safety for the wealthy overseas Chinese, yet allowed them to be
closer to their troubled home villages. In March of 1926, the association again
called a regional congress to be held at its new headquarters. This time the
congress received even more support and publicity. More than fifty overseas
Chinese made the trip to attend the meeting, and newspaper reporters and
representatives for the various counties of Minnan were also present for the
two-week assembly. Besides reemphasizing its various purposes and goals, this
congress also passed several key propositions, including urging Chinese gentry in the various counties to voluntarily prohibit opium cultivation, help with
the organization of local militias, and most importantly, extend the Zhang-Xia
railway to Longyan as proposed by the Indonesian "sugar king" Huang Yizhu.
A committee of eleven luminaries, including Huang himself, Li Qingquan, and
Lim Boon Keng, president of the Amoy University (Xiamen University), was
specially formed to take up the last project.

As is evident from the account above, the Association and the village salvation movement were spearheaded by same group of Chinese community leaders from the Philippines who fended off the Bookkeeping Law. Moreover, it was the Fujianese in the Philippines, whose willingness to loosen their purse strings in answer to the association's myriad calls, who kept the home village salvation movement going for as long as it lasted. During 1930–1931, to help organize local militias in Quanzhou and Yongchun, Chinese in the Philippines raised 30,000 pesos and donated 600 rifles with 30,000 rounds of ammunitions.[65] In 1932, they initiated a fund-raising drive to help arm the 19th Route Army in China. The 19th Route Army came to the attention of the overseas Chinese because of its role in the Shanghai Incident. In the night of January 28, 1932, Japanese forces conducted a sneak attack on Shanghai, expecting Chinese resistance to crumble there as everywhere else under superior Japanese fighting forces. To their surprise, the 19th Route Army not only fended off the initial attack but held out for another thirty-three bloody days, withdrawing only when massive new Japanese reinforcements arrived.[66] The Philippine Chinese raised US$800,000 in the end, amounting to 16 percent of the total US$5 million that the 19th Route Army received from overseas Chinese around the world.[67] Considering the fact that the Chinese in the Philippines were hard hit by global depression in the early 1930s and that there were only about 100,000 of them,[68] the sum raised was indeed remarkable.

Our purpose here is not to question the generosity or sincerity of the Philippine Chinese. What we wish to suggest, however, is that they were motivated not only by "love of the homeland" but also other concerns. And as our next section will show, not all of the association's courses of action were wholly selfless.

A Railway and a Bandit

Among the various undertakings of the association, the Zhang-Long Railway project was the most ambitious and the one that best exemplified the resolve, resourcefulness, and passion of its supporters. Yet it was the one that suffered the most setbacks.

At the time when the association was founded, Minnan already had a Zhang-Xia railway linking Zhangzhou and Xiamen, but it had long fallen into disrepair. The association passed a resolution to revive the existing railway and to lengthen it to Longyan. This extended Zhang-Long railway would run from Xiamen across the Jiulong River via Jiangdong Bridge to reach Anhua, Zhangping, and Longyan. Then it would turn south toward Kanshi and Yongding. A branch line would also connect Zhangzhou with Punan. The proposed Zhang-Long railway would be 347 miles in length.[69]

Like so many progressives at the time, the association took to railway building because of a belief in its relevance to the economic well-being of Fujian. Its members believed that the new mode of transportation could help rejuvenate the dilapidated province by facilitating fundamental construction. As Huang Yizhu, the main proponent of the project, put it:

> Railroads to the world are like blood vessels to a person. Once the blood flow is smooth, then whatever external infections or internal injuries exist may be cured one by one. Similarly, with railroads constructed, transport and communication will be convenient. Whatever we wish to promote, including education, manufacturing, industries, and self defense, we will get twice the result with half the effort.[70]

It was agreed that the association would raise 16 million yuan to complete the construction of the railway.[71] But this Zhang-Long Railway was not to be based on charitable contributions. As the association envisioned, the railway system was meant to be developed in tandem with the furtherance of the mining industry right from the start. Though Fujian was often remembered by overseas Chinese as a barren land, the association was well aware that Fujian actually had rich mineral reserves hidden in its hinterland.[72] Longyan in particular had a coal seam that a Japanese prospecting team estimated to be 120 miles in length, 60 miles in width, and four to six feet thick.[73] According to one French engineer, once excavated, Longyan alone could supply coal to the world for fifty years.[74] The Zhang-Long railway was designed with this huge coal reserve in mind. If completed, it not only could pay for its own construction, but also alter the economic landscape of Fujian and improve the lives of southern Fujianese. For the association investors, experts estimated that a 4 million yuan investment in coal mining—as agreed upon during the 1926 Gulangyu congress—could generate a total return of 7million yuan, or a 175 percent profit.[75]

With great expectations for their railway project, the association proceeded with much gusto. In 1926, Li Qingquan met with Du Xigui, prime minister of the government in Beijing, and received oral consent from the latter for the project. In August the same year, Huang Yizhu and Chen Peikun, head of Fujian's Finance Department, tendered their proposal to the ministry of transportation in Beijing. Huang was granted the rights to operate railways in the whole of Fujian province, and to mine coal in an area of not more than six hundred square miles in Longyan, Zhangping, and Ninyang. But before any concrete work could take place, Chiang Kai-shek's Northern Expedition forces took over Fujian province and refused to accept any agreement reached between Huang and the ousted Beijing government.

The Zhang-Long railway project was shelved for five years because Chiang's new Nanjing government did not allow private entrepreneurs to own or manage railroads. In 1932, after the 19th Route Army led by Cai Tingkai was sent to govern Fujian, the association rekindled a glimmer of hope and again put the railway project on their agenda. Jiang Guangnai, the new chairman of the Fujian provincial government, was excited with the association's initiative and specially ordered the creation of a Zhang-Long Railway Preparatory Committee, which consisted of members of the original railway committee.[76] Thrice between June and August of 1933, members of the committee met in Gulangyu to discuss specific details on how to proceed. Li Qingquan then made special trips to Shanghai and Nanjing to scout for qualified professionals to survey the proposed route and begin prospecting in the mines along the railway. A geologist and a mineralogist were hired for the job, and for two months beginning in September 1933, they trekked the entire length of the proposed railway, measuring the roadbed and collecting several dozen cases of mineral samples.[77] In November the same year, Huang Yizhu also hired a German pilot to perform an air survey of the region.[78] With detailed ground measurements and aerial photographs, a precise topographical map was prepared. It is noteworthy that Li and Huang footed the expenses for the surveys out of their own pockets; and of the proposed 20 million yuan to be raised for the project, they each shouldered half of the responsibility.[79]

Again, the mercurial political environment of the Chinese Republic put an unexpected halt to the project. In November of 1933, Jiang Guangnai and Cai Tingkai initiated the Fujian Rebellion, declared Fujian to be autonomous, and proclaimed the establishment of the People's Revolutionary Government. The Rebellion was short-lived as Chiang Kai-shek's superior forces crushed the rebels with little difficulty and brought the revolt to an end in mid-January, 1934.[80] Losing their patrons, Li and Huang were forced to shelve their pet project again, this time permanently.

While the ambitious plan to improve people's livelihood through the railway-cum-mining project remained unrealized, the association was more successful in restoring some sense of order to Minnan. Fully aware that the passive measures of organizing local militia could not guarantee complete safety, the association actively pursued the eradication of roving bandits and rebel armies. First on its list of targets was Chen Guohui, the most powerful among a host of "local despots"(*tu huangdi*) in Minnan.

To say that Chen Guohui was "exceedingly unpopular"[81] in Southern Fujian was an understatement. Headquartered in Longyan, Chen Guohui controlled much of Quanzhou and Yongchun. At his height, he commanded in excess of 15,000 men, and owned comparable number of rifles, more than seventy machine guns, several cannons of various makes, and two airplanes.[82] Better equipped than most units of the government's army in the region, it is small wonder that Chen was called the "King of Minnan" (*Minnan wang*), and he had almost a free rein to act as he pleased in Southern Fujian.

A man who acknowledged little authority and brooked no opposition, Chen Guohui showed how much destruction an insensitive man with an army at his disposal could carry out. Chen squeezed the peasants mercilessly as he raised existing taxes and imposed dozens of supplementary taxes. It has been determined that Chen created as many as twenty-six different taxes and levies in the eighteen years he was active in Minnan.[83] To be sure, taxes were a major source of money; in 1930 and 1931, the opium tax alone swelled his coffers by four to five million yuan. However, they did not always produce all the revenue he wanted. Southern Fujian was thus dotted with illegal tax stations to collect *likin*—a tax on goods in transit—from traveling merchants. And at Chen's whim, he might "borrow" three to five years of taxes in advance simply "to cover military expenses."[84]

Chen's propensity for destruction and disregard for the people were evident as he allowed his troops to ransack large and small towns, often with ruthless thoroughness. In the spring of 1930, a thousand of Chen's men raided Wufeng in Yongchun, killing thirty-three people in the process, burned forty-three houses, and held several hundred people for ransom. A few months later, they looted Huyang, another town in Yongchun, and caused over ten million yuan in damages. Ten townspeople were killed, over a hundred were kidnapped, and numerous young girls were taken captive and sold.

Seeing the destitution and tremendous hardships wrought by Chen Guohui, overseas Chinese bristled with hatred for this "local despot."[85] Adding to their fury was Chen's fondness of kidnapping returned overseas Chinese or their family members in China for high ransom. Hence as soon as the association was formed, Li Qingquan immediately telegrammed the government in Beijing and the provincial government in Fujian, appealing for troops to be dispatched to fight Chen Guohui. In response, Beijing ordered Zhou Yingren, then governor of Fujian, to suppress Chen. Zhou in turn delegated the responsibility to Kong Zhaotong, commander of the government forces in Quanzhou, who launched an attack on Chen's headquarters on Chinese New Year's Day, 1926. Caught by surprise, Chen retreated into the deep mountains of Anxi after having lost more than half his men through death, surrender, or flight. But Chen still had a thousand men by his side, enough to be a continual menace in southern Fujian.[86]

When the Northern Expedition forces entered Fujian in 1927, Li Qingquan wrote to its commanding officer beseeching him to come south to exterminate Chen once and for all. After the Nanjing government was established, Li again wrote Generalissimo Chiang Kai-shek with the same request. Both entreaties fell on deaf ears. As it turned out, the chaos that followed Chiang's Northern Expedition gave Chen Guohui the breathing space to expand his forces and reestablish himself in Southern Fujian, and his power reached a new height at the beginning of the 1930s. In 1931, Li again brought Chen's many crimes against the people to the notice of the Nanjing government, but the Nationalist Party was too preoccupied with national affairs to pay heed to the ravages of a local bandit.[87]

In 1932, the joint request from the association, the Philippines Chinese National Crisis Support Association, and the Xiamen Overseas Chinese Association, to have the 19th Route Army transferred to govern Fujian was surprisingly agreed to by Chiang Kai-shek. The gallantry of the 19th Route Army during the Shanghai Incident had propelled them to national heroes' status.[88] Not surprisingly, they were not favored by Chiang. Chiang was undoubtedly aware that any military unit enjoying such popularity in China and abroad represented a threat to his own power, and the open letter issued by the 19th Route Army complaining about the lack of support from his government during the Shanghai Incident did not endear them to Chiang either. Thus barely a month after the ceasefire agreement with the Japanese, Chiang transferred the 19th Route Army away from Shanghai to Fujian on May 5, 1932, under the pretext that they were needed to fight the communists there.[89]

Regardless of Chiang's intention toward the 19th Route Army, the Fujianese, including those abroad, received their arrival with much ecstasy and great expectations. After a congress of overseas Fujianese was held in August of 1932 in Hong Kong, Li Qingquan and other foremost members of the association formally filed charges against Chen and appealed for help from the 19th Route Army. Owing to the generous financial and public support overseas Chinese had showered on them since the Shanghai Incident, the 19th Route Army was rather receptive to overseas Chinese grievances and petitions. In September of 1932, employing treachery worthy of Cao Cao—in Lloyd Eastman's assessment[90]—the 19th Route Army lured Chen Guohui to Fuzhou where he was summarily arrested and charged for "ordering the cultivation of opium, levying arbitrary and exorbitant taxes, and harassing merchants and people."[91] Chen's troops quickly surrendered after his capture and on December 23, 1932, much to the immense gratification of onlookers, Chen Guohui was publicly executed.

The failure of the Zhang-Long railway-cum-mining project but the successful elimination of Chen Guohui remind us that as mere civilians, overseas Chinese depended heavily on the endorsement and support from military leaders in China to help them instigate change in their home villages. It would be rash to over-celebrate their role in the transformation of southern Fujian during the Republican era.[92] However, by keeping up persistent pressure on the national and provincial authorities and liberally using their wealth, overseas Chinese were still able to bring some of their bold intentions to bear and made some real and positive impact on the lives of people in their home villages.

"The Pillar of the Overseas Chinese"—Li Qingquan

As the Zhang-Long railway-cum-mining project revealed, business opportunities could also be sought and found when overseas Chinese turned their gaze to China. Compared to the chaos and dilapidation in the rural areas, Xiamen, the commercial hub and gateway to the wider world for southern Fujian, was undergoing a rigorous urban development plan in the 1920s and 1930s.[93] As city walls and marshy lands were giving way to macadamized roads and concrete houses, opportunities for profit abounded. It was during this period that overseas Chinese investments in industrial and commercial enterprises in Fujian reached its peak.[94] According to Chinese scholar Dai Yifeng, it is common for overseas Chinese to invest in China to seek profit at the same time they were promoting social and economic progress in their home villages.[95] Perhaps nobody exemplified this mode of thought better than Li Qingquan, the man at the helms of both the protest against the Bookkeeping Law and the Home Village Salvation movement.

Li Qingquan was born in 1888 in Shizhen, a small village belonging to Jinjiang city. Typical of coastal villages in southern Fujian, Shizhen was cursed with infertile soil and a paucity of fresh water. According to the genealogy of the Li lineage, members of their clan began to look for better prospects overseas as early as the late seventeenth century. Taiwan was the logical choice considering its proximity, but later generations were increasingly drawn to the Philippines given the better economic prospects there.

Li Qingquan's great-grandfather survived the perilous voyage to the Philippines in the late eighteenth century, and he was followed by Li's grandfather and father. Li Qingquan's father initially ran a small furniture shop with his uncle. But as it was unfortunately burned down, they decided to switch to the lumber business and set up a lumber-processing factory that they named Chengmei. The elder Lis' new venture coincided with Spain's decision to open the Philippines to world trade and promote economic growth. Their business quickly took off, and it laid the foundation for Li Qingquan's business empire in the early twentieth century.

Li Qingquan was groomed to take over the family's business at a young age. After some private education in one of the village schools, he was sent to Xiamen's American-run Tongwen Academy at age eleven. After two years of English, mathematics, and other subjects essential to a Western education, he had his first exposure to the running of the lumber business when he was summoned by his father to the Philippines. One year later, seeing that Li's passion for study did not fade, his father enrolled him in the Saint Joseph Institute in Hong Kong. For four years, Li received further instruction in Western education, and it is also believed that the rapid transformation of Hong Kong from a fishing village to a major commercial hub in East Asia left some favorable impressions on the young man in his mid-teens.[96]

Despite being only eighteen when he returned to the Philippines, Li Qingquan showed his business acumen during his first business transaction—the acquisition of several hundred hectares of land in Manila.[97] He soon won unreserved trust from his father and uncle who handed over the reins of their company to young Li in 1907, still shy of his twentieth birthday. As if to repay the faith entrusted him, Li worked tirelessly to expand the family business. In less than one decade after he took charge of Chengmei, he turned the company from a small lumber retailer to a firm that owned its own timberland, processing mills, and distribution networks. It was estimated that by 1916, Li Qingquan was worth well over 11 million pesos.

Having firmly established himself as the undisputed "lumber king" of the Philippines, Li began to diversify into the pharmaceutical industry, the aluminum industry, the paint industry, and other ventures.[98] Most significantly, he established the Chinese newspaper, *Huaqiao shangbao* (Chinese commercial news) in 1919, and formed, in the following year, the Philippines' first Chinese private bank, the China Banking Corporation, with strong support from Huang Yizhu.

With wealth, came power. In 1919, Li was elected chairman of the Philippine Chinese General Chamber of Commerce and held this position for six consecutive years. It was in his capacity as leader of the Philippines' Chinese business community that Li carried the fight to preserve their economic interest in the Philippines on the one hand, and led the charge to help save their home villages in Southern Fujian on the other.

It should be noted, however, that Li Qingquan did not reappear in southern Fujian only after acquiring the official savior role. As a matter of fact, Li had a personal and intimate tie to his hometown that was never broken. Like many overseas Chinese before him, Li was ordered home by his mother to marry a girl from a neighboring village in 1910, who bore him a son the following year.[99] In 1913, Li funded the establishment of Shizhen's first modern school, which featured a curriculum including English, mathematics, geography, and science. This Longmen School was to be the first of Li's many philanthropic contributions to his birthplace, which included a couple more schools, a public library, and a bridge. Li was also remembered for using his wealth and influences to help prevent a dispute between Shizhen and an adjacent village from escalating into an armed feud.[100]

As early as 1923, Li sought to improve the general economic well-being of his home village by joining with a few fellow overseas Chinese from Jinjiang to establish the Quan-Wei Transport Company. Though moderate in size and limited in scope, the transport company not only facilitated the movement of people from the southern parts of Jinjiang to key commercial and communication centers of the province, especially Fuzhou, Quanzhou, Zhangzhou, and Xiamen, but also provided Li with the first taste of business success in China. We do not know how much confidence in the investment environment of China Li gained from this small business pursuit, but the opening of a branch of the China Banking Corporation in Xiamen in 1925 truly signaled his intention to expand his business empire to China.

In 1927, Li Qingquan set up in Xiamen the Li Mingxing Company with an initial capital of 1.9 million yuan.[101] Unlike smaller investors who speculated in property prices, Li's intention was to establish a business stronghold in Xiamen. Between 1927 and 1933, he pumped well over 2.2 million yuan into Xiamen[102] for the acquisition of two tracts of land along the bank of Lu River (Lujiang),[103] the construction of a bund along the bank (the Lujiang Boulevard), and the development of shophouses, buildings, and a marketplace in downtown Xiamen or by the sea. According to the recollection of Li's agent in Xiamen, Li had a grand design for the land he acquired. He was prepared to expend another one million yuan to erect a department store building in the proposed Lujiang Boulevard that would outclass similar edifices in Hong Kong and Shanghai. The scale of his plan may be seen from the fact that a section of land by the bank of the Lujiang would be set aside specifically to build wharves and warehouses so as to support the operation of the department store.[104]

In today's Xiamen, however, only the shophouses that Li raised and his magnificent villa in Gulangyu still stand as a reminder of Li's impressive wealth and vigor. Unfortunately, due to the bursting of the speculative bubble in real estates in the early 1930s and the Japanese occupation of Xiamen after 1938, most of Li's ambitious plans remained unfulfilled, and his investments in Xiamen were ultimately a failure. An estimate made in 1953–1954 revealed that Li Qingquan's property in Xiamen was worth only a paltry 96,000 yuan. Not only could Li find no buyer for his land after World War II, he could only rent it out to petty vendors who sold coffee and tea out of the simple plank shops they built on his land. Despite losing millions of yuan in China in the 1930s and 1940s, Li could perhaps find solace in the fact that the main reasons for his failure were all beyond his control: world depression, political turmoil in China, and Japanese invasion.[105]

Li Qingquan's investments in Xiamen revealed another dimension to overseas Chinese's relations with China. At the same time he was fighting on two fronts to protect his interests and those of his fellow Fujianese, Li was also strategizing to establish a permanent foothold in Xiamen in order to build another business empire in China. China, then as now, notwithstanding its many deficiencies, was still a land with many opportunities, especially for someone with the wealth and connections of Li Qingquan.

One must not, however, jump to the quick conclusion that Li's interests in China caused him to drop his business abroad. As a matter of fact, Li never gave up his business base in the Philippines. It is a little ironic that while Li lost a huge amount of money in Xiamen, it was his foundation in the lumber business in the Philippines that saved him from collapsing during the Great Depression. According to Li's associate, Li still controlled the lumber industries in the Philippines in the 1930s with his five lumber processing factories and one trading firm. It is believed that Dee C. Chuan & Sons Inc., one of the five factories alone, had a capital of three million pesos and sales valued at ten million pesos annually.[106] In addition to the lumber industry, Li's China Banking Corporation was flourishing as well. In 1936, the Bank's total assets swelled from its starting capital of 10 million pesos to 26 million pesos, and its working capital also more than doubled from its initial 2 million pesos to 5.7 million pesos. Besides setting up branches in Xiamen and Shanghai, the China Banking Corporation also had foreign exchange agencies in major cities around the world.[107]

Conclusion

This chapter surveys an ostensibly patriotic village salvation movement and explores the motivations behind overseas Chinese's involvement in affairs in China, or more specifically, their native places. It has argued that the complex and multifaceted thought processes that underlay overseas Chinese's actions simply cannot be accounted for by the single explanation of overseas Chinese's undying love for the motherland. The "love of homeland" thesis is partially valid insofar as it is used to explain overseas Fujianese selective activism in providing alternatives when provincial and local government abdicated their responsibilities. For example, they contributed to the building of schools and roads, the organizing of local militias for self-defense, the setting up of local industries, and the establishment of public utility companies. Aimed at improving the standard of living of the people, these measures indeed manifest overseas Chinese's desire to better their home villages.

However, the "love of homeland" thesis does not necessarily describe the initial impetus that motivated overseas Fujianese to return to Fujian; in our case, their motivations are evident in the anti-Chinese campaigns in the Philippines. Neither is the thesis adequate in describing the full range of motivations of a collective organization (the Home Village Salvation Association) or even a single individual (Li Qingquan). As I have shown, the projects undertaken by the association served not only the interests of the inhabitants of Minnan, but the members of the association as well. They campaigned against Chen Guohui not only to rid their native place associates in Minnan of a freewheeling despot but also to make their home villages a more hospitable place should the overseas Chinese themselves decide to settle back in China. By the same token, although the construction of the Zhang-Long railway would help Southern Fujian economically, the first to reap benefit from the new mode of transport and the accompanying mining activities would be the investors from the association. The complex combination of rehabilitating Minnan and furthering one's own interest was especially evident in Li Qingquan's investment in Xiamen. With his wealth, Li was hoping to transform Xiamen into a modern city that could rival Shanghai and Hong Kong; but more importantly, Li took Xiamen as the beachhead from which he could extend his business empire to China. In all of these ways, overseas Chinese attempted to "salvage" their native villages not merely out of love for their homeland but also to exploit their comparative advantages there.

In her chapter on the overseas Chinese in French Indochina, Tracy Barrett argues that in order to make the most of their native place ties, overseas Chinese have to retain, or even reproduce through education, as many as possible of the linguistic, cultural, and social practices of the native place. While this may be true for the overseas Chinese abroad, this chapter has shown that as the overseas Chinese returned from the "margins" to the mainland, they did not seek to reconnect with their native place through traditional ties. Rather, they endeavored to reconstruct their home villages with their money and in accordance with the knowledge and visions they acquired abroad. In other words, not only were the overseas Chinese not dependent on China; they also played a central role in trying to shape the future of their homeland.

NOTES

1. The association was renamed the Chinese National Association in 1927. Despite the name change, the goals and principles of the association remained very much the same.
2. Wang Gungwu, "Upgrading the Migrant: Neither Huaqiao Nor Huaren," *Asian Culture* 19 (1995): 1.
3. Yen Ching-hwang, *Coolies and Mandarins: China's Protection of Overseas Chinese during the Late Ch'ing Period (1851–1911)* (Singapore: Singapore University Press, 1985), chapter 1.
4. Wang, "Upgrading the Migrant," 1.
5. Wang Gungwu, "The Limits of Nanyang Chinese Nationalism," in Wang Gungwu, *Community and Nation: Essays on Southeast Asia and the Chinese* (Kuala Lumpur: Heinemann Educational Books, 1981), 156–57.
6. Ibid.
7. Yen Ching-hwang, "Overseas Chinese Nationalism in Singapore and Malaya, 1877-1912," in Yen Ching-hwang, *Community and Politics: The Chinese in Colonial Singapore and Malaysia* (Singapore: Times Academic Press, 1995), 199–200.
8. Ibid.,199–228. See also Stephen Mun-Yoon Leong, "Sources, Agencies and Manifestations of Overseas Chinese Nationalism in Malaya, 1937–41" (University of California, Los Angeles, Ph.D. dissertation, 1976).
9. Yen Ching-hwang, *The Overseas Chinese and the 1911 Revolution: With Special Reference to Singapore and Malaya* (Kuala Lumpur: Oxford University Press, 1976).
10. Yoji Akashi, *The Nanyang Chinese National Salvation Movement, 1937–1941* (New York: Paragon Gallery Ltd, 1970); Wing Seng Pang, "The 'Double-Seventh' Incident, 1937: Singapore Chinese Response to the Outbreak of the Sino-Japanese War" (University of Singapore, B.A. honors thesis, 1972).
11. Lin Jinzhi and Zhuang Weiji, *Jindai huaqiao touzi guonei qiye shi ziliao xuanji—Fujian juan* [A sourcebook on overseas Chinese investment in Fujian in the modern era: Fujian province] (Fuzhou: Fujian renmen chubanshe, 1985).
12. Maurice Freedman, *The Study of Chinese Society* (Stanford: Stanford University Press, 1979).
13. George L. Hicks, ed., *Overseas Chinese Remittances from Southeast Asia, 1910–1940* (Singapore: Select Books, 1993).
14. C. F. Yong, *Tan Kah-Kee: The Making of an Overseas Chinese Legend* (Singapore: Oxford University Press, 1987).
15. Lin Jinzhi and Zhuang Weiji, 1–2.
16. See for example, *Xiamen huaqiao zhi* [The gazetteer of Xiamen's overseas Chinese] (Xiamen: Lujiang chubanshe, 1992); *Nanyang Siang Pau* (Nanyang shangbao) (July 2, 1925); Shi Xueqin, "Huaqiao yu qiaoxiang zhengzhi: 20 shiji ersanshi niandai feilubin minqiao yu

jiuxiang yundong yanjiu" [Overseas Chinese and native place politics: A study of the Philippines Chinese and their village salvation movement of the 1920s and 1930s], *Huaqiao huaren lishi yanjiu* 2 (1999): 43–49.

17. Dai Yifeng, "Jindai Fujian huaqiao churu guo guimo jiqi fazhan bianhua" [On the size and movement of Fujian's overseas Chinese and their development], *Huaqiao huaren lishi yanjiu* 2 (1988): 33–39.

18. Lin Jinzhi and Zhuang Weiji, 29, table 3.

19. In their book on the Fujianese diaspora, *Dongnanya de Fujian ren* [Fujianese in Southeast Asia] (Fuzhou: Fujian renmin chubanshe, 1993), Yang Li and Ye Xiaodun estimated that in 1990, about 78 percent of overseas Fujianese in the world come from southern Fujian. See Lynn Pan, ed., *Encyclopedia of the Chinese Overseas* (Singapore: Chinese Heritage Center, 1998), 33.

20. Quoted in Chang Pin-tsun, "Chinese Maritime Trade: The Case of Sixteenth-Century Fu-chien" (Princeton University, Ph.D. dissertation, 1983), 92.

21. Ng Chin-keong, *Trade and Society: The Amoy Network on the China Coast, 1683–1735* (Singapore: Singapore University Press, 1983), 21.

22. Lynn Pan, ed., 30.

23. Ibid. In the seventeenth, eighteenth, and nineteenth centuries, recorded incidents of famine numbered 228, 158, and 101 times, respectively.

24. Chi Xiumei, "Minguo shiqi Fujian zaihuang jiuji yanjiu" [A study of famine relief in Fujian Province during the Republican era] (Fujian shifan daxue, M.A. thesis, 2005).

25. Ibid.

26. Pan Shouzheng, Zhang Zongguo, Ye Chengqian, and Liu Xudong, "Li Houji zai Fujian" [Li Houji in Fujian], *Fujian wenshi ziliao* 9 (1985): 1–23.

27. Hong Shaolu, "Junfa tongzhi shiqi zhi Anhai" [Anhai under warlord rule], *Jinjiang wenshi ziliao*, 2 (1982): 77–101.

28. Goh Tjoei Kok, oral interview, National Archives of Singapore, B000082/11.

29. Ng Teow Yhee, oral interview, National Archives of Singapore, A000065/10.

30. Zhuang Guotu, "The Social Impact on Their Home Town of Jinjiang Emigrants' Activities during the 1930s," in Leo Douw and Peter Post, eds., *South China: State, Culture and Social Change During the Twentieth Century* (Amsterdam: North Holland, 1996), 169.

31. Zhang Youyi, *Zhongguo jindai nongye shi ziliao* [A sourcebook of modern Chinese agricultural history] (Beijing: Sanlian shudian, 1957), v. 3, 892.

32. Antonio S. Tan, *The Chinese in the Philippines, 1898–1935: A Study of their National Awakening* (Quezon: R. P. Garcia Publishing Co., 1972), 98.

33. Antonio Tan, 185.

34. Antonio Tan, 187; see also *Golden Book, 1955: A Fiftieth Anniversary Publication of the Philippine Chinese General Chamber of Commerce* (Manila: Philippine Chinese General Chamber of Commerce, 1955), v. 3, 21.

35. Antonio Tan, 187.

36. "Letter by Chinese Chamber of Commerce, Philippine Islands, to Governor General of the Philippines, February 15, 1921," in Chen Ta, *Chinese Migrations, with Special Reference to Labor Conditions* (Taipei: Cheng-wen Publishing Company, 1967), 187.

37. Antonio Tan, 191. *Golden Book, 1955*, v. 3, 21.

38. *Golden Book, 1955*, v. 3, 21.

39. Antonio Tan, 190.

40. Edgar Wickberg, "The Philippines," in Lynn Pan, ed., 192.

41. Antonio Tan, 188.

42. Ibid., 189.
43. *Golden Book*, v. 3, 21–22; Antonio Tan, 192–93.
44. *Golden Book*, v. 3, 21–22.
45. Ibid.
46. Antonio Tan, 191.
47. Ibid., 193.
48. Antonio Tan, 339.
49. Ibid., 340.
50. *Golden Book*, v. 3, 32.
51. Antonio Tan, 340.
52. Ibid., 343.
53. Ibid.
54. Between 1603 and 1762, there were five recorded incidents of Chinese massacres. In the first two massacres in 1603 and 1639 alone, 20,000 or more Chinese lost their lives.
55. Antonio Tan, 343.
56. *Xiamen huaqiaozhi*, 129; Shi Xueqin, "Huaqiao yu qiaoxiang zhengzhi," 45.
57. *Nanyang Siang Pau* (November 28, 1925).
58. *Xiamen huaqiao zhi*, 129.
59. Huang Xiaocang, ed., *Feilubin Minlila zhonghua shanghui sanshi zhounian jinian kan* [A book published in commemoration of the thirtieth anniversary of the Philippine Chinese General Chamber of Commerce of Manila] (Manila: Zhonghua shanghui chubanshe, 1936), v. 1, 46.
60. Ibid.
61. *Nanyang Siang Pau* (November 28, 1925).
62. *Xiamen huaqiao zhi*, 130.
63. *Nanyang minqiao jiuxianghui linshi dahui baogao shu* [A report of the ad hoc congress of the Southeast Asia overseas Fujianese village salvation association] (Xiamen: Minqiao jiuxianghui, 1926), 1–2.
64. *Nanyang Siang Pau* (December 2, 4, 7, 8, 9, 1925).
65. Huang Xiaocang, ed., v. 1, 47.
66. Lloyd Eastman, *The Abortive Revolution* (Cambridge: Harvard University Press, 1974), 91.
67. *The China Critic*, 5.35 (September 1, 1932): 908.
68. Antonio Tan, 285.
69. Chinese mile, roughly 1/3 of a statute mile.
70. *Nanyang minqiao jiuxianghui linshi dahui baogao shu*, 21.
71. Shi Xueqin, "Nanyang minqiao jiuxiang yundong yu Zhang-Long lukuang jihua" [The village salvation movement and the Zhang-Long railway-cum-mining project], in *Nanyang wenti yanjiu*, 4 (1995): 47.
72. *Nanyang minqiao jiuxianghui linshi dahui baogao shu*, 3.
73. Shi, "Zhang-Long lukuang jihua," 48.
74. Huang Yizhu, "Minban Fujian quansheng tielu gufen youxian gongsi yuanqi," in Zhao Dexing, *Huang Yizhu zhuan* [Biography of Huang Yizhu] (Changsha: Hunan renmin chubanshe, 1998), 366.
75. Shi, "Zhang-Long lukuang jihua," 48.
76. Zhao Dexing, 174.
77. Shi, "Zhang-Long lukuang jihua," 49.
78. Zhao Dexing, 174.

79. Shi, "Zhang-Long lukuang jihua," 49.

80. Eastman, chapter 3.

81. *Reports of the American Consulate, Amoy, China* (June 6, 1929).

82. Li Zhong, "Shijiu lu jun chujue Chen Guohui ji Chen bu fumie jingguo" [The extermination of Chen Guohui and his troops by the Nineteenth Route Army], *Fujian wenshi ziliao*, 3 (1964): 65.

83. *Nan'an wenshi ziliao*, cited in Shi Xueqin, "Huaqiao yu qiaoxiang zhengzhi," 44.

84. Li Zhong, 65–66.

85. An overseas Chinese whose native place of Yongchun was constantly ravaged by Chen Guohui vowed "not to live under the same sky" (*bugong daitian*) as Chen. See Shi, "Huaqiao yu qiaoxiang zhengzhi," 43.

86. Yang Yanying, "Zhou Yingren shilue" [Biographical sketch of Zhou Yingren], in *Fujian wenshi ziliao* 9 (1985): 44.

87. Shi, "Huaqiao yu qiaoxiang zhengzhi," 46.

88. So popular was the Nineteenth Route Army that the name Cai Tingkai, its chief commander, appeared, like the name of movie stars, as a brand name on cigarettes and other goods. Eastman, 92.

89. Ibid., 93.

90. Ibid., 98.

91. Ibid., 98. *Minguo ribao* (August, 2, 1932) as quoted in Shi, "Huaqiao yu qiaoxiang zhengzhi," 47. See also Cai Tingkai, "Gaizao Fujian yu huaqiao" [Reforming Fujian and overseas Chinese], in Huang Xiaocang, ed., v. 2, 71–72.

92. See for example, James A. Cook, "Bridges to Modernity: Xiamen, Overseas Chinese, and Southeast Coastal Modernization, 1843–1937" (University of California, San Diego, Ph.D. dissertation, 1998).

93. Zhou Zifeng, *Jindai Xiamen chengshi fazhanshi yanjiu* [A study of the urban history of Xiamen] (Xiamen: Xiamen daxue chubanshe, 2005).

94. Lin and Zhuang.

95. Dai Yifeng, "Southeast Asian Chinese investment in Xiamen: The Li Family during the 1920s and 1930s as a Case Study," in Leo Douw, Cen Huang and David Ip, eds., *Rethinking Chinese Transnational Enterprises: Cultural Affinities and Business Strategies* (Leiden: Curzon-IIAS, 2001), 102–22.

96. Ibid., 105.

97. Ibid.

98. Ibid., 106.

99. Li Rui, *Li Qingquan zhuan* [Biography of Li Qingquan] (Manila: Yu yi tong ji jin hui, 2000), 156.

100. Ibid., 60–68.

101. Ibid., 73. Lin and Zhuang, 468.

102. Dai, "Southeast Asian Chinese Investment in Xiamen," 111; Lin and Zhuang, 480–81.

103. The Lujiang was not really a river, but what locals call the bay that separates Xiamen island and Gulangyu.

104. Lin and Zhuang, 481; Dai, "Southeast Asian Chinese Investment in Xiamen," 111.

105. Lin and Zhuang, 481–82; Dai, "Southeast Asian Chinese Investment in Xiamen," 111–14.

106. Dai, "Southeast Asian Chinese Investment in Xiamen," 118.

107. Ibid.

12

PHONY PHOENIXES

Comedy, Protest, and
Marginality in Postwar Shanghai

Paola Iovene

On Friday, July 11, 1947, around nine o'clock in the morning, hundreds of people showed up at the Grand Theatre in Shanghai to attend the preview of the comedy *Jia feng xu huang* (Phony Phoenixes), produced by the Wenhua Film Studio and directed by Huang Zuolin.[1] The film, featuring Shi Hui as a barber and Li Lihua as a charming young woman in search of a husband, had been widely advertised. Invitations had been sent to journalists and local authorities, and preview slides had been shown in movie theaters for several weeks. Given this extended promotional campaign, viewers' expectations ran high, and disappointment ran deep when it became clear that no one would be able to watch the movie that day: a large group of angry men—hundreds of barbers, as they turned out to be—surrounded the building and formed human chains blocking all entrances. A student who attempted to break through was even injured. The barbers held out till the early afternoon, when they took to the streets nearby and slathered the movie billboards with paint.

The "Phony Phoenixes incident" (*Jia feng xu huang shijian*), as it was later referred to in memoirs and essays on postwar Shanghai cinema, provoked much sensation in the press and sparked a debate that lasted several days, eventually forcing the Wenhua Film Studio to change several scenes. It was also thanks to the protest, of course, that the comedy became an immediate hit, rivaling the box office success of the historical melodrama *Spring River Flows East* that was released in October that year.[2]

One of the rare instances of *documented* audiences' reactions to a popular movie, the barbers' protest provides a unique illustration of the social dynamics that shaped cinema production and reception in 1947 Shanghai. The purpose of this chapter is to contextualize this event in the film culture of the times, detailing the activities of the film-studio, exploring cinema venues and viewing habits, and delineating the social tensions that brought together, in the same dispute, filmmakers, critics, barbers, and representatives of native place associations. By shedding light on this particular incident and uncovering some of the reasons why the barbers protested, I hope to further our understanding of the movie-going experience in postwar Shanghai and to speak to the question of "China's margins" in relation to the difficult issue of cinema audiences in Republican China.

Filmmakers and film critics in Republican China often conflated cinema audiences with the elusive category of "petty urbanites" (*xiaoshimin*). But this term, initially coined by left-wing writers in the early 1930s to emphasize the supposedly conservative and low-brow tastes of the faceless majority, remains intrinsically vague and internally heterogeneous.[3] According to Perry Link, "the most anyone says is that the term includes clerks, primary school students, small merchants, and others of the so-called 'petty bourgeoisie.'"[4] Hanchao Lu, who prefers the translation "little urbanites," writes that this was "a blanket term popularly known and liberally used to refer, often with condescension, to city or town people who were of the middle or lower-middle social ranks. ... *Xiaoshimin* was never precisely defined. It was less clear who should be included in the category than who should be excluded. The elite at the top and the urban poor would never be referred to as *xiaoshimin*. It was the people who stood in between who were called 'petty urbanites.'"[5] In her study of the activities of the publisher Zou Taofen, Wen-hsin Yeh follows Link's definition of "petty urbanites" but identifies a specific subgroup, the "vocational youth" (*zhiye qingnian*), as the intended readership of Zou Taofen's periodical *Shenghuo Weekly*. Vocational youth was an equally heterogeneous category composed of shop clerks and employees of small enterprises who had a few years of schooling under their belt but had not had the opportunity to go to college. In publishing the immensely popular *Sheng-huo Weekly*, Yeh argues, Zou Taofen helped the vocational youth to "constitute themselves as a new kind of reading audience." Such popular periodicals created a sense of communality among readers, linking personal concerns to national issues and paving the way for the Chinese Communist Party's appropriation of people's voices into a unified discourse.[6]

The notion of *xiaoshimin* continues to be invoked in recent discussions of cinema audiences but it remains problematic—not only because of its widely acknowledged elusiveness, but also because of the diversity of cinema venues in Republican China, which was likely to generate movie-going experiences that varied significantly according to one's specific social status and background. In this sense, the reception of cinema is hardly comparable to that of the kinds of popular fiction and journalism discussed by Perry Link and Wen-hsin Yeh. Magazines and books were widely circulated and shared—they were readily available even to people who could not afford buying a copy. This very form of almost simultaneous enjoyment of the written word might have helped disseminate norms and beliefs among heterogeneous urban groups. My hypothesis is that, in contrast, up to the late 1940s the movie-going experience to a certain extent reinforced social distinctions. In postwar Shanghai, a broad range of spectators—including intellectuals and other elites not readily associable with the *xiaoshimin*—attended different movie theaters scattered across the city and showing very different kinds of films. What was shown in first-run cinemas at a certain moment would become available to the patrons of peripheral, third-run cinemas only after several months. Therefore, while movie-going was a relatively common activity for people from many walks of life, it would generally not bring them together under one roof. Since the Grand was one of the most elegant movie theaters of the city and only showed first-run films, it seems safe to assume that barbers and other members of the lower rungs of the *xiaoshimin* were not among its most frequent patrons. These experiential dimensions of film-viewing and the unequal conditions in which it took place might have affected the ways a film was received, exacerbating rather than overcoming all sorts of social differences.[7]

And yet, as I shall detail further down in this chapter, in the late 1940s theaters such as the Grand were actively trying to expand their audiences by promoting themselves as places where people from *all* walks of life could convene to be enlightened and entertained. As film studios and theaters were opening their doors to less privileged viewers through free matinee tickets and other promotional campaigns, they were inevitably confronted with tensions and resistance regarding the very conditions of this process of inclusion. The Phony Phoenixes incident provides such an instance. It reveals how the strong immigrant component of Shanghai inhabitants—notably referred to as a city of "sojourners"—and its cultural and "ethnic" heterogeneity complicated film reception, precisely at the moment when the lower strata were no longer merely part of the urban cinematic imaginary but were beginning to participate as distinctive spectators in spaces that had generally been beyond their reach.

One of the elements that the barbers found offensive in the film was that one of its main protagonists, a barber played by Shi Hui—pronounced a few words in Subei dialect, which associated barbers with the less privileged immigrants from Subei. As we shall see, while most barbers were immigrants from Yangzhou, a city physically located in northern Jiangsu (Subei), they did not consider themselves as Subei people. By protesting, the barbers attempted to dictate the conditions of their presence in the cinematic imaginary of the city and to acquire a more prominent, if perhaps ephemeral, voice in the media. This involved distinguishing themselves from the lower strata of Subei immigrants, including the itinerant barbers who were not members of any professional association as well as from other sorts of manual workers who came from poorer areas within the region. The barbers' attempt to "demarginalize" themselves, in short, brings to light the complex social layering within the largely silent masses of Subei immigrants living on the margins of Shanghai urban life.

But before dealing in detail with the social issues motivating the barbers' protests, I shall discuss the main themes of the comedy and introduce the people involved in the Wenhua Film Studio and the spaces where the protest took place, so as to offer a mapping of the event that, in that hot summer of 1947, took barbers to the cinema and cinema to the streets.

Phony Phoenixes:
A Romantic Comedy in Postwar Shanghai

Based on a script by Sang Hu, *Phony Phoenixes* is a story of fake identities and mutual cheating, culminating in a double marriage that unites the main couple and two of their friends in the consolatory embrace of laughter and romance. Yang Xiaomao, a.k.a. "San Hao" (Number Three), is the most acclaimed barber in Shanghai in the late 1940s.[8] He has, however, grown weary of his meager income: he would like to change his business, become rich, and drive around in a big car, he confesses one day to one of his clients, general manager Zhang Yijing. But the manager himself is covered in debts due to the collapse of the stock market and replies with a request for help. He urges Yang Xiaomao to respond to a marriage ad, in which a Miss Fan, a young lady recently returned from the United States, is looking for a husband to share the responsibilities of administering a big fortune. Hoping to gain a portion of the woman's wealth for himself, the manager helps Yang to write a letter, which presents him (Yang Xiaomao) as a rich returned student holding a Ph.D. from Oxford University. A photograph of a glamorous Yang Xiaomao is enough to convince Miss Fan that this candidate is not only rich and cultured but handsome as well. The two meet, and a series of hilarious adventures ensue, because, as the viewer is informed from early on, the woman is not rich at all. She is a single mother (probably a divorcee) with a six-month-old baby to take care of. She has not paid the rent for months, and her landlord has sent the police to urge her to leave the house within two days.

Much of the film is shot in interiors, mostly in the barber shop and in the tastefully furnished apartment of Miss Fan. Miss Fan herself sports a series of fashionable dresses. She has obviously become poor only recently and can still exhibit the remnants of the comfortable life she was accustomed to before separating from her husband. When Yang Xiaomao goes to see her, together with his colleague "Number Seven" who pretends to be his "secretary," he is truly impressed and in turn attempts to show off. With the money that the general manager has given him, and accompanied by his "secretary," he takes Miss Fan and her own "secretary" (a friend of hers who has recently divorced) to dine at a fashionable French restaurant. Here Yang Xiaomao knots a napkin around the necks of each of the two women, out of professional habit, as if he were about to do their hair. Then, believing that "à la carte" is the name of a dish, he cheerfully orders: "We'll have an 'à la carte!' " In the end, the bill is so high that he has to call up the general manager to ask for more money.

Yang Xiaomao/Shi Hui is clearly a stranger to Shanghai international entertainments, especially in comparison with the much more cosmopolitan Miss Fan/Li Lihua. Yang is an attractive man, but he is also meant to appear hopelessly provincial. His incompetence in things foreign is also shown later on, when he receives the women in the manager's office: pretending that the office is his own, he answers a phone call and stammers a few words of jumbled French and Japanese, so as to show off his international business connections. Such failed attempts at cultural cosmopolitanism, of course, must have been a source of great amusement for those viewers who were familiar with foreign languages and things but were likely to be deemed offensive by barbers.

In any case, for all the ridiculous moments that should have revealed to Yang and Miss Fan that neither of them is what they purport to be, a reciprocal misrecognition keeps the cheating going for quite a long time. Both Yang Xiaomao and Miss Fan are too enchanted by the prospect that the other one is going to solve their respective economic problems to break the chain of mutual deception. Very soon, a wedding date is set, and, as it typically happens, on the very morning of the wedding the truth finally emerges. Miss Fan goes to pawn the engagement ring she has received from Yang in order to pay the rent, and there she sees Yang Xiaomao also entering to the pawnshop with the clothes and shoes that his colleagues have lent him to help him buy his wedding suit. At this point, Miss Fan not only discovers the bitter truth of Yang's poverty, but also finds out that the engagement ring he had given her is a fake. She therefore resolves that she cannot marry such a poor swindler, and in a state of utter desperation calls up a retired official who had also replied to her marriage ad. The man is rich indeed but extremely old and ugly. In one scene he is seen carrying huge sacks filled with money (a clear reference to the rampant inflation of the time), which he is willing to give her if only she lets him become a father. Eventually, Miss Fan renounces wealth and marries Yang Xiaomao. She joins him in the barber shop, and her divorced friend marries Yang Xiaomao's colleague.

Phony Phoenixes focused on an issue that was widely discussed in the media, namely the difficulties of single women (widows, ex-concubines, as well as divorced women) to support themselves due to the shortage of jobs at the time. For the women in the comedy, marriage is represented as *the* solution to economic distress, not because they finally find a husband who loves and supports them, but rather because it provides them with the possibility to live and work in a relatively nondegrading environment. More generally, the comedy conveyed a benevolent, if mildly ironic denunciation of decline of honesty in postwar Shanghai and an anxiety about being cheated.[9]

The theme of hoaxes and swindles was quite common in comedies of the war period such as Yang Jiang's *Swindle* (*Nong zhen cheng jia*), which was staged in Shanghai in 1943.[10] Similarly to Yang Jiang's comedy, *Phony Phoenixes* did not present the issue of cheating in a moralizing tone but rather suggested that particularly harsh circumstances forced everyone to cheat. Lack of sincerity should not simply be condemned: in order to survive, it was necessary to lie. Moreover, authentic feelings and a new life could emerge even from lies. The film thus voiced an ambivalent moral stance and ended on a cheerful note. Its final scene, which showed the two newly formed couples waving goodbye from behind the glass window of the barber shop, conveyed the hope of returning to one's routine daily work, a perspective that might have seemed tragically remote to many who had lost their livelihood because of war or inflation. This overall conciliatory tone and hopeful mood may well be among the reasons for the comedy's appeal to the Shanghai public at a time of social disintegration, economic crisis, and raging civil war in the rest of the country.[11]

Mimicking Hollywood romantic comedies such as Ernst Lubitsch's *The Shop Around the Corner* (1940), *Phony Phoenixes* provided a playful counterpoint to solemn representations of love, motherhood, and the raising of the future generation characterizing Chinese melodramatic movies since the 1930s. While medium shots prevail, the very few close-ups generally emphasize not so much depth of feeling but rather amazement or surprise and end up having a comic effect.[12] Even if Miss Fan eventually decides to marry San Hao because she likes him, the reciprocal affection is simultaneously overstated and understated, with emphatic declarations of love immediately slipping into farce.

In Chinese melodramas of the 1930s and of the postwar period, the representation of motherhood often took on allegorical meaning, sometimes alluding to a traditional idea of womanhood that was incompatible with the revolutionary struggle, at other times highlighting the contradiction between new ideas of women's liberation and a society that was unable to offer women the means to support themselves. Such melodramatic representations suggested that hope lay in the education of the children, and that for mothers themselves, there was often no way out apart from death.[13] In *Phony Phoenix*, however, the mother-child relationship is mostly a source of comic effect. For instance, when Yang Xiaomao goes to see Miss Fan without warning her in advance, she is holding her baby in her arms, and hastily hides him under the bed. At that point the child starts crying, but Yang is made to believe that it is a doll on the table that is crying. This is yet another proof of Yang Xiaomao's gullibility and Miss Fan's feminine resourcefulness, but the shot on the child lying under the bed might also offer an irreverent, if indirect, commentary on melodramatic representations of children.

In sum, drawing from the experience of wartime drama and seeking inspiration from Hollywood comedies, the filmmakers of *Phony Phoenixes* addressed social issues in an indirect, humorous fashion. In particular, the comedy destabilized the melodramatic treatment of romantic love and mother-child relations, which in earlier Chinese films often appeared inextricably connected with the issue of national salvation. This indirect mode of representing current political and social issues was one of the characteristics that set Wenhua apart from other studios especially in its first two years. And it is to the activities of the Wenhua Film Studio that I now turn, with the aim of providing a fuller picture of the cultural, economic, and social agents involved in the production of *Phony Phoenixes*.

The Wenhua Film Studio

The Wenhua film studio was founded in 1946 by Wu Xingzai, who in the late 1930s to early 1940s had comanaged such studios as Lianhua, Hezhong, and Chunming. The only private studio in postwar Shanghai that could rely on constant capital turnover and was able to engage in uninterrupted film production, Wenhua started its production in February 1947 and wasted no time, delivering twelve films in the following two years.[14]

I have mentioned above the thematic affinities between *Phony Phoenixes* and wartime theater. Several members of the studio, in fact, had strong links with theater, most notably the director Huang Zuolin (1906–1994), who had studied drama at Cambridge University in the early 1930s.[15] Zuolin had returned to China in 1937, and in the war years worked in Shanghai as theater director and producer, staging several important plays such as Cao Yu's *Metamorphosis* (*Tuibian*, 1941) and Yang Jiang's comedy *As You Desire* (*Chen xin ruyi*, 1943).[16] At that time, Zuolin had set up a troupe called "Hard Work" (sometimes translated as "Bitter Toilers' Troupe," *Kugan jutuan*) which counted among its members Shi Hui, Zhang Fa, and several other actors who were then hired by Wenhua when the theater company was disbanded at the end of the war.[17] Actor Ye Ming, who played Yang Xiaomao's colleague "Number Seven" in *Phony Phoenixes*, later recalled that several theaters were converted into cinema venues after the war, and therefore work opportunities in theater were scarce. For these actors, to join the Wenhua Film Studio meant making a direct transition from the stage to the silver screen without having had much previous experience of cinema acting.[18]

The Wenhua Film Studio was housed in the old location of the Lianhua Film Studio at Sanjiao Street in Xujiahui, on the western border of what used to be the French concession. Wenhua shared the compound with the Kunlun studio. All the different phases of film production were taken care of on location, apart from developing and printing of the film copies, which was initially done by the Shanghai Film Developing Cooperative and by the Zhongdian Film Lab.[19] However, to accelerate the printing process, in mid-1948 a small laboratory was set up in the Wenhua Film Studio itself.[20] Wenhua employed about 120 people, of which 40 were stable employees. The permanent staff included four actors, while stars such as Li Lihua would be employed on a yearly basis or for specific films.

Already in early 1948 the press celebrated the Wenhua Film Studio's fast-paced production and quick rise to success. An article in the April 1948 issue of *Cinema Pictorial* (*Dianying huabao*), for instance, explained that the amazing success of the Wenhua Film Studio was due to the talent and fame of the people involved, effective production planning, and efficient advertisement strategies. Its male actors were led by Shi Hui, Han Fei, and Zhang Fa, and its female stars included the much acclaimed Li Lihua and the popular actress-singer Zhou Xuan.[21] The scripts were authored by such prominent authors as Zhang Ailing (Eileen Chang) and playwrights Cao Yu and Sang Hu. Wenhua was so well organized that it managed to produce a film every two months, and roles were assigned well before starting shooting. Before a film came out, advertisement strategies were carefully planned. The billboards of the Wenhua film studio, conceived by the skilled artist Ding Xi, were particularly effective in catching the attention of passersby. In the concluding lines, the article also refers to *Phony Phoenixes* as a potential gold mine for the Wenhua studio: thanks to an article in the American magazine *Life*, the film was going to be distributed in London and possibly also in the United States. If the film was to be shown in all U.S. movie theatres, the article claims, it would earn US$3 million.[22]

The Wenhua Film Studio, with its efficient production and distribution structure and its strong connections with theatre and film critics, was exceptionally well positioned in the cinema world of postwar Shanghai. It is no wonder, therefore, that *Phony Phoenixes* was one the first Chinese films to be shown at the Grand, a first-run theater that had previously specialized in foreign films. A glittering place of entertainment and attractions, the Grand lured different kinds of spectators but also turned many of them away—a physical manifestation of the contradictory popular aspirations of the film industry in republican Shanghai.

The Grand Theatre

The Grand Theatre, located at 216 West Nanjing Road, was built in 1928 by the Chaozhou entrepreneur Gao Yongqing and named "Da Guangming yingxiyuan" (literally, Grand Light Movie Theater, rendered in English as "Grand Theatre") by the editor of the *Shenbao* supplement *Ziyou tan* Zhou Shoujuan (1895–1968).[23] The theater occupied two floors and had more than 1,400 seats. The extravagance of its décor, its bright yellow interiors, and the reliefs of female nudes that flanked the stage all contributed to the moviegoers' experience. Before the show, spectators could watch slide shows in the lounge on the second floor, sip tea in the tearoom, or have a drink at the bar. A "Euro-American style" band of twenty-one musicians, also located on the second floor, accompanied the screening of silent films.[24]

It was at the Grand that the famous protest against Harold Lloyd's *Welcome Danger* (translated in Chinese as *Bu pa si*) took place on February 21, 1930.

The film dealt with opium smuggling in San Francisco's Chinatown and was perceived as portraying the Chinese protagonists in a degrading way. During an afternoon screening, playwright and Fudan University professor Hong Shen stepped up on the stage and called on the audience to leave the movie theater and demand their money back. The English manager of the Grand pushed Hong Shen off the stage and called the police. Hong Shen was held at the police station for about three hours, but as a result of his action, a press campaign ensued that called for a ban on films that humiliated China and the Chinese. *Welcome Danger* was soon banned throughout China, and in the following months several newspapers refused to carry advertisements for the Grand.[25] According to recently published memoirs, it was due to this protest that the theater fell on hard times. It closed down in late 1931 and was demolished, but the Hong Kong entrepreneur Lokan (Lu Gen) soon commissioned the Hungarian architect L. E. Hudec to build a new theatre at the same location, which opened in June 1933 under the slightly changed name "Da Guangming da xiyuan" (the English name remained the same).

The new Grand Theatre was even more magnificent than the old. Its floor entirely covered with pure wool carpet, it had more than 1,900 comfortable seats, three large lounges, and three multicolored fountains, the most notable of which was located in a cubic glass construction above the main entrance. Its display of water under the rays of colored lights constantly distracted drivers and caused innumerable traffic accidents, so much so that the Ministry of Works finally had it removed.

At least until the mid-thirties the Grand only screened first-run American movies. In the early 1940s earphones were installed in all seats, through which simultaneous translation from English to Chinese was broadcasted. In the mid-1930s Percy Chu (Chu Bochuan), an executive with the Zhejiang Industrial Bank who had purchased both the Grand and the Cathay, persuaded the American distributors to allow Chinese films to be screened at the Grand but only during weekdays.[26] Yet several sources report that the Grand continued to screen mostly foreign films, and that *Phony Phoenixes* was the first Chinese film to be shown there since the end of the war, a result that was possible only after long and tough negotiations between Wenhua and the movie theater and that testified to the high quality of the film.[27]

The Grand changed management a few times in the 1930s and 1940s. In 1947 it was part of the Guoguang Corporation, which also managed the Cathay. From the few anecdotes that we have on the fortunes of the Grand in the postwar era, it appears that the management promoted the theater as an open and accessible place that welcomed audiences from diverse social and economic backgrounds. Starting from 1947, for instance, the Grand held matinee shows twice a month, distributing free tickets to military police and wounded soldiers through the Songhu Garrison Headquarters. On the occasion of these screenings, the cinema appointed two military policemen to maintain order, but incidents and small-scale protests happened all the same. For instance, at one of these matinees about ten wounded soldiers holding metal crutches and carrying weapons forced their way into the theatre; the military policemen tried in vain to keep them out but were beaten up by them. A reinforcement of ten policemen was sent in from a police station nearby and arrested the wounded soldiers as they came out of the theater at the end of the screening.[28]

The protest of the barbers, it seems, was not an isolated episode but rather part of a series of clashes that surrounded the introduction of marginal groups into Shanghai's more central movie-theaters. The dispute can be related to several previous episodes of popular protest against media representation of social or ethnic groups, and yet it went beyond them both in scale and effect.

The Grand Besieged

Weeks before *Phony Phoenixes* came out, there had been some contacts between Wenhua and representatives of barbers' professional organizations. It is unclear whether it was the film studio that initiated these contacts, but it is very likely that its management showed the film to the barbers before the official preview at the Grand.[29] Certainly the barbers' representatives knew of the film well before the date of its opening, and they did not appreciate what they saw or heard about it. In fact, they warned Wenhua that if the film was screened without their approval, they would enter the movie theater and destroy all the seats. The film studio, however, decided to go ahead with the preview, promising the Grand to pay for the damage should any seat be ruined.[30] Since Wenhua's managers had already started advertising, they had no intention of postponing the show. Billboards with "true-to-life" portraits of Shi Hui and Li Lihua had been painted and posted at the corner of Nanjing and Chengdu Road,[31] invitations to the first preview had been sent out, announcements were published in the press, and stills from the film, accompanied by the text "soon in this cinema," were shown in the Grand. In addition, neon lights flashing the title *Phony Phoenixes* and the names of the studio and the actors were mounted on the façade and in the hallway of the Grand.[32]

On the morning of July 11, 1947, hundreds of people showed up at the gates of the Grand. For a moment, it seemed that what the filmmakers and the management of the movie theatre had hoped for, namely that this comedy would bring together "people from all walks of life," was about to come true.[33] But it soon became clear that the theater was besieged by angry barbers, whose picket lines, four men deep, blocked all the gates.[34] The manager of the Grand immediately sent a telegram to the Bureau of Social Affairs (*Shehuiju*), an organ routinely involved in the mediation of labor conflicts. The bureau ordered the screening canceled, and signs announcing that "Negotiations are in progress, the preview is cancelled" were hung outside. Around noon, the police arrived and scattered the crowd, but by that point, some of the barbers had already taken to the streets and smeared the faces of Li Lihua and Shi Hui on the billboards with white, red, and blue paint. Under the names of the actors, turtles were painted in red.[35] The *Zhongyang Daily* also reported that barbers wrote on the posters the sentence "× tui qiangu."[36] The author of the article claimed that he did not know what the × stood for, but it could be "gou" (dog), and the sentence could mean "lackeys forever," possibly an allusion to the fact that Li Lihua had acted in pro-Japanese propaganda films produced by the Huaying Studio during the Sino-Japanese War.[37]

In the following weeks, the barbers' organizations and the film studio held separate press conferences and meetings with associations and groups that could help them strengthen their respective positions. On July 19, the Barbers Trade Guild and the Professional Union held a joint press conference on the ninth floor of the Jinmen Hotel, during which they distributed an issue of the *Guild Journal* listing the nine scenes which, in their opinion, were offensive and ought to be cut. One of the incriminating scenes was when Yang Xiaomao, the main character, said "*guai guai*" (cute) with a Subei accent.[38] Others showed Yang putting his hands on a woman customer's shoulders, a gesture that was considered "indecent and obscene," and then borrowing money, clothes, and shoes from his colleagues, which suggested that barbers were poor and lacked dignity. Another scene that was criticized showed how Yang sharpened his razor on his necktie (instead of the usual leather strop), apparently trying to commit suicide after Miss Fan had refused to marry him. Barbers claimed that such depiction was not only offensive to their profession but also a threat to social order.[39]

The chairman of the Yangzhou Native Place Association (*Yangzhou tongxiang hui*), Jiao Dingkai, intervened in the press conference declaring that "it is intolerable that the film with its ugly representation humiliates the category of the barbers and even uses words in Subei dialect."[40] The joint statement of the Yangzhou Native Place Association and the two trade organizations (i.e., the Barbers Trade Guild and the Professional Union) claimed that it was exactly because cinema was such an effective tool of social education that it was regrettable that it offended their profession. A film like *Phony Phoenixes*, they argued, would have an enormous impact on society at large, leading national and possibly even international audiences to look down on them. In this statement, the barbers' representatives positioned themselves as supporters of state educational policies and guardians of public mores, and criticized the film studio for failing to do the same. Since the state was promoting the use of a standardized national language (*guoyu*), they claimed, film studios should follow suit instead of fishing for cheap laughs by using Subei dialect. Finally, they found faults with the film in comparison with other narrative and dramatic genres. Fiction and opera, they went on to explain, extol the good and condemn the vicious. Even though they might include episodes of banditry and debauchery, in the end the villains are punished and the virtuous glorified. The barber in *Phony Phoenixes*, by contrast, was not sufficiently heroic or virtuous. He showed little moral decency in act or speech and even tried to use his professional tools to commit suicide.[41] In short, the barbers were making quite a strong aesthetic statement, claiming that the filmic representation of Yang Xiaomao lacked literary imagination: it failed to elevate him above imperfect humanity and did not manage to transcend the contingencies of daily life.

The *Phony Phoenixes* standoff lasted for several weeks. For all its rhetoric of inclusiveness, on July 22 Wenhua had to resort to a small private "closed-door" preview at the Guanghua Movie Theater, to which only film critics and journalists were invited and were asked for advice on how to change the film. That morning, the barbers' organization appealed to the Bureau of Social Affairs demanding the cancellation of this preview as well. When the bureau declared that the matter was outside its competence, about five hundred barbers went to picket the Guanghua. Eventually they came to an agreement with delegates from the Journalists' Association and the police, and the preview took place as planned.

In the Media: Too Touchy?

While the press was generally mildly sympathetic to the barbers, well-known intellectuals and foreign language media criticized their reaction. The *North China Daily News*, an English language newspaper, published a foreign resident's letter to the editor, which accused the barbers of being "touchy" and narrow-minded: did they not know *The Marriage of Figaro*? If only they did, they would realize that barbers were often the protagonists of opera pieces, which in fact endeared them to the public.[42] An article in the Chinese language *Zhongyang Daily* reported that a bystander had commented that "Such things did not happen in the past. From now on it will only be possible to make films about cats and dogs"[43]—a casual remark that revealed a problematic tension between people's desire to control the ways they were portrayed in the media, the desire of filmmakers to make a successful comedy, and censorship. Several playwrights, including Cao Yu and Ouyang Yuqian intervened in defense of the film. For instance, Li Jianwu, a well-known playwright and theater critic who had previously worked with Huang Zuolin, claimed that the film was sympathetic to barbers who made a living by working honestly. The people that the film really satirized, instead, were the manager who had lost all his money in the stock market, and the wealthy old official who had proposed to Miss Fan. In any case, Li Jianwu argued, the whole dispute derived from a misunderstanding of the aims of comedy as a form of art. When viewing a comedy, the public was expected to be detached, not to identify with the characters. Li Jianwu exhorted his readers to be broadminded and liberal enough to laugh about themselves and their weaknesses. Bringing in Aristophanes and ancient Greek to support his claims, he pointed out that the genre of the comedy ideally poked fun at everyone, and therefore its existence was a true sign of democracy.[44]

The well-known playwright Hong Shen, who had started the protest against the American film *Welcome Danger* right there at the Grand seventeen years before, also wrote in defense of the filmmakers. Hong Shen admitted that he had not seen the film. Judging from the script, he conceded that there might be a couple of shots that were truly offensive and needed to be cut. However, all artistic works aimed at educating by means of social criticism, and for criticism to be effective, invention was necessary. At the same time, he reminded readers that it was a great achievement of modern art that common people had finally gotten on center stage, replacing the emperors and nobles of the past. He then explained that comedy was based on the principles of "simplification" and "exaggeration" (in English in the text, which is otherwise in Chinese), and that *Phony Phoenixes* was not a satire of the barbers but of the falsity of Shanghai life. Hong Shen compared the barbers' conditions depicted in the movie with the much harsher life of the people in China's interior and concluded that the barbers were not represented as poor or lacking in personal dignity. Rather, the film reminded them that, under the present circumstances, it was a great privilege that they could support themselves by means of an "ordinary profession."[45]

In sum, such intellectuals as Hong Shen and Li Jianwu, who were both close friends of the filmmakers, defended the film by claiming that it was a humorous representation not of the barbers in particular but of the economic difficulties of Shanghai inhabitants in general. Both critics articulated their claims by mobilizing "cosmopolitan" cultural affiliations: Li Jianwu mentioned Aristophanes and Greek comedy and Hong Shen used English words in the text. In doing so, they implicitly reinforced the point that barbers had found so offensive in the comedy: that they were provincial and unrefined. Not only had barbers no notion of propriety and good manners, as shown by the comedy, but they also did not understand the international/universal artistic form of comedy itself. With memories of wartime censorship all too fresh in mind, these critics had every reason to see the dispute as yet another threat to artistic autonomy. However, claims to artistic license could not be easily accepted by the people who were the object of representation. The "truthfulness" or "realism" of filmic representation was, after all, an important aspect of the popular discourse on film aimed to attract large numbers of viewers to the movie theaters. How could the barbers believe that the film was not *really* about them?

A Question of Accent:
The "Ethnic" Factor in Film Reception

While the press of the time largely depicted the *Phony Phoenixes* events as a struggle concerning the barbers' "professional dignity," the protest had much to do with their geographical origin, their relative socio-economic marginality, and general prejudices and conflicts among different social and "ethnic" groups in postwar Shanghai.

Most barbers in Shanghai came from the Yangzhou region, immediately north of the Yangzi River. Indeed, as mentioned above, the Yangzhou Native Place Association joined the barbers' professional organizations to organize the protests against the Wenhua Studio.[46]

Immigrants from the area north of the Yangzi—including those from Yangzhou—were generally identified as Subei people, associated in the popular imagination with crime, poverty, and demeaning, low-status work. As recalled by the actor Ye Ming, "at that time, most of the people involved in the barbers' trade in Shanghai were natives of Subei who had a strong sense of local belonging. Whether society treasured them or not had always been a very sensitive psychological issue. The theme of this film touched on precisely this problem. Film art supposedly takes as its subject the common person, but the barbers focused on the external implications of the professional role of the protagonist."[47]

But in fact, people from Yangzhou felt that they did not belong to Subei at all. As one remarked, "Although Yangzhou people are located in Jiangbei [north of the Yangzi], they became 'Jiangnan-ized' early on. From the Sui [dynasty], they have represented the whole Jiangnan style. To say that Yangzhou is part of Jiangbei is totally absurd!"[48] Although in the eyes of other Shanghai residents Yangzhou was part of Subei, people from Yangzhou considered their hometown as superior to the rest of the region. Indeed, while most Subei people were usually employed as coolies and night soil haulers, Yangzhou natives were relatively better off, and were mostly employed as barbers, bathhouse pedicurists, and cooks.[49]

The barber Yang Xiaomao was depicted as an occasional speaker of Subei dialect. Not only was he shown borrowing clothes and shoes, which suggested that he was poor; he also lacked urbanity and refined manners and could boast no knowledge of foreign things. The film thus associated barbers with a social group that the barbers themselves considered inferior to their own. Once they had come into public view through the powerful medium of cinema, barbers wanted to make sure that viewers would not get the wrong idea about their group as a whole. They had to draw a clear line between themselves and the underprivileged category of *Subeiren*, and, interestingly, they did so by adopting the rhetoric of the state. By arguing against the use of Subei dialect in *Phony Phoenixes*, they positioned themselves as promoters of the national language; by complaining about the comedy's failure to take a clear moral stance, they represented themselves as guardians of the national mores and promoters of a healthy cinema.

In sum, by protesting against *Phony Phoenixes*, barbers aimed not only to assert their professional dignity but also to affirm their identity as distinct from Subei people and to reclaim a position that was at least one rung above the lowest on the social ladder. While the press portrayed the protest as an issue of professional identity, in fact, class, profession, and ethnicity were practically inseparable in 1940s Shanghai.⁵⁰ The film thus offered the barbers a pretext to redefine themselves as a specialized professional group distinct from the *Subeiren* and to claim a better place and role in the national space.

Toward a Resolution

The *Phony Phoenixes* dispute went up to the Movie Censorship Office of the Ministry of the Interior (*Neizhengbu dianying jianchachu*), which decreed that the filmmakers had not broken any law and were not required to modify the film.⁵¹ However, on July 24 the Bureau of Social Affairs stipulated that three scenes had to be cut, namely the sequence in which the barber put his hands on the woman customer's shoulder, the sharpening of the razor on the tie before the attempted suicide, and Number Seven eating at the restaurant in his undershirt. When representatives of the barbers insisted on their nine points, the head of the bureau provided detailed explanations why these were not considered as offences. On the question of Subei accent, for instance, he claimed that Subei was a local language like any other and therefore could not be considered an insult. The head of the bureau also met with Huang Zuolin and other representatives of the film studio, who agreed to implement the three requested changes. The Bureau of Social Affairs had an important role in mediating the dispute. On the one hand, it admonished the barbers that if they did not comply with the agreement, "they would most likely lose the sympathy of society (*shehui de tongqing*)," while on the other, it requested that the filmmakers add words of praise for the barbers' hard working spirit at the end of the closing credits.

The Wenhua Studio could not but comply with the demands of the Bureau of Social Affairs and accepted all three of its requests to modify the film.⁵² This was the conclusion of The *Phony Phoenixes* dispute, which lasted little more than two weeks in that hot summer of 1947 but greatly contributed to the film's box office success. As the American pictorial *Life* wrote in October that year, this "comedy about an amorous barber [broke] records in Shanghai."⁵³

Epilogue: Out of Shanghai, Out of the Margins?

In other Chinese cities *Phony Phoenixes* was also met first by barbers' protests and then by growing numbers of curious audiences. The Shanghai barbers' associations had sent telegrams and letters to their sister organizations in Nanjing, Tianjin, and other cities all over the country, calling on them to protest against the film. In Tianjin, the Hua'an Movie Theater invited a few inspectors from the Nationalist government's garrison headquarters to a free private screening, in the hope to obtain their protection in case rebellious barbers would show up on the opening day.

But this did not help much. On the day before the opening, several barbers from the five largest barber shops in town, apparently incited by the local guild, started picketing the movie theater. After discussions with the police, the barbers sent five representatives who demanded to be invited to "inspect the film" before any ticket could be sold. The movie theatre agreed, but reportedly the barbers stood up and started protesting when they were only half way through the show, going up to the stage and even attempting to tear down the silver screen. Eventually the Tianjin barbers were pressured by local authorities and public opinion to come to a compromise. News of their protest quickly spread in the city, attracting large crowds eager to watch the movie that was creating such uproar all over the country.[54]

Overall, the barbers' protest functioned as an effective advertisement campaign for the film. Wenhua had to issue a much larger quantity of prints than they had expected, raising the number from an initial eight to seventeen. This created problems on how to arrange distribution on such a large scale. For some time the actor Ye Ming would fly to such cities as Hankou and Changsha to bring the prints in person, but very soon the film company established distribution agencies to deal with local theatres in the major cities of the north and the interior.[55]

To conclude, the *Phony Phoenixes* dispute was one of the very few instances in which urban migrants came out of the back alleys "beyond the neon lights" and sought to control their representation in the media and find a voice in the national arena. Unlike Chinese migrant communities outside of China (see Ong's and Barrett's chapters), whose actions were discursively justified (if not motivated) by identification with a specific regional locality, in this case *internal* migrants who found themselves in a disadvantaged position could not find solutions by claiming to have an exclusive bond with their hometowns. Instead, they identified themselves with the national public discourse of morality and education and established a web of city-to-city relations that were based more on professional identity than on birthplace. By staging their protest as a defense of their professional dignity, rather than as a fight against regional stereotyping, they implicitly acknowledged that being from a place that was "too close" to Subei could not be publicly transformed into a source of pride.

The *Phony Phoenixes* incident offers rare documentation of film reception in China, illustrating how a film that was meant to promote social reconciliation ended up reinforcing social distinctions. The barbers used the movie-theatre as a venue to assert their identity as a group that was not to be conflated with the poorer migrant workers from Subei. In the process of becoming cinema audiences, they called attention to the multiple layers of marginality in postwar Shanghai. Many of the barbers acted as audiences without having actually seen the film they criticized, which reminds us of the variety of modes of reception that may supplement—and sometimes even disrupt and displace—the film-viewing experience itself. After those few weeks of protest some of the barbers probably all but forgot about the film and never went to see it. But many did, and perhaps enjoyed seeing charming

Shi Hui playing one of them on screen, even though he was not as morally upright and refined as they might have liked to imagine themselves to be.

NOTES

*An earlier version of sections of this essay was published in Italian as "*Jia feng xu huang e la rivolta dei barbieri di Shanghai*" [*Jia feng xu huang* and the Shanghai barbers' revolt], in M. Scarpari and T. Lippiello, eds., *Caro Maestro ... Scritti in onore di Lionello Lanciotti per l'ottantesimo compleanno* (Venezia, Libreria Editrice Cafoscarina, 2004), 655–66. I thank Libreria Editrice Cafoscarina for permitting me to draw on this article.

1. The film's initial title, *Yuanyang hudie* [Mandarin ducks and butterflies], was changed because it sounded "too frivolous." Lu Hongshi, *Zhongguo dianying shi 1905–1949: Zaoqi Zhongguo dianying xushu yu jiyi* [History of Chinese cinema 1905–1949: Stories and recollections of early Chinese cinema] (Beijing: Wenhua yishu chubanshe, 2005), 188. Like mandarin ducks, phoenixes are a traditional symbol of love and conjugal happiness but are less associated with excessive sentimentality. *Phony Phoenixes* is the translation used in the English language reviews of the film. Paul G. Pickowicz nicely translates it "*Fake Bride, Phony Bridegroom*." See his "Acting like Revolutionaries: Shi Hui, the Wenhua Studio, and Private-Sector Filmmaking, 1949–1952," in Jeremy Brown and Paul G. Pickowicz, eds., *Dilemmas of Victory: The Early Years of the People's Republic of China* (Cambridge: Harvard University Press), 256–87.
2. Ye Ming, "Wenhua yingpian gongsi de huiyi (1947–1951)" [Recollections of the Wenhua Film Studio, 1947–1951], *Shanghai dianying shiliao* 1 (October 1992): 34.
3. Mau-Sang Ng, "Popular Fiction and the Culture of Everyday Life: A Cultural Analysis of Qin Shouou's *Qiuhaitang*," *Modern China* 20.2 (April 1994): 150–54, and Laikwan Pang, *Building a New China in Cinema. The Chinese Left-Wing Cinema Movement, 1932–1937* (Lanham: Rowman and Littlefield, 2002), 150–58.
4. Perry Link, *Mandarin Ducks and Butterflies: Popular Fiction in Early Twentieth-Century Chinese Cities* (Berkeley: University of California Press, 1981), 189.
5. Hanchao Lu, *Beyond the Neon Lights: Everyday Shanghai in the Early Twentieth Century* (Berkeley: University of California Press, 1999), 61.
6. Wen-hsin Yeh, "Progressive Journalism and Shanghai's Petty Urbanites," in Frederic Wakeman and Wen-hsin Yeh, eds., *Shanghai Sojourners* (Berkeley: Institute of East Asian Studies, University of California, Berkeley, 1992), 186–238.
7. These observations are inspired by a conversation I had with Paul Pickowicz in San Diego, June 2007. For a detailed description of the Shanghai "class-based exhibition system" see Poshek Fu, *Between Shanghai and Hong Kong: The Politics of Chinese Cinemas* (Stanford: Stanford University Press, 2003), pp. 33–38. The social composition of early cinema audiences remains one of the most elusive issues in film studies of China as elsewhere. For interesting points of comparison see Miriam Hansen, *Babel and Babylon. Spectatorship in American Silent Film* (Cambridge: Harvard University Press, 1991), and Jacqueline Stewart, *Migrating to the Movies: Cinema and Black Urban Modernity* (Berkeley: University of California Press, 2005).
8. In fact, Yang Xiaomao and his colleagues serve both male and female clients, so strictly speaking they should be called "hairdressers" or "hairstylists."

9. See the review "Phony Phoenixes" in *Cinema of Two Cities: Hong Kong-Shanghai* (Hong Kong: Eighteen Annual Hong Kong International Film Festival, 1994), 121.

10. The title of Yang Jiang's comedy "more literally reads 'turning truth into jest', a reversal of the phrase 'turning jest into truth', which more amply suggests the fruitfully ambiguous play with sincerity and truth in the comic action." Edward Gunn, *Unwelcome Muse: Chinese Literature in Shanghai and Peking 1937–1945* (New York: Columbia University Press, 1980), 234.

11. On the ways in which the traumatic experiences of the war and a sense of social disintegration were depicted in postwar cinema, see Paul G. Pickowicz, "Victory as Defeat: Postwar Visualizations of China's War of Resistance," in Wen-hsin Yeh, ed., *Becoming Chinese: Passages to Modernity and Beyond* (Berkeley: University of California Press, 2000), 365–98.

12. On the conventions of love scenes in Hollywood romantic comedies of the 1940s, which mostly show lovers in motion and from a distance, see Thomas Schatz, *Hollywood Genres: Formulas, Filmmaking, and the Studio System* (Philadelphia: Temple University Press, 1981), 162.

13. See for example, *Shennü* [Goddess] (1934), *Xin nüxing* [New women] (1935), and *Liren xing* [Women side by side] (1949), which feature quite similar types of "vanishing women," i.e., women who have to disappear for the sake of the future generation. For a recent theoretical elaboration of the trope of the "vanishing woman" in visual media and cinema, see Karen Beckman, *Vanishing Women: Magic, Film, and Feminism* (Durham: Duke University Press, 2003).

14. In the following months the Wenhua Studio opened a branch in Beijing. In collaboration with Jin Shan and others, Wu also established Qinghua Studio in Beijing and Huayi Studio in Shanghai. Cheng Jihua et al., eds. *Zhongguo dianying fazhan shi* [History of the development of Chinese cinema] (Beijing: Zhongguo dianying chubanshe 1963), v. 1, 256, 472–473. Ma Jingyuan, "Wenhua yingpian gongsi yange" [The evolution of the Wenhua Film Studio], *Shanghai dianying shiliao* 1 (October 1992): 54.

15. Huang Zuolin often appeared simply as "Zuolin" in closing credits. *Phony Phoenixes* was his first film. On this occasion, he probably worked very closely with the scriptwriter and director Sang Hu. Sang Hu was the director of notable Wenhua productions such as *Taitai wansui* [*Long live the wife*] (1947) and *Aile zhongnian* [*The joys and sorrows of middle age*] (1949).

16. Zhang Yingjin, ed., *Encyclopedia of Chinese Cinema* (London: Routledge 1998), 196. On Cao Yu's *Metamorphosis*, see Poshek Fu, *Passivity, Resistance, and Collaboration: Intellectual Choices in Occupied Shanghai, 1937–1945* (Stanford: Stanford University Press 1993), 96.

17. Huang Shaofen, Xu Jiehua, "Wo suo zhidao de Wenhua yingpian gongsi" [The Wenhua Film Studio that I know], *Shanghai dianying shiliao* 1 (October 1992): 67.

18. Ye Ming, 31.

19. Ma Jingyuan, 56–59.

20. Ye Ming, 31. Ye Ming also reports that when Shi Hui's yearly contract expired in 1948, he asked the manager Wu Xingzai to be given the opportunity to direct his own films.

21. Some episodes in the private life of these actors, such as the love story between Shi Hui and Zhou Xuan, also attracted the audience's sympathy.

22. Jian Hui, "Cong lupai guanggao shuo dao 'Wenhua'" [From street billboards to "Wenhua"], *Dianying huabao* (April 10, 1948): 6.

23. Until 1945 this stretch of Nanjing Road was called Jing'ansi Street. Wu Hehu, "Da

Guangming yingxiyuan yishi gouchen" [Lost and found anecdotes on the Grand Theatre], *Shanghai dianying shiliao* 5 (December 1994): 106.

24. Cao Yongfu, "Shanghai Da Guangming dianyingyuan gaikuang" [Some basic facts on Shanghai Grand Theatre], *Shanghai dianying shiliao* 1 (October 1992): 207–11. Wu Hehu, "Da Guangming yingxiyuan yishi gouchen," 105–7.

25. Wu Hehu, 105–7. All of Harold Lloyd's movies were subsequently banned in China. See Zhiwei Xiao, "Anti-Imperialism and Film Censorship during the Nanjing Decade, 1927–1937" in Sheldon Hsiao-peng Lu, ed., *Transnational Chinese Cinemas: Identity, Nationhood, Gender* (Honolulu: University of Hawai'i Press, 1997), 39–41.

26. Marie Cambon, "The Dream Palaces of Shanghai: American Films in China's Largest Metropolis Prior to 1949," *Asian Cinema* 7.2 (Winter 1995): 34–45.

27. Li Duoyu, *Zhongguo dianying bainian, 1905–1976* [Hundred years of Chinese cinema, 1905–1976] (Beijing: Zhongguo guangbo dianshi chubanshe, 2005), v. 1, 192.

28. Wu Hehu. According to Zhiwei Xiao, "incidents involving unruly soldiers were so frequent that the military police began to patrol the city streets—with a particular focus on the movie theatres, which were viewed as "trouble-spots." These incidents reflected "the general collapse of law and order in postwar Shanghai." Zhiwei Xiao, "Movie House Etiquette Reform in Early-Twentieth-Century China," *Modern China* 32.4 (October 2006): 530.

29. An article published in 1988 states that a preview for the barbers was held on June 13. Yu Zhi, "Dui '*Jia feng xu huang* shipian shi fengbo' yi wen de bu yi" [An addendum to the article "The storm around the preview of *Phony Phoenixes*"], *Dazhong dianying*, (November 1988), 25. According to Paul Pickowicz, "films were often shown privately and informally to small interest groups (especially with politically sensitive films) for preliminary feedback. Minor changes could be easily made to the film afterward." Quoted in Lu Liu, "*Sorrow after the Honeymoon*: The Controversy over Domesticity in Late Republican China," *Modern Chinese Literature and Culture* 13.1 (Spring 2001): 1.

30. Shen Nong (pseud.), "*Jia feng xu huang* fengbo shimo" [The whole story of the *Phony Phoenixes* storm], *Shanghai dianying shiliao* 1 (October 1992): 71-74. Shen Nong specifies that two barbers' organizations, the Lifaye tongye gonghui (Barbers trade guild) and the Zhiye gonghui [Professional union] led the protest.

31. Wenhua rented an advertisement space on the billboard in front of the Xianlesi dancehall for one *liang* of gold a month. Some sources report that the Wenhua posters were painted by the famous painter Zhao Xikui (1903-1984), and that they were generally lit up till midnight. See Shen Nong, 71. See also Ma Jingyuan, 60.

32. Neon lights were installed well in advance of the film opening and would initially run the text "This theatre is *not* currently showing." This would then be changed into "This theatre *is* currently showing ... " The neon lights were kept for the entire period in which the film was shown; they would be then pulled down and used at second-run cinemas. See Ma Jingyuan, 60.

33. Wu Hehu, 106-7.

34. *Shenbao* (July 12, 1947) reported that more than 1,000 viewers gathered outside the Grand, 800 of whom were barbers. "Lifashi fengsuo da guangming: Li Lihua Shi Hui ban guilian" [Barbers blockade the Grand: Li Lihua and Shi Hui made up as monsters], *Shenbao* (July 12, 1947). See also Ye Ming, 33, and Shen Nong, 72.

35. "Lifashi fengsuo da guangming." Jeffrey Wasserstrom has argued that the turtle, meaning "cuckold" or "bastard," was a recurrent image used by students in patriotic demonstrations to insult those who collaborated with foreigners or bought foreign goods. See

Jeffrey N. Wasserstrom, *Student Protests in Twentieth-Century China: The View from Shang-hai* (Stanford: Stanford University Press, 1991), 222–23. On turtles and tortoises see also Endymion Wilkinson, *Chinese History: A Manual* (Cambridge: Harvard University Press, 1998), 383.

36. "Titou siwu baowei 'Da guangming': *Jia feng xu huang* shiying zhanqi" [Barbers sur-round the Grand: *Phony Phoenixes* is postponed], *Zhongyang ribao* (July 12, 1947).

37. "Li Lihua shi zenyang chengming de?" [How did Li Lihua become famous?] *Dianying* 8 (June 1, 1947): 14–15.

38. Throughout the film the barbers speak standard mandarin. On only two occasions do Yang Xiaomao and his colleague Number Seven pronounce a couple of words with an exaggerated local accent. I thank Ling Zhang for bringing these instances to my attention.

39. "*Jia feng xu huang* jiufen shehuiju jinri tiaojie" [The Bureau of Social Affairs inter-venes today to mediate in the *Phony Phoenixes* dispute], *Shenbao* (July 14, 1947). The other scenes the barbers criticized were the following. (1) Yang Xiaomao tells manager Zhang that his wife believes that he (manager Zhang himself) has a lover. (2) When manager Zhang lends the fake ring to the barber, he says: "The ring is fake on a barber's hand, but it is real on a manager's hand." (3) Barbers in the film are called "*lifajiang*," but according to the bar-bers themselves they should be called by the more respectful term of "*lifashi*," i.e., "master barber." (4) When Yang Xiaomao goes to visit Miss Fan, he puts the cigarette he is smoking behind his ear, which is probably a reminder of his professional habits of keeping a comb or other tools behind his ears. (5) When the protagonists go to the French restaurant, Yang Xiaomao's colleague Number Seven takes his jacket off, showing that he is only wearing an undershirt. The reports in the press of the time only list three or four of these scenes. The entire list can be found in Yu Zhi, "Dui '*Jia feng xu huang*' shipian shi fengbo' yi wen de bu yi" [An addendum to the article "The storm around the preview of *Phony Phoenixes*"], *Da-zhong dianying* (November 1988), 25.

40. Shen Nong, 72; Ye Ming, 33. The native place association that intervened in the dispute was in fact called "Native Place Association of the Seven Counties of Yangzhou" [Yangshu qi xian tongxiang hui]. Its members included migrants from Yangzhou and surroundings who were mostly employed in the service sector. In 1946 the association counted 2,784 members, but it later grew to more than 10,000. The Chairman Jiao Ding-kai came from the town of Jiangdu, some ten miles northeast of Yangzhou. He was an accountant and held a public school degree. For details, see Guo Xuyin, *Lao Shanghai de tongxiang tuanti* [Native place organizations in old Shanghai] (Shanghai: Wenhui chu-banshe, 2003), 775–840.

41. Shen Nong, 76.

42. "Too Touchy? To the Editor of the *North-China Daily News*," *North-China Daily News* (July 16, 1947).

43. "Titou siwu baowei 'Da guangming.'"

44. Li Jianwu, "Cong *Jia feng xu huang* shuo minzhu" [What *Phony Phoenixes* tells us about democracy], *Dagongbao* (July 19 and 20, 1947), reprinted in Ding Yaping, ed., *Bai-nian Zhongguo dianying lilun wenxuan* [One hundred years of Chinese film theory: An anthology] (Beijing: Wenhua yishu chubanshe, 2002), v. 1. 307–13.

45. Hong Shen, "Lun *Jia feng xu huang* yu yiban ju zhong ren de shenfen" [On *Phony Phoenixes* and the dignity of commoner protagonists], *Dagongbao* (July 24, 1947).

46. "*Jia feng xu huang* jiufen shehuiju jinri tiaojie."

47. Ye Ming.

48. Quoted in Emily Honig, *Creating Chinese Ethnicity: Subei People in Shanghai, 1850–1980* (New Haven: Yale University Press, 1992), 23.

49. Ibid., 85.

50. See also Elizabeth J. Perry, *Shanghai on Strike: The Politics of Chinese Labor* (Stanford: Stanford University Press, 1993), and Bryna Goodman, *Native Place, City, and Nation: Regional Networks and Identities in Shanghai 1853–1937* (Berkeley: University of California Press, 1995).

51. "Dianjianchu zuo biaoshi yijian" [Yesterday the Movie Censorship Office expressed its views], *Dagongbao* (July 22, 1947). "Barbers Continue Film Attack; Insult Denied," *The North-China Daily News* (July 24, 1947).

52. Shen Nong, 78–79. "*Jia feng xu huang* jiufeng jiejue" [The *Phony Phoenixes* dispute is settled], *Zhongyang ribao* (July 27, 1947). The scene in which Yang Xiaomao says "guai guai" with a Subei accent was also cut out (at least, it is not in the extant version of the film), but reports of the time do not mention it.

53. "Chinese Movie," *Life* (October 27, 1947): 75–78.

54. Jin Lishan, Xie Hesheng, "Hongdong Tianjin de dianying *Jia feng xu huang* de shijian [The *Phony Phoenixes* incident that caused a stir in Tianjin], *Congheng* 11 (2003): 61. For more details on how the events developed in Tianjin, see Zhiwei Xiao, "Social Activism during the Republican Period: Two Case Studies of Popular Protests against the Movies," *Twentieth-Century China* 25.2 (April 2000): 63.

55. Ye Ming, 64.

13

RURAL POLICY IN FLUX

Lai Ruoyu's Challenge to the
Party Center in the Early 1950s

Xiaojia Hou

The immediate aftermath of the founding of the People's Republic (1949–1953) was a time of uncertainty and fluidity. Communist Party (CCP) leaders, in the course of adapting to their new role as rulers of the nation, constantly asked themselves "Why should we adopt this kind of policy and not another?" The long-term goal was a wealthy and powerful socialist nation; a broad consensus was quickly reached on industrialization and social transformation towards the Soviet model, yet how the model should be adjusted to Chinese conditions or the pace of the transition was not resolved. Moreover, no one possessed definitive knowledge of the exact nature of the first step. In the coming years, a tension would surge between an emphasis on securing economic revival on the one hand, and the desire to establish firm control and quicken the steps to planned development and transformation on the other.[1] The only unchallenged authority in the party, Mao Zedong, for a while did not articulate his vision. In the early 1950s, as Teiwes rightly observes, "while reserving the right to insist on his own way in matters of prime concern such as the Korean decision, Mao's general approach was to encourage broad discussion in order to reach a consensus," especially in areas where he acknowledged his inadequacies.[2] Economy was certainly one of them. The rest of party leaders discussed, debated, and clashed on various policies, while working tirelessly to woo Mao. Political luminaries at all levels sought to define their new political positions and fought with each other to demarcate their zones of influence, a process accompanied by growing identification of individuals with the institutions and departments they worked for as the new system took shape, while at the same time the party Central Committee struggled to establish its authority with respect to national issues and to extend its control down to the local level. Hierarchies were reconfiguring.

Under such circumstances, specific policies could be rather easily cobbled together by local actors far from the party center in Beijing in order to deal with local realities. And individuals, even those of relatively low rank, could on occasion make a significant impact on the region and even the nation. This reality is not well understood in much of the scholarly literature. Consequently, a stereotype that dwells excessively on rigid hierarchies and strict control from above still prevails. This essay will discuss a fascinating case in which a provincial politician not only challenged Liu Shaoqi, second only to Mao in the party's chain of command, but actually succeeded in having his agenda promoted across the entire nation.

In 1949, the Central Committee officially adopted the "New Democracy" policy, a strategy recommended by Joseph Stalin in 1948 and articulated in China by Liu Shaoqi. The goal was to foster a mixed economy, to encourage the development of capitalism during a transition period and to secure broad acceptance through some concessions to social groups like capitalists. With respect to the rural sector, New Democracy acknowledged a grand future of collectivization of agriculture, but "both at present and during a relatively long period of time in the future our agricultural and handicraft industry are and will remain dispersed and individualized in terms of the basic form."[3] Peasants were encouraged to accumulate family wealth. Rich peasants were to be protected.[4] Deep in Mao Zedong's heart, he was not fully convinced of the virtues of the New Democracy policy and he warned it was wrong to let peasants take this course.[5] But for the time being, he did not involve himself much in rural issues and did not challenge Liu Shaoqi's rural policy. Challenges for Liu were to come from cadres of lower ranks. This policy was not unanimously supported among CCP cadres. On the contrary, many cadres were confused. Lai Ruoyu, the vice secretary of the CCP Shanxi provincial party branch, was one of them.

Assumptions and Challenges on Peasant Issues

Lai Ruoyu and his fellow provincial leaders in Shanxi were duly impressed by Soviet collectives. After the CCP won the civil war, some members of the party began at once to think about how to build socialism. A socialist countryside should move in a socialist direction, they believed.[6] Unlike Liu Shaoqi, who suggested holding off for a while on building a socialist countryside, Lai Ruoyu declared on September 1, 1949, the day the Shanxi provincial government was established, that "Our grand goal is modernization and collectivization. Without collectivization, there is no modernization. Those two are mutually related. We should now step by step move toward this goal."[7]

Four days later, Lai instructed his subordinate, Wang Qian, who was about to assume the post of party secretary of Shanxi's Changzhi prefecture, to carry out investigations in this old liberated area.[8] Wang's assignment was to find out what people were thinking, what kinds of problems they had encountered, and what methods the CCP should employ to take the party's work one step further. Lai explicitly told Wang Qian "You can ask other people to deal with other matters; you must take this mission very seriously and find the correct answer."[9] Lai did not explain clearly what kind of answer he was expecting, but Lai's trusted subordinate, Wang Qian, was likely well aware of Lai's hopes. Upon his arrival in Changzhi in late 1949, he initiated a series of investigations of rural conditions. What he discovered was an unpleasant surprise.

The Changzhi area was an old liberated region. Between the winter of 1948 and the spring of 1949, 96.3 percent of villages in its territory completed land reform, and land had been nearly equally distributed. Taking Yaozizhen village in Tunliu county as an example, of the 88 households in this village, the average landholding was 4.1 mu per person, and the average per capita output of grain was 3.6 dan (540 catties).[10] According to Tanaka's estimation, after land reform many peasants in Shanxi province could not make their livings merely on their land's output.[11] In accordance with Tanaka's estimation, aid organizations and economists generally define "self-sufficient" as equivalent to 45 to 51.1 catties of unhusked grain per month, 600 catties per year.[12] Peasants themselves considered 700 catties of unhusked grain per year as the standard of subsistence.[13] The secret for peasants' survival was income from sideline work and from the hidden lands. However, the party's standard was much lower; it considered 400 catties per year as the minimal income. Generally speaking, in the party's view, between 1949 and 1951 peasant livelihood improved. However, from the point of view of the government, the situation was not so encouraging.

The biggest problem was rural cadres. Officially, only cadres of township (*xiang*) and higher levels were considered state employees receiving salaries from the state payroll.[14] So village cadres were not financially compensated by the government. When the civil war was over, many village cadres believed their mission was accomplished and that it was time to work for themselves. Like other peasants, most of them desired to be left alone, to prosper as farmers and to dispose of their produce as they saw fit. Working for the party was increasingly considered a burden. Quite a few CCP village cadres asked to resign. For example, in Suyu village of Changzhi prefecture, during land reform there were sixty-eight CCP members and thirty-six activists who petitioned to join the party believing that "only the CCP can save China." But by 1951, there were only twenty-two CCP members, half of whom did not engage in party affairs and many of whom believed they would be able to live a happier life without the CCP.[15] Wang Qian was particularly shocked by the fact that one party branch in Xianghuan county declared its own dissolution. The branch head said, "We have participated in fighting against the Japanese and against Chiang Kai-shek. Now the land has been redistributed, and Japan and Chiang have been defeated. Our mission is over. Therefore our branch is dissolved."[16] Wang Qian considered such erratic behavior to be extremely dangerous and regarded the problem as the most troubling issue.[17]

Agricultural production was another issue of concern. After the war, the party articulated a new mission for rural cadres: to guide peasants as producers. Many cadres did not understand this assignment very well. They said peasants knew how to farm their land and required no guidance from the party. Or, more practically, they claimed they did not know how to guide peasants since there was no detailed party directive from above. In the era of land reform the CCP issued oceans of directives, and so long as cadres followed those directives, there was no need to worry about making mistakes.[18] But now that land reform was completed, how to encourage cadres to be involved in guiding agricultural production became an "urgent and large issue that had to be addressed."[19]

Peasant attitudes did not please the party either. The CCP had anticipated that once peasants obtained their own land, they would be willing to purchase new tools, apply new technologies, and invest in the land. Contrary to this prediction, however, in most cases, post-land reform peasants, especially middle peasants, were reluctant to focus all their efforts on farming or to invest in production. As a result, unit yields had not significantly increased. First, peasants had a living memory of the land reform of 1946–1948 and feared that their property would be "socialized" (equally redistributed) in the near future. In addition to their fears of being "socialized," there was something more deeply rooted in farming culture that prevented tillers from applying new technologies. James Scott convincingly shows that, based on his research in Southeast Asia, peasants "typically prefer to avoid economic disaster rather than take risks to maximize their average income."[20] Peasants tended to resist innovations because adopting new strategies might mean abandoning a system that they knew well and that involved minimal risks. Moreover, after land reform in north China, family holdings were fairly small and households contained fewer members.[21] A family with fewer laborers and smaller plots saw itself as being in a tenuous situation and was risk adverse. A common attitude was "safety-first." Increasing production was not a high priority for such a family.[22] Although probably unaware of this sort of peasant psychology, the CCP was quite clear about the fact that few peasants could afford the cost of new farming tools. What state agents could do, Wang Qian soon figured out, was to organize peasants to buy tools collectively.

After receiving some property allocations and being relieved of paying rents, a large number of peasants did experience improved livelihoods. But from the point of view of the state, the changes that had taken place did not directly benefit other parts of the nation. Grain availability on the free market dropped off considerably. In pre-land reform times, it was not uncommon for a small group of wealthy households, mainly small landlords and so-called rich peasants, to supply as much as one-half or more of the entire surplus marketed by villages.[23] As those rich groups vanished, so did their surplus grains. In Hanbi village of Changzhi prefecture, for instance, annual marketed grain in the prewar period amounted to over 800 dan, while in 1950 it dropped to 409 dan.[24] Peasants were unwilling to sell their grain. They preferred to eat better and live better, or just build up their surplus supplies.[25] Studies show that on average peasant consumption of grain increased from 370 catties per capita in 1949 to 440 catties per capita in 1952.[26] Grain procurement to assure nationwide consumption became the CCP's major concern.

Meanwhile, not all peasants had improved their lives after land reform. Changzhi prefecture officials were now keenly aware that factors other than the lack of land, namely natural disasters, increases or decreases in labor power, marriage, laziness, and excessive indulgence, all could lead to poverty.[27] These sorts of factors seemed unavoidable. But some investigators asked: was there a better way to deal with them?[28] The CCP did not want to leave people to starve. However, the customary relief system had been destroyed and the new one not yet established. The party itself did not want to directly assume the full responsibility of feeding the needy, partly because it did not possess adequate financial resources at that time. A new method was needed to accommodate the unfortunate and feed the hungry.

Peasants not only decided how much to sell on the market, they also decided what kinds of crops should be planted. Conditions varied in different regions. It was not uncommon for peasant planting patterns to conflict with party plans. Finding a way to keep peasant planting practices in line with the needs of the state was a constant concern for provincial leaders. Making a concrete production plan seemed a solution. Within the framework of the sort of centrally planned economy the CCP intended to build in the early 1950s, each level of the system was required to make a plan and move ahead accordingly. Agriculture was no exception. Each spring, local CCP cadres took tremendous pains to create production plans. Because of customary culture and illiteracy, peasants were reluctant, if not downright unwilling, to make plans of this sort. Pressed too hard, peasants or rural cadres fabricated plans. And peasants rarely followed that phony plan. Instead, they laughed at such attempts. In short, for all practical purposes, individual family farming was inconsistent with a centralized national economy.

All of these were new and unanticipated phenomena. Under such conditions, Wang Qian concluded that new policies and restructuring were necessary to move peasants along a socialist path once again. What he had in mind was a new organizational model that could organize peasants around economic issues and at the same time facilitate party political control.[29]

Having discussed this with Lai Ruoyu in advance, Wang Qian's first response was to advocate the building of Soviet-style collective farms. However, knowing something about the tremendous damage done to the agricultural economy of the Soviet Union during the rapid collectivization, Wang hesitated. He decided instead to move ahead step by step, starting from the mutual aid team, a form Mao Zedong had fervently advocated in the mid-1940s,[30] which was being promoted by Gao Gang in the northeast, a place that influenced the ideas of key party leaders and informed national economic policy in the early 1950s.[31]

Upgrading Mutual Aid Teams

Wang Qian soon obtained support from the Shanxi provincial government for his proposal. In essence, Shanxi provincial leaders were closely following trends in the northeast and on occasion went even further in the direction of collectivization. All along, though, Shanxi leaders offered numerous local data to convince the central leaders in Beijing of their regional wisdom.

Gao Gang's advocacy of building mutual aid teams amounted to resistance to New Democracy policies and thus angered Liu Shaoqi. When Shanxi provincial leaders sided with Gao Gang's economic projections, they too came into conflict with Liu Shaoqi. Unfortunately for the Shanxi locals, the direct superior of the Shanxi organization in the party hierarchy was the North China Bureau, which was under Liu's direct influence. Inevitably, as Shanxi provincial leaders marched toward collectivization, they consistently encountered obstacles and constraints that originated with the North China Bureau and Liu Shaoqi. Past research, mainly based on Bo Yibo's memoir, has focused mostly on the heated disputes between Shanxi provincial leaders and Liu Shaoqi in the middle of 1951.[32] But well before 1951, Shanxi provincial leaders chose to confront the North China Bureau.

On January 4, 1950, *Northeast Daily* published a speech by Gao Gang in which he declared a determination to upgrade mutual aid organizations and to offer them financial incentives. Inspired by Gao Gang's proposal, Shanxi leaders, in March 1950, developed a new slogan about "combining organizational mobilization with improving technology" to boost production and to guide peasants towards collectivization.[33] But on April 28, the North China Bureau sent directives requesting "the rectification of simple notions of agrarian utopian socialism," making it clear that the right direction for rural development among peasants was a New Democracy in which the private economy was the main force.[34]

The North China Bureau's directive had nearly no effect on Changzhi prefecture. From May to June, at local conferences at various levels, the direction of rural development toward collectivization continued to be highlighted. According to Tunliu county estimates, in 1950 approximately two to three thousand people had attended conferences hosted by the county focusing on the issue of rural development and stressing the need to organize peasants into mutual aid teams as a way of moving toward collectivization. But the report from Tunliu county also showed that at the village level, most party members did not comprehend the meaning of the message, and nearly all peasants still wanted to work individually in a manner chosen by themselves.[35]

On June 7, *Shanxi Daily* published Gao Gang's speech in which he again emphasized the building of mutual aid teams. In the same month, *Shanxi Daily* responded enthusiastically to Gao Gang's call by publishing several articles that introduced success stories about mutual aid team experiments and discussed details about how to operate such mutual aid teams. One article questioned the notion that after land reform peasants tended to withdraw from mutual aid teams. By contrast, this article argued that peasants withdrew from mutual aid teams because these teams could not meet their demands for enlarging and expanding development. So this article recommended that the party expand the function of mutual aid teams and recommended the practice of collectively opening up wasteland.[36] One month later, another article in *Shanxi Daily* advocated a new form of organizing peasants that was called the "agricultural cooperative," in which peasants pooled their private land and farmed it collectively, although land and output remained the property of owners. This was considered by the prefecture as an advanced form, and local leaders were encouraged to extend it to other areas.[37]

The North China Bureau promptly fought back. On July 10, it published in *People's Daily* an editorial entitled "Striving for the Wealth of Peasants in North China." It asserted that the most urgent problem with respect to peasants was their reluctance to work harder due to fear of further redistribution of private property, so the solution was to assure peasants that accumulating wealth by working hard was fully justified, glorious, and encouraged by the government. A rich peasant economy was protected by the law. The party's job was to convince peasants that socialism would come along only in the very distant future and mutual aid teams and co-ops should never be forced on people. The article forbade rural cadres from imposing hollow political instructions on peasants.[38] On August 26, the North China Bureau once again sent out a directive calling for the curbing of "agrarian utopian socialism" and criticizing the practice of forcing peasants to "get organized." Without identifying the target, this directive stated, "Some branches have not seriously implemented the North China Bureau's directive on rectifying the simplistic idea of agrarian utopian socialism. They are expected to carry out a deep investigation and thoroughly overcome this problem."[39] It was not hard to figure out who "some branches" referred to.

Shanxi provincial leaders again chose to ignore the directive. Instead, they turned in a report (that will be analyzed later in this essay) to the North China Bureau stating that many peasants did not want to withdraw from mutual aid teams. So, according to Shanxi leaders, what the party should do was actually to expand their functions.[40] In November, Changzhi prefecture was able to publish a report on its achievement of forming mutual aid teams in *People's Daily*, the most authoritative newspaper in China.[41] This article was a landmark in the Shanxi provincial leaders early, some said premature, march toward coopertivization, as will be discussed later. It brought national attention to Changzhi.

One fact that was not noted in those promising reports was that local cadres in Changzhi prefecture had been reported to higher-ups and accused of ignorance and commandism. Cadres of district and lower levels knew little or nothing about central policies. Believing that "communism" would arrive within two to three years, they did not care about peasant rights to private property. Predominantly siding with poor peasants, they did not hesitate to infringe on the rights of middle peasants. They regarded mutual aid teams as administrative organizations designed to control peasants. As for how to deal with peasants, that was easy. Peasants were "like pecans, you have to smash them to get what you want." Other cadres said, "Thousands of words do not work as well as one lash." Eight cadres in Changzhi were exposed as leaders who had oppressed people to death. In addition to violence, they had also organized numbingly long conferences to "persuade" peasants. When it came to organizing mutual aid teams, they simply asked peasants, "The Chairman requested you to get organized, so why don't you follow his instruction?" "What kind of people do not support Chairman Mao?"[42] Few peasants dared to be labeled as anti-Mao and thus many meekly followed orders. Certainly, the attitudes of local cadres toward peasants and socialism produced high rates of "organized peasants," which provided Changzhi prefecture with the sort of "positive" data it wanted.

Losing Touch with Reality

Changzhi got its national reputation because of a series of reports. Acting on Wang Qian's orders, counties in Changzhi prefecture submitted numerous reports supporting the development of mutual aid teams. Quite a few of them reached the central committee of the CCP in Beijing and some were even published in the *People's Daily*. But during the transmission of the reports from the counties to the central government, messages that were already tendentiously formulated were further distorted to meet the needs of various groups. This process of distortion becomes clear when one compares three such reports and understands how the information was spun and thus "perfected" during the transmission from the local level to the newspaper-reading level.

One of the major investigations Wang Qian ordered was carried out in six villages in Wu county, Changzhi prefecture. The statistics based on this investigation generated several influential reports. On August 7, 1950, Wu county submitted a summary entitled "Investigation of the Movement to Organize Mutual Aid Teams and Agricultural Production in Six Villages in Wu County" to the agricultural department of Shanxi province. Based on this report, on August 25, Shanxi province submitted a report entitled "Investigation of Villages in the Old Liberated Areas of Wu County" to the North China Bureau. This report was later published by *Shanxi Daily* on October 12, 1950. On November 14, a Changzhi prefecture report "On the Current Situation and Problems Associated with Getting Organized" was published in *People's Daily*.

The original Wu county report summarized developments and new problems in the six villages under investigation. After land reform, rural production had recovered and agricultural output in 1949 had surpassed the prewar record by

9.1 percent. Peasants consumed much more food than previously, but marketed grain dropped substantially. Now, 3.14 percent of households were able to store 10 dan of surplus grain, another 6.7 percent stored over 5 dan, and yet another 33.5 percent stocked over one dan of surplus grain. At the same time, 47.2 percent of households could barely feed themselves and 6.5 percent could not meet their needs. The main problems, as far as this report was concerned, were the increase in labor surpluses and the need to enlarge rural investment. So the report suggested expanding investments in agriculture and putting more effort into careful planting in order to absorb surplus laborers. It mentioned that class polarization had begun and land sales were taking place. 4.33 percent of households were involved in land sales, a few had even sold all their land. This report noted that in areas where peasants had been organized and were helping each other, the pace of class differentiation was somehow slower, and the scale smaller. But it also acknowledged that the pace and scale of polarization were closely related to whether peasants could acquire loans and credit. Thus the report petitioned the state to grant peasants more credit and loans.

This report discussed next the issue of mutual aid teams. The fact was that mutual aid teams were shrinking. Fewer households participated in them. Investigators also noticed that peasants of the same economic status were more likely to form a mutual aid team. But these groups tended to deny access to seniors and females, and failed to make long term production plans. The report noted that the peasants feared that their property would be socialized in the near future, thus they did not want to invest in farming. Second, with more surplus labor, there was no need to get organized to overcome difficulties. Finally, rural cadres did not place much emphasis on organizing peasants.[43]

This report acknowledged the fact that most peasants did not want to form mutual aid teams, and explained the economic considerations involved. It affirmed neither any peasant desire for mutual aid teams nor any call by them for party guidance. Quite the contrary, it implied that many peasants had refrained from withdrawing from mutual aid teams simply because they were afraid of being labeled laggards by the party. They chose to maintain the form in name only. Agreeing to the necessity of organizing peasants into mutual aid teams, this report did not highlight the socialist future or the long term goal of collectivization. Rather, it suggested that the party should provide more economic incentives in order to attract peasants into mutual aid teams so as to get them to produce more. The original report regarded the mutual aid team as an economic form, and nothing more.

At the provincial level, in Shanxi's report to the North China Bureau, the basic statistics were in accord with the Wu county report, but its focus was on the nature of peasant problems. And its analysis of the issues was different. The focus shifted to the alleged problem of class polarization and the phenomenon of land concentration, and it urged the party to be alert to such a trend. As for the mutual aid teams, it claimed, after investigating certain cases and reviewing the overall picture, that all villages that had "gotten organized" had fewer or no land transactions. It insisted certain teams were developing fast and very well. Acknowledging that many mutual aid teams were in decline, the Shanxi report stated that the downswing did not mean that peasants were unwilling to join mutual aid teams. Quite the contrary, peasants were reluctant to leave mutual aid teams. A common reaction of peasants was said to be, "Chairman Mao is right, we must get organized." The writers asserted that after the party had led peasants to acquire land, peasants had improved their political consciousness and had gradually formed the habit of working collectively. Thus they offered the conclusion that although peasants as small producers were inclined to work individually, they had the potential, even the desire to be organized along more socialist lines. They were confident: "When we did it right, there was no problem getting peasants organized."[44]

Unlike the internal Wu county report, this provincial one was published in *Shanxi Daily*. It told of peasant aspirations regarding mutual aid teams and proposed the nurturing of peasant culture in the direction of increasingly collective work styles. It also portrayed the reemergence of class polarization as an urgent issue in the countryside and called on the party to focus on and eradicate the problem. As a consequence, many other problems in the countryside were downplayed in the article, if not totally neglected.

At the national level, the *People's Daily*, made selective use of the Changzhi prefecture reports to paint an even simpler picture. First, it presented rural life as filled with abundance and wealth. Without providing supporting statistics, it said that in the Changzhi area advanced villages had produced 50 percent more, or even doubled their prewar output. Peasants were getting rich and had more surplus grain. For example, in Wulihou village the majority of village households had stocked surplus grain in amounts greater than 5 dan. Also, the article asserted, there was abundant "idle money" or capital available in the countryside which needed to be properly channeled by the party. The present situation was one in which the peasants were demanding further developments, yet the party could not offer the guidance they needed. So, peasants embraced the idea of "working individually" and mutual aid teams were falling apart. If such phenomena were allowed to continue, only a few peasants would become rich while most peasants would go bankrupt. Rural cadres, the report warned, must not ignore such a situation. The Changzhi report quoted Mao's writings from the mid-1940s and claimed that the party must fight the idea of "leaving peasants alone" and resolve to put peasants on the road to collectivization. Shanxi employed two methods. One was to combine mutual aid teams with new technology, another was to have peasants purchase farm tools collectively in mutual aid teams. According to the article, these methods had been shown to work well and a revolution in agricultural production had already started.

This *People's Daily* report was quite different from the first two. For instance, the statistics it used were inconsistent with those cited in the first two reports. Even if the numbers were valid, they did not represent the typical situation depicted by most archives I have accessed. Second, the report did not rely on data to make its claims. Instead, it simply quoted Mao's words to prove its points. Moreover, the *People's Daily*'s version of the Changzhi report was ideologically driven, and discussed the long term goal of collectivization. From this point of view, the peasant tendency to work individually and the presence of rich peasants in mutual aid teams were considered "bad" elements. The report in the *People's Daily* formally declared that those who preferred to work individually stood in opposition to the goal of collectivization, and it expressed a clear resolve to curb the trend. Of all the reports, this one reflected the least about rural realities. Sadly, this was the most influential report, and when it was published in *People's Daily* its message reached the whole nation.[45]

By comparing the three reports, it is possible to see that during the process of transmission of information from the local to the central level, and from internal circulation to the public circulation, reality was sacrificed and findings were distorted further and further. The development of agricultural production in the countryside was exaggerated, especially in the *People's Daily*'s Changzhi report, to convey a single message: it was time to give priority to ideological agendas since the economy had already been improved. It is likely that Changzhi prefectural leaders were aware of the exaggerations. In an internally circulated summary of the agricultural production of Changzhi prefecture, a note was added underscoring the fact that agricultural production in 1949 was only slightly higher than prewar levels, and that the data showing an increase of over 40 percent were not reliable at all. This summary concluded that one-third of villages had not yet reached their prewar levels of production.[46]

Step by step, in the three reports, such phenomena as alleged class polarization and land sales were increasingly highlighted, while their complex causes, such as natural disaster, personal difficulties, and the lack of credit, were entirely overlooked. The causes were not analyzed, yet the solution was said to be crystal clear: form mutual aid teams and get peasants organized. The diversity of views among peasants was not explored. Instead, peasants were simply categorized into two groups: those who wanted to work individually to accumulate family wealth and those who wanted to form mutual aid teams but did not receive meaningful assistance from the party. Although no data or research findings were provided to support the claim, the *People's Daily*'s presentation of the Changzhi report argued that once well guided, most peasants had a desire to enroll in mutual aid teams and move toward collectivization. So it was the responsibility of the party to work ever harder to educate and lead peasants. The fact that many peasants were in desperate need of credit and loans was not mentioned. On the contrary, it was the myth of abundant idle money floating around in the countryside and available for investment that was underlined. In sum, the story was that peasants had reached a bottleneck in rural production and were in need of guidance for further development. Only mutual aid teams could help peasants ultimately improve their lives by putting them on the right road in the direction of collectivization. Mao's writings on mutual aid and China's socialist future were reiterated and regarded as self-evident.

Once the task of guiding peasants toward collectivization became a central issue, mutual aid teams were no longer viewed as merely economic organizations, but as political and ideological symbols. Many pressing issues in the countryside were neglected, and the need to move toward collectivization in the future justified the necessity of developing mutual aid teams in the present. The disbanding and breakup of mutual aid teams was thus increasingly regarded as a serious concern. The party was assigned the political task of swinging into action.

The higher level a report reached, the simpler its message was. The complex problems encountered by the peasants in Wang Qian's internally circulated investigations were increasingly downplayed, if not totally overlooked. During the process of communication and channeling, politically motivated interpretations with a specific purpose were injected, one after another. Although real peasant mentalities and conditions were not accurately presented, nearly all reports left the misleading impression that they represented the views of peasants and often quoted peasant voices and language. Plans, suggestions, and innovations were commonly presented as coming directly from peasants.

The challenge for scholars who seek the truth is to pay more attention to the intentionally ignored messages contained in the reports. But contemporary leaders did not have easy access to grass roots reports. In the case of Mao Zedong, a large number of reports he saw had been subjected to round after round of censorship, editing, and interpretation. The complexity of rural realities faded away in the process of communication. What the reporters' thought peasants should have been thinking was reported as though it was what the peasants really were thinking.

In fact, even the original Wu county report was produced for a specific purpose: to promote mutual aid teams. It did not fully reflect what peasants were thinking and what peasants were in need of. We can say with certainty that the situation was far more diverse and complex than the picture crafted for the reports at every level. Moreover, the situation varied dramatically in the different regions of China. In short, peasant problems could not be resolved by any one solution. But it is still worth asking whether any peasant was interested in forming mutual aid teams.

The answer is, yes, there were such peasants, like Geng Changsuo and his followers in Wugong village in neighboring Hebei province.[47] But generally speaking, in 1950 the overwhelming number of peasants were reluctant, if not resistant, to joining mutual aid teams. A case in point is peasant Li Shunda of Changzhi prefecture. In the cooperativization movement of the mid-1950s Li Shunda emerged as the most recognized labor hero of the nation; there was even a documentary film about him. But earlier in 1949 his mutual aid team was in the process of disintegration and Li was considering moving out of the countryside and into town. His plan deeply worried Changzhi prefecture leaders who decided to redouble their special guidance of Li and his village. In late 1949, the party branch of Wu county had sent cadres to help Li. A work team of cadres from different levels had been established in Li's village. This team had given Li suggestions, helped him conduct research, discussed issues with him, made working plans for him, and most importantly, manufactured reports for him. In addition to personnel, a large amount of material support had also been sent Li's way.[49] It was thanks to such elaborate support that Li Shunda had become a national star in the early 1950s.

Decades later, an interview with Tao Lujia, the present day propaganda minister of Shanxi, shed considerable light on the situation in the early years. Tao was asked, "Did peasants practice cooperative farming or have such aspirations?" He replied candidly, "Peasants themselves did not have such aspirations. The key was our guidance."[50]

Clashing with Liu Shaoqi and the North China Bureau

Following Changzhi prefecture's November declaration, on December 30, 1950, the Shanxi provincial government submitted another summary of its mutual aid movement to the North China Bureau. According to this report, mutual aid teams flourished. For example, in the Changzhi area, up to 75 percent of peasants had joined mutual aid teams, and agricultural production had increased substantially. As mutual aid teams deployed new farming implements and made efficient use of labor, unit yield improved significantly. Moreover, according to this survey, in order to meet the needs of increasing production, quite a few mutual aid teams had collectively purchased large farming implements, and some teams took the initiative to collect communal funds for further investment and group welfare. Everything appeared promising.[51]

Nevertheless, the truth was not so reassuring—as Shanxi leaders knew all too well. The idea of combining mutual aid teams with new technology was rather hollow and did little to reverse the trend of mutual aid team breakups.[52] Meanwhile, as some mutual aid teams increased in number, there were cases of well-off peasants making use of the form to exploit the poor. Since hiring laborers was considered politically risky, "cunning" rich peasants set up mutual aid teams and recruited poor peasants to work in them. This constituted another trend. Changzhi prefecture was not comfortable with this development and decided to restrict the activities of richer peasants who were enrolled in mutual aid teams. The method Wang Qian proposed was to collect community funds according to the amount of private property held by peasants. If a member withdrew from a team, he could not take away his share of communal funds.

Beginning in December 1950, this method was enforced in Changzhi. Peasants resisted it. Despite peasant misgivings, Wang Qian concluded that communal funds might possibly guide peasants in the direction of agricultural cooperatives while keeping rich peasants out of the mutual aid teams.[53]

Lai Ruoyu endorsed the method of increasing communal fund collections and further suggested putting into effect the socialist principle of "distribution according to labor." In his report to the North China Bureau and Chairman Mao in March 1951, Lai proposed setting up experimental agricultural cooperatives (co-ops) in the counties of Changzhi prefecture. In these co-ops, peasant households would pool their land and farm collectively; net profits would be distributed according to both labor and land input, and communal funds would be collected.[54]

Following Lai Ruoyu's proposal, Changzhi prefecture convened a mutual aid and co-op conference of heads of mutual aid teams to discuss the details of operating semi-socialist co-ops. Wang Qian concluded that the ultimate goal was collectivization and modernization. Communal purchases of farm implements would advance collectivization, the acquisition of communal funds would allow for the accumulation of more collectively owned goods and equipment, and group farming would undermine the age old peasant tendency to work individually. In sum, "Our agriculture would move toward collectivization." Not only did he draw up the general blueprint for co-ops, Wang Qian also spelled out specific rules. He recommended that peasants pool at least two-thirds of their land into the co-ops and farm it collectively. Profits would be distributed mainly according to labor, supplemented by a component linked to individual land input. Approximately 20 percent of output should be put aside as communal investment funds, public welfare funds, and education funds. If members withdrew from the co-op, they could not take any of the funds with them. Wang Qian promised loans and reduced taxes as financial incentives. After the conference all attendees were said to agree that co-ops could improve rural productivity and asked to sign up for the experiment.[55]

Lai Ruoyu's report instantly upset the North China Bureau. During the course of the Changzhi mutual aid and co-op conference, a North China Bureau inspection team arrived on the scene. The work team did not challenge the essential idea of agricultural co-ops, but it cautioned about the timing of implementation. It was the spring planting season, and peasants were totally unprepared for such a form of organization. The work team suggested postponing the trials. They also questioned whether the exaction of communal funds would discourage prosperous peasants and raised concerns about the very nature of mutual aid organizations.[56] But Wang Qian did not change his plan. And no compromise was reached. Instead, the opinions of both sides were written down and submitted to the North China Bureau. When the work team discussed this issue with Lai Ruoyu, Lai unequivocally sided with Changzhi and reasserted his claim that the disagreements were related to different attitudes toward private ownership.[57]

The North China Bureau pressed to place some constraints on Shanxi leaders and decided to convene a conference on mutual aid and co-ops in five provinces and cites in North China to discuss the issue of building co-ops. Informed of this upcoming conference, Shanxi provincial leaders met and approved Lai Ruoyu's draft regarding "Upgrading Mutual Aid and Cooperative Organization" and promptly submitted it to the North China Bureau. In this report, Lai claimed that mutual aid teams had reached a turning point. They might decline to become rich peasant organizations, or they might be promoted in ways that advanced a socialist agenda. Lai proposed upgrading mutual aid and cooperative organizations in order to check the "the spontaneous tendency" of the individual peasants and to further destabilize and eventually eliminate the private ownership system. He insisted that accumulating communal funds and distributing profits according to labor were two key principles.[58] But such efforts to weaken the private sector touched Liu Shaoqi's sensitive nerves. Liu and the North China Bureau retaliated immediately. The North China Bureau first questioned the data contained in the Shanxi report and then directly and personally criticized the Shanxi representatives.

During the conference on mutual aid and co-ops convened by the North China Bureau, the majority of attendees criticized the Shanxi report because it was inconsistent with New Democracy policies and because agricultural co-ops were said to be manifestations of utopian socialism. Under New Democracy, it was wrong to eliminate private ownership. There could be no true collectivization without mechanization. Some participants blasted Wang Qian for "cutting a fine figure" (chu fengtou). After the conference, Liu Lantao, head of the North China Bureau, told the Shanxi representatives that "Comrade Liu Shaoqi does not agree with Shanxi's report. When you return, tell the provincial branch not to endorse the errors in the report. You should read some related books and report back to the North China Bureau."[59]

The North China Bureau's critique generated disputes among Shanxi provincial leaders. In a standing committee meeting of the CCP Shanxi branch, Cheng Zihua, the chairman of the Shanxi provincial government, supported the North China Bureau and said Shanxi should follow the instructions of the North China Bureau. Lai disagreed. Wang Qian then gave a particularly important speech. Referring to some model cases in Changzhi prefecture as relevant examples, he asserted that rural cadres who did not actively lead peasants were the cause of the decline of mutual aid teams. He highlighted positive peasant affiliations with mutual aid teams. More importantly, he widely quoted Mao's earlier writings and CCP directives of the 1940s that advocated mutual aid teams and collectivization to underscore the necessity of getting peasants organized. In the end he concluded that insuring the right direction of rural development meant doing more than forming mutual aid teams; co-op formation should be initiated.[60]

Lai Ruoyu won his debate with Cheng Zihua. As a matter of fact, Cheng Zihua was soon transferred to a post outside Shanxi largely because of this debate.[61] Lai drafted a reply to the North China Bureau in which he rejected nearly all of the charges, which immediately enraged Liu Shaoqi.[62] The disputes between Lai Ruoyu and Liu Shaoqi from May 1951 to July 1951 have been well recounted by Bo Yibo.[63] Briefly speaking, Liu Shaoqi took a position that adhered strictly to the policies for economic construction that the party had adopted in 1949. He introduced two principles that lower levels were to follow. First, no attempt should be made to undermine private ownership in the countryside, and, second, mechanization was a prerequisite for full scale collectivization. Liu Shaoqi further accused those who wanted to begin collectivization in the countryside of pursuing "utopian socialism." But Bo Yibo's writings do not do full justice to the extent of Liu's anger. On May 7, Liu Shaoqi asserted at a national propaganda conference that it was virtually impossible to guide China's agriculture toward socialism by organizing mutual aid teams or agricultural cooperatives. Liu actually identified the target of his criticism when he declared that "Comrade Lai Ruoyu did not accept the critique of the North China Bureau, therefore he made huge mistakes." Liu sternly advised other comrades to maintain their faith in the party, refrain from embracing localism, and avoid fighting against the center. Otherwise the central CCP would exert organizational discipline and punishment.[64] In the next two months, and on several different occasions, Liu attacked Lai Ruoyu and the Shanxi government.

However, Lai Ruoyu was not intimidated. During his debate with Liu Shaoqi, Lai sent petitions to the central CCP and particularly to Mao himself. He instructed Shanxi officials to ignore directives from the North China Bureau and proceed as previously planned until they received a reply from Mao.[65] One explanation for such boldness was that at this moment Lai was in contact with Chen Boda, Mao's former secretary and close friend. Chen implied to Lai that Mao was indeed interested in Gao Gang's northeastern experiments of building socialism in the countryside and Mao was increasingly discontent with Liu Shaoqi on the matter.[66]

In response to Liu Lantao's order to read more books, Shanxi leaders read more Marxist classics, but they did so for the purpose of further supporting their own proposal. They discovered that in *Capital* Marx had said "All fully developed machinery consists of three essentially different parts, the motor mechanism, the transmitting mechanism, and finally the tool or working machine," and "The tool or working machine is that part of the machinery with which the industrial revolution of the eighteenth century started."[67] Lai Ruoyu concluded that new "tools" such as big farm equipment made of iron and pulled by horses were the "working machines" Marx had referred to. Compared to China's traditional farming tools made of wood, the new tools represented a significant improvement. Tractors, he quipped, should not be regarded as the only modern machine of relevance to rural people. As for the question of when to start moving peasants into collective farms, Shanxi leaders found yet another theoretical text. Engels once said, "It will serve us nought to wait with this transformation until capitalist production has developed everywhere to its utmost consequences, until the last small handicraftsman and the last small peasant have fallen victim to capitalist large-scale production."[68] In this way, Liu Shaoqi's support of the development of New Democracy capitalism was rebutted. Further, in order to justify their views about the rules that should govern co-op formation, Shanxi leaders highlighted Engel's ideas about the transformation of small peasant private enterprises and private property into cooperative enterprises and property as the best method of liberating peasants.[69] Taking Marx and Engels as their theoretical forefathers, Shanxi leaders were confident that their plan had nothing to do with utopian socialism.

In summer 1951 the debate between the North China Bureau and Shanxi leaders continued. During the debates, Liu Shaoqi made his ideas increasingly clear. He did not see agricultural co-ops in the near future, and he believed for the next decade or more the party should not think about building socialism in the rural sector. By stating that the mutual aid team was not a form that paved the way for socialism, Liu Shaoqi eventually crossed the line in the eyes of Mao Zedong.[70]

In July, Mao held a private talk with Liu Shaoqi, Bo Yibo, and Liu Lantao. He explicitly endorsed the Shanxi leaders. Presumably impressed by the success of the Shanxi leaders in finding theoretical support in the Marxist classics, Mao based his own position on Stalin's statements in *Foundations of Leninism*. Mao asserted that just as the British putting-out system had provided the foundation for a new set of production relations associated with industrialization, the Chinese mutual aid teams could perform a similar function in the creation of new production relations associated with socialism.[71] Convinced or not, Liu Shaoqi, Bo Yibo and Liu Lantao appeared to have been "persuaded by Mao's arguments" and abruptly abandoned their viewpoints.

Mao then instructed Chen Boda to convene the First National Mutual Aid and Cooperation Conference in September 1951. Liu Shaoqi wrote a keynote speech, but it was shelved and never discussed. Instead, Chen Boda's draft was adopted as the keynote message. From then on, Liu Shaoqi ceased to actively comment on the co-op issue and seldom published his thoughts about it. Indeed, at the time and in subsequent years, Liu made repeated self-criticisms of his "mistakes" on the issue of co-ops.

In Chen Boda's draft, peasant desires to work collectively and join mutual aid teams were highlighted. After the conference, Mao consulted with Zhao Shuli, a highly respected writer on peasant affairs, about Chen's draft. Zhao replied candidly and simply: peasants had no desire to join mutual aid teams; they only wanted to work individually. Stimulated by Zhao, Mao instructed that the draft should also affirm that many peasants preferred to work individually. Consequently, the "Resolution on Mutual Aid and Cooperation in Agriculture (Draft)" was rewritten. The first paragraph of the revised version declared that the enthusiasm of peasants after land reform was related to a combination of aspects of both the individual economy and cooperative labor. This draft approved the building of trial agricultural co-ops.

The production of this draft was rather arbitrary. It simply neglected an important reality: most peasants were not enthusiastic about forming co-ops. Peasant preferences for working individually were only recognized after Zhao Shuli's frank feedback. The draft was heavily influenced by the series of reports that were generated in Shanxi and was based more on what the party wanted peasants to be than on what peasants themselves wanted. Nevertheless, this draft served as the foundation of a series of future movements, and its assertion of the dual natures of peasants was never questioned for the next quarter century during the Mao era. The notion that peasants were willing to work collectively inspired the party's expressed desire to guide them, while the notion that peasants were traditionally inclined to work individually alerted party members to their responsibilities to guide peasants. The first wave of mutual aid team and co-op movement in the early 1952 was thus launched.

Lai Ruoyu vs. Liu Shaoqi—Margin vs. Center

This case is of particular significance considering its geographical factors and the issue it dealt with. Shanxi, located in the middle of nowhere, had been near the central area for the CCP when it was based at Yan'an before liberation. But as the CCP conquered the whole nation, the political center moved eastward from Yan'an to Beijing, and Shanxi lost its charmed location. How did the provincial leaders deal with such a change? The case described here is about farming issues, which were a key component of CCP policy until 1949. But in 1949, Mao declared that "the centre of gravity of the party's work has shifted from the village to the city,"[72] and the party indeed turned to urban issues, paying much less attention to the rural. For a prefecture like Changzhi with no modern industry or big cities, how could officials there attract attention from above and get promoted?

It is still not fully clear what drove Lai Ruoyu to so persistently advocate the building of agricultural co-ops and to so boldly challenge Liu Shaoqi, the second most powerful figure in the CCP. Recently his former colleagues, including Tao Lujia and Wang Qian, all highlight Lai's deep faith in Soviet-style collectivization. Another explanation is that Lai was keenly aware of Mao's long-term preference for mutual aid teams since the early 1940s and his lack of enthusiasm for New Democracy policies, so Lai chose to challenge Liu Shaoqi and to win Mao's favor. This view has its merits. In retrospect Lai Ruoyu seems to have taken a well calculated risk. Ultimately his proposal was fully endorsed by Mao and applied to the whole country. Ironically, however, Lai Ruoyu himself did not benefit much politically from this victory. In 1952 he was appointed secretary of the National Labor Union, a position that carried little power or influence. Lai Ruoyu was purged in 1958 and died the same year.

The 1951 episode had a direct impact on the political careers of other Shanxi leaders. Cheng Zihua, who had opposed Lai Ruoyu on the issue of mutual aid teams, was transferred out of Shanxi province to an inconsequential post. This change was intentionally executed to facilitate the launching of the co-op movement in Shanxi.[73] Other Shanxi cadres who were supportive of Lai Ruoyu were rewarded. Wang Qian, for example, had provided Lai Ruoyu with theoretical support and statistical backup at several critical moments and had been especially good at theorizing Shanxi's plans in terms of Mao's most authoritative writings. Wang Qian became well known and continued to build his reputation as a specialist on co-ops. He was soon promoted to the office of chief of the Policy Research Center of the North China Bureau and subsequently appointed vice minister of the Rural Work Department of the North China Bureau. Between 1954 and 1956 he assumed the post of vice secretary of the central Rural Work Department. In 1956 he was appointed vice secretary of the CCP Shanxi provincial branch. Given the fact that both Lai Ruoyu and Wang Qian had deliberately twisted the facts in their favor, it is safe to conclude that political ambitions for moving up to higher positions must have played a role in their decision to support the co-op movement.

At the top, the role played by Mao Zedong is worth some discussion. Certainly, his undisguised interest in mutual aid teams in the 1940s and his deep faith in Soviet collectivization provided Lai Ruoyu and his fellows with whatever political incentives they needed to advocate their radical policies. But Mao himself did not move actively in the early stage of the mutual aid and co-op movement. There is no evidence at present that Mao himself hinted to Gao Gang or Lai Ruoyu that they should push mutual aid teams; he did not clarify his own position until he was presented with what appeared to be well-documented reports showing the effectiveness and popularity of cooperatives. It is fair to say that it was the Shanxi leaders' action from relatively low levels in the administrative hierarchy that provided Mao with the inspiration, evidence, confidence, and even theories that convinced the Chairman to support a nationwide co-op movement—not Mao taking the initiative from the top down at this time.

This essay shows how reports were modified and twisted to meet the specific purposes of certain groups. Rural reality was complex and varied, but the images presented to higher-level CCP leaders were one-dimensional and simplified. It is rather astonishing to consider how a policy that would transform millions of people's lives was grounded on intentionally fabricated reports. The fundamental reason might be traced back to the dichotomy between Mao Zedong's constant use of the word "mass line" as part of the legitimate foundation of the party and the elite leadership the CCP had built after 1949. Following the Leninist tradition, the people "were in the end to be made to embrace, and to interiorize ideas" and "if left to themselves, they were quite incapable of elaborating in systematic form."[74] So people's willingness to participate from below could be overtly appreciated by Mao Zedong and even considered to have a degree of legitimacy. Such circumstances created a powerful impulse for local cadres to twist the reality to their favor. The pattern continued, and as a matter of fact grew in intensity, as economic issues were coated with ideological stamps, as higher political stakes became more involved with economic performance, and as Mao was getting more careless about expressing his preferences. The same patterns finally were followed to a ridiculous and tragic extent during the Great Leap Forward (1958–1961), resulting in millions of deaths, mostly of peasants.

This does not mean we should demonize all CCP cadres. The practical difficulties they encountered created day in and day out pressures. Constrained by ideological strictures and their limited experiences, they turned to the Soviet model as an easy way out, a way that would not entail any ideological risks. In brief, personal ambitions, every day pressures, and ideological obligations caused some CCP cadres at intermediate levels to push Mao and the party onto the collective road at this early stage.

NOTES

1. Frederick Teiwes, *Politics at Mao's Court* (Armonk: M. E. Sharpe, 1990), 16.
2. Ibid., 17.
3. Zhu Yonghong, "Reflections on the Party's Policy Toward the Rural Individual Economy During the First Seven Years of the State," in Frederick Teiwes and Warren Sun, eds., *The Politics of Agricultural Cooperativization in China* (Armonk: M. E. Sharpe, 1993), 29.
4. For Stalin's role in the making of the New Democracy policy, see Li Hua-yu, *Mao and the Economic Stalinization of China 1948–1953* (Lanham: Rowman and Littlefield, 2006); Arlen Meliksetov, "'New Democracy' and China's Search for Socio-Economic Development Routes (1949–1953)," *Far Eastern Affairs*, 1(1996): 80.
5. Mao Zedong, "Zai Zhongguo gongchandang di qi jie zhongyang weiyuan hui di er ci quan ti huiyi shang de baogao" [Report to the Second Plenary Session of the Seventh Central Committee of the Communist Party of China], in *Mao Zedong xuanji* [Collected works of Mao Zedong] (Beijing: Renmin chubanshe, 1991), vol 4.
6. Unpublished transcript of Gao Jie's interview of Tao Lujia, Beijing, April 19, 2007.
7. Lai Ruoyu, "Zai shengwei kuoda huiyi shang de jianghua" [Report at the enlarged provincial conference] (September 1, 1949), Shanxi Provincial Archive (hereafter SPA), 00.29.1.
8. Old liberated areas refer to the regions that were occupied by the CCP during the war against Japan (1937–45). Nearly all of them were located in north China.
9. Wang Qian, "Weishenme yao shiban nongye shengchan hezuoshe" [Why did we try to build agricultural producers' cooperatives], in Shanxi sheng yanjiu yuan [Research institute for local history in Shanxi province], ed., *Shanxi nongye hezuohua* [Agricultural cooperatives in Shanxi] (Taiyuan: Shanxi renmin chubanshe, 2001), 656.
10. 1 dan = 150 catties = 167 pounds; 1 mu = 1/6 acre.
11. Tanaka Kyoko, "Mao and Liu in the 1947 Land Reform: Allies or Disputants?" *The China Quarterly*, 75 (1979): 590.
12. Jean C. Oi, *State and Peasant in Contemporary China* (Berkeley: University of California Press, 1989), 47.

13. Gao Wangling, *Renmin gongshe shiqi Zhongguo nongmin fanxingwei diaocha* [Investigation on peasants' oppositional behavior during the people's commune period] (Beijing: Zhongguo dang shi chubanshe, 2006), 38.

14. In 1950, the administration ladder within a province rose from low to high through village, township, district, county, prefecture and to province.

15. "Zhengzhi diaocha baogao" [Political investigation report] (June 22, 1951), Jincheng City Archive (hereafter JCA), 1.1.48.

16. Wang Qian, 657.

17. Ibid., 655–58.

18. "Shanxi sheng chunji shengchan jiancha baogao" [Report on the investigation of the spring farming in Shanxi province] (March 31, 1950), SPA, C55, 1002, 64.

19. Ibid.

20. James C. Scott, *The Moral Economy of the Peasant: Rebellion and Subsistence in Southeast Asia* (New Haven: Yale University Press, 1976). The question persists as to whether Scott's thesis applies to China.

21. In land reform, peasants in extended families were usually divided into smaller core families to keep the land size per family smaller and thus avoid being labeled landlords or rich peasants.

22. Scott, 19.

23. Ramon H. Myers, "The Agrarian System," in John Fairbank and Albert Feuerwerker, eds., *The Cambridge History of China* (Cambridge: Cambridge University Press, 1986), v. 13, pt. 2, 254–55.

24. 1 dan = 150 catties = 167 pounds.

25. "Wuxian liu ge cun jingji diaocha" [Investigations on the economy of six villages in Wu county] (August 7, 1950), JCA, 024.11.

26. "Wuxian liu ge cun nongye shengchan zhong zuzhi huzhu de kaocha baogao" [Investigations on the movement of organizing mutual aid teams in agricultural production in six villages of Wu county] (August 7, 1950), SPA, C 77. 04. 0002.

27. Jin Guantao and Liu Qingfeng, "Zhongguo gongchandang weishenme fangqi xin minzhuzhuyi" [Why the CCP gave up New Democracy], *Ershiyi shiji* 13 (October 1992): 17.

28. As for the cause of poverty, Chayanov emphasizes that the high ratio of consumer and laborer was the fundamental factor. Shanin highlights the multidirectional and cyclical mobility of peasants and the fatal effects of accidents. Daniel Thorner, Basile Kerblay and R. Smith, eds., *A.V. Chayanov on the Theory of Peasant Economy* (Homewood: Richard D. Irwin, 1966); Teodor Shanin, *The Awkward Class* (Oxford: Oxford University Press, 1972).

29. "Changzhi diqu wu ge cun tugai shengchan zhong jieji bianhua de diaocha" [Investigation of the changes of class statuses during land reform and production in five villages of the Changzhi area] (January 10, 1950), in *Changzhi diqu shiban he fazhan nongye shengchan hezuoshe de ruogan lishi ziliao* [Several historical documents on building experimental agricultural producers' cooperatives in the Changzhi area] (Shanxi: Nongcun zhengzhibu, 1977).

30. Wang Qian, 655–58.

31. Xiaojia Hou, "The Impact of Soviet Models on the CCP's Rural Economic Strategy: 1950–53," a paper presented at the conference on The Soviet Impact on China: Politics, Economy, Society, and Culture, 1949–1991, Columbia University, June 22–23, 2007.

32. Li Hua-yu, 69.

33. Bo Yibo, *Ruogan zhongda juece yu shijian de huigu* [Recollections of some important decisions and events] (Beijing, Zhonggong zhongyang dangxiao chubanshe, 1991).

34. *Shanxi ribao* (March 5, 1950).

35. *Zhonggong zhongyang Huabei ju zhongyao wenjian huibian* [Collections of important documents of the North China Bureau of the CCP], SPA, v. 1, 638–39.

36. "Nongcun fangxian guanche zhuanti baogao" [A special report on carrying out the direction of rural development] (October 30, 1950), JCP, 24.1.1.

37. *Shanxi ribao* (June 11, 1950).

38. *Shanxi ribao* (July 22, 1950).

39. *Renmin ribao* (July 10, 1950).

40. *Zhonggong zhongyang Huabei ju zhongyao wenjian huibian*, v. 1, 638–39.

41. "Laoqu Wuxian nongcun kaocha baogao" [Investigation of villages in the old liberated region of Wu county] (August 25, 1950), in Shanxi sheng nongye hezuo shi bianji weiyuan hui, ed., *Shanxi sheng nongye hezuo shi wenjian huibian juan* [Collections of documents on the agricultural cooperation movement in Shanxi province], SPA, 258–65.

42. *Renmin ribao* (November 14, 1950).

43. *Neibu cankao* (February 28, 1951). *Neibu cankao* is a multivolume collection of reports written by Xinhua wire-service reporters from 1950 to the 1960s.

44. "Wuxian liu ge cun nongye shengchan zhong zuzhi huzhu de kaocha baogao."

45. "Laoqu Wuxian nongcun kaocha baogao," 258–65.

46. *Renmin ribao* (November 14, 1950).

47. "Changzhi diwei 1949 nian yilai nongye shengchan zongjie" [Changzhi prefecture's summary of agricultural production in 1949], JCP, 004. 2.

48. Edward Friedman, Paul G. Pickowicz and Mark Selden, *Chinese Village, Socialist State* (New Haven: Yale University Press, 1991).

49. "Youguan Li Shunda he Xigoucun xiang shengwei he Huabei ju de baogao" [A report on Li Shunda and Xigou village to the provincial government and the North China Bureau] (June 10, 1951), JCA, 44.1.1.

50. Gao Jie's interview with Tao Lujia.

51. "Zhonggong Shanxi shengwei xiang Huabei ju zhuanbao nongye ting guanyu 1950 nian shengchan huzhu yundong de zongjie baogao" [CCP Shanxi branch report to the North China Bureau on the development of mutual aid teams in 1950] (December 30, 1950), in Shanxi sheng shizhi yanjiu yuan, ed., *Shanxi nongye hezuohua*, 49–57.

52. Lai Ruoyu, "Guanyu Changzhi qu shiban nongyeshe de yijian" [Opinions on the experiment to build agricultural cooperatives in the Changzhi area] (March 1951), *Zhonggong zhongyang Huabei ju zhongyao wenjian huibian*, 273.

53. "Changzhi zhuanqu huzhuzu zhong de gonggong caichan yu gongjijin wenti" [Problems with communal property and communal funds in mutual aid teams in Changzhi prefecture] (February 21, 1951), *Zhonggong zhongyang Huabei ju zhongyao wenjian huibian*, 271–73.

54. "Zhonggong Shanxi shengwei shuji Lai Ruoyu guanyu sheng di'erci dang daibiao huiyi zhuyao neirong xiang Huabei jubing Mao zhuxi de baogao" [Lai Ruoyu's report to the North China Bureau and Chairman Mao on the CCP's second congress in Shanxi] (March 5, 1951), in Shanxi sheng shizhi yanjiu yuan, ed., *Shanxi nongye hezuohua*, 63–64.

55. "Wang Qian tongzhi sanyue 29 ri zai huzhu daibiaohui shang de zongjie baogao" [Comrade Wang Qian's report at the mutual aid and cooperation conference for heads of mutual aid teams on March 29] (March 29, 1951), SPA, C77. 4.5.

56. "Chungeng gongzuodui Shanxi xiaozu guanyu Changzhi zhuanqu huzhu daibiao

huiyi qingkuang de baogao" [The report of the spring planting work teams in Shanxi on the mutual aid and cooperation conference of heads of mutual aid teams in Changzhi prefecture] (March 30, 1951), SPA, C 54. 2003. 47.

57. Tao Lujia, "Mao zhuxi zhichi Shanxi sheng shiban hezuoshe" [Chairman Mao supported Shanxi province in the building of trial cooperatives], in Shanxi sheng shizhi yanjiu yuan, ed., *Shanxi nongye hezuohua*, 635–54.

58. "Ba laoqu huzhu zuzhi tigao yibu" [Upgrading the mutual aid organization one step further in the old liberated areas], *Nongye jitihua zhongyao wenjian huibian* [Collection of important documents on the agricultural collectivization] (Beijing: Zhonggong zhongyang dangxiao chubanshe, 1981), 35–36.

59. Tao Lujia. "Mao zhuxi zhichi Shanxi sheng shiban hezuoshe."

60. *Shanxi sheng nongye hezuo shi wenjian huibian juan*, 282–92.

61. Gao Jie's interview with Tao Lujia.

62. For details of this report and the North China Bureau's feedback, see Bo Yibo.

63. Ibid.

64. Shi Dongbing, *Gao Gang hunduan Zhongnanhai* [Gao Gang's failure in zhongnanhai] (Xianggang: Tiandi tushu youxian gongsi, 1995).

65. Ibid.

66. Ibid.

67. Karl Marx, *Capital*, cited by Tao Lujia, *Mao zhuxi jiao women dang shengwei shuji* (Chairman Mao taught us how to be provincial governors) (Beijing: Zhongyang wenxian chubanshe, 1996).

68. Frederick Engels, "The Peasant Question in France and Germany," cited by Tao Lujia, *Mao zhuxi jiao women dang shengwei shuji*.

69. Tao Lujia, *Mao Zhuxi jiao women dang shengwei shuji*, 205–6.

70. In 1943, Mao Zedong clearly asserted that mutual aid teams were the sprouts of socialism and embodied the progressive nature of socialism. Mao Tse-tung, "Get Organized," *Selected Works of Mao Tse-tung* (Peking: Foreign Languages Press, 1965), v. 3, 156.

71. Bo Yibo, *Ruogan zhongda juece yu shijian de huigu*.

72. *Selected works of Mao Tse-tung*, v. 4, 363.

73. Gao Jie's interview with Tao Lujia.

74. Stuart Schram, *The Thought of Mao Tse-tung* (Cambridge: Cambridge University Press, 1989), 98.

Contributors

Tracy C. Barrett	Assistant Professor of History, North Dakota State University
David Cheng Chang	Ph.D. candidate, University of California, San Diego
Sherman Cochran	Hu Shih Professor of Chinese History, Cornell University
Xiaojia Hou	Assistant Professor of History, University of Colorado, Denver
Paola Iovene	Assistant Professor in Chinese Literature, East Asian Languages and Civilizations, University of Chicago
Justin Jacobs	Ph.D. candidate, University of California, San Diego
Amy Kardos	Assistant Professor of History, Northern Kentucky University
Judd Kinzley	Ph.D. candidate, University of California, San Diego
Peter Lavelle	Ph.D. candidate, Cornell University
Tai Wei Lim	Assistant Professor of Japanese Studies at the Chinese University of Hong Kong
Jeremy Murray	Ph.D. candidate, University of California, San Diego
Soon Keong Ong	Assistant Professor of History, University of Missouri
Paul G. Pickowicz	Distinguished Professor of History and Chinese Studies, and Modern Chinese History Endowed Chair, University of California, San Diego
Elya J. Zhang	Assistant Professor of History, Fordham University

INDEX

Abrogation, in China and Japan, 103, 108, 113(n23)
Academia Sinica, 65, 79, 83
actors/actresses, banned from voting, 203
"Advice from Yunnan's Population," 229
"age of the gold pack animal," 24
Agricultural centers, 6
agricultural cooperatives, of peasants, 295, 302, 310(n52)
Agricultural Treatise from the Pavilion of Pucun (Zuo/Pucun), 46
agriculture
  in Chinese hinterland, 3
  collectivization of, 290, 311(n58)
  Zuo Zongtang's effects on, 43–60
Ala-tau Mountains, 20
Algeria, French in, 229
American archeologists, Duanhuang Caves and, 73–77
Amoy University, 253
Analects of Confucius, 80
An Analytical List of the Tunhuang Manuscripts in the National Library of Peiping Remaining after the Plunder (Chen), 65
An Index of the Dunhuang Manuscripts Remaining after the Plunder, 65
An Guangxue, 127
Ang Watawat, riot news in, 251
Anhai, army retreat to, 247
Anhua, 254
Anhui province
  revenues of, 164, 165, 166
  Zuo Zongtang as ruler of, 43
Ansu county, elections in, 211
anti-imperialism, 95, 108
  of Chinese intellectuals, 97
Anti-Opium Society, 206
antiquarian officials, reaction to archeologists, 66–73

antiquities, Chinese, 173
Anxi, Chen Guohui's retreat to, 257
Archaeological Society (Beijing University), 77
archaeology
  Chinese, 75,76, 84
  of Dunhuang caves, 6–7
  Egyptian, 84
archaeological plundering
  of China, 88(n24)
  of Dunhuang, 65
area-field system, for agriculture, 47, 60(n11)
Aristophanes, 278
Asia Theatre (Manila), 243
Association du Lycée Franco-Chinois, current existence of, 242(n47)
As You Desire (play), 273
Australia, gold strikes in, 29
aviation gasoline, 124
avoidance system, 174, 192(n23)

Baiyanghe, oil wells in, 118
ballot box, use to draw voters, 208–213
bamboo, cultivation of, 47
banditry
  in Fujian, 247
  Fujian suppression of, 243
  officials dismissed for, 163, 188–189
bandits, gold-digging, 26, 31, 84
Baojun, dismissal of, 188
Bao Tianxiao, as *Shibao* commentator, 199, 203, 205, 206, 207
Baoxin Company, 34
barbarism, Chinese, 67
barbers
  demarginalization of, 269
  film preview for, 285(n29)
  protest of film by, 267–287
barbers' revolt, 223–224
Barbers Trade Guild and the Professional Union, 277, 281
Barlyk Mountains, 20
Barret, Tracy C., 2, 4, 10, 11, 221–242, 262, 282, 313

Beijing, in 170, 171, 174, 249, 252
  CCP in, 296
  as Chinese capital, 2, 5, 6, 8, 11, 43, 81
  print media in, 195
Beijing Spring movement of 1989, 91, 96
Beijing University, 71, 73, 75, 76, 79, 93, 95, 118, 125
Beiyang arsenal, 164
Bian Baodi, dismissal of, 188
Bingtuan, 141, 142, 143, 148, 149, 154,
Bonhoure, 232,233
Bookkeeping Law, 248–250, 253, 254, 259
Book of Rites, 80
border disputes, Russian-Chinese, 26
bordering states (Chinese), as centers with margins, 2
"Boxerism", 98–99
Boxer Uprising, 67, 98, 188, 197, 235, 236
Boxer Rebellion/debacle, officials dismissed in, 86, 164,
Bo Yibo, 294, 304, 305
Brahmi-Chinese Dunhuang stele, 84–85
brigands, miners as, 5, 18
British Malaya, 252
British Museum, 79
bronze coinage, revenue from, 166
Buddhism, as voting restriction, 202
Buddhist literature. *See also* Duanhuang Thousand-Buddha Caves
  in Duanhuang Thousand-Buddha Caves, 68, 81
"Build a Garden on the Gobi" (song), 151
Bureau of Social Affairs, film protest and, 276, 278, 281, 286(n39)
Burhan Shähidi, 137
Burma, 119, 120
"Butcher Yuan", Yuan Shikai as, 169

313

CORNELL EAST ASIA SERIES

CORNELL
East Asia Series

Order online at www.einaudi.cornell.edu/eastasia/publications or contact
Cornell University Press Services, P. O. Box 6525, 750 Cascadilla Street,
Ithaca, NY 14851, USA.
Tel: 1-800-666-2211 (USA or Canada), 1-607-277-2211 (International)
Fax: 1-800-688-2877 (USA or Canada), 1-607-277-6292 (International)
E-mail orders to: orderbook@cupserv.org

CPSIA information can be obtained
at www.ICGtesting.com
Printed in the USA
LVHW090708301219
641963LV00015B/17/P